THE WILEY BICENTENNIAL–KNOWLEDGE FOR GENERATIONS

Each generation has its unique needs and aspirations. When Charles Wiley first opened his small printing shop in lower Manhattan in 1807, it was a generation of boundless potential searching for an identity. And we were there, helping to define a new American literary tradition. Over half a century later, in the midst of the Second Industrial Revolution, it was a generation focused on building the future. Once again, we were there, supplying the critical scientific, technical, and engineering knowledge that helped frame the world. Throughout the 20th Century, and into the new millennium, nations began to reach out beyond their own borders and a new international community was born. Wiley was there, expanding its operations around the world to enable a global exchange of ideas, opinions, and know-how.

For 200 years, Wiley has been an integral part of each generation's journey, enabling the flow of information and understanding necessary to meet their needs and fulfill their aspirations. Today, bold new technologies are changing the way we live and learn. Wiley will be there, providing you the must-have knowledge you need to imagine new worlds, new possibilities, and new opportunities.

Generations come and go, but you can always count on Wiley to provide you the knowledge you need, when and where you need it!

WILLIAM J. PESCE
PRESIDENT AND CHIEF EXECUTIVE OFFICER

PETER BOOTH WILEY
CHAIRMAN OF THE BOARD

VISUALIZING

ELEMENTARY SOCIAL STUDIES METHODS

John K. Lee

North Carolina State University

In collaboration with

THE NATIONAL GEOGRAPHIC SOCIETY

CREDITS

VICE PRESIDENT AND PUBLISHER Jay O'Callaghan
MANAGING DIRECTOR Helen McInnis
ACQUISITIONS EDITOR Robert Johnston
DIRECTOR OF DEVELOPMENT Barbara Heaney
DEVELOPMENT EDITOR Ann Greenberger
PROGRAM ASSISTANT Eileen McKeever
EXECUTIVE MARKETING MANAGER Jeffrey Rucker
MEDIA EDITOR Lynn Pearlman
PRODUCTION MANAGER Kelly Tavares; Full Service Production Provided by Camelot Editorial Services, LLC
CREATIVE DIRECTOR Harry Nolan
COVER DESIGNER Hope Miller
INTERIOR DESIGN Vertigo Design
PHOTO EDITOR Hilary Newman
PHOTO RESEARCHER Stacy Gold, National Geographic Society
SENIOR ILLUSTRATION EDITOR Anna Melhorn
COVER CREDITS **Top photo:** © Joel Sartore/NG Image Collection; **Bottom photos (left to right):** © NG Maps; Hugh Sitton/Getty Images; Charles Thatcher/Stone/Getty Images; Martin Puddy/The Image Bank/Getty Images; Robert Manella/Iconica/Getty Images

This book was set in New Baskerville by Preparé, Inc., and printed and bound by Quebecor World. The cover was printed by Phoenix Color.

Wiley 200th Anniversary logo designed by Richard J. Pacifico.

To order books or for customer service, please call 1-800-CALL WILEY (225-5945).

ISBN 8: 0471-72066-6
ISBN 13: 978-0471-72066-9

Printed in the United States of America
10 9 8 7 6 5 4 3 2 1

FOREWORD *From the Publisher*

isualizing Elementary Social Studies is designed to help your students learn effectively. Created in collaboration with the National Geographic Society and our Wiley Visualizing Consulting Editor, Professor Jan Plass of New York University, *Visualizing Elementary Social Studies* integrates rich visuals with text to direct students' attention to important information. This approach represents complex processes, organizes related pieces of information, and integrates information into clear representations. Beautifully illustrated, *Visualizing Elementary Social Studies* shows your students what the discipline is all about, its main concepts and applications, while also instilling an appreciation and excitement about the richness of the subject.

Visuals, as used throughout this text, are instructional components that display facts, concepts, processes, or principles. They create the foundation for the text and do more than simply support the written or spoken word. The visuals include diagrams, graphs, maps, photographs, and illustrations.

Why should a textbook based on visuals be effective? Research shows that we learn better from integrated text and visuals than from either medium separately. Beginners in a subject benefit most from reading about the topic, attending class, and studying well-designed and integrated visuals. A visual, with good accompanying discussion, really can be worth a thousand words!

Well-designed visuals can also improve the efficiency with which a learner processes information. The more effectively we process information, the more likely it is that we will learn. This processing of information takes place in our working memory. As we learn, we integrate new information in our working memory with existing knowledge in our long-term memory.

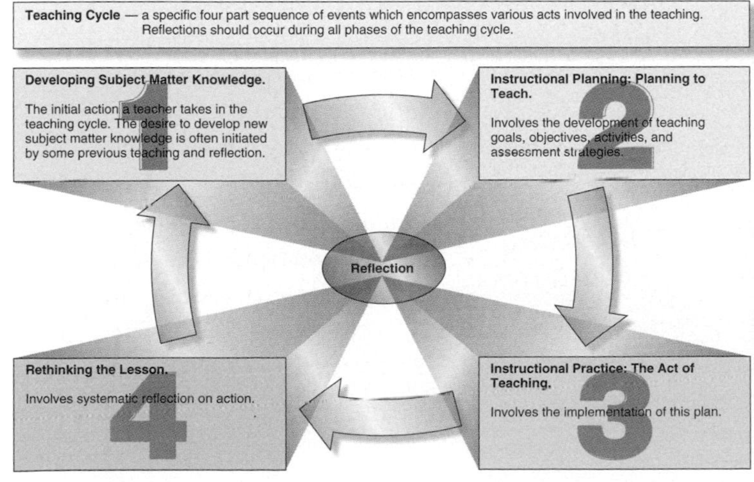

Have you ever read a paragraph or a page in a book, stopped, and said to yourself: "I don't remember one thing I just read?" This may happen when your working memory has been overloaded, and the text you read was not successfully integrated into long-term memory. Visuals don't automatically solve the problem of overload, but well-designed visuals can reduce the number of elements that working memory must process, thus aiding learning.

You, as the instructor, facilitate your students' learning. Well-designed visuals, used in class, can help you in that effort. Here are six methods for using the visuals in the *Visualizing Elementary Social Studies* in classroom instruction.

1. **Assign students visuals to study in addition to reading the text.**
   Instead of assigning only one medium of presentation, it is important to make sure your students know that the visuals are just as essential as the text.

2. **Use visuals during class discussions or presentations.**
   By pointing out important information as the students look at the visuals during class discussions, you can help focus students' attention on key elements of the visuals and help them begin to organize the information and develop an integrated model of understanding. The verbal

explanation of important information combined with the visual representation can be highly effective.

3. **Use visuals to review content knowledge.**
   Students can review key concepts, principles, processes, vocabulary, and relationships displayed visually. Better understanding results when new information in working memory is linked to prior knowledge.

4. **Use visuals for assignments or when assessing learning.**
   Visuals can be used for comprehension activities or assessments. For example, you could ask students to identify examples of concepts portrayed in visuals. Higher-level thinking activities that require critical thinking, deductive and inductive reasoning, and prediction can also be based on visuals. Visuals can be very useful for drawing inferences, for predicting, and for problem solving.

5. **Use visuals to situate learning in authentic contexts.**
   Learning is made more meaningful when a learner can apply facts, concepts, and principles to realistic situations or examples. Visuals can provide that realistic context.

6. **Use visuals to encourage collaboration.**
   Collaborative groups often are required to practice interactive processes such as giving explanations, asking questions, clarifying ideas, and arguing a case. These interactive, face-to-face processes provide the information needed to build a verbal mental model. Learners also benefit from collaboration in many instances such as decision making or problem solving.

Visualizing Elementary Social Studies aids student learning through extraordinary use of photos,

Authentic Learning
Highly focused learning that revolves around student interests and resources from the historical period being studied

Active Learning
More focused learning activities that require students to reorganize or re-represent background material

Direct Learning/Transmission
Facts and details that provide background for later learning activities

3
2
1

maps, and other materials from the National Geographic Society collections and other sources. Students using *Visualizing Elementary Social Studies* also benefit from the long history and rich, fascinating resources of National Geographic.

National Geographic has also performed an invaluable service in fact-checking *Visualizing Elementary Social Studies:* they have verified every fact in the book with two outside sources, ensuring the accuracy and currency of the text.

Given all of its strengths and resources, *Visualizing Elementary Social Studies* will immerse your students in the discipline, its main concepts and applications, while also instilling an appreciation and excitement about the richness of the subject area.

Additional information on learning and instructional design is provided in a special guide to using this book, *Learning from Visuals: How and Why Visuals Can Help Students Learn*, prepared by Matthew Leavitt of Arizona State University. This article is available at the Wiley Web site: www.wiley.com/college/visualizing. The online *Instructor's Manual* also provides guidelines and suggestions on using the text and visuals most effectively.

PREFACE

This debut edition of *Visualizing Elementary Social Studies* offers students a unique way to explore issues and ideas about how to teach social studies using text, pictures, and graphics brought together in a stimulating and thoughtful design. In this book, content and pedagogy are blended to take advantage of the rich visual context that National Geographic images provide. Students who use this book will explore central teacher education topics in elementary social studies along with concepts and ideas from social studies disciplines including history, geography, political science, economics, and behavioral sciences. *Visualizing Elementary Social Studies* is infused with explorations of how to teach in subject matter contexts given the democratic purposes of social studies.

Visualizing Elementary Social Studies begins with a consideration of the parameters and purposes of social studies. The book then examines the special role that social studies can play in the elementary classroom. As a field, social studies often receives less instructional time than other core areas such as math and literacy. We made a special effort in this book to situate social studies in the core area of literacy as being particularly well suited for inquiry and reflective learning. In *Visualizing Elementary Social Studies,* instruction in social studies is presented as central to the elementary classroom. Through an emphasis on the integrative and interdisciplinary nature of social studies, this book makes an argument for authentic and regular social studies teaching and learning in the elementary classroom.

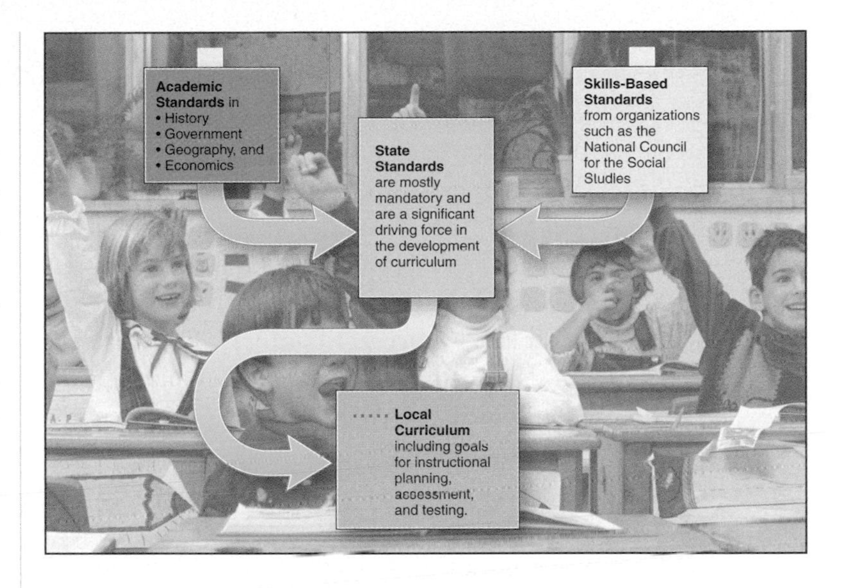

As methods books go, *Visualizing Elementary Social Studies* might seem a bit different. Although many of the chapters deal with typical sorts of topics you might expect in a methods book (e.g., curriculum, assessment, technology), the visual style and subject matter emphasis are by no means ordinary. Through rich visual presentations, we present social studies teaching methods and issues as embedded in social studies subject matter. For example, we discuss a method for reading instruction called "Challenge Reading" in the context of the archeological debate over the arrival of the first humans on the North American continent. In Chapter 4, we look at the impact of standards and

curriculum on the way teachers approach instruction in the context of the Dolley Madison story. Both of these examples include visual representations of the subject matter that enhance the context for the discussion of social studies teaching methods and issues. *Visualizing Elementary Social Studies* does not include exhaustive lists of instructional approaches or lockstep procedures for implementing particular approaches to instruction. Instead, we present contextualized and authentic methods of instruction with as much attention to how instruction looks in the classroom as to the distilled steps in a procedure.

Given the wide range of backgrounds that students will bring to the experience of using this book, we made no assumption about the subject matter background of readers. *Visualizing Elementary Social Studies* instead suggests that pre-service and beginning teachers can learn how to teach best when they consider the purposes, methods, and issues associated with social studies in authentic and subject-based contexts. Readers will find singular subject matter references throughout the book—for example, the Xosha people of South Africa, life for children in Georgia Colony, the story of John

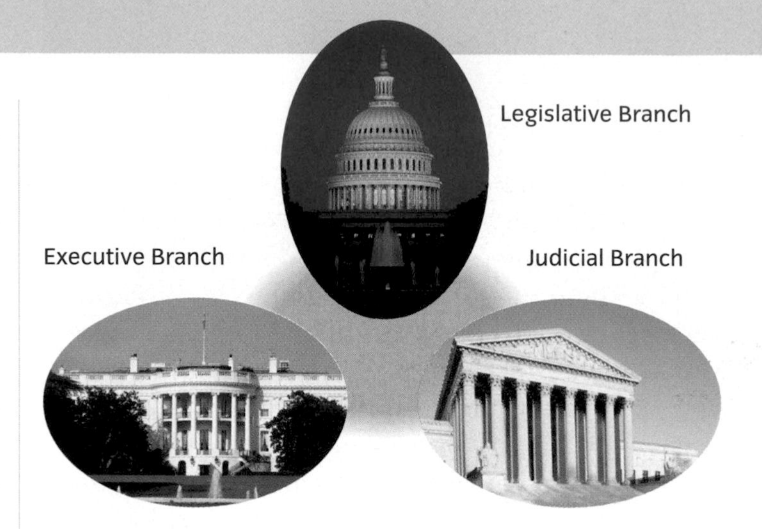

Henry, the Vietnam Veterans Memorial, Salish Indian totem poles, Ponce de Leon and the Fountain of Youth, climate and the Earth's movement around the Sun, and advantages and disadvantages of nuclear technology. These subject matter references reflect both curriculum and the times in which we live. Some subject matter topics appear in multiple places; Abraham Lincoln, immigration, and colonial American history are three such thematic subject matter points of focus. Each of these symbolizes an important way of representing subject matter in social studies: Lincoln represents biography; immigration is a concept; and Colonial American history is an episodic period. Using the rich visual resources of National Geographic we explore these three topics, along with others, in multiple social studies contexts. *Visualizing Elementary Social Studies* can be used in a one-semester class devoted to social studies or as part of a general methods course that includes social studies.

ORGANIZATION

Visualizing Elementary Social Studies is organized around the notion that social studies is best taught in elementary school grades when it is deeply integrated into the larger curriculum. We believe that readers will find the social studies content presented in *Visualizing Elementary Social Studies* to be purposeful, authentic, integrative, and rich. The book contains four main sections that specifically address: (1) the purposes of social studies, (2) the relationship between social studies subject matter and methods, (3) the interdisciplinary nature of social studies, and (4) the planning, teaching, and assessing processes involved in successful elementary school teaching.

The first section of *Visualizing Elementary Social Studies* includes Chapters 1–3 and focuses on the purposes and ideals of social studies. Chapter 1 addresses the question, *what is social studies?* and presents various definitions of social studies as well as the history of the field and descriptions of social studies as it is currently taught and learned. Chapter 2 presents the notion that teaching social studies is a particularly reflective endeavor. The special focus on human relationships in social studies makes reflection a particularly important activity. Chapter 3 considers inquiry as a central method and means of organizing social studies. We see inquiry, in its various forms, as fulfilling the ultimate purpose of social studies: citizenship preparation.

The second section, Chapters 4–7, deals with methods in social studies by considering authentic subject matter contexts for teaching at the elementary school level. Chapter 4 considers curriculum, standards, and testing as subject matter contexts that inform the development of instructional ideas. This chapter pays special attention to the manner in which teachers can construct rich and detailed subject matter–based instructional activities in curricular environments that might not on the surface seem to enable such teaching and learning. Chapters 5–7 focus on methods that are related to the three most common academic subject matter areas in social studies: history, geography, and civics. Chapter 5 examines the ways that instruction can facilitate historical understanding. Chapter 6 centers on teaching for geographic awareness. Chapter 7 deals with teaching and learning in elementary social studies for civic awareness.

Chapters 8–10 form the third section, addressing the integrative and interdisciplinary nature of social studies at the elementary level. Chapter 8 considers direct instructional approaches in social studies, while Chapter 9 focuses on collaborative ways to incorporate social studies into the elementary classroom. Chapter 10 considers literacy as a context for social studies teaching and learning given the important role of literacy instruction in elementary grades.

The fourth section, Chapters 11–14, presents social studies instruction as a process that involves planning, teaching, and assessing given a variety of unique contexts. Chapter 11 presents planning, teaching, and assessing in social studies in the context of active student involvement in the learning process. Chapter 12 discusses planning, teaching, and assessment in diverse cultural contexts, and Chapter 13 focuses directly on assessment as an essential and often underemphasized part of the instructional process. Chapter 14 considers the role of technology in planning and teaching.

ILLUSTRATED BOOK TOUR

A number of pedagogical features using visuals have been developed specifically for *Visualizing Elementary Social Studies.* These features reflect and highlight the interdisciplinary nature of social studies. The **Illustrated Book Tour** on the following pages provides a guide to the diverse features that contribute to the *Visualizing Elementary Social Studies* pedagogical plan.

ILLUSTRATED

CHAPTER INTRODUCTIONS illustrate a particular idea in the chapter with relevant stories as a way to heighten and initiate a consideration of the main theme of the chapter. These narratives are featured alongside accompanying photographs. The chapter openers also include illustrated **CHAPTER OUTLINES** that use thumbnails of illustrations from the chapter to refer visually to the content.

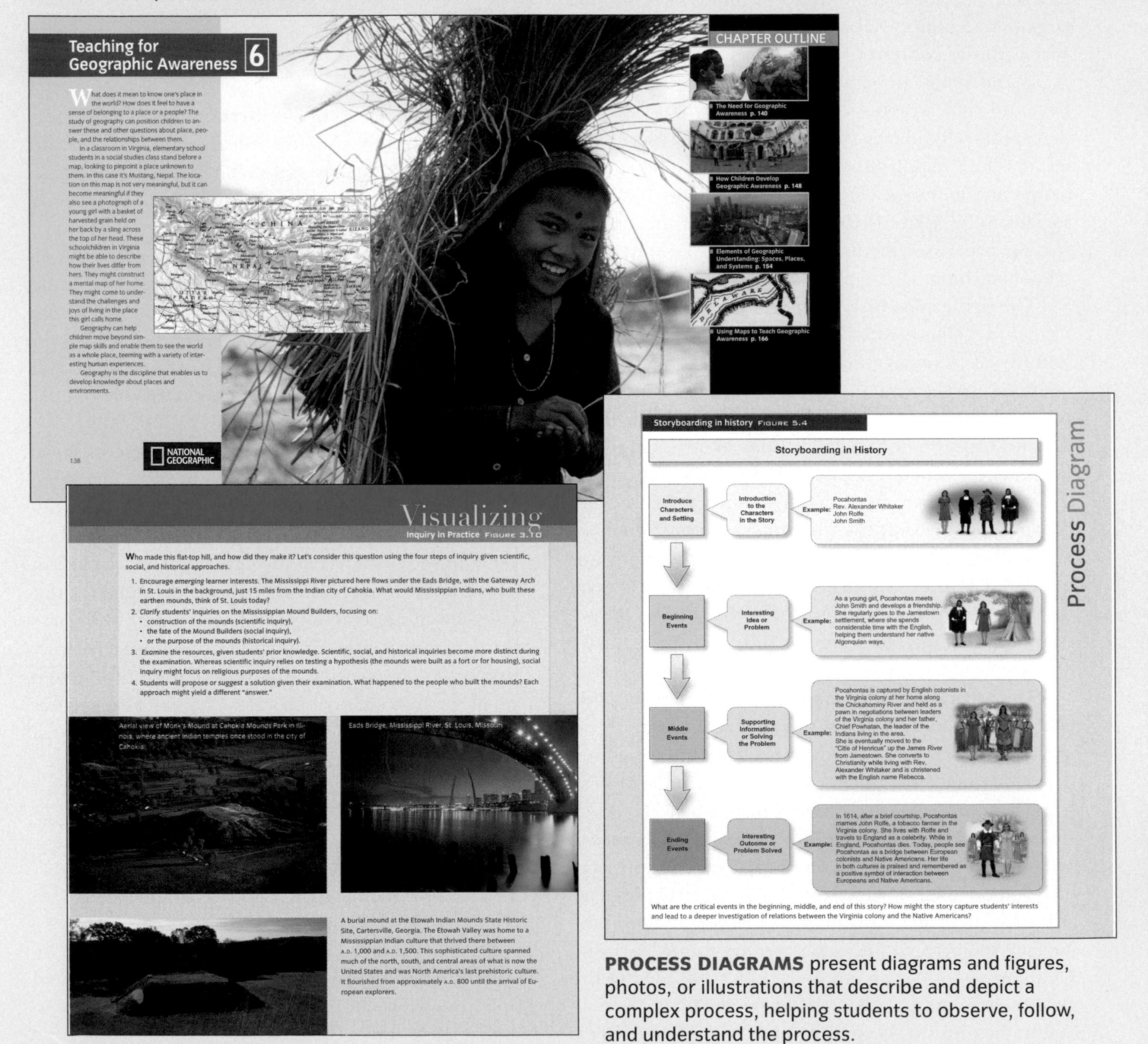

PROCESS DIAGRAMS present diagrams and figures, photos, or illustrations that describe and depict a complex process, helping students to observe, follow, and understand the process.

VISUALIZING features are specially designed multipart visual spreads that focus on a key issue, concept, or topic in the chapter, exploring it in detail or in broader context using a combination of photos.

BOOK TOUR

LESSON

The Abrahamic Religions: Judaism, Christianity, and Islam

INTRODUCTION

The three religions of Judaism, Christianity, and Islam share a striking similarity. All three religions believe in the same God. Despite this similarity, many people think of these religions as being different or even in conflict. In fact they have not always lived easily together, but there were times of harmony—most notably in Islamic Spain, when the three religions mostly coexisted side by side. All three religions trace their spiritual heritage to one person named Abraham and all share a belief in one God—the God of Abraham. In this activity, children will describe the genealogical relationships between Judaism, Christianity, and Islam. Consider the following fourth- or fifth-grade lesson on the three Abrahamic religions (Judaism, Christianity, and Islam). As you read the lesson, reflect on the complications that accompany teaching about religion.

INSTRUCTIONAL GOALS AND OBJECTIVES

The overall goal of this lesson is to identify events relating to similarities between Judaism, Christianity, and Islam. Students will use this information in either a story or a series of illustrations to show the relationships between Judaism, Christianity, and Islam.

PROCEDURES

In this lesson students will develop a timeline of events related to the origin of each of the Abrahamic religions. Students should incorporate the events listed below into a timeline. Also, all of the dates for these events are based on a Christian calendar. Students should know this and should be challenged to consider why we use a Christian calendar.

- Abraham is born in Ur, a city in Mesopotamia (modern day Iraq)—about 1991 B.C.
- Abraham has two sons, Isaac and Ishmael—about 1905 and 1891 B.C., respectively
- The Jews, who were Abraham's descendents from his son Isaac, travel to Egypt and are enslaved—1500 to 1300 B.C.
- Abraham's descendents from his son Ishmael settle to the south of Mesopotamia, establishing Arabia—1500 to 1300 B.C.
- Jewish exodus from Egypt led by Moses—1300 B.C.
- Saul, David, and Solomon establish the Jewish Kingdom of Israel—1000 B.C.
- Jesus (the founder of Christianity) is born in Israel to a Jewish family descended from Isaac—1 A.D.
- Jesus dies—33 A.D.
- Roman Empire adopts Christianity—300 A.D.
- Muhammad (founder of Islam) is born in Arabia to an Arab family descended from Ishmael—570 A.D.
- Muhammad dies—632 A.D.
- The Crusades—1095 to 1291 A.D.
- Islamic Spain—1150 to 1492 A.D.

When the timeline is complete, students should study their work and answer the following question:

Given your timeline, what are the connections between Judaism, Christianity, and Islam?

To some degree, all of the events in the timeline are controversial and unsettled. For the most part, the closer in time an event is to today, the more evidence we have to support that event. For example, we have plenty of evidence from various sources to verify that the Crusades occurred from about 1000 to 1200 A.D. and that Muslims controlled Spain from 1150 to 1450 A.D.. We have much less evidence about Abraham's birth and the lives of his sons Isaac and Ishmael. After

La Mezquita Mosque in Cordoba, Spain. Originally built as an Umayyad Islamic mosque in the 9th century, it represents a unique and historic confluence of Islamic, Christian, and Jewish culture. After over 400 years as a mosque, a Christian church was built inside; all the while Jews dominated the intellectual and cultural scene in Cordoba. For centuries, these three religions existed and in many ways thrived side by side in Cordoba.

students complete the timeline, they should write an explanation for why the older events are less historically certain than the more recent events and also should explain the consequences of the uncertainty of the older events.

After students have completed their work on this question, the teacher should lead a class discussion about the similarities between the religions and introduce other similarities including the following:

- All three religions are monotheistic (belief in one God).
- The story of creation is consistent in all three religions.
- All three feature basic laws, given by God.
- They all describe a route to personal salvation.
- All three religions include ideas of heaven and hell.

ASSESSMENT

The primary assessment should be a separate activity in which students write a story or draw an illustration that describes how Judaism, Christianity, and Islam are similar. The teacher should give students very clear expectations about what to write or draw. One possible criterion, which could be provided to students, might include the following:

Your story or drawing should include a main idea and at least three pieces of evidence supporting your main idea.

The teacher can also assess the timeline for accuracy (was the event copied correctly) and event placement on the timeline (was it placed in the correct proportion to other events).

LESSONS explain a specific instructional plan for teaching using one of the approaches presented in the book. Each lesson includes illustrations and photos and focuses on authentic and curriculum-based subject matter for age-appropriate elementary audiences. Lessons include background subject matter information, goals and objectives, procedures, and assessment ideas.

In the Classroom A BRIEF CASE STUDY ON TEACHING ABOUT THE CONSTITUTION

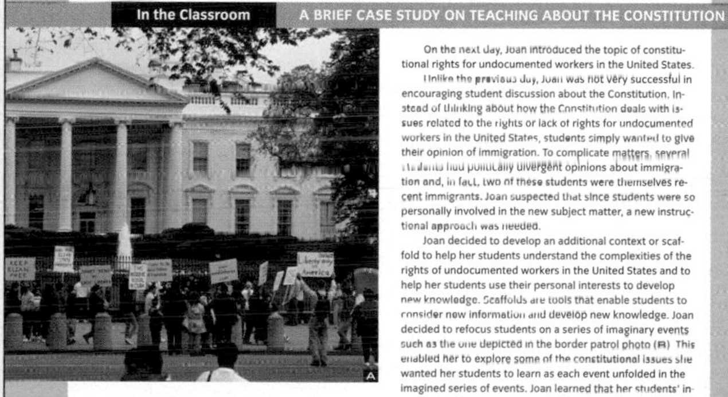

Joan Childress finished an undergraduate teacher education program and started her first teaching job four months ago. She has a passion for teaching that is partly driven by her love for children as well as her insatiable appetite for learning new things. On this day, Joan was teaching about the United States Constitution. She provided students with visual prompts to get them to think about how the Constitution addressed particular actions.

Joan became interested in the case of Elian Gonzales, a young boy from Cuba living in the United States who was about the age of students in her class. Elian was being deported as an illegal alien against the wishes of some of his family who were legally in the United States. Elian was ultimately returned to Cuba, which angered some of his U.S. supporters, who are shown in the photo (A) of protestors in front of the White House. Joan used this photo to illustrate protected rights in the Constitution; most students can readily identify the rights to free speech and assembly. Her students not only successfully identified these First Amendment protections, they also were able to describe why we need such rights. Joan extended the discussion to talk about the limits of free speech and the consequences of restricting free speech. Joan was so confident in her students' responses that she continued to teach about additional constitutional rights.

On the next day, Joan introduced the topic of constitutional rights for undocumented workers in the United States.

Unlike the previous day, Joan was not very successful in encouraging student discussion about the Constitution. Instead of thinking about how the Constitution deals with issues related to the rights or lack of rights for undocumented workers in the United States, students simply wanted to give their opinion of immigration. To complicate matters, several students had politically divergent opinions about immigration and, in fact, two of these students were themselves recent immigrants. Joan suspected that since students were so personally involved in the new subject matter, a new instructional approach was needed.

Joan decided to develop an additional context or scaffold to help her students understand the complexities of the rights of undocumented workers in the United States and to help her students use their personal interests to develop new knowledge. Scaffolds are tools that enable students to consider new information and develop new knowledge. Joan decided to refocus students on a series of imaginary events such as the one depicted in the border patrol photo (B). This enabled her to explore some of the constitutional issues she wanted her students to learn as each event unfolded in the imagined series of events. Joan learned that her students' interest in subject matter was important, but such interest required a different instructional approach than when students might not be as personally interested.

50 CHAPTER 2 Reflective Social Studies Teaching

NATIONAL GEOGRAPHIC

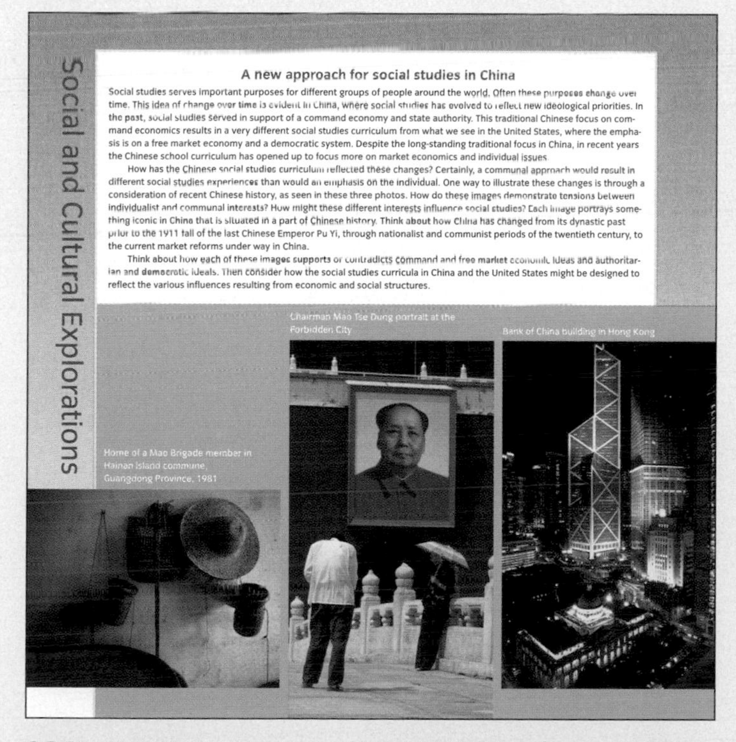

Social and Cultural Explorations

A new approach for social studies in China

Social studies serves important purposes for different groups of people around the world. Often these purposes change over time. This idea of change over time is evident in China, where social studies has evolved to reflect new ideological priorities. In the past, social studies served in support of a command economy and state authority. This traditional Chinese focus on command economics results in a very different social studies curriculum from what we see in the United States, where the emphasis is on a free market economy and a democratic system. Despite the long-standing traditional focus in China, in recent years the Chinese school curriculum has opened up to focus more on market economics and individual issues.

How has the Chinese social studies curriculum reflected these changes? Certainly, a communal approach would result in different social studies experiences than would an emphasis on the individual. One way to illustrate these changes is through a consideration of recent Chinese history, as seen in these three photos. How do these images demonstrate tensions between individualist and communal interests? How might these different interests influence social studies? Each image portrays something iconic in China that is situated in a part of Chinese history. Think about how China has changed from its dynastic past prior to the 1911 fall of the last Chinese Emperor Pu Yi, through nationalist and communist periods of the twentieth century, to the current market reforms under way in China.

Think about how each of these images supports or contradicts command and free market economic ideas and authoritarian and democratic ideals. Then consider how the social studies curricula in China and the United States might be designed to reflect the various influences resulting from economic and social structures.

Home of a Mao Brigade member in Hainan Island commune, Guangdong Province, 1981

Chairman Mao Tse Dung portrait at the Forbidden City

Bank of China building in Hong Kong

IN THE CLASSROOM features a specific event or series of events from an elementary classroom that highlight or provide an in-depth view of a specific idea from the chapter.

SOCIAL AND CULTURAL EXPLORATIONS focus on social studies methods and issues through the lens of culture and society using images of people from diverse places in the world.

OTHER PEDAGOGICAL FEATURES

Elements of Civic Competence

LEARNING OBJECTIVES

Recognize and distinguish between the rights and the responsibilities afforded to children in the United States.

Describe the role of government and what children in elementary grades should know about government's function.

Explain the role of reasoning in a multicultural democracy.

UNDERSTANDING RIGHTS AND RESPONSIBILITIES

Children's ability to understand their rights and responsibilities as citizens in

gests that children should learn about both personal and civic responsibilities.

Personal responsibilities:

- Taking care of themselves
- Accepting responsibility for the consequences of their actions
- Taking advantage of the opportunity to be educated
- Supporting their families

Civic responsibilities:

- Obeying the law
- Respecting the rights of others

LEARNING OBJECTIVES at the beginning of each section head indicate in behavioral terms what the student must be able to do to demonstrate mastery of the material in the chapter.

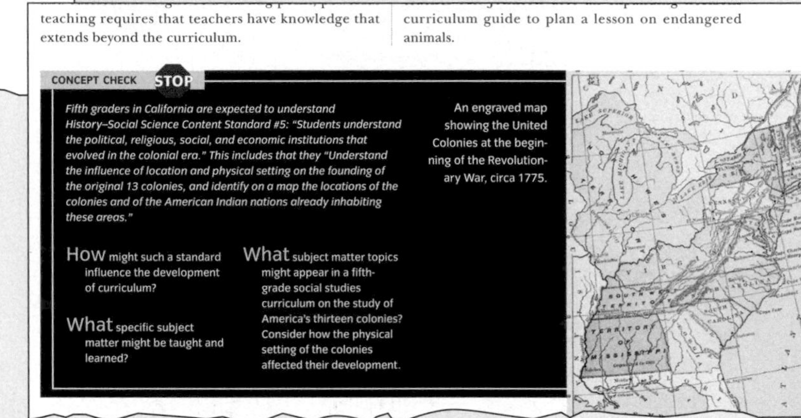

teaching requires that teachers have knowledge that extends beyond the curriculum.

curriculum guide to plan a lesson on endangered animals.

CONCEPT CHECK STOP

Fifth graders in California are expected to understand History–Social Science Content Standard #5: "Students understand the political, religious, social, and economic institutions that evolved in the colonial era." This includes that they "Understand the influence of location and physical setting on the founding of the original 13 colonies, and identify on a map the locations of the colonies and of the American Indian nations already inhabiting these areas."

How might such a standard influence the development of curriculum?

What specific subject matter might be taught and learned?

What subject matter topics might appear in a fifth-grade social studies curriculum on the study of America's thirteen colonies? Consider how the physical setting of the colonies affected their development.

An engraved map showing the United Colonies at the beginning of the Revolutionary War, circa 1775.

CONCEPT CHECK questions at the end of each section give students the opportunity to test their comprehension of the learning objectives.

Civic competence The knowledge and skills needed to actively and productively participate in democratic life.

Civic virtue The necessary moral nature of participation in a democracy.

MARGINAL GLOSSARY TERMS (IN GREEN BOLDFACE) introduce each chapter's most important terms.

What is happening in this picture ?

Teaching children about patriotism is complicated. Teachers often rely on iconic representations of national unity or national identity. How does this image represent either patriotic notions of national unity or identity?

The Statue of Liberty on Liberty Island, New York City. What messages about Americans do we associate with the Statue of Liberty, in the sense of both its physical and its emotional characteristics?

WHAT IS HAPPENING IN THIS PICTURE? presents students with a photograph that is relevant to a chapter topic but that illustrates a situation they are not likely to have encountered previously. The photograph is paired with questions designed to stimulate creative thinking.

END-OF-CHAPTER FEATURES

VISUAL SUMMARY

1 What Is Reflection?

Good teaching requires reflection. Without reflection, teaching can become stale and stagnant. Donald Schön classified reflection as occurring during an event (reflection in action) or after (reflection on action). Reflection can occur during all thinking about teaching. The processes involved in teaching can be thought of as a teaching cycle. This cycle includes developing subject matter knowledge, planning to teach, teaching, and reconsidering what was taught. Reflection can and should occur during all parts of the teaching cycle.

2 Reflection Prior to Instruction

In order to be effective, teachers must continually develop their subject matter knowledge throughout their professional career. Given the interdisciplinary nature of teaching, elementary teachers have a particular need to stay on top of subject matter. When developing subject matter knowledge, teachers must consistently reflect on their personal interests, the curriculum, and the misunderstandings that emerge from teaching and learning.

Teaching is a process that might be compared to artistic performance. Donald Schön called this artful doing. As teachers "perform" they must give themselves opportunities to grow. This is best achieved through reflection.

3 Reflection During and After Instruction

The delivery of meaningful and effective instruction also requires consistent reflection. Reflection during instruction enables teachers to be more dynamic and enables them to better meet the needs of learners. Reflection on teaching is part of a teaching cycle that includes the processes of learning new subject matter, planning for instruction, teaching, and deliberate reflection.

4 Using Reflection to Increase a Teacher's Professional Knowledge

Teachers must reflect not only about subject matter and instruction, but also about other elements of teacher knowledge. Teachers must consider their learners, the curriculum, the community, the contexts for education, and the ends of education. All of these areas are part of what is called teacher knowledge.

5 Reflection as Inquiry

As we reflect on teaching and in teaching experiences, we must plan our reflection to achieve the most desirable outcomes. John Dewey suggested that we can inquire through reflection, but cautioned that the circumstances surrounding our reflections are in constant flux. Given that there is not a formal body of teacher knowledge, a good source for learning about how to teach is case studies of teaching episodes. We can use these case studies to conduct reflective in-... developing our teacher knowledge.

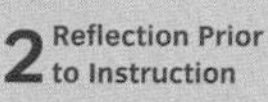

KEY TERMS

- **citizen**, p. 176
- **civic**, p. 176
- **civic competence**, p. 177
- **tolerance**, p. 178
- **conscience**, p. 180
- **patriotism**, p. 182
- **democratic reasoning**, p. 189
- **ideology**, p. 196

The **CHAPTER SUMMARY** revisits the learning objective and provides a brief review of each major section. The summaries are illustrated with a relevant photo from the respective chapter section. A list of **KEY TERMS** is also included.

SELF-TESTS provide a series of questions, a number of them incorporating visuals from the chapter, that review the major concepts.

SELF-TEST

1. What is civic competence? How is this image representative of a form of civic competence?

2. How can teachers avoid civic self-centeredness through social studies experiences?
   a. require students to behave in class
   b. test students on civic knowledge
   c. develop a sense of community in the class
   d. encourage students to do their homework
3. ______________ is the capacity to recognize and respect the beliefs or practices of others.
4. Which of the following is most important in a democracy?
   a. civic competency
   b. patriotism
   c. personal conscience
   d. all of the above
5. Which of the following forms of talk is most common in a teacher-centered classroom?
   a. conversation
   b. discussion
   c. dialogue
   d. discourse
6. Which of the following is least important in a democracy?
   a. appreciating and respecting authority
   b. developing an affection for country
   c. understanding how to contribute to political campaigns
   d. participating in civic dialogue and conversations
7. How does democratic reasoning relate to civic competence in a multicultural or pluralist society such as the United States?
8. Which is not a branch of government?
   a. legislative
   b. judicial
   c. appeals
   d. executive
9. How does ideology affect learning civic competency?
10. What is democratic reasoning? How might students engage democratic reasoning to address the pollution problem illustrated in this photo?

CRITICAL AND CREATIVE THINKING QUESTIONS

The work of government is complicated and in a democracy is seemingly inefficient. Consider the following montage of images that represent the three branches of government in the United States.

- How can social studies teachers help children understand why the framers of the United States Constitution created a system of government with three separate branches of government that in operation is complicated and seemingly inefficient?

CRITICAL AND CREATIVE THINKING QUESTIONS encourage critical thinking and highlight each chapter's important concepts and applications. Each feature uses a prominent photo as the context for a central question that is designed to elicit an extension of a concept or issue in the chapter.

NATIONAL GEOGRAPHIC MAPS appear through the book in a variety of contexts and for a variety of purposes.

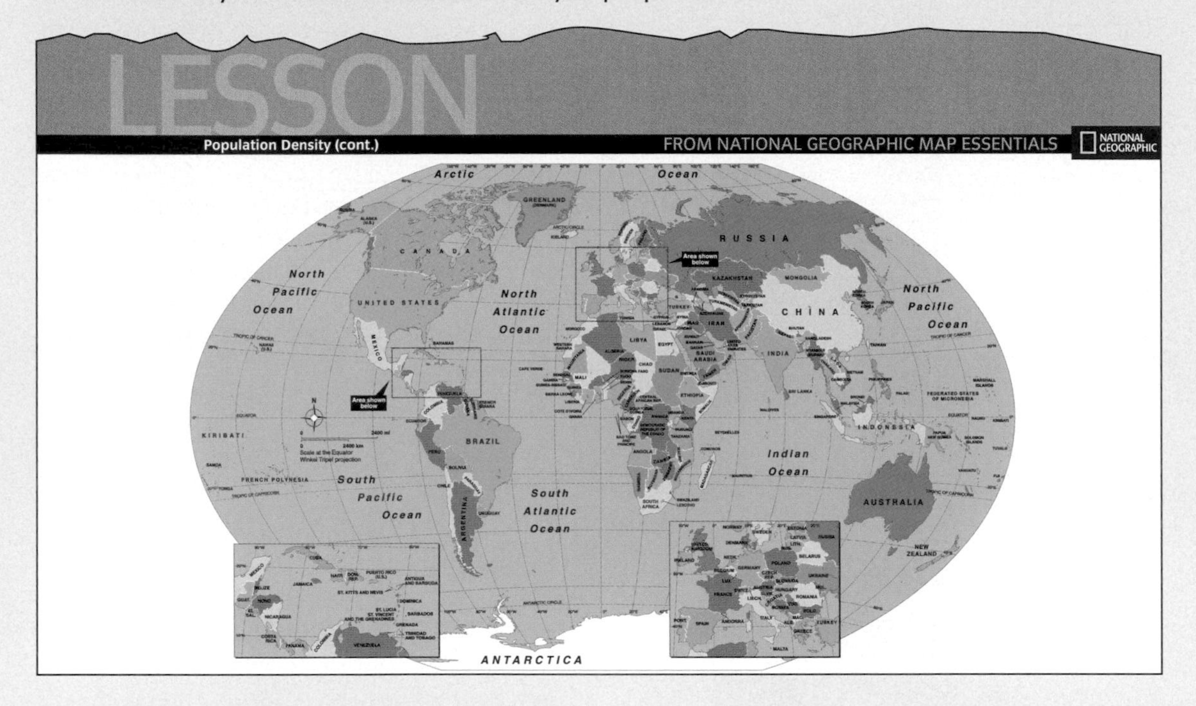

The Vietnam Veterans Memorial FIGURE 4.5

The Memorial includes the Three Servicemen Statue (A), the Nurse Comforts a Soldier (B), and the famous Wall of Names (C), designed by Maya Ying Lin, which contains the names of the 58,220 men and women who were killed or remain missing from the war. The enormous size of the wall with tens of thousands of names combined with the beauty of the reflective black granite leaves most people who visit the wall deeply moved. Students might study the symbolism of the Wall of Names by comparing it to other national symbols or by describing how they feel when they look at images of the Wall.

ILLUSTRATIONS AND PHOTOS support concepts covered in the text, elaborate on relevant issues, and add visual detail. Many of the photos originate from National Geographic's rich sources.

BOOK COMPANION SITE

(www.wiley.com/college/Lee)

Instructor resources on the book companion site include an Instructor's Manual by Amy Good, East Carolina University, and all illustrations and photos in the text in jpeg format.

ACKNOWLEDGMENTS

PROFESSIONAL FEEDBACK

Throughout the process of writing and developing this text and the visual pedagogy, I benefited from the comments and constructive criticism provided by the instructors and colleagues listed below. My sincere appreciation to these individuals for their helpful reviews:

Margaret Beddow, *California State University at Sacramento*

Geraldine Brown, *Drexel University*

Sandra Byrd, *University of North Carolina at Ashville*

Allan Cook, *University of Illinois at Springfield*

Mary Couillard, *Saginaw Valley State University*

Kristie Fowler, *Hollins University*

Jeri Gillin, *Providence College*

Amy Good, *East Carolina University*

Susan Gooden, *University of Southern Indiana*

Thomas B. Goodkind, *University of Connecticut*

Peter Hester, *Rider University*

Betty Kansler, *College of Notre Dame*

Sandra Kaser, *University of Arizona*

Laurie Katz, *Ohio State University*

Marilyn May, *Brenau University*

Cathy Nelson, *University of St. Francis*

Debbie Noyes, *Greenville College*

Crystal Olson, *California State University at Sacramento*

Donna Pearson, *University of North Dakota*

Joan Purkey, *Newman University*

Sandy Rakes, *Delta State University*

Yolanda Ramirez, *University of Texas of the Permian Basin*

Beverly Ray, *Idaho State University*

Lois Schaefer, *Trinity Baptist College*

Julia Shahid, *Austin College*

Jean Spears, *Monmouth University*

Reese Todd, *Texas Tech University*

Scott Waters, *Emporia State University*

Saundra Wetig, *University of Nebraska*

FOCUS GROUPS AND TELESESSION PARTICIPANTS

A number of professors and students participated in focus groups and telesessions, providing feedback on the text, visuals, and pedagogy. Our thanks to the following participants for their helpful comments and suggestions:

Sylvester Allred, *Northern Arizona University*

David Bastedo, *San Bernardino Valley College*

Ann Brandt-Williams, *Glendale Community College*

Natalie Bursztyn, *Bakersfield College*

Stan Celestian, *Glendale Community College*

O. Pauline Chow, *Harrisburg Area Community College*

Diane Clemens-Knott, *California State University, Fullerton*

Mitchell Colgan, *College of Charleston*

Linda Crow, *Montgomery College*

Smruti Desai, *Cy-Fair College*

Charles Dick, *Pasco-Hernando Community College*

Donald Glassman, *Des Moines Area Community College*

Mark Grobner, *California State University, Stanislaus*

Michael Hackett, Westchester *Community College*

Gale Haigh, *McNeese State University*

Roger Hangarter, *Indiana University*

Michael Harman, *North Harris College*

Terry Harrison, *Arapahoe Community College*

Javier Hasbun, *University of West Georgia*

Stephen Hasiotis, *University of Kansas*

Adam Hayashi, *Central Florida Community College*

Laura Hubbard, *University of California, Berkeley*

James Hutcheon, *Georgia Southern University*

Scott Jeffrey, *Community College of Baltimore County, Catonsville Campus*

Matther Kapell, *Wayne State University*

Arnold Karpoff, *University of Louisville*

Dale Lambert, *Tarrant County College NE*

Arthur Lee, *Roane State Community College*

Harvey Liftin, *Broward Community College*

Walter Little, *University at Albany, SUNY*

Mary Meiners, *San Diego Miramar College*

Scott Miller, *Penn State University*

Jane Murphy, *Virginia College Online*

Bethany Myers, *Wichita State University*

Terri Oltman, *Westwood College*

Keith Prufer, *Wichita State University*

Ann Somers, *University of North Carolina, Greensboro*

Donald Thieme, *Georgia Perimeter College*

Kip Thompson, *Ozarks Technical Community College*

Judy Voelker, *Northern Kentucky University*

Arthur Washington, *Florida A&M University*

Stephen Williams, *Glendale Community College*

Feranda Williamson, *Capella University*

SPECIAL THANKS

I am extremely grateful to the many members of the editorial and production staff at John Wiley and Sons who guided me through the challenging steps of developing this book. Their tireless enthusiasm, professional assistance, and endless patience smoothed the path as I found my way. I thank in particular: Robert Johnston, Acquisitions Editor, who directed the process; Helen McInnis, Managing Director, Wiley Visualizing, who oversaw the concept and development of the book; Eileen McKeever, Editorial Assistant, who was always unfailingly responsive; Kelly Tavares, Associate Production Manager, who stepped in whenever I needed expert advice; Jay O'Callaghan, Vice President and Publisher, who oversaw the entire project; and the marketing team of Jeffrey Rucker and Emily Struetker, who adeptly represent the Visualizing imprint.

I wish also to acknowledge the contributions of Vertigo Design for the interior design concept; Harry Nolan, Wiley's Creative Director, who gave art direction and refined the design and other elements; and Hope Miller, who designed the cover. I appreciate the efforts of Hilary Newman in obtaining some of the text photos, and Anna Melhorn, Senior Illustration Editor, for her expertise in managing the illustration program.

I especially want to thank Stacy Gold, Research Editor and Account Executive at the National Geographic Image Collection, for her valuable expertise in selecting NGS photos.

Many other individuals at National Geographic offered their expertise and assistance in developing this book: Francis Downey, Vice President and Publisher, and Richard Easby, Supervising Editor, National Geographic School Division; Mimi Dornack, Sales Manager, and Lori Franklin, Assistant Account Executive, National Geographic Image Collection; Dierdre Bevington-Attardi, Project Manager, and Kevin Allen, Director of Map Services, National Geographic Maps. I appreciate their contributions and support.

Lastly, I would like to thank my family and personal colleagues who have given me invaluable suggestions and support. Their encouragement, ideas, and patient considerations have made this project a tolerable and in fact enjoyable endeavor.

CONTENTS *in Brief*

CONTENTS

5 Teaching for Historical Understanding 110

6 Teaching for Geographic Awareness 138

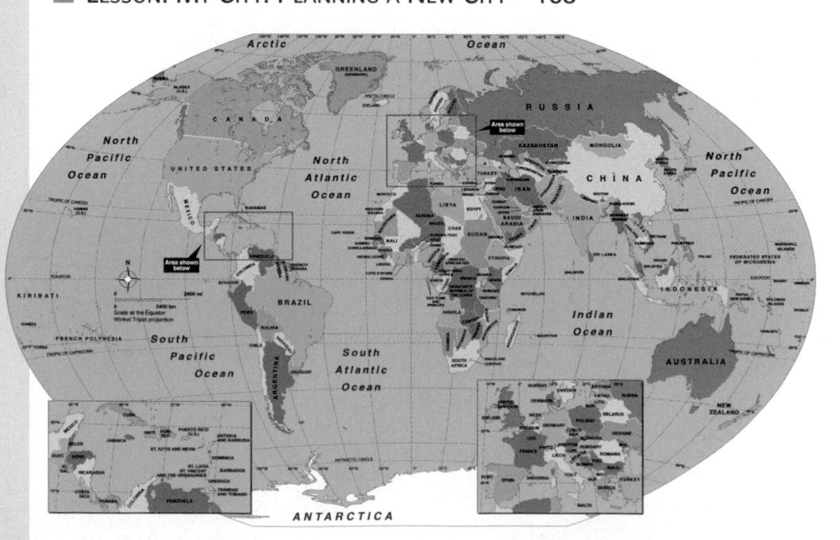

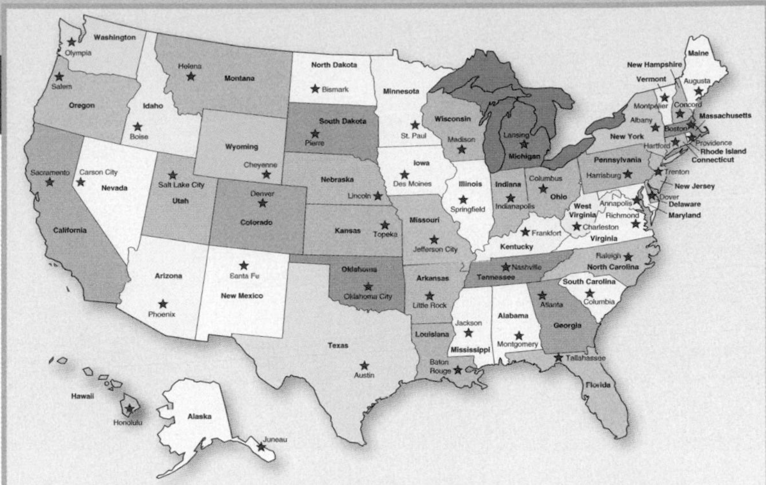

1:45-2:30 Math
2:30-2:45 Read Aloud
ABRAHAM LINCOLN

11 Planning for Active Learning 288

12 Teaching Social Studies in a Diverse Society 314

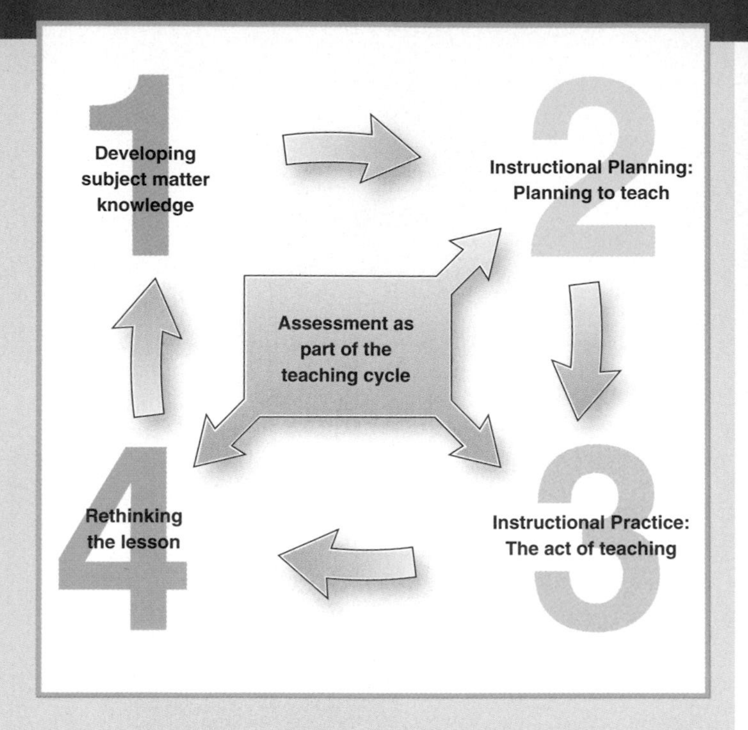
1
Developing subject matter knowledge
2
Instructional Planning: Planning to teach
Assessment as part of the teaching cycle
3
Instructional Practice: The act of teaching
4
Rethinking the lesson

VISUALIZING FEATURES

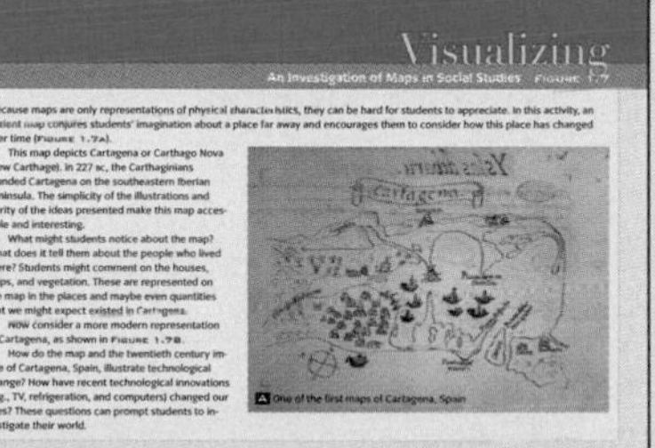

PROCESS DIAGRAMS

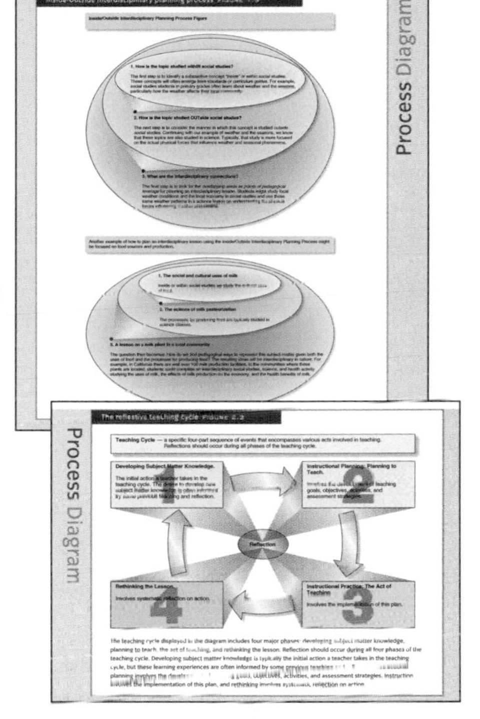

The *National Council for the Social Studies* (NCSS) offers the broadest definition for social studies. In 1992, the Board of Directors of NCSS adopted this definition:

> **Social studies** is the integrated study of the social sciences and humanities to promote civic competence. Within the school program, social studies provides coordinated, systematic study drawing upon such disciplines as anthropology, archaeology, economics, geography, history, law, philosophy, political science, psychology, religion, and sociology, as well as appropriate content from the humanities, mathematics, and natural sciences. The primary purpose of social studies is to help young people develop the ability to make informed and reasoned decisions for the public good as citizens of a culturally diverse, democratic society in an interdependent world.

Social studies The integrated study of the social sciences and humanities to promote civic competence.

THE NATURE OF SOCIAL STUDIES

The NCSS definition attempts to include three distinct dispositions about the field. First, NCSS claims that social studies is designed to promote *civic competence.* Second, the NCSS definition involves a *multiple disciplinary approach* to social studies. Third, the definition puts forth a rationale for social studies aimed at a *public or common good.* In the following sections we explore each of these dispositions.

Social Studies for Civic Competence

The knowledge and skills needed to be an effective citizen in a **democracy** are multifaceted. Some organizations, such as the *Core Knowledge Foundation,* have suggested that a core body of knowledge is a prerequisite for meaningful civic dialogue and action. What that body of knowledge includes is less important than agreement that a body of knowledge is commonly developed by school children in an academic setting. This approach is embodied in national standards movements in the United States and national curriculums in countries all over the world.

Democracy Most typically thought of as government by the people, either in direct or representative form, but also meant to refer more broadly to principles of social cooperation and individual rights.

Civic competence has also been conceptualized by a host of national and international organizations as including not only knowledge components, but also skills. The *Center for Civic Education* has developed a range of programs for developing civic competence in young people in the United States focused on **civic virtue**, civic participation, and civic knowledge and skills. Other organizations such as *CIVITAS International,* which focuses on strengthening civic education in new and established democracies around the world, aim to extend civic education beyond formal schooling to include public and private organizations acting to promote civic democratic practices.

Civic competence The knowledge and skills needed to actively and productively participate in democratic life.

Civic virtue The necessary moral nature of participation in a democracy.

Multiple Disciplinary Social Studies

For many teachers and researchers, social studies is **multidisciplinary**. For some this means that social studies is a collection of discrete disciplines, while others approach it as a synthesis of academic disciplines or some combination of both. NCSS views the academic disciplines of anthropology, archaeology, economics, geography, history, law, philosophy, political science, psychology, religion, and sociology as collectively contributing toward the delivery of effective social studies learning.

Other organizations have taken the separate disciplines approach and attempted to exert more extensive control over social studies curriculum, knowledge, and practice. Organizations within the discipline of history have been particularly active in trying to shape social studies. In its infancy, social studies was deeply influenced by historians in the *American Historical Association* (AHA) who called for history to be the focus of the social studies. Today the AHA, the *Organization of American Historians* (OAH), and the *World History Association* (WHA) continue to recommend that history be the focus of social studies. Likewise, the *National Council for Geographic Education* (NCGE) has called for the discipline of geography to occupy a central place in the social studies curriculum.

FIGURE 1.3

These children are working together to solve a problem related to land use. How can such activities be focused on the common good?

Social Studies for the Common Good

In its 1994 standards publication, NCSS defined the **common good** as "the general welfare of all individuals and groups within the community." This definition reflects some significant differences in how teachers approach teaching for the common good. What does the term "common good" actually represent and how can social studies teachers promote a common good? (See FIGURE 1.3.)

Common good The general welfare of all individuals and groups within a community.

In order to understand the NCSS definition of the common good, we must consider the role of ideology—specifically, as it relates to individuals and communities. Liberals tend to want to focus on community group action when thinking about the common good, and many liberal educators believe that the common good must ultimately take form through community group–based social action. Such a belief might suggest that social studies teachers should prepare their students for social action. Conservatives tend to be more concerned with the improvement or welfare of individuals as opposed to groups. Thus, an instructional focus on individual learning outcomes and personal responsibility is typically more in line with conservative approaches to promoting the common good. NCSS has deliberately attempted to weave through the complications of potential ideological discord by endorsing the common good as dependent on both individual (conservative) and collective (liberal) action.

CONCEPT CHECK STOP

NCSS sees the common good as central to social studies instruction. What types of common good are evident in this image?

What contradictions emerge when considering social studies for the common good as opposed to social studies as a discipline?

In what ways can these two purposes be unified or made more similar?

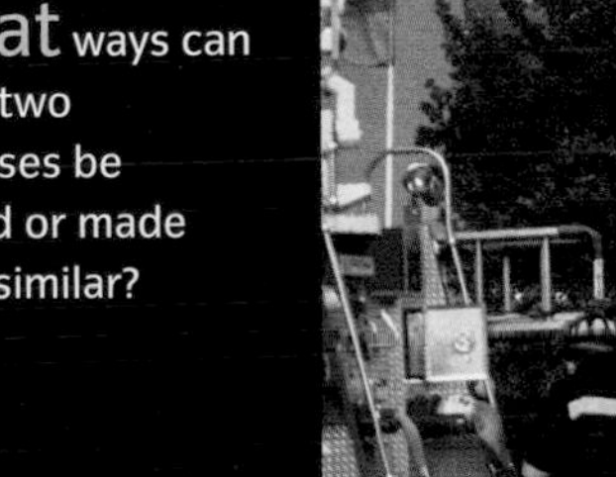

Firefighters in an Oakland, California, residential area battle a blazing fire that killed, 24 people and destroyed 2,500 homes.

Social Studies as a School Subject

LEARNING OBJECTIVES

Describe when and why social studies first emerged as a school subject.

Explain the early evolution of social studies in the public schools.

Recognize the origins of current perspectives on social studies purposes.

THE HISTORY OF SOCIAL STUDIES

Social studies appeared by name in the public schools in the years just before World War I. The concept of social studies and the social studies course both have a long and interesting history. David Warren Saxe (1991) has argued that social studies has its roots in the Social Welfare movement, which emerged in Britain in the 1820s. The movement provided a starting point for organized efforts to address and consider social problems in democracies. This movement would eventually lead to the development of an academic field of study called social science as well as social science organizations. By the 1880s, the formal study of social sciences had been introduced in British and American schools. An Episcopal minister and scholar named R. Heber Newton coined the term "social study" in 1887 to refer to studies within the social sciences directed at improving conditions for poor urban workers (**FIGURE 1.4**).

By 1900, calls for "social education" in public schools and "social-centered" education were proliferating. One of the first formal programs in social studies was founded by Hampton University professor Thomas Jesse Jones, but public school social studies programs did not emerge until after a 1916 recommendation for the inclusion of social studies in public school curriculum by committees working through the National Educational Association.

Initial social studies courses were very similar to what we see in schools today—primarily history, geography, and civics courses focused on factual recall. How-

FIGURE 1.4

Two girls, one seated at a sewing machine and the other standing, work in a textile mill. How do the working conditions depicted in this image illustrate the problems R. Heber Newton might have seen in society?

ever, between 1916 and today, there have been two major efforts to change social studies education. In the 1930s, **social reconstructionists** such as George Counts and Harold Rugg aimed to redirect social studies practice toward collective action and social change. The impact of their work was moderate, but quickly faded with the outbreak of World War II. In the 1960s, a movement called the *New Social Studies* (FIGURE 1.5) refocused the field, this time on inquiry. We still see the legacy of new social studies in schools today, but the national standards movement of the 1990s resulted in a return to the fact-and-recall social studies of the early 20th century.

Social reconstructionists Activists who aimed to redirect social studies practice toward collective action and social change.

EARLY PURPOSES OF SOCIAL STUDIES

From 1913 to 1916, Progressive Era committees organized by the National Education Association formally called for social studies courses in the public schools. These committees conducted their work in the wake of great social change brought on by the rapid industrialization of large urban centers in the United States and northern Europe, as well as the influx of immigrants to the United States from all parts of Europe.

The influx of immigrants into the United States in the late 19th century resulted in a different kind of education—one that could help set the context for the assimilation of new immigrants as well as establish a means for social control. In this environment, the National Education Association's Committee on Social Studies through its mammoth Reorganization of Secondary Schools project introduced "social studies" to the mainstream educational community in 1916 by recommending a course in social studies as part of the standard curriculum.

Although the Committee on Social Studies was more likely to be in favor of a social education approach to the social studies, the implementation of social studies was decidedly more conservative. Instead of focusing on social problems and the improvement of social conditions, as the committee's report implied, most social studies instruction continued to be academic in nature and focused on teaching students about concepts and generalizations in various disciplines such as history and geography. Conservatives and liberal progressives disagreed over how social studies should be taught. Despite consistent efforts to bridge the differences over how social studies should be conceptualized and taught, this gulf is still with us today.

FIGURE 1.5

How might the protest outside the 1968 Democratic National Convention, pictured here, be used in a "New Social Studies" classroom? Think about how students might inquire into sixties-era upheaval in the United States over the Vietnam War and civil rights.

A new approach for social studies in China

Social studies serves important purposes for different groups of people around the world. Often these purposes change over time. This idea of change over time is evident in China, where social studies has evolved to reflect new ideological priorities. In the past, social studies served in support of a command economy and state authority. This traditional Chinese focus on command economics results in a very different social studies curriculum from what we see in the United States, where the emphasis is on a free market economy and a democratic system. Despite the long-standing traditional focus in China, in recent years the Chinese school curriculum has opened up to focus more on market economics and individual issues.

How has the Chinese social studies curriculum reflected these changes? Certainly, a communal approach would result in different social studies experiences than would an emphasis on the individual. One way to illustrate these changes is through a consideration of recent Chinese history, as seen in these three photos. How do these images demonstrate tensions between individualist and communal interests? How might these different interests influence social studies? Each image portrays something iconic in China that is situated in a part of Chinese history. Think about how China has changed from its dynastic past prior to the 1911 fall of the last Chinese Emperor Pu Yi, through nationalist and communist periods of the twentieth century, to the current market reforms under way in China.

Think about how each of these images supports or contradicts command and free market economic ideas and authoritarian and democratic ideals. Then consider how the social studies curricula in China and the United States might be designed to reflect the various influences resulting from economic and social structures.

Home of a Mao Brigade member in Hainan island commune, Guangdong Province, 1981

Chairman Mao Tse Dung portrait at the Forbidden City

Bank of China building in Hong Kong

CONCEPT CHECK **STOP**

How would the influx of immigrants at Ellis Island affect what was taught in school social studies programs at the time?

When might immigration have influenced how social studies was taught and what was taught in social studies?

The Registry Room at Ellis Island

Approaches to Social Studies

LEARNING OBJECTIVES

Recognize three common approaches to teaching social studies.

Apply knowledge of the subject matter to different teaching situations.

Make choices about how to represent your knowledge for pedagogical purposes.

Describe the inside/outside process for thinking in an interdisciplinary way about concepts.

Throughout this book, we will be looking at models and specific examples of how teachers develop pedagogical knowledge by transforming their knowledge of social studies subject matter into knowledge of how to teach social studies. In this section, we will start with some basic approaches to teaching social studies that emerge from the central purposes of the discipline.

Social studies is a complex subject. As teachers we can represent this complexity for children through the presentation of stories, investigations, and deliberations. The "In the Classroom" feature on page 12 describes a storytelling activity from a first-grade classroom about Christopher Columbus and the Taíno Native Americans. The "Visualizing" feature on page 15 explains how students might investigate changes over time in Cartagena, Spain, using a variety of sources. The "Lesson" on pages 16–17 describes how students might deliberate about problems and opportunities associated with mining and drilling in the Amazon River Basin. Each of these features highlights one of three unique approaches to social studies and is focused on specific subject matter adaptations that are part of a larger **pedagogy** of the subject.

Pedagogy Most broadly, the act or art of teaching; also the substance of the knowledge of how to teach.

THREE APPROACHES TO SOCIAL STUDIES

Teachers craft social studies experiences for students to reflect their own talents and to take advantage of resources in the school and the community. Social studies practice should include practices with which teachers are comfortable and confident. These can be thought of as practical pedagogical approaches to teaching content. Jerome Bruner (1999) calls such practical approaches folk pedagogies and views this form of teacher knowledge as emerging from the experiences of those who are teaching or have taught. These teachers' ideas about teaching are not formalized, but instead are passed on as traditions of success in the classroom.

In the Classroom TEACHING ABOUT CHRISTOPHER COLUMBUS

In a recent class, Mr. Gregory told the story of Columbus's first contact with Native Americans to his first-grade students. The story is well known, but, like much of social studies, it is full of complexity, including conflict and violence. Mr. Gregory knows that if he includes too much of this conflict and violence, he may create anxiety among his young students, so he decides to cast the story as one of missed opportunities. In his story, Mr. Gregory describes Columbus as a man who was motivated to do good, but also was limited by greed and self-centeredness. He describes the Taíno Native Americans whom Columbus encountered as relatively naïve, simple, and primitive, but also brave in the face of this unknown group of Europeans.

Alonso de Hojeda, an agent of Columbus, cuts off an ear of a Taíno Indian during a trek to reinforce the inland fortress of Santo Tomas on Hispaniola Island. The incident, portrayed in a watercolor painting by Arthur Shilstone, occurred after one of the Indians was accused of stealing clothes from some Spaniards. How does this image illustrate the complexities of the relationship between the Spanish and Taíno?

Three practical pedagogical approaches for elementary social studies include the following:

1. *Storytelling*
2. *Investigating*
3. *Deliberating*

1. **Storytelling** is a teaching approach that takes advantage of what educators call "direct" instructional pedagogical practices. You will read more about direct instruction later. For now we can think of this approach to teaching as capitalizing on teachers' capacities as storytellers and lecturers. Levstik and Barton (2001) describe effective storytelling as engaging children's interests as well as reflecting multiple interpretations. Children must understand that history is not based on a single narrative or a sole perspective. Every person has his or her own story and all stories have some value.

Let's look at an example of how we might develop a story from subject matter that might interest children. Consider the topic of famous women in the twentieth century. Two such women, Mary McLeod Bethune and Eleanor Roosevelt, worked to address social problems in the 1930s and 1940s. This picture of Bethune and Roosevelt illustrates the closeness of their relationship (FIGURE 1.6). Bethune was Roosevelt's "Special Advisor on Minority Affairs" for 1935–1944. The story of their friendship is also the story of African American emancipation and political involvement in the middle of the 20th century.

If we were to use the storytelling approach to teaching this subject matter, students might hear a ten-minute story about Bethune and Roosevelt using the women's friendship as an organizing framework. Casting the work of these women in the frame of friendship should help students better relate to the subject matter and thus potentially lead to better retention of the facts presented in the story. As students relate to subject matter, they begin to see themselves as part of the stories they are being told. Students might be more likely to remember the story of Bethune and Roosevelt, as well as assorted facts related to their lives, if they associate these facts to something meaningful to them, such as the concept of friendship. Cognitive psychologists call this process semantic elaboration.

FIGURE 1.6

Mary McLeod Bethune (left) and Eleanor Roosevelt (right)

2. **Investigating** is a student-centered teaching approach that enables learners to consider problems, topics, people, places, events, and other social phenomena that have some meaning or relevance to them. To better explain this teaching approach, look at the feature on page 15 titled "Visualizing: An Investigation of Maps in Social Studies" (FIGURE 1.7). This feature describes an exercise on geographic and physical changes that occur over time in a place. Investigation exercises such as this are based on questions or unexplained events or ideas. An investigation requires the use of sources such as maps or pictures and should result in students better understanding something that was previously unknown or misunderstood.

3. **Deliberating** is a teaching approach to social studies that focuses on the development of students' dispositions about social problems. In this approach, students clarify what they think is most important in situations and places where conflict or limited resources are present. For example, much controversy has existed over how humans have used and continue to use natural resources.

Students can deliberate about the uses of natural resources in social studies. Consider the cost and benefits of mining and drilling in the Amazon River Basin and how teachers can facilitate their students' deliberations. First, let's look at some of the issues involved in the controversy over the Amazon River Basin.

For decades, conservationists and environmentalists have expressed alarm at the rate at which the world's forests are being depleted. Indigenous populations in Southeast Asia, Indonesia, Central Africa, and Central and South America are particularly concerned about deforestation and the related gradual loss of their way of life. A significant portion of deforestation has been attributed to the mining and petroleum industries. One of the most celebrated examples of native protest against deforestation has been in the Amazon region, where indigenous populations have garnered a tremendous amount of worldwide support.

Environmentalists are concerned about the loss of natural habitats and the acceleration of species extinction that accompanies deforestation. The mining and petroleum industries believe that they can steward the land in efficient and effective ways. Many corporations involved in drilling and mining have made concerted efforts in recent years to consider the cost of new exploration on biodiversity and indigenous people. At the same time, demand for oil and precious metals continues to rise, with consumers in countries such as the United States, India, and China pushing for new sources of these resources. See the "Lesson" on pages 16–17 for an in-depth explanation of how a teacher might guide students through a deliberation about drilling and mining in the Amazon River Basin.

How might you encourage a student investigation about the subject matter suggested in FIGURE 1.8?

How would your lesson be different if you used a direct instructional approach or a student-centered approach?

Investigating
FIGURE 1.8

A Sioux medicine man offers a ritual prayer to the buffalo.

Visualizing

An Investigation of Maps in Social Studies FIGURE 1.7

Because maps are only representations of physical characteristics, they can be hard for students to appreciate. In this activity, an ancient map conjures students' imagination about a place far away and encourages them to consider how this place has changed over time (FIGURE 1.7A).

This map depicts Cartagena or Carthago Nova (New Carthage). In 227 BC, the Carthaginians founded Cartagena on the southeastern Iberian Peninsula. The simplicity of the illustrations and clarity of the ideas presented make this map accessible and interesting.

What might students notice about the map? What does it tell them about the people who lived there? Students might comment on the houses, ships, and vegetation. These are represented on the map in the places and maybe even quantities that we might expect existed in Cartagena.

Now consider a more modern representation of Cartagena, as shown in FIGURE 1.7B.

How do the map and the twentieth century image of Cartagena, Spain, illustrate technological change? How have recent technological innovations (e.g., TV, refrigeration, and computers) changed our lives? These questions can prompt students to investigate their world.

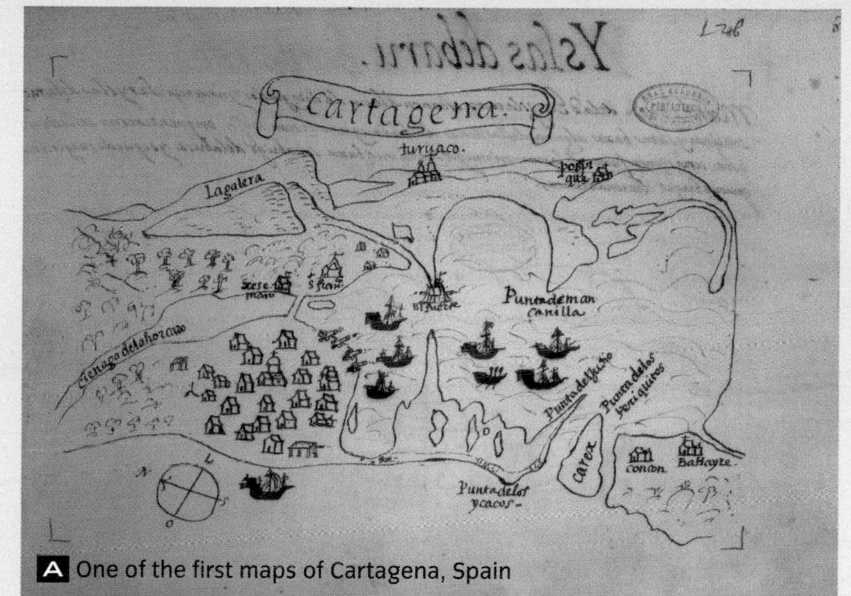

A One of the first maps of Cartagena, Spain

B A man fixes a TV antenna on a rooftop in modern Cartagena. In the background is the city, enveloped in pollution from local industry, against the outline of a mountain.

Jamestown example. What would a geographer want to know about the location of Jamestown? How does this knowledge help children understand the social story of the Jamestown settlement? By using the discipline of geography, students can answer these questions. Geographers describe a location in terms of its value for humans. In the case of Jamestown, the location was along a major waterway that extended in such a way that protected the settlement from attack. It was also easily accessible for ships coming from England. This knowledge helps us understand the precarious circumstances that the Jamestown settlers faced. They were far from home in a potentially hostile site and were dependent on a landscape they knew little about.

CIVICS

Part of the purpose of social studies is to instill in students a sense of civic responsibility. When children learn civics, they learn about how their government works, as well as the rights and responsibilities of citizens who live in this democracy. The students we teach in social studies are emerging citizens in the American democracy. To be productive citizens, they must participate in civic life. Civic life demands that we take positions on issues that are often contested and sometimes ideologically driven (e.g., Who should be the next president? How do we reduce the number of drunk drivers on the road?). The knowledge and skills that students develop in school support them in pursuing a meaningful civic life, and thus in carrying out democracy. Students construct their civic knowledge within the discipline of political science. Political scientists study the processes, principles, and structures of government. They study politics and political behavior and institutions. The knowledge they construct is the basis for civics in social studies.

Again, we devote a full chapter to civics, so let's think about our Jamestown example with special attention on political science or civics. What would a political scientist think about the construction of a fort as one of the first actions of the settlers of Jamestown? A political scientist would focus on the relationships that existed between the colonists and the native Indians as well as the political forces that compelled the Jamestown settlers to go to the Americas. The construction of a fort at Jamestown reflected the hostility that existed between European settlers and natives as well as the expansionist political environment in England. Students can use the processes used by political scientists as well as the content knowledge they develop to better understand the Jamestown story, elements of which are relevant in social studies.

ECONOMICS

Economics is the study of the production, distribution, and consumption of goods and services in a cultural setting. Most of us never think about how economies function, but understanding the process is central to a transparent and fair economy. If we do not understand how people get money and why some people have more than others, we may be less able to enrich our own lives or live comfortably within our means. Societies that are structured to protect small groups who control most of the wealth in the society do not allow citizens to learn about and participate equally in the economy. Students must develop a certain level of economic knowledge that will enable them to participate as economic actors, protecting their interests while understanding their responsibilities. Students must also understand how to manage their personal economics (e.g., balancing a checkbook), while developing an understanding of the larger macro forces that shape economic thought and action on a global scale.

How might teachers integrate the economics of Jamestown into social studies? How would an economist evaluate the value or potential value of the Jamestown settlement? An economist would look at the costs incurred when developing the colony and would compare them to the benefits that resulted from the settlement. For the first few years, Jamestown lost money and human resources. Hundreds of people died and the investors spent more than they got back. After time, the colony began to pay off. In the long run, the value of the Jamestown colony in paving the way for future settlement is incalculable. Such an analysis is of course only one side of the story. An economic evaluation of the Jamestown settlement from the Powhatan native Indian perspective would yield almost opposite findings. The Indians lost everything including their land, their culture, and ultimately their lives.

BEHAVIORAL SCIENCES

The behavioral sciences include psychology, anthropology, and sociology. Although subject matter from these disciplines is rarely if ever formally studied in elementary social studies, concepts and topics common in the fields are part of most social studies curriculums. For example, social studies curriculums often include concepts from sociology, such as family and culture. The behavioral sciences investigate human behavior, each using a different technique to explain human action. Psychology focuses on human actions and cognition in the present. Anthropologists look at human cultures, both past and present. Sociologists attempt to explain collective human action and behavior. For example, we study the reasons why people wanted to settle in Jamestown. What would a psychologist or anthropologist or sociologist find interesting about the work of William Kelso at Jamestown (see Figure 1.10)? Behavioral scientists can help us understand how the social structures of the English settlers conflicted with the natives who already lived in the area. For example, the natives did not understand the notion of private property. The English had constructed an entire culture around the protection of private property. Conflict over land reflected the differences the two groups had over how humans should interact with the land.

FIGURE 1.12

An American scientist and local Krongs in Burma study animal species around a fire.

Now, consider another case of two groups that have come together, the situation of an American scientist in Burma. How might the subject of this American scientist in Burma (FIGURE 1.12) prompt teaching in the social studies disciplines (history, geography, civics, economics, and behavioral sciences)? Think beyond the subject matter depicted in the picture to consider the place, the broader activity taking place, the different cultures represented, and the possible roles of each person in the activity.

CONCEPT CHECK STOP

How might a teacher present this image of an untouchable woman and child at a weaving loom as subject matter in each of the social studies content disciplines?

What are some of the economic, political, and geographic influences of the caste system in Indian history?

The untouchables are at the bottom of the caste social system that orders much of life in India. Although the caste system was banned in 1947, vestiges are still present.

Standards-Based Social Studies

LEARNING OBJECTIVES

Describe how standards have influenced social studies.

Compare the five major social studies-related standards projects.

Contrast positive and negative consequences of social studies standards.

Social studies, like all school subjects, has been deeply influenced by the recent development of national, state, and local **standards**. In many ways, the standards movement has been beneficial. National standards have helped teachers and researchers focus their understanding of the syntactic structures that provide rules to guide how the academic disciplines within social studies are organized. The standards projects have also pushed experts to grapple with what substance should be taught, and unfortunately this has often resulted in significant conflict. Despite the short-term conflicts, the resulting standards have been a positive force in helping to clarify and unify social studies and the related academic disciplines.

Standards
Criteria or goals by which one can judge the quality of educational achievement.

National standards have had some negative side effects for social studies educators. Critics argue that standards limit flexibility and creativity in the classroom. Some educators are concerned that their ideas or voices are left out of standards. Others worry that standards projects tend to focus on a lowest common learning denominator, or that standards pressure teachers and students to do too much with too little depth in a school year. Despite the criticisms, well-written standards establish reasonable benchmarks for subject matter understanding. They also help us to argue for challenging academic experiences for all children, regardless of race, ethnicity, or socioeconomic status. When standards are used to develop local curriculum and ultimately lessons and activities, children from diverse backgrounds have similar opportunities to learn similar things. In theory, this form of equal treatment can level the educational experiences for children who are potentially at risk.

There are five major national social studies standards documents, and all fifty states have developed additional social studies standards. Four of the five national projects were a product of a congressional mandate to develop academic standards in major school subject areas. Social studies was not included; instead, history, geography, government/civics, and economics standards were developed (FIGURE 1.13). A brief description of each of those standards documents follows. Although these standards were created through an act of Congress, the adoption of the standards by states is voluntary.

1. **National History Standards from the National Center for History in the Schools.** The National History Standards came to life amid a swirl of controversy. Conservative critics panned a first draft as anti-American and overly pessimistic. At the direction of the United States Senate, the National Center for History in the Schools redrafted the standards, which were overwhelmingly approved. The document puts forth

FIGURE 1.13

This ancient map and these navigation tools are representative of the major social studies disciplines (history, geography, political science, economics, and behavioral sciences). Consider how each discipline might develop standards related to some element of knowledge derived from this image.

separate standards for grades K–4 and 5–12 in historical thinking and historical understanding.

Available online at http://nchs.ucla.edu/standards/

2. **Geography for Life: National Geography Standards from the National Council for Geographic Education.** In 1994 the Geography Education Standards Project (a partnership of four major geography groups) published Geography for Life: National Geography Standards. Geography for Life was offered as a replacement for the "Five Themes of Geography" developed by a Joint Committee on Geographic Education of the National Council for Geographic Education (NCGE) and the Association of American Geographers (AAG). The new geography standards focus on six essential elements of geography: the world in spatial terms, places and regions, physical systems, human systems, environment and society, and the uses of geography.

   Available online at http://www.nationalgeographic.com/xpeditions/standards/

3. **National Standards for Civics and Government from the Center for Civic Education.** Separate K–4 and 5–12 standards for civics and government teaching are organized around five central questions. (1) What are civic life, politics, and government? (2) What are the foundations of the American political system? (3) How does the government established by the Constitution embody the purposes, values, and principles of American democracy? (4) What is the relationship of the United States to other nations and to world affairs? (5) What are the roles of the citizen in American democracy?

   Available online at http://www.civiced.org/stds.html

4. **Voluntary National Standards in Economics from the National Council on Economic Education.** The National Standards in Economics are a concise package of twenty standards that consist of detailed explanations and benchmarks for achievement at the fourth, eighth, and twelfth grades. These standards focus on concepts such as scarcity, supply and demand, markets, and entrepreneurs. The overall emphasis of the standards is to encourage economic literacy directed at children learning how to participate in economic life.

   Available online at http://www.ncee.net/ea/standards/

5. **Curriculum Standards for Social Studies from the National Council for the Social Studies.** These are a separate, nonmandated set of social studies standards developed by the National Council for the Social Studies (NCSS).

   NCSS standards focus on ten themes and draw from a wide range of humanities-based academic knowledge. The ten themes include Culture; Time; Continuity and Change; People, Places, and Environment; Individual Development and Identity; Individuals, Groups, and Institutions; Power, Authority, and Governance; Production, Distribution, and Consumption; Science, Technology, and Society; Global Connections; and Civic Ideals and Practices.

   Available online at http://www.ncss.org/standards/

States and communities use each of these five sets of standards differently. Since adoption is voluntary, some states have chosen to simply use the five national standards documents in social studies to inform the development of their own state social studies standards.

CONCEPT CHECK STOP

Can you find a topic in each of the five social studies standards that relates to this image of a soldier in the conflict-riddled Middle East?

Which of the NCSS themes can you see in this image?

U.S. Army troops and Iraqi civilians search for a downed U.S. pilot during the Iraq War in 2003.

What is happening in this picture?

Describe how we might teach about the people in this photo in an elementary social studies class, given the various purposes for social studies set forth in this chapter.

A slave family in a Georgia cotton field, c.1866

VISUAL SUMMARY

1 Defining Social Studies

The National Council for the Social Studies (NCSS) defines social studies as a school subject that helps prepare students to be effective participants in a democratic society. According to NCSS, good social studies instruction should promote civic competence using a multiple disciplinary approach. Furthermore, social studies instruction should be aimed at the promotion of a common good.

2 Social Studies as a School Subject

Social studies emerged as a formal subject well over one hundred years ago. The origins of social studies are sometimes situated in the social reform movement of Britain in the late 19th century. The National Educational Association (NEA) suggested the creation of a school subject called social studies in its 1916 report on the reorganization of public schools.

3 Approaches to Social Studies

Educators and the general public have conflicting opinions on how best to teach social studies. Some argue that social studies should involve the transmission of cultural ideas and knowledge, while others argue for a more active approach focused on social action and change. Still others see social studies as a combination of academic disciplinary activities. No matter what approach is selected, social studies is well suited for interdisciplinary work. Subject matter in social studies draws from the vast repository of life experiences and can be easily formed or adapted for study from disciplines including the language arts, mathematics, and science.

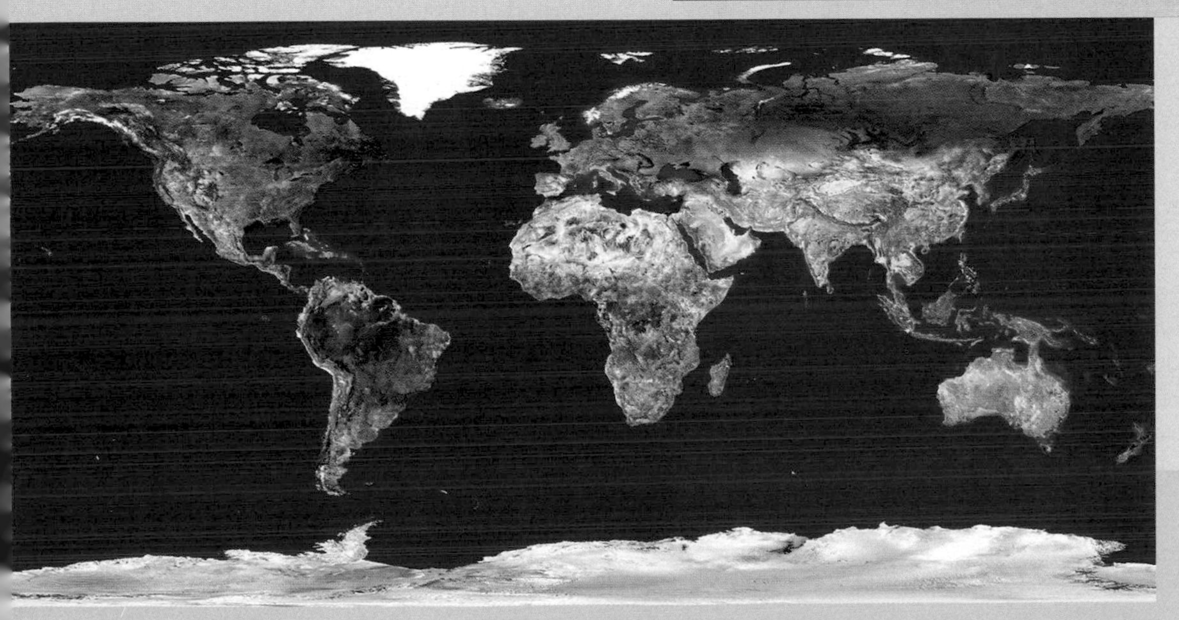

4 Social Studies and Content Disciplines

Social studies is often considered a collection of academic or content disciplines including history, geography, government (civics), economics, and the behavioral sciences, which include psychology, sociology, and anthropology.

s. Suez's experience teaching her students about the concept of time demonstrates that effective teaching is a process that requires consistent reflection on practice and a willingness to act on one's reflections. Acts of reflection, such as Ms. Suez's realization that her students needed help understanding a seventy-five-year period, are most appropriately embedded in the pedagogical practices of planning and teaching. As teachers implement their plans through acts of teaching, they are establishing contexts for **reflection**. Whether a teacher reflects during or after a planning and teaching period is not central to the process. What is central is that the reflection take place and that teachers act on their reflections in some meaningful and productive manner. This chapter argues for consistent and deliberate reflection and provides examples of how reflection informs social studies planning and teaching.

Reflection To reflect or think about something carefully; formal reflection may include the use of particular repeatable procedures for careful thinking.

Given the nature of the subject matter in social studies, reflection is particularly important. Elementary social studies curricula tend to be vague and less emphasized than other areas such as math and language arts. Elementary teachers must think very carefully about how to teach and integrate social studies in their classrooms.

What Is Reflection?

LEARNING OBJECTIVES

Identify the need for reflection in everyday teaching.

Distinguish between reflection in action and reflection on action.

Analyze how reflection fits into the teaching cycle.

In the 1980s, Donald Schön introduced the idea that reflection is a critical component of professional practice in education and other professions. Schön (1983) suggested that professionals should consistently and systematically reflect in action and reflect on action. Reflection in action might be thought of as thinking on your feet. We certainly can appreciate the importance of this in an elementary classroom. A class full of energetic children might be one of the most dynamic and fluid professional environments that exists. Without the ability to "think on her feet," a teacher would be severely limited, but professional reflection includes more than just thinking on your feet. It must also include a reasoned post-event action. In other words, teachers must also reflect after they teach—what Schön called reflect on action. Reflection in and on professional practice in education allows teachers to adapt to changing educative conditions and account for new ideas and unforeseen circumstances.

REFLECTION IN ACTION

How can teachers actually reflect during their instructional practice? Often teachers will pause, physically or mentally, to rethink something that is not working. This kind of adaptation is in fact a hallmark of good teaching. Essentially, it means that teachers understand that action in the classroom is not static and can never be perfectly predicted. Instead of trying to predict what will happen in a class, reflective teachers maintain flexibility by preparing a variety of options for what they plan to teach. This allows teachers to choose what will work best in their classroom.

The most common forms of reflection in action are informal. We expect teachers to respond to new conditions as they emerge in the classroom, but at the same time we do not want teachers to just react to problems. Reflection is not simply putting out fires. Instead, reflective teachers need to expect the unexpected during their teaching. As is illustrated in FIGURE 2.1, reflec-

FIGURE 2.1

The teacher in Figure 2.1 is willing to listen to her student as he tries to make sense of a story in his textbook. Why is it important for the teacher to reflect as she works with her student?

tive teachers can solve teaching problems in a positive and productive way by opening themselves to the idea that teaching can be adaptive and even experimental.

REFLECTION ON ACTION

After a teaching and learning episode, one of the most important intellectual tasks confronting a teacher is systematic reflection. Reflection on action allows teachers to consider what went right and what went wrong. Far too often teachers get stuck in the rut of looking ahead and planning for the next lesson without considering where they have been. In order to prepare for the next day, teachers have to consider what their students have achieved to date, and that requires reflection. Meaningful reflection on action should include a deliberate effort to see the teaching and learning events that just unfolded as a narrative, or story. Just like the events in a story, teaching and learning episodes are full of unexpected occurrences, twists, and turns. When teachers reflect, they are thinking about unforeseen events, mistakes, or unresolved problems from a classroom teaching experience and trying to generate some resolution (just like the resolution to a story!).

What does reflection on action look like? Read the following internal monologue of a student teacher thinking about teaching and consider the purpose of the reflection and what this teacher resolved through reflection.

Leaders and Followers: Coaxing Participation of Shy Students, by Jenelle Smith

I thought my students were going to love my lesson on colonial Georgia. I developed what I thought was an interesting and personal lesson on comparisons between life in colonial Georgia and life in Georgia today. I planned for students to learn about clothing, housing, schooling, and employment and to think about the advantages that they may have today over children who lived in colonial times. First, I gave students a letter written by a young girl named Elizabeth who lived at that time. In the letter, Elizabeth talks about colonial schools, transportation, clothing, and housing. The students answered questions comparing Elizabeth's life to their own everyday lives today.

For the main activity, students sat in groups. I gave each group a laminated card, which displayed a colonial item they were to assemble. The items included a horn book, a quill pen, a pomander ball, and a whirligig, along with assembly instructions. Each group took turns describing their object to the other students. They appeared to really enjoy this lesson, but that is not to say it went over without incident. As happens often with group work, there were students who completed the majority of the work for the group, and students who sat back and let the others finish the task. I thought this happened because my grouping strategy did not compel shy students to participate.

In an attempt to adjust this lesson for the following periods, I selected the groupings before the students came to class. These groups were based on the students' personalities and work habits. I placed students that were less likely to take charge with those I was certain would do just that. In a further effort to guarantee participation of all students, I assigned a group leader, based on past behavior and participation habits. The leader was in charge of making sure each group member had a job in the activity. I hoped that this would improve participation for those students who were more likely to leave the work to others, whether it was through laziness or shyness. I found that participation was much higher with the prearranged grouping and the group leaders. The students I selected as leaders did a great job at keeping their classmates motivated.

In a further effort to ensure equal group participation, especially from those who were shy, each student was to complete a step in the construction of their assigned item. The instructions I gave to each group were arranged by steps, so this adjustment was an easy one to make. To avoid bickering over the steps, the students counted off. Their number was the step assigned to them. Giving each student a specific job really helped ensure participation. Ultimately, I found that what I tried worked pretty well, and I really learned how important it is to constantly think about my teaching.

Schön's ideas about reflection in and on action are only two ways to conceptualize the act of reflection. We might also think about reflection as being part of a cycle of thinking. Reflection is one critical component in the development of knowledge about how to teach—what we call pedagogical knowledge. In fact, pedagogical knowledge cannot be developed or sustained without reflection. The **reflective teaching cycle** Process Diagram, FIGURE 2.2, describes a process for teaching with reflection.

Teaching cycle A specific four-part sequence of events that encompasses various acts involved in teaching.

Process Diagram

The reflective teaching cycle FIGURE 2.2

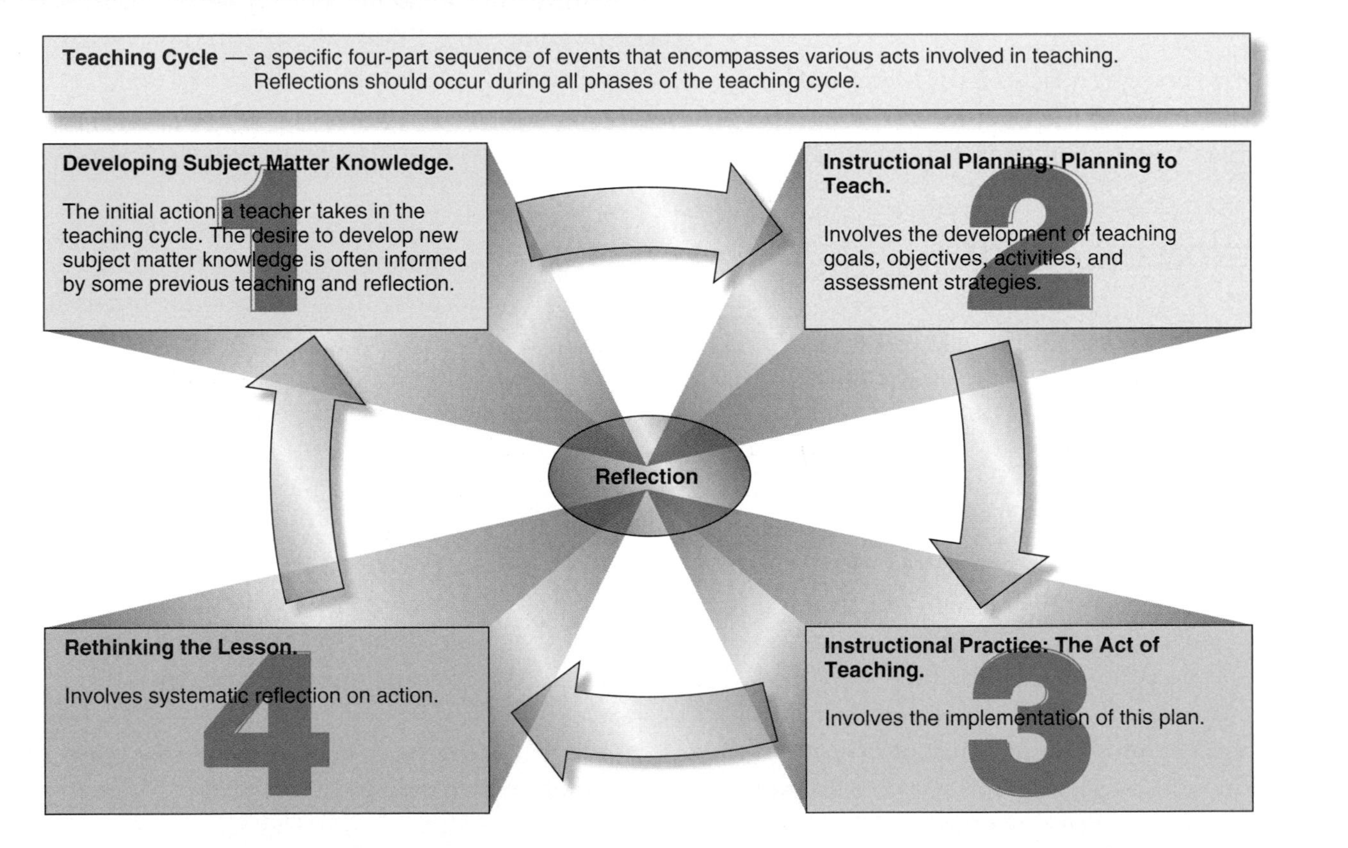

The teaching cycle displayed in the diagram includes four major phases: developing subject matter knowledge, planning to teach, the act of teaching, and rethinking the lesson. Reflection should occur during all four phases of the teaching cycle. Developing subject matter knowledge is typically the initial action a teacher takes in the teaching cycle, but these learning experiences are often informed by some previous teaching and reflection. Instructional planning involves the development of teaching goals, objectives, activities, and assessment strategies. Instruction involves the implementation of this plan, and rethinking involves systematic reflection on action.

CONCEPT CHECK STOP

Imagine you are teaching about 1950s culture in the United States. The image of this Washington, D.C., diner represents this unique period of time in American cultural life.

How might students with different cultural backgrounds react differently to the image?

How might reflecting on possible student reactions play out in a teaching episode?

What adjustments might you make if not all students recognize this image as a soda shop?

What if some students have never heard of a soda shop or a diner?

Reflection Prior to Instruction

LEARNING OBJECTIVES

Identify how to reflect on subject matter knowledge derived from personal interests.

Distinguish between curricular and personal subject matter.

Analyze the reflective process as it relates to subject matter misunderstandings.

Identify the role of reflection in instructional planning.

ne specific form of reflection for all teachers occurs in the process of developing **subject matter knowledge**. For example, teachers often reflect on their personal interests in the process of learning new subject matter. Think about your favorite topic in social studies and why you are interested in the topic. Your interests can serve as a starting point for reflection. Think about why people who live in your city would be interested in the history of the area. Your thinking about those interests is reflection on subject matter. At the same time, teachers must develop curricular-based subject matter knowledge regardless of their personal interests. The interplay between personal interests and the demands of curriculum is also a subject of reflection for teachers. Teachers constantly make decisions about how to spend their time learning new material. These decisions occur during and after reflection.

Subject matter knowledge Understanding about content in a specific academic area, such as history.

Reflection on subject matter presumes that we are always seeking to enhance or improve our understanding of some topic. Reflection on subject matter focuses not just on what we know and what curriculum requires us to teach about, but also our misunderstandings of that subject matter. These reflections on misunderstandings allow us to improve our knowledge about what we teach and thus be better able to teach. One commonly misunderstood area is the causes of the American Civil War. Often people try to distill these causes to a short list or even a single cause. Reflection generally leads people to a realization that the causes of the Civil War were complex and, as historian Edward Ayers has said, emotional and uninformed.

Reflection allows teachers to consider what they know about their students, the curriculum, and the community in which they teach. Through reflection, teachers begin to reshape and reform their knowledge of subject matter for pedagogical contexts. Knowing about the American Civil War is one thing, but knowing how and what to teach about the Civil War is another. Reflection on what you know about the Civil War given a need to teach about the subject should change what you know about the subject.

PERSONAL SUBJECT MATTER INTERESTS

Each of us has a set of personal likes and dislikes, experiences, and interests that drive our personal quests for knowledge. Professional growth is dependent on using our personal interests of subject matter to motivate us to continually develop our knowledge. Unless we have some well-developed context, such as personal interests, into which we place our new understandings, we will most likely be limited in our opportunities for growth. Consider planning for a lesson on space. A teacher who is interested in space or space travel will be compelled by his or her interest to study a wide range of topics related to space. Absent that personal interest, teachers must rely on external motivators such as curriculum, parental expectations, or school administrative requirements for turning in lessons.

Sometimes our quest for new knowledge is driven by a desire to address a subject matter knowledge deficit. There are many events that might help us realize our subject matter deficiencies. Often these events are social or academic. For example, we might have a conversation with another teacher or a friend and realize that our knowledge is limited. Or, we might take a class in college and find out that there are large gaps in our knowledge of content. As teachers, we should continually give ourselves opportunities to find out what we do not know. These opportunities to grow in our knowledge of subject matter will make us better teachers.

FOCUSING ON CURRICULAR SUBJECT MATTER

Teachers have a professional obligation to continually develop their knowledge of curricular subject matter. Teachers who are employed by a school system are contractually obliged to "know" what they are teaching about as well as morally responsible to not mislead their students and others about the subject matter. Elementary teachers have considerable responsibilities with regard to what they know. They must develop knowledge in all academic areas and consider how these bodies of knowledge interact. Given these conditions, reflection on understanding of curricular subject matter is particularly important in elementary settings.

How can teachers enhance their knowledge of curricular subject matter through reflection? First, the process requires engagement with curriculum at local, state, and national levels. Let's look at a specific example of how teachers might reflect on some curricular subject matter. Consider the curricular requirement that social studies should include instruction about major world religions. One way to approach religion in elementary social studies is to focus on the three major world religions, which were all founded in the Middle East and, in some way, owe their origin to Abraham (see "Lesson" on pp. 38–39). A lesson on a topic such as religion will often generate questions from students. Such questions can promote reflection and, if engaged, should lead to a deeper understanding of the pedagogy of the subject matter.

REFLECTING ON SUBJECT MATTER MISUNDERSTANDINGS

We all have misunderstandings about subject matter. We considered misunderstandings about the causes of the Civil War earlier. Think of a subject matter misunderstanding you might have corrected at some point in your life. For example, maybe you could not remember the original 13 American colonies or confused the dates of historical events. If you have corrected these misunderstandings (or when you correct them!), it will probably be because you were either unsatisfied with your knowledge or unsure about what you knew. Being unsatisfied or unsure usually results from reflection, or taking the time to think about what we know and do not know. Too frequently, teachers develop subject matter knowledge at a hurried pace—without enough time to reflect. It is often an unfortunate reality that teachers are trying to stay a day ahead of students. Reflection can help ameliorate the problem of limited or shallow subject knowledge that results from teaching conditions in which teachers, particularly new teachers, have to learn subject matter as they teach.

Reflection aimed at uncovering misunderstandings requires that teachers are willing to recognize their limitations. When working with children who are developing new knowledge, teachers must have confidence in their own subject matter knowledge, but of course there is a danger with not being open to our knowledge limitations. Accepting what we do not understand and then considering why we do not understand something can lead us to the pursuit of new knowledge, which might correct a misunderstanding or extend our knowledge in unforeseen ways.

For example, it is not uncommon for people to misunderstand regional climate due to mistaken generalities about expected temperatures. A teacher might encounter this misunderstanding when planning to teach or while actually teaching. The goal is not to get everything right the first time, but to be reflective enough to realize when something is wrong. Let's consider one specific misunderstanding about climate in the United States.

If we look at a map such as the one in **FIGURE 2.3**, we might expect places such as Flagstaff, Arizona, and Charlotte, North Carolina, to have similar climates.

Both cities are about 35 degrees north of the equator, but Flagstaff has much colder winters with an average temperature that is 10 degrees colder than that of Charlotte. Flagstaff also averages over 100 inches of snow per year, while Charlotte only averages 6 inches. So, if the two cities are at about the same place relative to the equator, why are the climates so different? The climate difference between the two cities is due to Flagstaff's elevation at 6,905 feet above sea level. In this case, the simple application of the principle of climate similarity based on latitude resulted in a misunderstanding. As this example illustrates, we must always be willing to consider new knowledge.

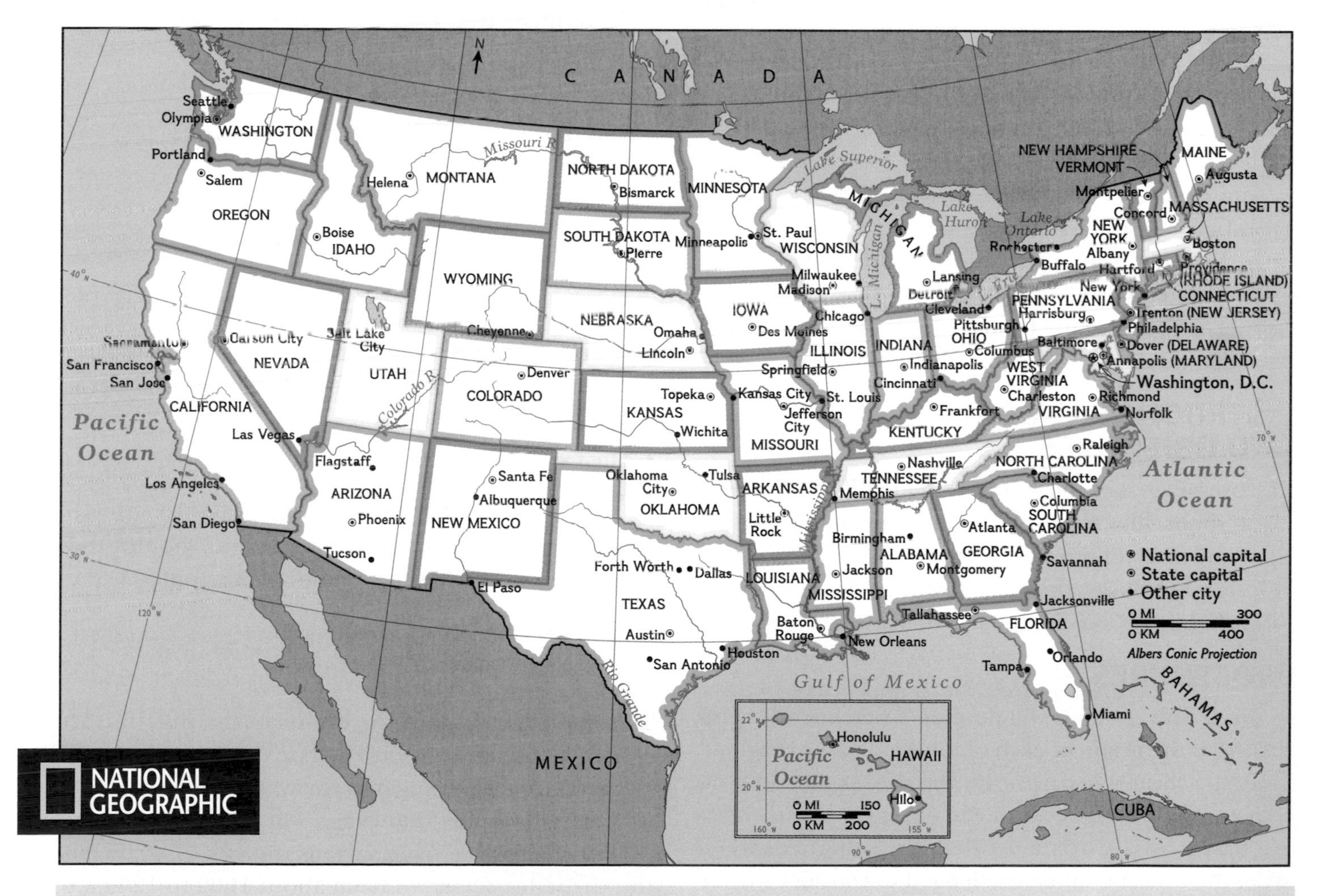

Climate in the United States FIGURE 2.3

Common misunderstandings about climate can occur due to mistaken generalizations. When viewing this map, students might assume that Flagstaff, Arizona, and Charlotte, North Carolina, have similar climates, but that is not the case. Other factors affect the climate.

TRANSFORMING SUBJECT MATTER INTO PEDAGOGY

Pedagogical content knowledge (PCK) Unique forms of knowledge about how to teach that take into account a teacher's knowledge of subject matter, curriculum, learners, and communities, as well as contexts and ends for education.

The processes involved in transforming subject matter into pedagogy should include opportunities for reflection. Lee Shulman calls the results of this transformation **pedagogical content knowledge (PCK)**. Pedagogical content knowledge consists of understanding how to teach certain subject matter. PCK is professional knowledge, but it is not necessarily in the form of a lesson plan. For example, a teacher may know that some parts of the story of Cinque, a North American slave who led a slave rebellion in 1839, are not appropriate for younger learners. Before a certain age (perhaps fifth grade) the story of Cinque often takes shape as a heroic tale of a group of people who refused to be enslaved. Later, children might learn more about the conditions that led to the rebellion or may study the legal struggle that resulted from Cinque's capture and subsequent trial for murder.

As teachers transform their knowledge of subject matter into pedagogy, they have to reflect on what they know and why they know it. Teachers might reflect on the students who will be involved in the lesson about Cinque. Should the teacher make any specific adaptations for students? Younger learners might focus on the wrongness of slavery and the struggle of slaves to improve their condition. Older children might study about the complexities of the social system that supported slavery and resisted efforts to end the practice of slavery. These considerations are important because

A Grand Teton, Wyoming.

This visual narrative from a third-grade social studies classroom describes how a teacher might reflect on general misunderstandings about places in the United States as she prepares for a lesson about states in the U.S.

Consider how these images represent knowledge about specific places in the United States. In some ways, the images represent stereotypes and communicate narrow understandings of the place. What are some stereotypes these images convey? How do these images tell a story about places in the United States? Consider climate, recreation, work, and geography of each place.

What might happen in the classroom when students learn about states, and in particular, look at images such as these? Students of different ages and diverse places will have different reactions. Some may see the image of a plantation in South Carolina (**B**) and think plantation life was the typical "story" of the American South. However, the Hopsewee Plantation is atypical and in some ways represents a mythology about the South.

How can we plan for reflection in action in a lesson about culture when students' prior knowledge stories may be informed by historical myth? What changes are needed to plan a lesson about U.S. states considering how students might react? This thinking is a form of reflection and is a part of planning and teaching.

they cause teachers to think about the scope of their knowledge and the extent to which students should possess the same forms of knowledge.

REFLECTION WHEN PLANNING FOR INSTRUCTION

Meaningful reflection when planning a lesson allows teachers to rethink the fundamental purpose and shape of an instructional lesson. We typically think about instructional lessons as a plan for action in a classroom. They are often written to include certain parts, such as procedures and materials. These lesson parts can be generally applied to multiple classroom settings. This approach to lesson planning is easy to learn and is in fact often distilled into routine procedures.

Some of the more common components of a lesson plan include a lesson opening, a listing of behavioral objectives, connections to standards, procedures, materials, and assessment. All of the information in these categories is essential to quality instruction, but when teachers think in the boxes that confine the categories, they often lose a dynamic character in their lessons. When the planning process is more open and active, lesson plans can be adapted and take shape as learning conditions change.

Reflection during lesson planning should result in lessons being more of a plan of action than a recipe for action. A recipe prescribes a how-to procedure, with little room for adaptation. A reflective lesson plan is structured without closing avenues to possible alterations in the plan. See **FIGURE 2.4** "Visualizing: Reflecting on Stereotypes of Places in the United States" for an example of reflecting on teaching students about states in the United States.

Visualizing

Reflecting on Stereotypes of Places in the United States FIGURE 2.4

B Hopsewee Plantation, South Carolina.

C Craftsbury Common, Vermont.

CONCEPT CHECK STOP

Given your knowledge of South Africa,

How do these images of Ndebele men compare with "typical" representations of South Africa?

What misconceptions could arise if one of these pictures were used as a sole representation of Ndebele men?

Reflect on the differences between the two images.

How might these images, if viewed separately, lead to an incomplete understanding of the Ndebele people?

S.S. Skosana was chief minister in the 1980s of KwaNdebele, a region of South Africa inhabited primarily by Ndebele people.

Young Ndebele men in South Africa after a traditional rite of passage: a two-month initiation marking their passing into manhood.

Reflection During and After Instruction

LEARNING OBJECTIVES

Recognize the importance of reflecting during instruction.

Identify formal and informal means for reflection during instruction.

Consider how and why teachers should reflect after instruction.

Teaching can be a solitary endeavor. During a lesson, the teacher might be the only adult in the classroom. In elementary classes, teachers have very few opportunities to talk with others about the progress of their lesson. Consider other professions—how many of them require that practitioners operate in such an isolated setting? Can you imagine an accountant who could not immediately consult with another accountant when preparing a tax return? How about a lawyer who would be made to argue a case in a courtroom without assistance or opportunities for on-the-spot professional consultation? Teachers, typically, do not have such luxuries, so they have to develop routines and habits of mind that enable them to support themselves while acting without other professionals in the room. An important part of this procedure is developing the habits of reflection.

REFLECTING DURING TEACHING

Earlier in this chapter, we learned about Schön's notion of reflection in action. Schön imagines that professional practice is "artful doing," a particular way of thinking about professional action. For teachers, this means that instruction can be envisioned as a performance, where teachers direct their actions for an audience of student learners. Of course, there are numerous nuances to teaching as performance. For one thing, teachers interact with their students on a number of levels: individually, in small groups, or as a whole class. Reflecting during the act of teaching enables teachers to capitalize on the moment and to address many instructional concerns in the moment.

A significant part of reflection in action triggers a process that results in teachers developing new ideas about instruction. These instructional insights might result from a poorly conceived method or an unexpected amount of time being required for an activity. They might also be a product of an unplanned-for level of student misunderstanding or unexpected outcomes.

What do you think of when you see the image in FIGURE 2.5? In a second-grade classroom that is studying weather, children might ask for an explanation of how lightning works. A lot of good social studies teachers might not know the answer. A teacher who is not willing to reflect on this question might just say "I don't know."

A reflective teacher who takes time to think about the consequences of dismissing the question might respond that lightning is a common occurrence, but many people do not know how or why it happens. She might have to admit to not knowing the exact reasons why and how lightning occurs, but could tell students that since lightning is so powerful and potentially harmful, they should find out the answer. What other types of questions would you expect students to ask about lightning in that second-grade class? In a classroom where reflection is not valued, specific facts are taught and questions rarely emerge. Children in classrooms where reflection is valued learn that it is acceptable to explore and ask questions even when the teacher might not know the answer.

REFLECTING AFTER A LESSON

Reflection after a lesson allows teachers to rethink how and why a lesson went the way it did. The most important thing to remember during reflection is that a good lesson plan should look different after it has been taught compared to before. No matter how much teachers know about their students, no lesson can actually predict learning circumstances. It is vital to the process of professional and pedagogical growth for teachers to think about what went right and what went wrong in a lesson. Too often, teachers are unwilling or even afraid to think about what went wrong. But considering the limitations of a lesson does not have to be the same as admitting failure. Most often, problems in the implementation of a lesson are the product of not anticipating some circumstance of learning. Rethinking the lesson plan with knowledge of what happened should result in new pedagogical understandings and growth. In fact, reflection often prompts teachers to seek out new knowledge.

A thunderstorm in New Mexico FIGURE 2.5

This image might provoke children to ask a host of unforeseen questions.

In the Classroom — ACCOUNTING FOR STUDENTS' PRIOR KNOWLEDGE

Valeria June's fifth-grade social studies class was studying India. To help her students understand the diversity of life in that country, Ms. June showed her students three images of India. Each image represented something that Ms. June wanted the students to learn about—the modern India, the historical India, and the traditional India.

The first image (A) was of modern Mumbai. Most of her students thought this image of Mumbai was of New York City. The students thought that India did not have high-rise buildings or metropolitan cities like the United States.

A Mumbai, India.

The next image (B) represented India's past. Most students recognized the Taj Mahal and were either able to name it or place it in some location outside of the United States.

B Taj Mahal at sunrise, Agra, India.

C Residents and pilgrims bathe in the Ganges River to purify body and soul.

The third image (C) was of a ritual Hindu cleansing in the Ganges River. Many of Ms. June's students thought the people in the photo were caught in a flood, and very few were able to place the people in India.

Ms. June began to think about why her students had these impressions about India. She realized that they were informally learning about India outside the classroom. The fact that some of her fifth graders, who had never formally studied India, recognized the Taj Mahal and were able to place it in India was important. Ms. June began to think about how media in the United States create simple representations of places like India using iconic images like the Taj Mahal, but the Taj Mahal by itself gives only a narrow view of India's long history. The building was built by Shah Jahan, a Mughal (Mongolian Muslim) ruler of India. The Mughals ruled India for just over 200 years of India's rich 3,000-year history. During the instruction, Ms. June realized that she needed not only to teach her students something new, but also to help them expand their prior conceptions and ideas about India. This type of reflection was a product of Ms. June's direct and purposeful reflection on her students' actions during class.

Ms. June quickly adapted her lesson to address students' prior misconceptions of Indian culture. She started with a simple graph that illustrated the percentage of Hindus and Muslims, which is about 80% and 14%, respectively. Ms. June had recently read Salman Rushdie's book *Midnight Children* in which two children, one Hindu and one Muslim, are switched at birth and grow up in opposite cultural environments. She shared a simple version of the story with her students and also reviewed the division of Pakistan and Bangladesh from India and noted that both Pakistan and Bangladesh are over 90% Muslim. Her goal was to provide students with an opportunity to explore the diversity of the Indian subcontinent and to expand on students' prior knowledge.

CONCEPT CHECK **STOP**

Think about "artfully doing" a lesson on community services.

What community services must be in place for the girl in the photo to safely push her baby carriage down the street?

Reflect on your own experiences with community services. How might your experiences with community services influence a lesson on the topic?

Using Reflection to Increase a Teacher's Professional Knowledge

LEARNING OBJECTIVES

Describe how reflection relates to the development of professional teacher knowledge.

Compare various forms of reflection that increase professional teacher knowledge.

Being a teacher demands knowledge in areas other than subject matter and pedagogy. Teachers must possess professional knowledge about the learners in their classes, the communities from which these learners come, the curriculum for the classes they teach, and the broad purposes of education. Each of these areas provides context and opportunities for deliberate reflection directed at purposeful growth in **teacher knowledge**.

Teacher knowledge A formal body of information that comprises our understanding of how to teach.

PROFESSIONAL DEVELOPMENT AND REFLECTING ON THE LEARNER

When we think about children in our classes, we are confronted with a wide range of considerations. Teachers must determine the prior knowledge of their students, the skills they possess, their dispositions to learn, and the sociocultural contexts within which they live. Teachers, schools, and school systems try to systematically collect this information through surveys, assessments, counseling, and conferencing, but teachers can never have too much information about the students in their classroom. For this reason, teachers must reflect on the specific needs of the learners in their classes. This type of reflection is, in practice, a reconsideration of what teachers know about their students in the context of classroom activities.

A teacher may develop an activity, for example, designed for a child or group of children who are interested in a particular subject—say, airplanes. In the pursuit of these students' interest in airplanes, the teacher might develop a small activity related to a unit on inventions. The teacher could provide pictures of various airplanes, such as the one in FIGURE 2.6, and

The "Silver Dart" FIGURE 2.6

The Silver Dart biplane 6, in Hammondsport, New York, was designed by Douglas McCurdy of the Aerial Experiment Association and was the first airplane to fly in Canada.

ask her students to draw their own picture of an airplane and write a description of how the airplane manages to stay aloft.

The teacher could extend the activity by working with students to consider how air transportation changed life in the United States in the 20th century. The lesson has curricular relevance (the importance of air travel) and came about as a result of the teacher's knowledge of her students' interest. She could have chosen a number of different inventions on which to focus, but selected airplanes upon reflection on the learners in her class.

PROFESSIONAL DEVELOPMENT AND REFLECTING ON COMMUNITY NEEDS

Teachers must also reflect on the needs of the community at large. As is the case with learner needs, schools typically make a deliberate effort to engage communities through focus groups and advisory councils. These vehicles provide school personnel with valuable insight into what the community wants and expects from their school, but teachers must do more. Teachers must continually think about their actions in community contexts.

Each community has unique needs and wants. Teachers should be aware of these needs and wants and should try to address them through their teaching. Consider a community with a high immigrant population. Teachers in such environments must provide their students with special opportunities to learn what we may otherwise take for granted with our students. These children and their parents may need special help getting around the community or learning how to get services from the school or other agencies.

Other communities have special needs that result from patterns of development or historical inequities. Jonathon Kozol's powerful book *Savage Inequalities* details the problems ingrained in poor communities all across the United States. Teachers in such environments must know about the conditions in which their children live, how these conditions emerged, and what they can do to support children who are trying to learn there.

PROFESSIONAL DEVELOPMENT AND REFLECTING ON CURRICULUM

Every day, teachers wonder how they will facilitate **curriculum** through their teaching. This planning is very important and time consuming. Social studies scholar Stephen Thornton talks about this process as "gatekeeping" (Thornton, 2004) and suggests that teachers must make active and informed decisions about how to implement curriculum. When teachers reflect on curriculum, they are essentially assessing the extent to which a lesson meets particular curricular goals. This type of reflection can help a teacher make adjustments to a lesson given the requirements of the curriculum. Far too often, we think about curriculum as being received from authorities (the school district, for example) and unable to be altered or reworked. However, most curriculums leave significant room for interpretation. For example, the National History Standards state that students in grades K through 4 should be able to "describe local community life long ago, including jobs, schooling, transportation, communication, religious observances, and recreation."

Curriculum
Courses of study in an academic discipline or the scope and sequence of specific subject matter within a single academic course.

How might a teacher encourage students to consider transportation or recreation among the Eskimo Indians? Consider the picture of Inuit Eskimos from the early 20th century in **Figure 2.7**. Look at the dress and consider what you already know about the climate of the Eskimo Indians' homeland. For example, the climate would limit year-around water transportation. If we add information about the learning context, such as a first-grade class located in the Deep South, how does your curricular thinking change? The changes that you are thinking about are a product of reflection, which occurs as new contexts and information are added to the thinking process.

Inuit Eskimos in 1909 FIGURE 2.7

A mixed group of Inuit Eskimo men, women, and children pose for this informal group portrait taken by Robert Peary in front of Red Cliff House in McCormick Bay, Greenland.

PROFESSIONAL DEVELOPMENT AND REFLECTING ON THE PURPOSES OF EDUCATION

Conversations about the purposes of education take place in multiple contexts. Teachers talk with colleagues at their schools and in larger professional communities. These conversations enable us to expand our beliefs about the purposes of social studies. Some teacher leaders might serve on curriculum or textbook selection committees charged with making important decisions based on beliefs about the purposes of education. All of these activities should occur through dialogue and as such are a form of public professional reflection. For example, the last several years have seen a dramatic decrease in the amount of time spent on social studies instruction in elementary school. Discussions about the consequences of these changes are influenced by public opinion and public discourse.

In early 2006, the Center on Education Policy released a study that found that almost three quarters of schools nationwide had cut back on social studies instruction. Some schools, according to the study, allocated as little as 30 minutes a week to social studies. Conversations about the purpose of education and specifically the purpose of social studies became national news with the release of this report, and elementary school teachers across the country played (and continue to play) an important role in the national dialogue over the proper place of social studies in school.

CONCEPT CHECK STOP

Reflect on a common topic in elementary social studies, such as farming. How has farming changed in the last hundred years?

How might a lesson on changes in farming relate to community interests?

This threshing machine is in cornfields in the hills above the Platte Valley north of Shelton, Nebraska. How does the context of this photo shape our understanding of the needs of children who live in Platte Valley?

Reflection as Inquiry

LEARNING OBJECTIVES

Recognize the relationship between inquiry and reflection.

Describe ways that inquiry can be informed and enhanced by reflection.

Analyze case studies of teacher knowledge using reflective inquiry methods.

Reflective inquiry combines the inquiry approach to learning with the idea that reflection is a way of knowing things. In his 1910 book *How We Think*, John Dewey talked about reflective inquiry as "the elaboration of an idea, or working hypothesis, through conjoint comparison and contrast, terminating in definition or formulation." In other words, Dewey thought that reflective inquiry in a democracy was a process that enabled learners to learn something given ever changing conditions related to that knowledge. For example, students in social studies who learned about space and time in the early 20th century learned that space and time were absolute. After Einstein's theory of relativity, we now learn about time as relative to motion. Other forms of knowledge change over time due to changing perceptions. In the past, some teachers taught about slavery as a benign parochial system that was eventually dismantled

Reflective inquiry A process of developing new knowledge, which is contingent upon a procedure that assumes knowledge is ever changing and evolving.

through a natural course of events. Today, students learn about the brutality of slavery and the struggles (including the Civil War) that resulted in the end of slavery.

We can even reflect on the purposes of social studies. Consider the democratic purposes of social studies that were suggested in Chapter 1. What does the image in **FIGURE 2.8** of an Iraqi woman voting suggest about the purposes of social studies? Given the complexity of democracy and various global experiences with democracy, what do you think are social studies educators' responsibilities in preparing young people to participate in democratic life? Consider what changes you are making in your thinking about social studies as you read and learn more about social studies.

FIGURE 2.8

An Iraqi woman puts her vote into a ballot box.

LEARNING ABOUT TEACHING FROM CASE STUDIES

One condition for reflective inquiry is that there is a body of knowledge upon which to reflect. Unfortunately, we do not have a formal body of knowledge about how to teach. Other professions—for example, the professions of law, accounting, and medicine—have this formal body of knowledge. However, an emerging body of knowledge taken from case studies of teaching practice can be used as a source for reflective inquiry.

In the last twenty years, cases of teacher practice have been assembled as a foundation for general knowledge about how to teach. Cases on teaching are most appropriately what social studies scholar O. L. Davis calls "wise practice" (Davis & Yeager, 2005). These "wise practice" **case studies** are exemplars that entail elements of successful teaching in local situations, and also enable us to explore how the teaching episode can be extended or even improved. When inquiring using these cases, teachers transfer meaningful knowledge about how to teach from the situations described in the case to their own teaching situations. The "In the Classroom" feature on page 50 describes a case study of a first-year fifth-grade teacher's efforts to teach about the Constitution. Consider what you and other social studies teachers can learn from this case.

> **Case studies**
> Descriptions of professional action, such as teaching, that have some explanatory qualities.

By reading case studies, teachers can begin to learn about common problems such as the one Joan faced. What did Joan learn that might be useful in other situations? Perhaps Joan's experience adapting her lesson given her students' interests can be transferred to other teaching and learning situations. As teachers read more case studies, they begin to form generalizations, which in turn inform their planning and teaching. Although case studies can be powerful, we have to be careful not to directly apply the lessons learned in a case. Rather, the key is to transfer the knowledge gained by reading the case into a personal body of knowledge that we can then apply in new and unique settings.

he teacher/student dialogue about gas prices demonstrates how we can use real-world contexts to encourage elementary social studies inquiry. Inquiry skills enable students to explore their interests, address meaningful problems, and work with real-world, authentic resources. In this chapter, we will explore inquiry as an instructional approach in social studies.

Inquiry as Learning

LEARNING OBJECTIVES

Define inquiry.

Describe the four steps of the inquiry process.

Explain how the learning cycle and the inquiry process are similar.

WHAT IS INQUIRY?

nquiry holds different meanings depending on the discipline. For example, in the legal field, an inquiry is an activity centered on justice, right, and wrong. In science, inquiry is equally precise, but more focused on improving human conditions through technical advancement. In social studies, inquiry is both of these things and more. **Inquiry** is a way of learning and teaching that uses real-world resources to investigate authentic and meaningful topics and problems.

Inquiry A method of teaching and learning that makes use of authentic resources in the investigation of meaningful topics and problems.

Inquiry, in its broadest sense, is simply a questioning and answering process infused with purpose and meaning. Inquiry has been a part of educational practice almost since the inception of social studies at the start of the twentieth century. Early promoters of social studies such as John Dewey believed in inquiry, and Dewey's work in particular has influenced the development of inquiry in practice. In his book *How We Think* (1910), Dewey described inquiry as being rooted in experience and reflection. For Dewey, reflective inquiry or thought emerges from experiences that are driven by human curiosity. Dewey felt that curiosity occurs naturally in young children as they try to make sense of the strange aspects of the world around them. Experiences that emerge from children's curiosity result in learning, and these experiences lead to intellectual knowledge. Teachers can facilitate experiential learning opportunities by grounding their students' work in relevant, interesting, and meaningful problems (**FIGURE 3.1**).

Effective inquiry models should be based in students' interests. Bertram Bruce and Judith Davidson (1996) argue for a literacy-based inquiry model that is centered on student interests. They view inquiry as beginning with students understanding their own role in learning or seeing a need to learn. The process then moves into a web of activities that include reflection, dialogue, writing, experimentation, observation, draw-

FIGURE 3.1

What does this real-life context offer with regard to learning in social studies? Consider questions about how the food in the market was produced and the means by which it got to market. How does the vendor set the prices? How does the consumer decide what to purchase?

Learning cycle A self-perpetuating learning system in which new learning opportunities result from existing learning experiences.

ing, music, or any other action resulting from immersion in an inquiry activity. Other specific approaches to inquiry will be explored later in this chapter, but first, let's look at the process of inquiry (FIGURE 3.2).

As early as first grade, children can participate in purposeful inquiry activities. The inquiry process in social studies exists within a self-propelling **learning cycle**, which is much like the reflective teaching cycle as presented in Chapter 2. David Kolb and Roger Fry (1975) developed one of the first theoretical learning cycle models. Their model includes four parts:

- Concrete experience
- Observation of and reflection on that experience
- Formation of abstract concepts based upon the reflection
- Testing the new concepts

The inquiry process FIGURE 3.2

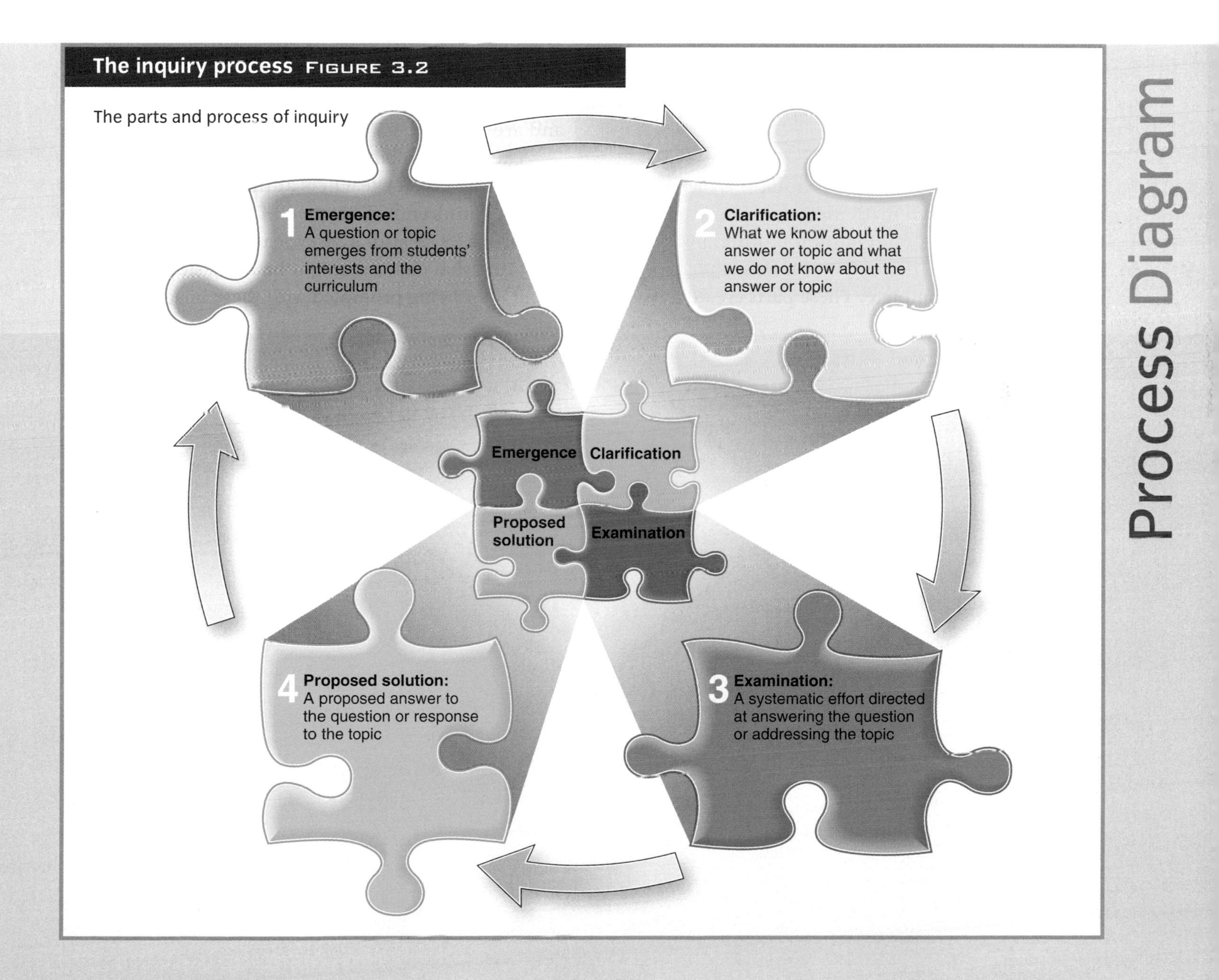

Forms of Inquiry

LEARNING OBJECTIVES

Describe social science inquiry.

Discuss the unique qualities of social inquiry.

Explain the role of historical inquiry in social studies.

lthough social studies inquiry is a unique form of teaching and learning, it is dependent on inquiry in other areas. In this section, we will review related forms of inquiry—social science inquiry, social inquiry, and historical inquiry. Each of these types of inquiry is practiced in social studies classes.

SOCIAL SCIENCE INQUIRY

Social science inquiry Inquiry that involves disciplinary investigations focused on observation, hypothesis generation, data collection, and the proposal of a solution.

Social science inquiry is very similar to scientific inquiry and involves specific disciplinary investigations focused on observation, hypothesis generation, data collection, and the proposal of a solution. Social science inquiry in social studies is highly structured and aimed at answering direct questions about observable phenomena.

An example of social science inquiry is an investigation of the causes of homelessness. The method for social science inquiry parallels the scientific method; however, the social science inquiry is not attempting to replicate specific experiments. Social science inquiry begins with observation. In their observations, students find some incongruence or unexplained phenomenon and consider it in the form of a problem. Once a problem has been identified, students then proceed through the steps of scientific inquiry by defining a question, proposing a hypothesis, testing their hypothesis through some form of data analysis, forming conclusions from the data analysis, and proposing a theory.

Many schools and school systems have organized social science fairs designed to showcase students' social science inquiries. These experiences stimulate students' interests in social studies topics and motivate students through the public display of their work. A typical social science fair project might include the following components.

- The research question
- A physical project display describing the research process
- A research paper report on the results of an inquiry into the research question
- An oral presentation or Q/A about the process and research inquiry product

A social science project presentation is the culmination of student research on a guiding research question. Following are social science questions from award-winning projects in Virginia in 2006.

- How did the belief in the afterlife affect Egypt?
- Ancient Amish culture: Has it changed through the years?
- Holidays—How do you celebrate?
- Snake handling: What's all the hissing about?
- How did the 1970s fads and trends affect American culture?
- Plains and Pueblo Indians: How did the land determine their style of living?

SOCIAL INQUIRY

Social inquiry Inquiry that focuses on the investigation of common problems whose solution will improve the human condition.

Social inquiry is a distinctly different form of inquiry that focuses on the investigation of common problems whose solution will improve the human condition. It is often thought of as involving the following steps:

1. Identifying a problem
2. Determining the resources needed to solve the problem
3. Developing a potential solution
4. Implementing the solution

The most important characteristic of social inquiry is that it is focused on a problem that has real-world social characteristics. In fact, the problem being investigated is more important than the product of the inquiry. For example, an inquiry into the limits of civil liberties during wartime is a problem that has been and will continue to be very important in the United States. Students' inquiry-based understandings or opinions, while important, are not as important as their understanding that the United States has continued and will continue to struggle with this issue.

The social inquiry approach to learning values process and action as a form of understanding more than it values products and performance. Given that the "answers" are not easy to come by, involving students in their learning might present some complexities, but in the long run students will be more excited about their learning. As students take action on the problem they are addressing, either through their thinking or through some community action, they become invested in the solution and thus more interested in the outcome.

HISTORICAL INQUIRY

> **Historical inquiry** A specific form of asking and answering questions that makes use of historical resources and particular methodologies in order to construct an interpretation of the past.

Historical inquiry plays an important role in social studies instruction and requires students to construct an interpretation of the past. Historical inquiry is a specific form of asking and answering questions that makes use of historical resources and particular methodologies. For example, an inquiry about the effect of the 1930s Depression on families (FIGURE 3.9) might make use of photos from the time or letters and diaries written by people who lived through that time.

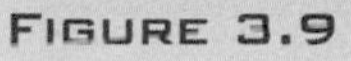
FIGURE 3.9

A breadline at the intersection of 6th Avenue and 42nd Street in New York City during the Great Depression that followed the Wall Street crash. What hardships must have faced the families of the men who were desperate enough to stand in lines this long just to get free bread?

Definitions and examples of inquiry in social studies TABLE 3.2

Type of inquiry	*Definition*	*Example of an inquiry question*
Social science inquiry	Investigations focused on observation, hypothesis generation, data collection, and the proposal of a solution	How does supply and demand affect the price of basketball shoes?
Social inquiry	The investigation of common problems whose solution will improve the human condition	What can be done to protect young people from secondhand tobacco smoke?
Historical inquiry	Asking and answering questions that make use of historical resources and particular methodologies	Why was President Richard Nixon impeached?

As early as second or third grade, children can participate in historical inquiries. The products of these inquiries can be very productive in helping children understand their social world. Historical inquiry requires that children develop an interest in a topic or historical problem, and then perform an analysis of resources. The analysis is directed at constructing an interpretation of the past. Doolittle and Hicks (2003) described the analysis of resources as including five distinct steps: summarizing, contextualizing, inferring, monitoring, and corroborating (SCIM-C). We will read more about the SCIM-C method in Chapter 5.

Historical inquiry, like social science and social inquiry, involves unique traits. Read "Visualizing: Inquiry in Practice" (FIGURE 3.10), and think about the differences and similarities among these three types of inquiry. TABLE 3.2 provides some ideas for different types of inquiry.

CONCEPT CHECK **STOP**

How might students conduct scientific, social, and historical inquiries about the trading of ivory from elephant tusks?

What are some of the potential inquiry questions that might arise from an investigation of this image?

Hunters and traders sitting atop elephant tusks in Zanzibar, Tanzania, in the late nineteenth century.

Visualizing

Inquiry in Practice FIGURE 3.10

Who made this flat-top hill, and how did they make it? Let's consider this question using the four steps of inquiry given scientific, social, and historical approaches.

1. Encourage *emerging* learner interests. The Mississippi River pictured here flows under the Eads Bridge, with the Gateway Arch in St. Louis in the background, just 15 miles from the Indian city of Cahokia. What would Mississippian Indians, who built these earthen mounds, think of St. Louis today?
2. *Clarify* students' inquiries on the Mississippian Mound Builders, focusing on:
   - construction of the mounds (scientific inquiry),
   - the fate of the Mound Builders (social inquiry),
   - or the purpose of the mounds (historical inquiry).
3. *Examine* the resources, given students' prior knowledge. Scientific, social, and historical inquiries become more distinct during the examination. Whereas scientific inquiry relies on testing a hypothesis (the mounds were built as a fort or for housing), social inquiry might focus on religious purposes of the mounds.
4. Students will propose or *suggest* a solution given their examination. What happened to the people who built the mounds? Each approach might yield a different "answer."

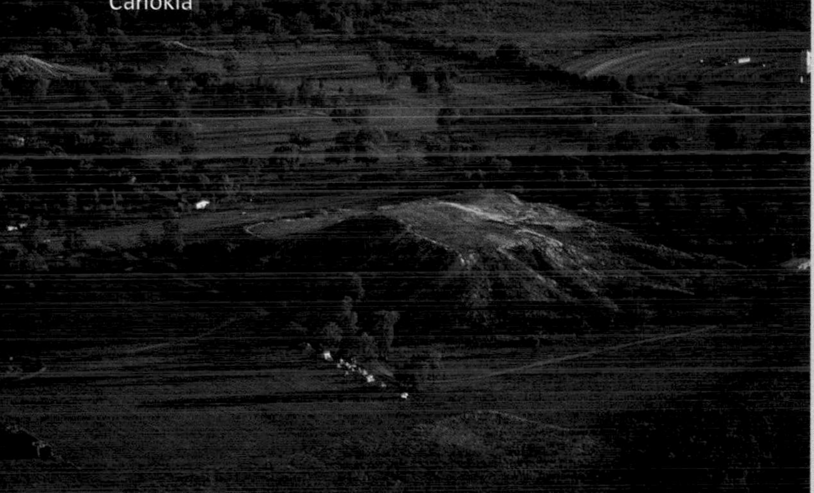

Aerial view of Monk's Mound at Cahokia Mounds Park in Illinois, where ancient Indian temples once stood in the city of Cahokia

Eads Bridge, Mississippi River, St. Louis, Missouri

A burial mound at the Etowah Indian Mounds State Historic Site, Cartersville, Georgia. The Etowah Valley was home to a Mississippian Indian culture that thrived there between A.D. 1,000 and A.D. 1,500. This sophisticated culture spanned much of the north, south, and central areas of what is now the United States and was North America's last prehistoric culture. It flourished from approximately A.D. 800 until the arrival of European explorers.

Inquiry and the Curriculum

LEARNING OBJECTIVES

Describe how inquiry can be successfully implemented in highly structured curricular contexts.

Identify how inquiry can be standardized in terms of testing and assessment.

INQUIRY-DRIVEN CURRICULUM AND STANDARDS

As noted earlier in this chapter, one of the most significant limitations to inquiry is the difficulty in reconciling the sometimes narrow curricular focus of inquiry activities with the need to cover a substantial amount of subject matter. There are many things social studies teachers can do when developing inquiry activities to ensure that the activity fits within the curriculum.

First, start planning for the inquiry within the bounds of curriculum and stay within the curriculum throughout the planning and teaching phases of the lesson. This also means that teachers need to encourage their students' interest in topics that are relevant to the curriculum.

National History Standards suggest that students in grades K–4 should "Analyze the dance, music, and arts of various cultures around the world." How might we make connections between the children in grades K–4 learning about the content suggested in this standard and the dancing tradition displayed by the young San Bushman women in Namibia (FIGURE 3.11)?

Let's look at a curriculum-based inquiry that includes some of the hallmarks of inquiry we have reviewed in this chapter. New Jersey Social Studies Core Curriculum Content Standards require students to explore basic concepts of diversity, tolerance, fairness, and respect for others by the end of the second grade. Elementary-grade teachers in New Jersey might develop inquiry activities related to this curriculum standard (see "Lesson" on pages 76–77).

INQUIRY, ASSESSMENT, AND STANDARDIZED TESTING

There is no one-size-fits-all approach to assessing inquiry activities. Each student's work in inquiry activities has to be considered on its own merits. This can

FIGURE 3.11

The San people partake in ritual communal dances, such as the one displayed here, that have spiritual and medicinal purposes. The energy of the dance is thought to heal both physical and psychological illnesses.

Sample rubric for assessing student work on the lesson about the meaning of "fair" TABLE 3.3			
Score	**1**	**2**	**3**
Criterion 1: Students construct a definition of the concept of fair that includes three ways to determine whether something is fair.	Definition includes 0–1 way(s) to determine whether something is fair.	Definition includes 2 ways to determine whether something is fair.	Definition includes 3 ways to determine whether something is fair.
Criterion 2: Students will apply their definition in a consistent manner with an explanation or reasons supporting their application.	Students do not apply their definition to new situations in a consistent manner.	Students apply their definition to new situations in a consistent manner.	Students apply their definition to new situations in a consistent manner and provide reasons why each example is or is not fair.

Assessment rubric A method for evaluating learning that includes multiple criteria and performance levels for each criterion.

be accomplished by using **assessment rubrics** that aid in determining the structural soundness of students' work. We will look at rubrics in detail in a later chapter. For now, let's review the basic assumptions behind rubrics.

Assessment rubrics are mechanisms for appraising students' work based on specific criteria. Typically, rubrics have numerous criteria and performance levels for each criterion. Teachers construct the criteria based on the objectives of the lesson and set performance levels based on expectations and prior knowledge.

In an inquiry activity, assessment criteria might relate to syntactic or process-oriented student knowledge as well as substantive content knowledge. Syntactic knowledge might be the student's thinking skills, while substantive knowledge might be facts such as dates or the names of famous people. Teachers should emphasize these forms of **discrete knowledge**, such as the names of famous people, in inquiry activities. These details are the facts that are typically found on high-stakes tests.

Discrete knowledge Ideas and concepts that share no obvious characteristics and are understood separately.

The sample rubric in TABLE 3.3 details how criteria and performance levels might be constructed for the lesson on the concept of "fair." Although this lesson does not include typical "facts," students are expected to achieve at fixed and clearly communicated levels. Rubrics provide teachers with a means to communicate expectations in a clear manner and are particularly important when using methods such as inquiry.

CONCEPT CHECK STOP

How might an inquiry about rural ways of life in the Ivory Coast be connected to the National History Standards, your state's social studies standards, or your local curriculum?

What are some discrete pieces of information that might emerge from an inquiry about life in the Ivory Coast?

In the Ivory Coast, rural food vendors sell pineapples, coconuts, and corn, among other items.

LESSON

"That's Not Fair": An Inquiry Lesson Into the Meaning of "Fair"

INTRODUCTION

All inquiry activities should begin with a question and take into consideration students' interests. A possible inquiry activity could be built around exploring the meaning of fairness.

LEARNING GOALS AND OBJECTIVES

In this lesson, students will create their own definition of "fair" and apply that definition to various situations.

PROCEDURE

The first task for teachers in this lesson is to nurture the *emergence* of student interest. To accomplish this, begin with a demonstration or explanation of an event or action in which a child thinks he is being treated unfairly. Here is an example.

> Leticia and Nadia were riding bikes together when the next-door neighbor Matthew came outside. "Can I ride with you?" asked Matthew. The girls did not want Matthew playing with them. They were planning to go to Leticia's house to play her new video game. "We're playing girl stuff," Nadia said. Matthew felt bad. He didn't think it was fair for the girls to not let him play.

After sharing this or a similar story, ask students what they think was or was not fair about the situation. This discussion should aid in the *clarification* of what students think is fair and not fair. Continue the discussion by asking students if they can think of times when they were treated unfairly, and make a list on the board of these incidents. After a few minutes of discussion, share with students the learning goal for the lesson (create your own definition of "fair").

As a result of this activity, students will create their own definition of what it means to be fair and compare their definition to others. The definition that students create needs to be set in their own experience. The next part of this activity requires students to use the list on the board, along with additional examples provided by the teacher, to *examine* some commonalities among the incidents. Questions to facilitate this part of the activity might include:

- What are some of the things that happened to people in the same way?
- Have any of the things we talked about in class happened to you?
- Which of the things we have talked about were the most unfair?

As students begin the process of narrowing the ideas about fairness, the teacher should introduce some fairness principles or an existing definition. Although research shows that children are more likely to be positively influenced by real-life examples than principles, the inclusion of principles will provide students with a starting point for developing their own beliefs about fairness. Following are a few existing definitions of fairness:

- Everyone gets what they need.
- A person is treated honestly.
- People follow the same rules.
- No one feels left out.
- The same rules are applied to everybody.

Following the presentation of these existing ideas about fairness, the teacher might want to give some historical and current examples of fairness. Historical examples might include episodes from the past when groups of people were treated differently. For example, we might suggest that it wasn't fair to exclude black children from white public schools in the early twentieth century.

Another example of fairness might be an anecdote about an activity children are familiar with, such as the following story about checkers:

These children are playing chess. How do issues of fairness arise when children play games? How can we use children's life experiences playing games as a context for learning about concepts such as fairness?

> Chris and Jorge are playing the game of checkers. When the game started, both boys thought the game was fair. Each player had the same number of game pieces and they would follow the same rules. After a few moves, Chris started to complain that the game was not fair. Jorge had quickly taken half of Chris's pieces. Chris complained, "You didn't tell me how good you were. That's not fair." Jorge wasn't happy either. He didn't want his friend to be mad, so he decided to change the rules and let Chris automatically have king pieces, even before he got to the end of the board. Jorge asked Chris, "Is it fair now?"

After sharing this short anecdote, ask students if they think this game of checkers as it unfolded was fair.

ASSESSMENT

The general question students are examining is, what is fair? At this point in the lesson, students should be asked to *propose their own solution* with a short description or definition of fairness. The definition should be written down by each student and then applied to the situations on the board. The teacher can review each of the situations listed and ask students whether the person was treated fairly or unfairly given their definition. As a culminating activity, students should be asked to revise and share their definitions of fairness.

Process Diagram

The influence of standards on curriculum FIGURE 4.2

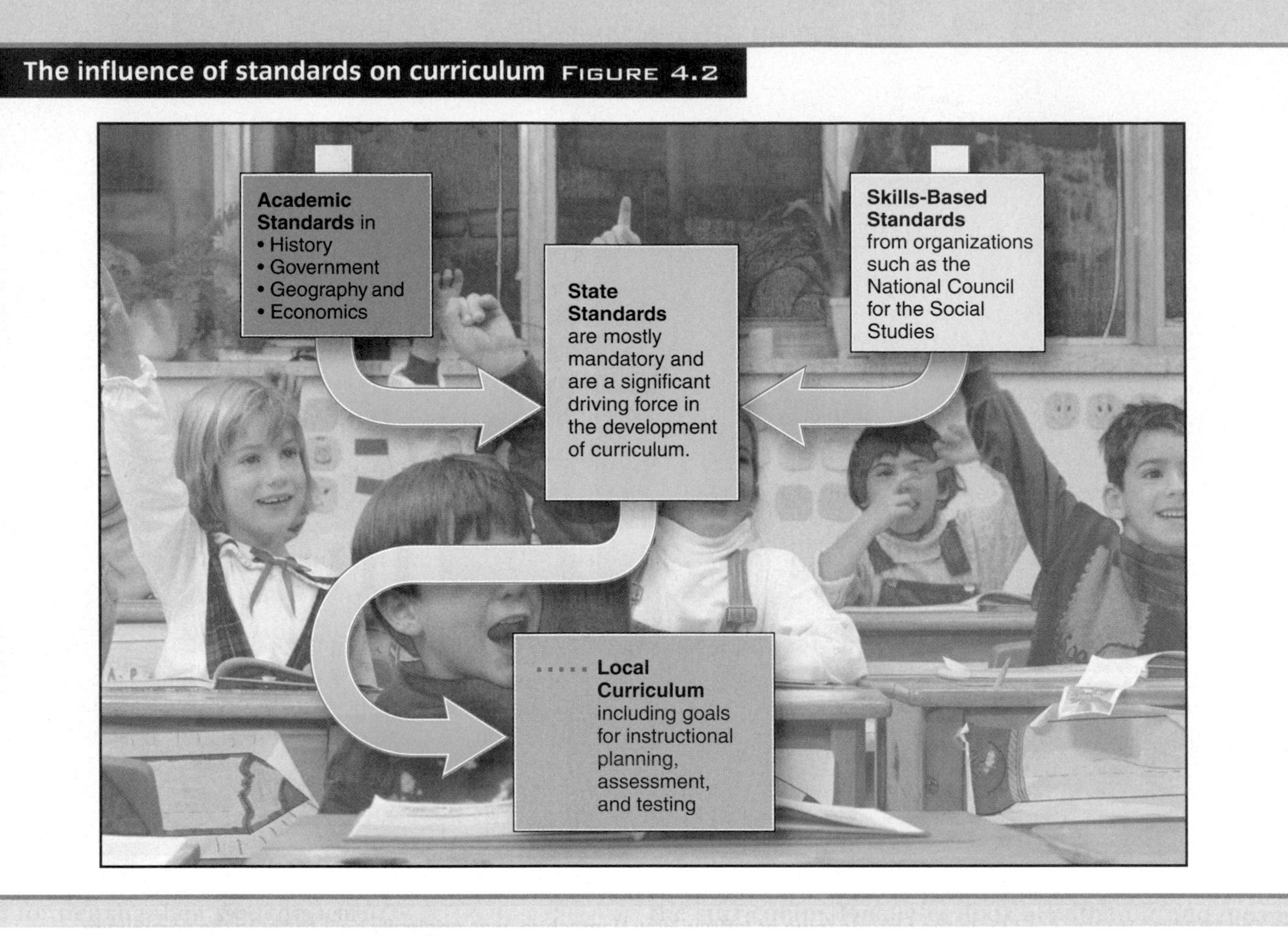

FIGURE 4.2 details the typical pattern of influence that national and state standards have in local schools. In Chapter 1, we looked at standards from five national social studies organizations:

- National History Standards from the National Center for History in the Schools
- Geography for Life: National Geography Standards from the National Council for Geographic Education
- National Standards for Civics and Government from the Center for Civic Education
- Voluntary National Standards in Economics from the National Council on Economic Education
- Curriculum Standards for Social Studies from the National Council for the Social Studies (NCSS)

Each of these standards projects influences, to some degree, the state standards. For example, the state standards in Arkansas, called the Arkansas Social Studies Curriculum Framework (revised 2000), are closely aligned with the National Council for the Social Studies standards with specific content standards arranged according to the ten NCSS themes. Other states' standards are organized more like the national standards in discipline areas. For example, Virginia and California have standards that are similar in structure to the National History Standards. Standards in states such as Arkansas, Virginia, and California serve as frameworks for local school systems in these states to develop curriculums. No state has a one-size-fits-all curriculum. Instead, states enable local school systems to develop their own curriculum that is based on the state standards.

STANDARDS AND CURRICULUM: THE STARTING POINT FOR POWERFUL TEACHING

How will standards and curriculum impact the way you teach in the classroom? The answer to this question influences much of the instructional planning and teaching process. The connections between curriculum and daily teaching are much more obvious than the connections between standards and teaching. Standards are most often too broad to actually influence the development of a daily lesson. But teachers need to understand standards, and in particular, how the standards have influenced the development of the local curriculum. Teachers are also often required to correlate their teaching objectives with state standards in order to ensure that the subject being taught is within the context of one or multiple standards.

The curriculum, on the other hand, is closely connected to planning and teaching. In fact, teachers often directly use local school system curriculum guides when planning their daily instruction. Curriculums, which are most typically developed at the school-system level, often include pacing guides, which help teachers understand what they should teach and when. If a pacing guide is not included, curriculums will typically include some general information about the amount of material to teach in a given period of time (scope) and the order in which to teach it (sequence). Teachers who are uncertain about their own pedagogical and subject matter knowledge might appreciate these details in a curriculum. Teachers who are very comfortable with their knowledge of teaching may find detailed curriculums more restricting. Consider how two teachers with different levels of knowledge might teach about the burning of Washington, D.C. during the War of 1812.

The approach of a novice teacher A novice teacher might know the story of Dolley Madison and her reported effort to save valuable items from the White House as the British marched on the city. State standards and local curriculums all across the United States mention this event, often as a tale intended to help children develop an understanding of the concept of courage. A novice teacher, with little knowledge of the Dolley Madison story, might plan a lesson about it, relying on what he learned directly from standards and supporting materials. Several standards/curriculum projects suggest using books about the event such as *Dolley Madison: First Lady (Spirit of American Our People)* by Cynthia Fitterer Klingel and Robert B. Noyed (2002). This 32-page book briefly describes the life of Dolley Madison, including her efforts during the War of 1812.

A novice teacher might have students read the book for the purpose of reconstructing the events of 1812 or reflecting on the courage of Dolley Madison (FIGURE 4.3). This reading could be part of a lesson that focuses on the reasons why the British and the Americans were at war. Madison's courageous actions in rescuing valuable documents and materials from the White House might serve as the central focus of the lesson. The novice teacher could implement these ideas in a meaningful way in a best effort to teach about a topic about which he knows very little.

Dolley Madison FIGURE 4.3

A This miniature painting of Dolley Payne Madison (1768–1849) shows her at age 26. The portrait was done the year of her courtship and marriage to James Madison. Does she have the appearance of a hero? Why might it be important to portray Dolley Madison as a hero?

B This plate memorializes Dolley Madison as a character of almost royal dimensions. Consider how the story of her heroics at the White House in 1814 might have influenced the production of this plate. How does the story of her actions influence our current perception of Dolley Madison?

Standards and Testing

LEARNING OBJECTIVES

Contrast high-stakes standardized testing with lower-stakes teacher-developed testing.

Identify how standards influence test item development.

Identify teaching methods for ensuring that students are prepared for standards-based tests.

he relationship between standards and testing is very important. Standards set the expectations for what students should learn, and tests measure what students learn.

Instruction and testing that are organized around standards provide students with the best opportunities to succeed. This section explores how teachers can deliberately connect testing to standards through curriculum and instruction.

HIGH-STAKES AND LOW-STAKES TESTS

Tests provide teachers, administrators, and the community around a school with valuable information about the progress of students. Many of the tests teachers give their students are directly connected to standards. Some of these tests are **high-stakes** and might be used to help determine a final grade or whether students can progress to the next grade level. These tests are standardized, meaning that all students in a school or district get the same test or at least similar versions of the same test. Other tests are more individualized. These are developed by individual teachers or possibly by a department in a school. Such tests are often used to assess students' knowledge at the end of a unit or even the end of a several-week period or a quarter. These tests are important, but have lower stakes than the school- and district-wide tests, which might determine whether a student goes to the next grade.

High-stakes tests Standardized assessments of student learning that are used to make decisions about, among other things, students' progress to the next grade level or another course, a school's standing at the local or state level, and/or the need for special services or instructional opportunities for students in a school.

Teacher-developed low-stakes tests should also be connected to standards. Understanding how standards are associated with high-stakes and more common teacher-developed low-stakes tests is an important part of ensuring student success on tests. To reach this goal, teachers need to learn how standards influence test item development. Teachers should consider offering students opportunities to take low-stakes tests with a structure similar to that of high-stakes tests, to give students practice with the format of high-stakes tests.

High-stakes tests are by their design tightly correlated with state standards. Students are more likely to experience success on high-stakes tests when teachers connect their own low-stakes testing program to state standards. **Low-stakes** tests assess students' knowledge in specific content areas on a regular basis. This means that students learn the state standards throughout the school year, not just in preparation for a one-time annual high-stakes test.

Low-stakes tests Tests that assess students' knowledge in specific content areas on a regular basis so that students learn the state standards throughout the school year, not just in preparation for a one-time annual high-stakes test.

In order to connect standards to teacher-developed tests, teachers must carefully consider the format of their tests and with some tests try to use the same format as a standardized test. For example, teachers can use mul-

How standards influence test item development FIGURE 4.4

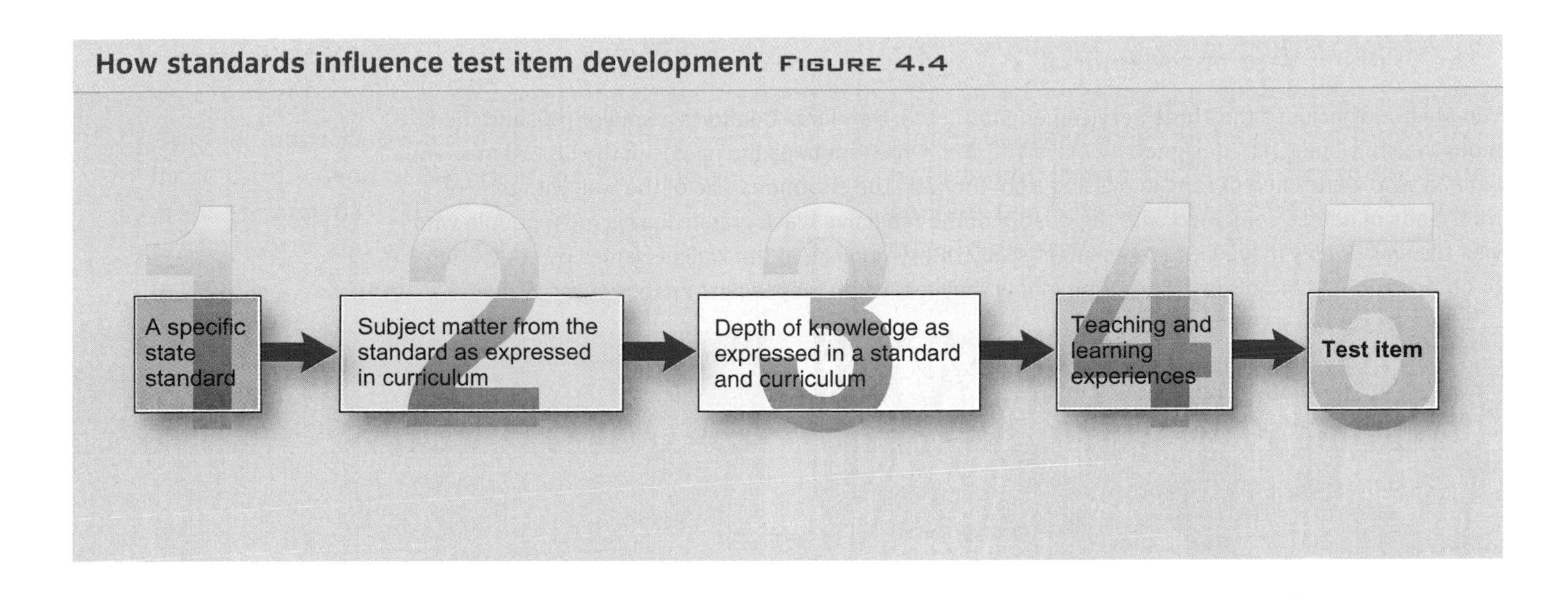

tiple choice, short writing samples, or other standardized test formats in developing their own tests. These tests are not the same as practice standardized tests. Instead, teachers can determine how standardized test formats might be used to check for student understanding of subject matter taken directly from classroom experiences.

Connecting standards to tests involves a systematic consideration of subject matter covered in learning experiences. Such subject matter needs to be based in standards and/or curriculum and should take into consideration the depth of knowledge expected of students. FIGURE 4.4 illustrates how standards should influence the development of a test item.

Let's look at a specific example of how standards influence test item development. In Illinois, students in upper elementary grades are expected to "identify major political events and leaders within the United States historical eras since the adoption of the Constitution, including the westward expansion, Louisiana Purchase, Civil War, and twentieth century wars as well as the roles of Thomas Jefferson, Abraham Lincoln, Woodrow Wilson, and Franklin D. Roosevelt." Of course, this standard is very broad, and much work must be done to determine the exact subject matter to include in a lesson.

In the Chicago, Illinois, city schools curriculum, this state standard has been expanded to include several areas of focus including the following: "Interpret the symbolism of the images/icons found on historical memorials, murals, or monuments."

Planning to teach about symbolism and memorials will require that the teacher make important decisions about the subject matter focus of the lesson. The subject matter selected might relate to the Vietnam Veterans Memorial (FIGURES 4.5A, B, and C) on page 92.

The Vietnam Veterans Memorial is one of the most powerful monuments in Washington, D.C. The monument combines statues of soldiers, nurses, and the famous granite Wall of Names inscribed with the names of fallen soldiers from the war. What kinds of symbolism are evident in the memorial? How might an elementary-level teacher use this memorial to teach about the symbolic value of images and icons?

Student work such as this can be tested in a number of ways. A test question might be very discrete or "fact" based. For example, "How many fallen soldiers' names are on the wall?" Or a teacher might move test items to a higher level by asking why such a memorial would be constructed or how it compares to other memorials such as the Washington Monument. Because most standardized tests are reduced to multiple-choice items, the teacher would have to carefully develop such a question to reflect meaningful instructional activities about the Vietnam Veterans Memorial.

s Professor Binns from the Harry Potter stories shows, bringing the past alive requires a good teacher. Good history teachers help their students see how the past is important, and understanding the past can help us in the present. Effective history teachers know how history is constructed and how we use history to improve the human condition. This chapter focuses on how to help children learn about local and national stories from the past and provides strategies for meaningful historical learning.

History in the Schools

LEARNING OBJECTIVES

Explain why we study history in school.

Describe some of the things students can learn about history in elementary school.

Analyze the role of history in the elementary curriculum.

THE NEED FOR HISTORY IN THE ELEMENTARY SCHOOLS

> People live in the present. They plan for and worry about the future. History, however, is the study of the past. Given all the demands that press in from living in the present and anticipating what is yet to come, why bother with what has been?
>
> Peter Stearns, 1998

Peter Stearns posed this question in an essay he wrote for the American Historical Association in 1998. Stearns wanted his readers to think about the purpose of history. For ancient historians, like the famous Greek historian Thucydides, history was a chronicle of the past, without much concern for cause and effect or how understanding the past can help us in the present. Unlike Thucydides, modern historians see their field as a workspace for understanding human experiences in many contexts. Yet, history in school is often just a chronicle, much like Thucydides writing about the Peloponnesian War—a simple listing of people, dates, and events.

History can and should be so much more than lists of facts. For young children, history helps them understand their place in the great sweep of human progress—from the discovery of electricity, to the advent of iPods; from a country of British settlers to a diverse culture of Asian, Hispanic, and African Americans. History is a compass that orients us for action in the present. Stearns, in response to his question, said that history "harbors beauty," and exposure to the beauty of history makes us better. For children, this might take form through studying role models and heroes (Abraham Lincoln, Martin Luther King, Jr., or Susan B. Anthony) or by learning about events that shaped our collective identity (the Civil War or the Civil Rights movement), or by seeing that tragedy occurs and can be overcome by persistence and courage (e.g., the stories of Joseph Cinque or Sitting Bull). By studying these stories and others, children can be inspired to act more responsibly, study harder, and even care more about their fellow humans.

WHAT DO ELEMENTARY SCHOOL CHILDREN NEED TO KNOW ABOUT HISTORY?

Trying to determine exactly what children need to know about the past has been the source of much controversy. Some of the more salient questions that generate disagreement include:

- Should elementary-age children study history at the local, state, national, and/or global level?
- Should history instruction focus on facts or stories, individuals or groups, memorization or inquiry?
- Can learning about history help us live better in the present?
- Are there certain people and events that all children should study?

Many of these questions raise dichotomies, which shape our thinking about history. Far too often these dichotomies, such as memorization versus inquiry, limit our ability to conceptualize appropriate subject matter and teaching methods. We might best answer the question of what to teach in history and how to teach it by considering why we study history.

If as teachers we want children to learn history so that they might distinguish themselves from others by their possession of knowledge, then children should memorize facts about the past. If we want children to independently use resources to learn, then we can provide children with historical documents and artifacts to make inferences about what has happened in the past. If we want children to learn lessons from the past so they might act with wisdom in the present, then we offer opportunities for children to study morally relevant and authentic stories from the past. All of these approaches to learning the past are equally appropriate. The question becomes, how do we select content for historical study that meets these wide-ranging goals?

HISTORY AND THE CURRICULUM

Curriculum is typically developed given standards for learning. All 50 states have their own standards projects, and many were influenced by the National History Standards. This project includes standards for historical thinking and understanding for grades K–4. The standards for understanding focus on five topics.

Topic 1—Living and Working Together in Families and Communities, Now and Long Ago

Topic 2—The History of the Students' Own State or Region

Topic 3—The History of the United States: Democratic Principles and Values and the Peoples from Many Cultures Who Contributed to Its Cultural, Economic, and Political Heritage

Topic 4—The History of Peoples of Many Cultures around the World

Ultimately, making determinations about what to study is a standards-based curricular question. Even though most curriculums are developed by small committees and then given to teachers for implementation, the process of curriculum development does not end with implementation. Teachers have to fill in considerable blanks when they implement a curriculum. For example, consider Westward Expansion, a common item in most clementary United States history curriculums. In Kansas, where studing westward expansion is personal, one specific reference to this subject matter in the State Curricular Standards reads as follows:

> Describe life on the Santa Fe and Oregon-California Trails (e.g., interactions between different cultural groups, hardships such as lack of water, mountains and rivers to cross, weather, need for medical care, size of wagon).

A scene such as the one depicted in **FIGURE 5.1** of covered wagons would have been familiar to nineteenth century pioneers traveling on the California or Oregon Trail.

Teachers might want their students to learn about the hardships that pioneers endured on the trail, just as the curriculum standard indicates. The question is how to go about doing this. Students could read first-hand accounts of life on the trail. They could listen to a teacher lecture. They could watch a video or slideshow. They could assemble evidence to construct their own interpretation of the hardships. Each of these approaches meets the curriculum standard. Ultimately, teachers make decisions about how their students will learn this material best and then select the appropriate method.

FIGURE 5.1

Several covered wagons pulled by mules string out across the desolate prairie in a historical recreation of a journey on the Oregon Trail.

CONCEPT CHECK STOP

Given your beliefs, why is it important for children to study history?

Why should students learn about commonly taught historical content, such as the Dust Bowl farm families?

What contradictions might there be in your reasoning about the importance of studying history?

A giant dust storm engulfs Goodwell, Oklahoma, in June 1937.

Constructing Historical Knowledge

LEARNING OBJECTIVES

Define historical understanding and historical thinking.

Describe how historical thinking complements historical understanding.

Explain the process for historical thinking.

Historical knowledge is what we know about the past that helps us live in the present. Although many historians are suspicious of the notion that we can learn any lessons from the past, studying the past allows us to engage our flaws, indulge our greatness, marvel at our wisdom, and genuinely reflect on our progress. Learning history is part of the human endeavor to better ourselves, what Keith Barton and Linda Levstik (2004) call the "**common good.**" Teachers can teach more effectively about the past when they have a clear purpose for studying the accumulated knowledge about the past.

Common good An agreed-upon vision of what best suits the multiple interests of people in pluralistic societies.

HISTORICAL THINKING AND HISTORICAL UNDERSTANDING

In their National History Standards project, the National Center for History in the Schools suggests that historical understanding and historical thinking are equally important and central to social studies instruction. **Historical understanding** develops out of an active interest in history. Histori-

Historical understanding Knowledge of the past that develops out of intrinsic interest and active interpretation.

cal understanding is at times both inordinately simple and quite complex. Historical understanding means knowing the importance of a historical event, for example. It's not just reciting the facts or recounting the story of the first Thanksgiving. Historical understanding means having a grasp on why that first Thanksgiving was important and what impact it had on the people involved. For example, a historian understands the causes of the Civil War as a web of interlocking social, political, and economic circumstances that played out over decades in countless places and in countless contexts—this is historical understanding. Knowing the names of the major battles in the Civil War is not historical understanding. School children often know these same complex causes as a short list of three or four distilled ideas, mostly unassociated from the contexts within which these ideas were set forth. Knowing a list of possible causes of the Civil War is not historical understanding. Historical understanding of the Civil War would include knowing which causes of the Civil War are most important and how we came to agree on a list of causes of the Civil War.

Historical thinking
Cognitive activities that help students develop historical understanding.

Historical thinking is a set of cognitive activities that help in developing historical understanding. The National Center for History in the Schools (NCHS) defines historical thinking activities as including

- Chronological Thinking
- Historical Comprehension
- Historical Analysis and Interpretation
- Historical Research Capabilities
- Historical Issues: Analysis and Decision-Making

Based on the NCHS report, students in the early elementary grades can use historical thinking skills—summarizing a document, for example—to develop an understanding of that piece of history. Historical thinking might include determining why a document was produced. "In the Classroom" (pages 116–117) looks at how students' thinking about history with the use of historical artifacts can result in meaningful historical understanding.

ENCOURAGING HISTORICAL UNDERSTANDING THROUGH DIRECT INSTRUCTION AND EXPLANATION

The most common teaching method for historical understanding is lecture or direct instruction. In elementary school, this approach often takes the form of storytelling, discussion, and conversation. All of these forms of direct history instruction should center on explanation as opposed to exploration, particularly in elementary grades.

Explanation is at the core of direct instruction in history. Explanations simplify and clarify. Good explanations make use of symbols, metaphors, analogies, descriptions, comparisons, and restatements. Explanations should focus on making known the unknown, but should also make use of what students already know. (It is not useful to give an explanation that contains an analogy to something students are not familiar with.) It is also important to involve students in the process, so an explanation takes shape more as a conversation than a lecture. Explaining to students requires patience, especially when they often need multiple restatements or descriptions of the idea or concept.

In the Classroom USING HISTORICAL ARTIFACTS

Robin Collingwood teaches fourth grade, and one of her favorite lessons is on ancient history. She knows that most students might balk at the idea of ancient history unless she makes it interesting. So, she takes every opportunity to help students learn about the past in active and meaningful ways. For a lesson on the Roman Empire and Christianity, Ms. Collingwood uses coins—an authentic resource—as historical evidence to help her students understand how the Romans lived. The coins will help her students develop historical understanding of topics such as religion, republican forms of government, Roman art and architecture, and the Roman virtues of *veritas* (truth) and *dignitas* (dignity).

Next, Ms. Collingwood shows students a coin that depicts a Roman ruler named Vespasian who ruled the Roman Empire from A.D. 69 to 79. One side of the coin shows Vespasian's head with the inscription "IMP CAES VESP AVG P M COS IIII," which is an abbreviation for Vespasian's official Latin title "Imperator, Caesar, Vespasianus, Augustus, Pontifex Maximus, Consul IIII." The other side of the coin depicts Vespasian riding in a four-horse chariot.

How would you describe the actions of the people depicted on this coin?

Does the person on this coin appear to be important? Why do you think so?

First, Ms. Collingwood shows her students an image of this Roman coin, above, which depicts a woman in mourning with the word "Judea" inscribed below. She asks students to begin their historical thinking by summarizing what they see when they look at the coin. Summarizing the content often initiates a historical investigation—what do their descriptions of the coin suggest about the Romans? Why would they have a coin with a woman mourning? Ms. Collingwood tells students that the coin is symbolic of the downfall of Judea to the Romans in the first century B.C. Judea was one of many Roman colonies. Students can develop a historical understanding of the reach of the Roman Empire by studying this coin and related materials such as a map of the Roman Empire.

After being provided a translation of the words on the coin and told the story of Vespasian, the teacher asks the students to summarize what they see. This summary and context can become the basis for students beginning to develop an understanding of Roman government, which vacillated between autocracy, dictatorship, and republic. Such an understanding would require that students continue to engage information about Rome that describes various examples of Roman rule. The story of Vespasian is part of the grand story of kings, political leaders, and emperors. Vespasian was one of Rome's early emperors (he ruled from A.D. 69–79). Among his most important accomplishments, Vespasian brought peace to the Roman Empire for the first time in dozens of years.

Another coin that depicts a temple excavated in Caesarea Maritima serves as a starting point for an investigation of Roman religion. Ms. Collingwood asks her students to describe the coin.

What do you see on this coin?

Students typically do not recognize the structure on the coin as a temple, so Ms. Collingwood tells them about the gradual adoption of Christianity by the Romans. When the Romans produced this coin, they worshiped a variety of gods at temples such as the one depicted. Thinking about the image on this coin can prompt students to consider how the Romans' views of religion changed during the first two centuries. The following dialogue illustrates how the coin can be used as a starting point to describe the Roman adoption of Christianity.

Ms. Collingwood: Can someone tell me what you see on this coin?

Student: Is it a building?

Ms. Collingwood: Yes, it is a building. What kind of building is it?

Student: Maybe an outdoor building.

Ms. Collingwood: OK, what do you think people did in this building?

Student: Is it a house or maybe . . .

Ms. Collingwood: This was a public building, where a lot of people might go. What kinds of buildings are used by big groups of people?

Student: Schools?

Other Students: A store, a club, a church?

Ms. Collingwood: Yes, a church, or as the early Romans called it, a temple. Temples were public buildings where the early Romans would worship their gods. Remember learning about all the Roman gods?

Student: Yes, like Jupiter and Apollo?

Ms. Collingwood: Correct. Toward the end of the Roman Empire, they gave up their worship of multiple gods and started to worship a single God. Does anyone remember what religions worship a single God?

Student: Christianity?

Ms. Collingwood: Yes, as well as Judaism. Christians worshiped one God the same as Jews, and over time Romans adopted this approach to religion themselves. In fact, toward the end of the Roman Empire about A.D. 300, the Romans officially adopted Christianity.

There are many other techniques for direct instruction, such as lecture, which will be reviewed in upcoming chapters, but for now we continue the focus on explanation. A specific teaching example that makes use of explanation appears at right: "Social and Cultural Explorations: Life along the Cuyahoga River."

FOUR WAYS TO THINK HISTORICALLY

Encouraging historical thinking can provide students opportunities to develop meaningful historical understanding. Because young children bring very little in the way of prior knowledge and skills to the task of developing historical understanding, they must be provided with systematic thinking strategies. These strategies revolve around four ways to think historically:

- Comprehension
- Awareness
- Investigation
- Judgment

In order to develop meaningful and consistent historical understanding, teachers should provide their students as many opportunities as possible to think historically using these four methods. Teachers can structure historical thinking exercises to support their students' work toward understanding the past.

First and foremost, teachers can support students in comprehending essential information about the topic they are studying. To comprehend something means that you grasp the meaning or importance of that thing. *Historical comprehension* requires students to identify and recall, as well as to describe, explain, and compare. For example, consider students in Vermont learning about Ethan Allen. What might we expect these students to comprehend about Ethan Allen? Why was Ethan Allen important? Why do we need to know about Ethan Allen? Answering these questions enables students to comprehend Ethan Allen as an historical figure.

Historical awareness allows people to be well informed about the past. An awareness of Ethan Allen would mean that students are familiar with when and where Allen lived and the contributions that make him famous. We might think of this knowledge as factual, but those facts are situated in a context. Facts are often maligned in social studies as boring, but when applied to real historical settings (a context), factual knowledge contributes to students' awareness of historical significance.

The image in **FIGURE 5.2** suggests important factual information about Ethan Allen. Allen is shown in the middle of the image with a sword in his right hand. If students use this image along with other resources, they will learn that Ethan Allen was a citizen of Vermont who commanded a local militia group called the Green Mountain Boys during the American Revolution.

While the facts of Allen's life are important and can lead to an awareness of his significance, these facts have more meaning when we ask about their historical relevance. Such work can be facilitated through *historical investigation*, by enabling students to determine the importance, or relevance, of the contributions of Ethan Allen in the American Revolution using specific historical resources like this picture. An investigation of the image should result in students understanding that Ethan Allen is famous because he was promoted as a hero by writers and historians during the American Revolution and just after. Students conduct historical investigations not only to learn the facts, but also to learn why certain facts are important.

FIGURE 5.2

American Colonel Ethan Allen (1738–1789) (second left), leader of the Green Mountain Boys, a Continental paramilitary group, surprises British Captain William Delaplace outside his chambers as the Americans capture the British garrison at Fort Ticonderoga during the American Revolution, Ticonderoga, New York, May 10, 1775. How does this image promote historical awareness of Ethan Allen?

Life along the Cuyahoga River

In the state of Ohio, students study how the history of human development has impacted and is impacted by the surrounding environment. One example of this human relationship with the land involves the Cuyahoga River.

These two dramatically different images are both pictures of the Cuyahoga River, one taken outside Cleveland in 1969 (A) and the other at Brandywine Falls over 20 years later (B), but just 20 or so miles from the site of the first picture.

A teacher in Ohio might want to use the Cuyahoga River and these images to explain how humans interact with the environment. Following is an explanation of how Native Americans, Europeans, and Americans have used the Cuyahoga River throughout history.

A Industrial activity along the Cuyahoga River, just south of Cleveland in 1969. What does this photo tell you about how people interact with the environment?

> The Cuyahoga River is a source of food, transportation, and energy. Seneca and Cayuga Native American Indians settled along the river many hundreds of years ago. So did European settlers just over two hundred fifty years ago. More recently, Americans have built factories and the city of Cleveland along the banks of the river. Over the years, Native Americans, European settlers, and Americans have developed villages, towns, and cities along the river. Each of these groups has made use of something the Cuyahoga has to offer. For the Native American and European settlers, this was transportation and food. For Americans, the Cuyahoga was used for transportation and food sources as well as a source of energy.

The habit of settling close to rivers helps explain growth patterns across the United States. As they explain how people have used rivers throughout history, teachers can continue to situate their explanations in examples from Native American Indian and white settlements. These general ideas simplify the complexity of settlement and growth and thus serve to help *explain* the past rather than just describe it.

Ultimately, students need to learn how to construct explanations themselves. In fact, elementary school students in Ohio are expected to "explain the impact of settlement, industrialization, and transportation on the expansion of the United States." Staying with our example, a teacher might want to prompt students to think of specific examples of how rivers provide sources of food and energy and can be used for transportation. This work might require that students access additional historical resources and will most certainly require that students engage in systematic historical thinking aimed at developing historical understanding.

B A view of the Cuyahoga River at the 33,000-acre Cuyahoga National Recreational Area from the top of Brandywine Falls. What explanation might an elementary school student need in order to compare these two photos and therefore gain historical understanding of the Cuyahoga River?

Historical judgment requires that students make decisions about the value or importance of people and events from the past. Students are essentially filling in the blanks from historical sources. The record of the past is always tentative, and when working with historical sources, students have to make decisions that result in a more complete understanding of the past. For example, students might see the depiction of Ethan Allen in the middle of this image as heroic, positioned to take the British leader William Delaplace captive. Allen's most notable military accomplishment was the capture of Ticonderoga, which was manned by only 50 British soldiers, but his greatest military challenge was a miserable defeat—namely, the 1775 attack on Montréal during which he was captured by the British. Ethan Allen was perhaps best known for his inspirational writing. His book *Narrative of Colonel Ethan Allen's Captivity* (written in 1779) was one of the most popular books of its time and served as an inspiration to American colonists during the Revolutionary War. Students learn to appreciate the importance of careful consideration of historical information when they are given potentially contradictory evidence (such as the painting and reports of the attack on Montréal).

Using historical judgment results in students making decisions about what to believe and what to not to believe. Should we believe that Ethan Allen is a hero? Should we promote this belief among our students? The best approach is to allow students to decide for themselves. As students consider Allen's legacy by comprehending information, developing an awareness of his legacy, examining information, and making judgments, students can begin to understand the past as a more complete story.

CONCEPT CHECK **STOP**

Consider the distinctions between historical thinking and historical understanding.

How might a teacher encourage students to use historical thinking skills to develop their historical understanding of the African salt trade?

What explanations or resources might students need to support their work?

A view of a salt camel caravan outside the Fachi oasis in Niger. What does this image tell you about the lifestyle and culture of these West African salt traders?

Forms of Historical Understanding: Timelines, Stories, and Empathy

LEARNING OBJECTIVES

Describe how to use timelines and stories in history instruction.

Evaluate the role of empathy in developing historical understanding.

Explain how presentism can limit historical understanding.

Remember that students practice thinking about history by comprehending information, increasing their awareness, investigating historical information, and making judgments. All of these lead to students' understanding of history. But what does an understanding of history "look like"? Historical understanding takes shape in a number of ways. Students might understand the past as a chronology, as a story, or through empathetic experience. They also understand the past as a series of significant events and as explanations of the present. Each of these approaches and contexts requires different types of instruction that reflect varying beliefs about why we study the past.

HISTORICAL UNDERSTANDING AS CHRONOLOGY

Understanding the past through chronology is probably the most obvious and common way to learn history. We tell the stories of our life using chronology, and we use stories to help children make sense of the past. Timelines and storyboards are two chronologically oriented learning structures that help students develop their understanding of the past.

Timelines are a very important pedagogical tool for social studies teachers. The timeline incorporates discrete subject matter into patterns. Timelines help students remember events from the past and consider cause and effect. A good timeline should be clearly focused on a specific body of subject matter and should have sensible and meaningful beginnings and ends. See **FIGURE 5.3**, "Visualizing: Timelines" for an example of how students can investigate timelines.

Visualizing

Timelines FIGURE 5.3

Timelines display visual and numerical characteristics. Teachers can emphasize these visual factors for students for whom English is a second language, or for students with language deficits. Following is a very simple visual timeline depicting famous buildings over time. Each structure represents some human effort to glorify, entertain, or govern. Students might investigate these concepts by studying the structures and the contexts in which they were built.

c. 3000 B.C. The Pyramids of Giza, Egypt. Why are these pyramids famous?

A.D. 82. The Colosseum in Rome, Italy. Why was the Colosseum built? What were the Romans hoping to accomplish?

A.D. 1973. The Sydney Opera House in Sydney, Australia. How do you think the people of Sydney feel about the Opera House? What does this building tell us about their culture?

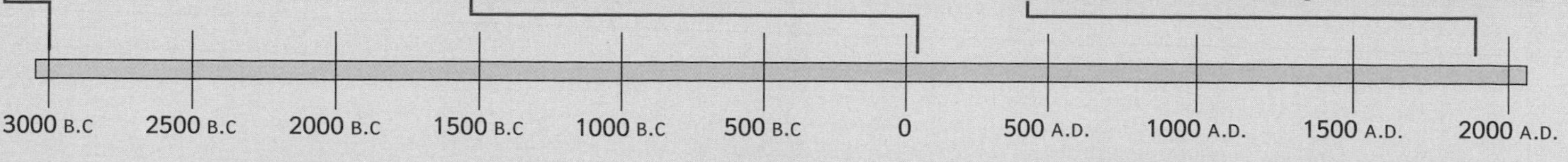

HISTORICAL UNDERSTANDING AS STORY

Storytelling is another form of historical understanding that is central to social studies teaching. Good storytellers keep their listeners' attention by building a sense of suspense and drama that is typically resolved at the end of the story. Drama can be a powerful context for teaching history. Students can participate in dramatic role-playing activities and simulations. Such activities require varying levels of scaffolding. Small role-playing activities can often be constructed by students with very few teacher scaffolds. Larger simulations require more scaffolding and support. At the extreme, teachers can write scripts for students. More effective and authentic simulations should involve some student work in developing the content of the simulation.

Story structure plays an important pedagogical role in education. Stories have a beginning, middle, and end, and they often have a dramatic turning point in the middle. Because stories develop in patterns that are somewhat predictable and easy for students to manage, they are ideal for introducing unfamiliar material. Stories about families and schools also provide a good pedagogical construct for students to begin to develop meaningful understanding about the past. Children might interview their parents, grandparents, or elders in their community to learn about events from the past that were important or relevant for these participants in history.

Historical fiction is another powerful way to engage students in stories about the past. This special form of literature blends information about the past with a fictional literary form to create engaging stories. Works such as Esther Forbes's *Johnny Tremain* provide students with access to the past through engaging storylines. Johnny Tremain is the fictional story of a young apprentice silversmith who injures his hand and joins the *Boston Observer*, a local newspaper. At the newspaper, Johnny stands witness to the dramatic events of the mid-1770s alongside Sam Adams, James Otis, and other members of the Sons of Liberty. Teachers can use this fictional work as a context for elementary school children to learn about the events leading to and the outbreak of the American Revolution.

Children's books that are set in the past can also be valuable contexts for learning history. For example, Alan Armstrong's 2005 book *Whittington* is a retelling of an English folktale called "Dick Whittington and His Cat." The tale is told by a cat to a group of barnyard animals who are stuck in a barn during a snowstorm. Along with the animals is a young boy named Ben. The book weaves the story of Ben, who has dyslexia and is trying to learn how to read, with the actual folktale about Dick Whittington. The folktale is set in medieval England and can be a context for learning about this period in history. Such an approach can be used with virtually any book set in a historical context. All the events and people in these books can be windows into a past that teachers and students can construct around the story.

Social studies teachers can work with their students to develop storyboards about historical events—using historical events, or historical fiction. A storyboard is a visual layout for the progression of events in a story. FIGURE 5.4, "Process Diagram: Storyboarding in history," shows a typical storyboard structure. A historical storyboard should convey ideas about the past and help others understand something by presenting it in an interesting format. Storyboards should begin with an introduction to the characters in the story as well as the setting for the story. Following the introduction, the student should sequence the beginning, middle, and ending events according to the goals for the story. A student may want to use the story to explore a problem or simply an interesting idea. Figure 5.4 includes an example of a storyboard that a student might develop on the story of Pocahontas. The extent to which students assemble the information for the story or teachers provide scaffolds for their students' work is dependent on the age and prior knowledge of the students.

HISTORICAL EMPATHY

People experience the emotion of empathy in different ways. By definition, empathy is the identification with and understanding of another person's situation, feelings, and motives. When a child empathizes with people or historical figures from the past, the child is seeking to understand the past in a personal way. Empathy can result in students feeling happy or sad; encouraged or discouraged; motivated or dejected. The degree to which a child might have an empathetic experience varies significantly, but in history we might

Process Diagram

Storyboarding in history FIGURE 5.4

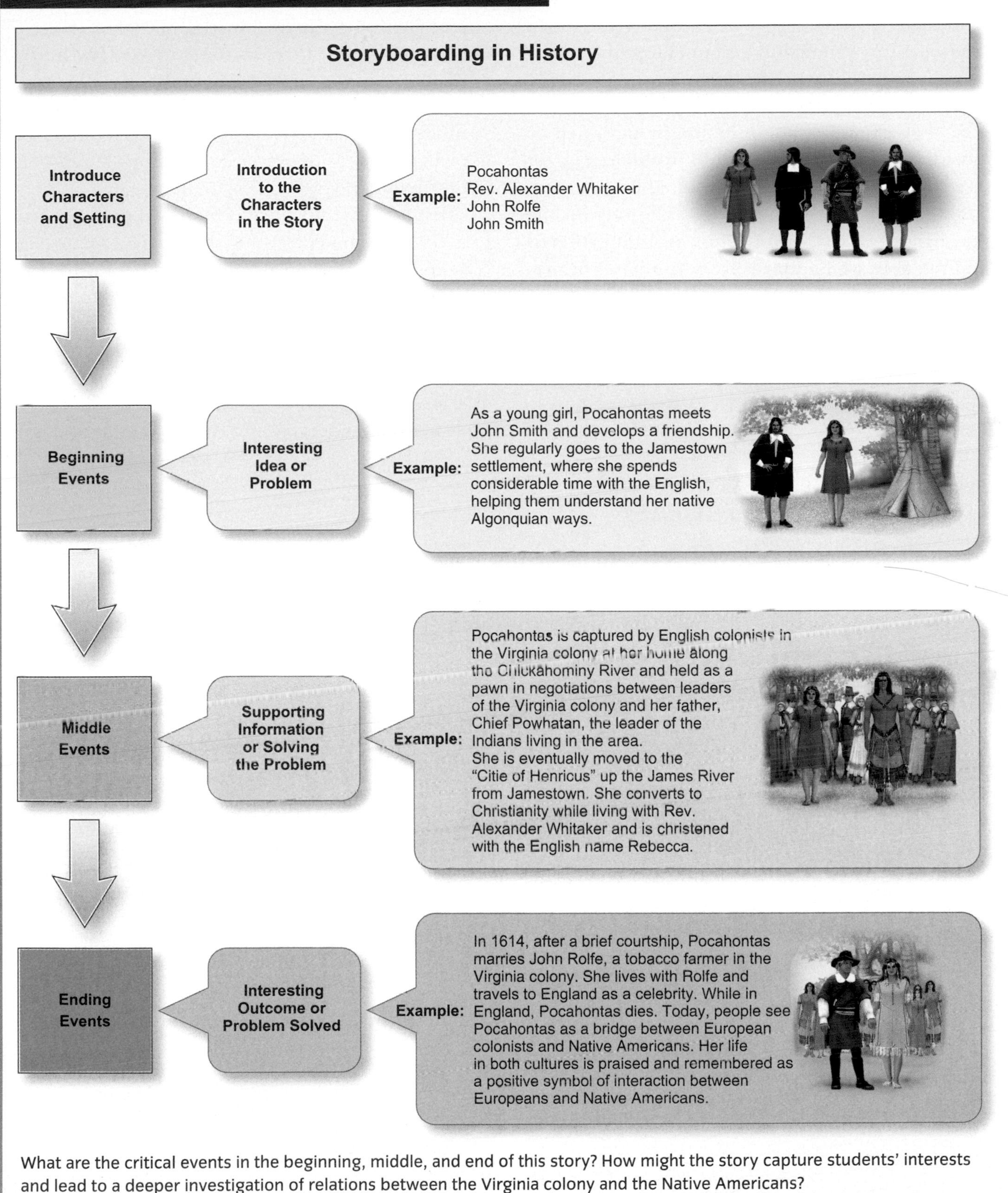

What are the critical events in the beginning, middle, and end of this story? How might the story capture students' interests and lead to a deeper investigation of relations between the Virginia colony and the Native Americans?

want to encourage students to engage in limited empathy. Ideally, students need to be uplifted and encouraged through empathy, particularly at younger ages.

Students can be encouraged to empathize with a range of historical figures. The more interesting or personal the figure, the more likely children are to empathize. For example, students might be asked to consider the images in **FIGURE 5.5** of children in various social settings. Each child lives in a historical context that is depicted in the image. The boy on the donkey lives in Luxor, Egypt. The children gathered around the pole are Buddhists from Yunnan Province, China. How might students consider the historical contexts of the children in these photos, while still empathizing with the children depicted? Can you empathize with any of the people in these photos? Explain.

UNDERSTANDING WHAT IS SIGNIFICANT FROM THE PAST

As students progress in their understanding of the past, they can make determinations about what is significant and what is not. Assigning significance is an extraordinarily complex act. Students will learn to take into account a range of factors that influence historical significance. First, they can decide what yardstick to use for measuring significance. In some instances, they will want to use very personal measures, such as how it makes them feel or whether it has local or community significance. On other occasions, students will need to use external measures given to them by the teacher as put forth in standards and curriculum.

Historical significance is included in the curriculum, but when implementing the curriculum, teachers have to make decisions about which details to teach. Essentially, this means that teachers have to read between the lines in the curriculum. For example, if they are expected to teach about historical biographies (an expectation from the National History Standards for K–3 grades), which specific biographies would be significant? Consider students learning about the American Civil War. If they are learning about military planning, the records of President Abraham Lincoln might be more significant than the letters of a Civil War solider. If the topic is the life of a soldier, then the letters might be a better tool.

Let's think about how to look at the significance of a common curricular item such as the Emancipa-

FIGURE 5.5

A A young Egyptian boy rides a donkey along a dirt road in Luxor. Where do you think the boy is going, and why?

B Five Chinese Dai students dressed in the orange robes of a Buddhist monk in Yunnan Province

The Emancipation Proclamation FIGURE 5.6

A Close-up of a copy of the Emancipation Proclamation

A Proclamation.
Whereas, on the twenty-second day of September, in the year of our Lord one thousand eight hundred and sixty-two, a proclamation was issued by the President of the United States, containing, among other things, the following, to wit:
"That on the first day of January, in the "year of our Lord one thousand eight hundred "and sixty-three, all persons held as slaves within

B African-American Union soldiers of the 29th Regiment from Connecticut, 1864. Why was the Emancipation Proclamation particularly significant for these African-American Union soldiers?

tion Proclamation (FIGURE 5.6A). Some teachers might simply want to emphasize the words in this document by requiring that students memorize the text or give dramatic readings. Other teachers might want to extend this activity by having their students consider how the Proclamation affected different groups of people such as the African-American Union soldiers (pictured in FIGURE 5.6B).

The Emancipation Proclamation had a different significance for the African-American men in FIGURE 5.6B than it did for other people. Students have to weigh this information as they make determinations about assigning significance to past events.

UNDERSTANDING THE RELATIONSHIP BETWEEN THE PAST AND THE PRESENT

Most of us have heard the common notion that "history repeats itself." Although scholars might disagree about the extent to which this maxim is valid, on some level people are pressed to take certain actions in the present because of their impressions about the past. It is important to position students to understand the past in such a way that will result in actions in the present that are thoughtful and productive. We do this by selecting what we want students to understand about the past with care for how it projects into the present. For example, we expect students to study about George Washington as a hero and a moral character, so as to provide an example of good judgment for students. We do not study other characters from the time such as Vice President Aaron Burr, who killed Alexander Hamilton in a duel and went on to attempt a coup in the western territory of the United States. We must be particularly careful, when considering the past, not to indulge in **presentism**, or overemphasizing our present values and beliefs when developing an understanding of history.

CONCEPT CHECK STOP

Consider how children might understand Benjamin Franklin's contributions to science.

How might we develop a timeline or a story depicting Franklin's work with electricity?

What might be some empathetic approaches to studying Franklin?

How significant was Franklin's work with electricity?

How can we judge the work of Franklin given modern expectations for science?

Politician and inventor Benjamin Franklin discovers that lightning is electricity in this painting of the famous 1752 experiment in Philadelphia.

Three Approaches to Teaching History

LEARNING OBJECTIVES

Describe the basic procedures involved in transmitting information through direct learning.

Explain the expectations of active instruction.

Identify how to use authentic resources in teaching history.

Approaches to teaching history FIGURE 5.7

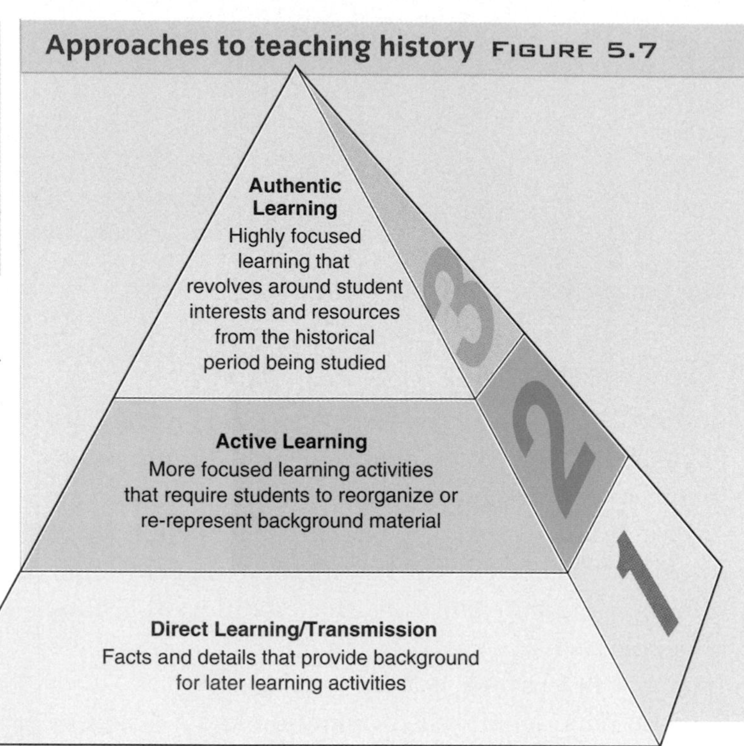

In this section, we discuss three increasingly sophisticated learning activities in history (FIGURE 5.7):

1. Direct Learning/Transmission
2. Active Learning
3. Authentic Learning

DIRECT LEARNING IN HISTORY

Direct learning involves a form of instruction known as **transmission**. Instructional procedures that support transmission assume that a teacher is in possession of some knowledge and can effectively transfer his understanding to learners using direct instructional methods. The most common transmission-oriented instructional method is lecture, but transmission might also include discussion, individual and small group self-guided work, and multimedia presentations. The central idea behind transmission is that a fixed body of knowledge is being transferred as a whole, without critical examination. Transmission instruction is well suited for curriculum and standards that focus on low-level forms of knowledge such as the dates of events and names of important characters in history. Ideally, transmission of historical knowledge should precede more sophisticated historical explorations. The Lesson on pages 128–129 on The First Thanksgiving is an example of a very common historical story that is often transmitted to students, but can also serve as the opening for an in-depth investigation.

Transmission The delivery by a teacher to students of predetermined knowledge intended to be learned as a whole by the student.

ACTIVE LEARNING IN HISTORY

After students have begun to learn historical information through transmission, they can more actively engage this information. Active learning enables students to assign meaning to facts (FIGURE 5.8). Teachers might use inquiry methods to facilitate active learning. Such learning helps students make connections between otherwise disconnected information. Teachers can help their students create meaning and make connections so they will better remember the information. Too often, curriculum and standardized tests emphasize subject matter without encouraging students to make these active connections. Consider the following test items from the New York State Grade 5 Elementary Social Studies Test.

FIGURE 5.8

Children in a social studies class constructing a replica of a historical building. How are these students engaging in active learning in history?

How many immigrants came to the United States between 1840 and 1849?

A. 200,000

B. 500,000

C. 1,500,000

D. 2,800,000

What do the stripes on the United States flag represent?

A. The Presidents of the United States

B. The immigrants from around the world

C. The original 13 colonies

D. The wars the United States has fought

Both of these questions reflect something important, but is knowing the answers what is important? Certainly, students should understand that immigration increased in the 1840s due to the Irish potato famine, but the exact number of immigrants approaches a triviality. Was it half a million, 1.5 million, or 2.5 million—do you know? Knowledge about the North American British colonies that rose up in revolt is important, but it is significant because of the context of the American Revolution. It is less important to be certain of why that many stripes are on the flag.

Students need to possess historical knowledge that has meaning and context, and this is best developed through active learning. For example, students are encouraged to know that the United States is a nation of immigrants, and historical examples of our rich history of immigration can be found throughout American history. Students will benefit from understanding some of the challenges that confronted the United States as it incorporated hundreds of thousands of Irish immigrants into the national fabric in the 1840s and hundreds of thousands more, this time from Eastern Europe (FIGURE 5.9), in the 1890s. We live in another period of massive immigration in the first decade of the twenty-first century. Students need to know how this continuing process of immigration has changed the United States over its history.

FIGURE 5.9

Immigrants heading for New York City in 1893 huddle in blankets outdoors in the steerage class of the Red Star Line's *S.S. Pennland*.

Developing this knowledge requires an active application of factual information. For example, immigration to the United States continues to be a dynamic and polarizing issue (FIGURE 5.10). In order for students to make sense of issues surrounding immigration and its impact, they need historical understanding.

Many of the same issues in play today were significant in the 1840s. But far too often adults who express opinions about topics such as immigration and who commit political acts based on these beliefs, lack the context that historical understanding provides. Unfortunately, remembering that 1.5 million people immigrated to the United States in the 1840s does not, on its own, help with developing such a context. Actively engaging information about immigration in the 1840s in the context of questions about immigration today does help students develop more meaningful understandings about the past.

Also consider the question about the stripes in the U.S. flag. Students need to know that there were thirteen colonies, which, despite their significant social, political, and economic differences, joined in a rebellion against British rule. The significance of the number thirteen is that it was such a large and diverse group—more than two, more than five—13 colonies! Students use this fact in the act of assigning significance to the scope of the rebellion, which helps them understand a series of political events that has shaped our current political lives. This is an active process that requires that students reorganize information to suit their needs.

LEARNING IN HISTORY USING AUTHENTIC RESOURCES

All learning in history should make use of authentic historical sources, and recent research suggests that children as young as those in first and second grade can reason historically using historical resources. This

FIGURE 5.10

Immigrant Salvadorians building a house in Fairfax County, Virginia. "Without this influx of immigrant labor, we wouldn't come close to meeting the demand for housing in this area," says Craig Havenner, former president of the Northern Virginia Building Industry Association.

recognition is changing elementary social studies and necessitates a careful consideration of the nature and appropriate uses of historical sources. Authentic historical sources are fragments from the past that can serve as evidence for understanding more complete interpretations of the past. Whether the authentic source is a letter from a soldier in the Civil War, or a government transcript from the Watergate hearings, or a picture of Martin Luther King, Jr. giving a speech, these documents become important and meaningful when they are studied in the classroom. An authentic historical source is not static. These resources are given meaning by the learners who are using them as they seek to learn about and from the past. Types of authentic historical sources include:

- Government records and documents
- Oral histories
- Historical photos
- Letters and diaries
- Physical artifacts

How might students engage in active consideration of authentic historical resources? David Hicks and Peter Doolittle have developed a method for analyzing authentic historical sources they call **SCIM-C** (**s**ummarize, **c**ontextualize, **i**nfer, **m**onitor, **c**orroborate). The process involves students completing the following tasks:

- **S**ummarize the content of a resource;
- **C**ontextualize the emerging knowledge in broader historical knowledge;
- **I**nfer from this knowledge some new information;
- **M**onitor the process of summarization; and when multiple resources are involved,
- **C**orroborate emerging understandings by considering the historical document.

Students can and should engage in this process in primary grades, as early as first and second grade.

The processes students follow when thinking historically with authentic historical resources lead to more thoughtful historical understanding. Consider all of the steps in Hicks and Doolittle's SCIM-C process as you look at the authentic historical document in **FIGURE 5.11**. How might a student summarize the content of the immigration passport? How might a student contextualize it in broader historical knowledge, and infer new knowledge from it?

FIGURE 5.11

This is the 1923 passport of Greek immigrants Kalotina Kakias Fatolitis and her daughter Eleni who entered the United States through Ellis Island. What does the document tell us? (name of the individual, date of arrival, home country) The answers to these questions can initiate an historical examination using Hicks and Doolittle's SCIM-C method. What steps would come next in the SCIM-C process?

The process of working with this immigration passport using the SCIM-C model might unfold as follows:

Summarize—This passport document includes text, a photo, an official stamp, and several signatures. Students can literally copy this information given the limited text, even using the same format. They would have to describe the picture, seal, and signatures.

Contextualize—Students need to understand that this document is an official record that enables the person listed to enter the United States. The concept of immigration is an important part of the context, as is the relevant history of immigration. Teachers can provide students this information in a brief lecture or through helpful hints, or maybe even through guided questions.

Infer—Any inference made about this document would require a question being raised. Proposing an answer to the question would compel students to make guesses or inferences. Students might ask what the woman who owned the passport did when she arrived in New York. A proposed answer to this question would require an educated guess based on the students' understanding of the document itself (e.g., her age can be summarized from the document) and the general context of the times (e.g., many women who entered the United States at this time worked in factories).

Monitor—As they work, students have to double-check their work. This means returning to the summary while developing the context and returning to the context while making inferences. This interplay between each step is essential and allows new information to constantly emerge.

Corroborate—Students need to compare this document to others as they make inferences. If another document supports this one, then the inferences are stronger.

Now, consider the excerpts of a letter in which Walt Whitman tells of his visits to wounded Civil War soldiers in Washington, D.C. (**FIGURE 5.12**). How can students use the SCIM-C model to learn about death and dying during the American Civil War?

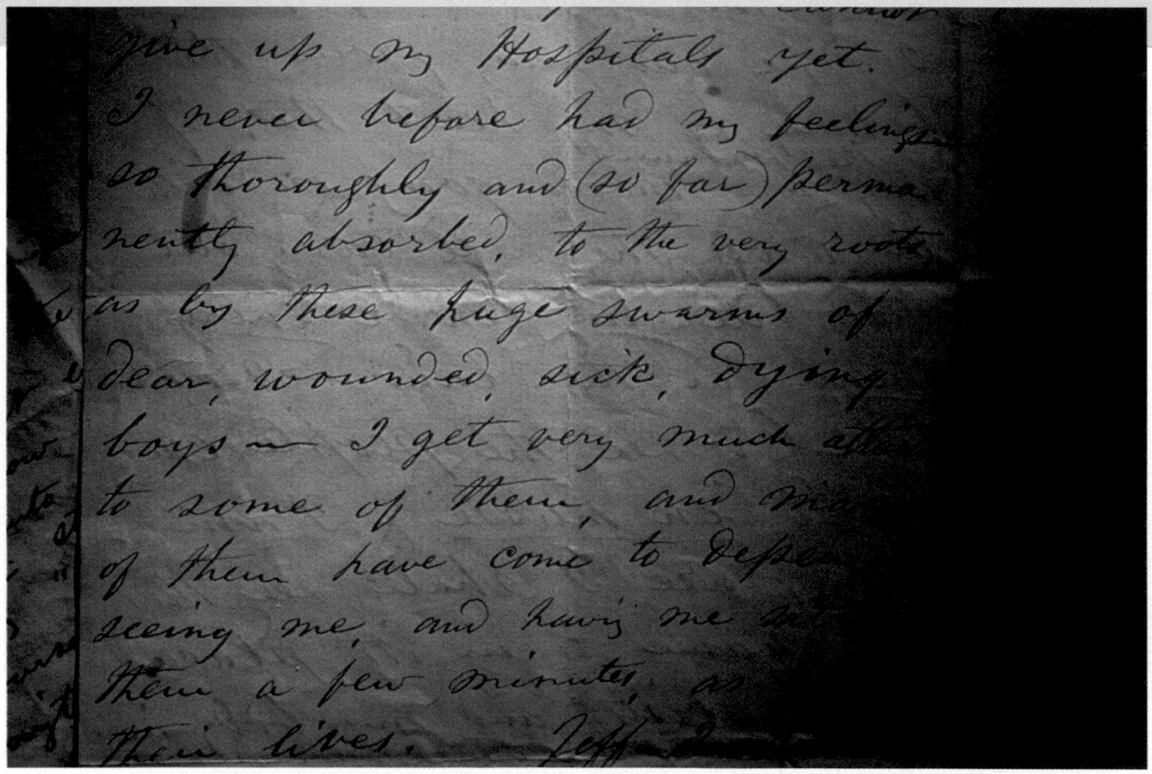
give up my Hospitals yet.
I never before had my feelings
so thoroughly and (so far) permanently absorbed, to the very roots
as by these huge swarms of
dear, wounded, sick, dying
boys — I get very much att
to some of them, and ma
of them have come to depe
seeing me, and having me
them a few minutes, as
their lives.

FIGURE 5.12

Passage excerpted from a Walt Whitman letter in which he tells of his visits to wounded Civil War soldiers in Washington, D.C.

TRANSCRIPTION: "I have never before had my feelings so thoroughly and (so far) permanently absorbed to the very roots as by these huge swarms of dear, wounded, sick, dying boys. I [give] very much attention to them, and many of them have come to depend on seeing me, and having me sit by them for a few minutes, as if for their lives."

FIGURE 5.13

The Ta Lama (left of center), Grand Lama of Chung tien, and his Tibetan party at luncheon in the Yangtze Gorge above Ashi, May 1923, Northwest Yunnan

Using Historic Photos Historic photos often include important clues about how people live and what they are able to do and not do in their daily lives. What can you infer about the subject in FIGURE 5.13? Who is in this picture? What do you think they were doing when the picture was taken and before and after the picture was taken? Why do you think this picture was taken? What does it tell you about the lifestyles of the people shown there? What else would you need in order to learn more about these people?

In order to make any inferences you will need to do some background research on Buddhism, particularly the role of the Ta Lama. While engaging in this exercise, consider how you will conduct your research and how you can facilitate students in elementary grades in doing this type of background research.

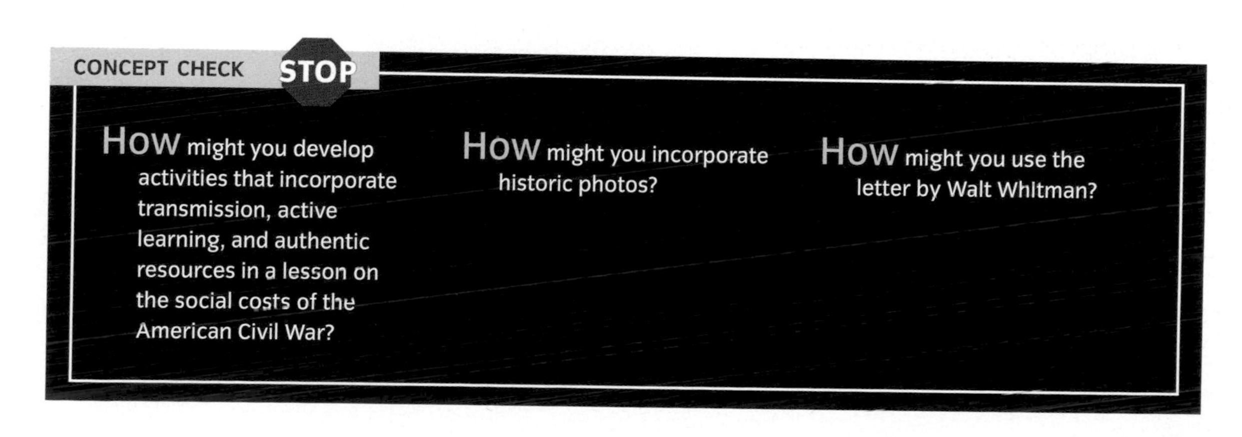

Teaching for Geographic Awareness 6

What does it mean to know one's place in the world? How does it feel to have a sense of belonging to a place or a people? The study of geography can position children to answer these and other questions about place, people, and the relationships between them.

In a classroom in Virginia, elementary school students in a social studies class stand before a map, looking to pinpoint a place unknown to them. In this case it's Mustang, Nepal. The location on this map is not very meaningful, but it can become meaningful if they also see a photograph of a young girl with a basket of harvested grain held on her back by a sling across the top of her head. These schoolchildren in Virginia might be able to describe how their lives differ from hers. They might construct a mental map of her home. They might come to understand the challenges and joys of living in the place this girl calls home.

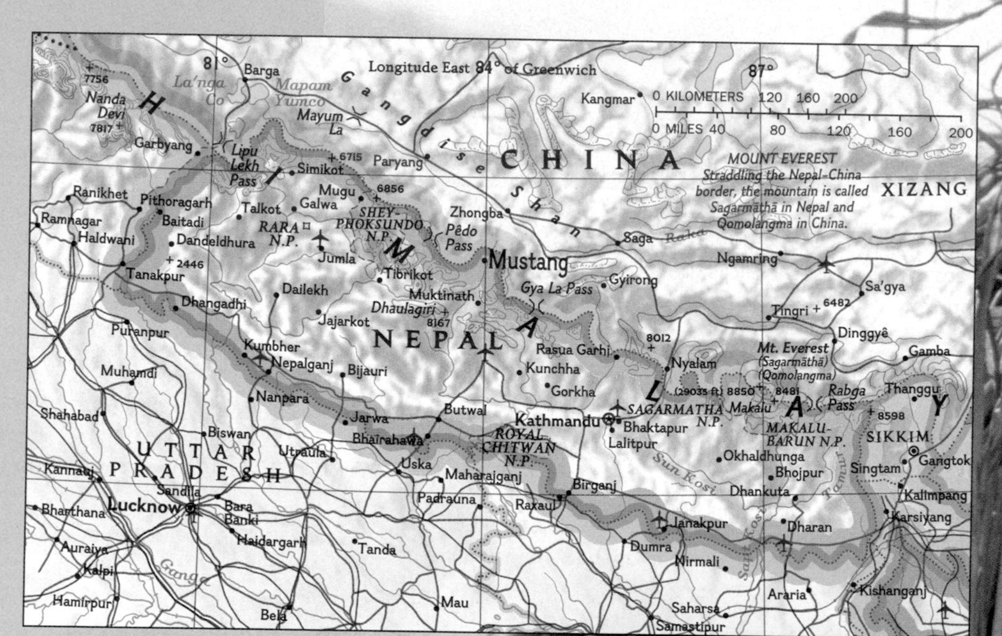

Geography can help children move beyond simple map skills and enable them to see the world as a whole place, teeming with a variety of interesting human experiences.

Geography is the discipline that enables us to develop knowledge about places and environments.

NATIONAL GEOGRAPHIC

CHAPTER OUTLINE

This young girl in Mustang, Nepal carries a basket using a sling on her head. What does the image suggest about life in Nepal?

We use geography to make sense out of the world as well as to come to a greater understanding of its complexities and its difficulties. By studying places, we can learn about human achievement and tragedy. Students might study the Colorado River and the Hoover Dam or Hiroshima, Japan, and the dropping of the atomic bomb. By struggling to understand complex relationships, we can be motivated to create a better place to live.

This chapter focuses on ways to think about geography and the most effective strategies for enabling children to make use of geographic knowledge. We will explore what it means to have geographic awareness and how this geographic awareness enriches and enhances daily civic life.

The Need for Geographic Awareness

LEARNING OBJECTIVES

Understand why we study geography in the schools.

Develop a personal rationale for studying geography.

Analyze how geography is situated in the elementary school curriculum.

WHAT IS GEOGRAPHIC AWARENESS?

Did you know that most people cannot accurately estimate distances? In part, this is due to limited experience accurately measuring distance. Unfortunately, most of our "incidental" geographic knowledge is limited and often incorrect. Geography professor Reginald Golledge talks about geographic awareness as both "incidental" and "intentional." **Incidental geography** is the knowledge we have developed from our everyday life and experiences. As we navigate life, we develop an awareness of the space around us and how we interact with that space. This may result in having a sense of direction, or knowing how to get from one place to another. It might also mean that we sense that pollution is a problem or that some places have limited natural resources.

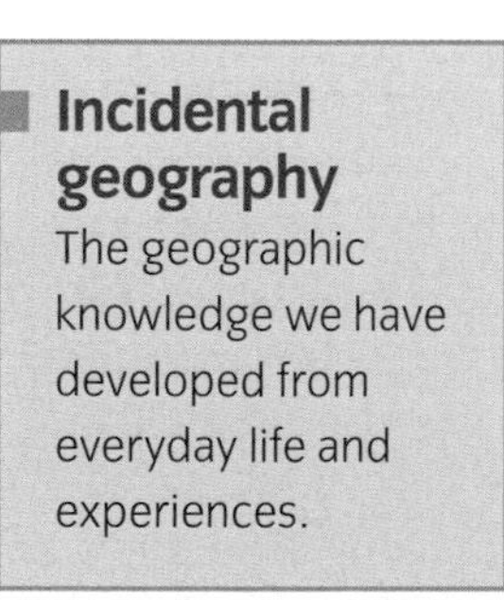

Incidental geography The geographic knowledge we have developed from everyday life and experiences.

We teach about geography to fill in the gaps and correct misperceptions. We can teach students geography skills, such as how to properly estimate distance, to help children understand the physical and cultural world around them. This learned or **intentional geographic** knowledge can improve our quality of life and enrich our personal experiences. For example, if we can properly estimate distance, we can better plan our day and perhaps avoid being late to events and gatherings (**FIGURE 6.1**). To be geographically aware means that we understand how our knowledge about geography is constructed, what its limitations are, and how to correct our misunderstandings.

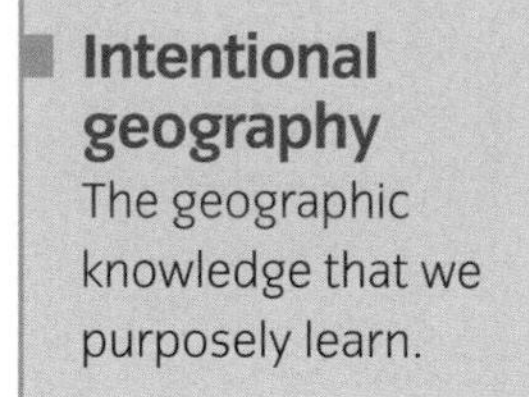

Intentional geography The geographic knowledge that we purposely learn.

Children do not come to school with a tabula rasa. Instead, they have ideas that are often poorly formed or misinformed and we teach to help them advance their knowledge. For example, a first-grade child may be able to tell you how far away something is, maybe one mile or ten miles away, simply by remembering what he was told or by reading sign posts. However, children often do not understand the difference between distances such as one mile and ten miles. Most adults conceptualize one mile as a distance that is covered on foot at its fastest in four or five minutes but more commonly by walking 20–25 minutes. We do not consider ten miles to be a distance that we would travel on foot; consequently we tend to think about this distance as being

FIGURE 6.1

Children can learn spatial values such as the distance that one or ten miles covers in early elementary grades. Think about how children learn these distances and how teachers can help children develop this knowledge.

traversed in a car or train, or we might think of ten miles as the distance from our home to some landmark. This adult knowledge is incidental, based on experience, and it is developmentally situated.

Children often struggle to consider what "distance" means. One way we can help them understand the concept of distance is to use life experience. How far is one mile? We can help children understand by mapping a mile around the school campus or perhaps on a track close to the school. We can do the same with ten miles measured as a distance from school to a particularly well-known place in the community.

Geography can help us answer virtually any question about human interaction. If students want to know why people live where they do, geography can help. If they want to understand why people in some areas are wealthy and others are poor, geography can help. When studying geography, students can investigate relationships between people, places, and environments and marvel at the beauty of our world and its people. Geography is both local and global, focused on helping us understand our backyard and the other side of the world.

Geography The discipline that teaches knowledge about places and environments.

Human geography A branch of geography that deals with people, their environment, and their interactions.

GEOGRAPHIC CONCEPTS AND IDEAS FOR ELEMENTARY SCHOOL CHILDREN

Children need to understand a range of concepts and ideas about geography in order to be contributing citizens in our democratic society. Children need to learn human geography, spatial understanding, and systems-based understanding. We discuss each of these geographic concepts in this chapter. Students' understanding in these areas takes shape through the development of knowledge, skills, and values.

Human geography includes all the considerations about how people interact with the land and use natural resources. Human geography is about the places and regions that humans have constructed and the meaning we have given to these places. The study of geography often overlaps the study of human systems. We can study about human interaction separately—in courses about sociology, for example—but geography is often an integral part of studying people and their cultures and behaviors. For example, we cannot study the history of a place such as Iceland without taking into account its very unique and sometimes harsh physical geography. Iceland's isolation from other areas and its long periods of light and day in winter and summer have deeply influenced the history of the place.

Spatial understanding enables humans to place themselves and other natural and human-made things in space. We can represent our understanding using a variety of personal and formal methods. For example, maps are spatial representations that most often conform to certain conventions (FIGURE 6.2). We can teach students these conventions by emphasizing legends, directional orientation, and other skills. We also construct personal representations of space. These might include mental maps or might take form in personal drawings or photographs.

Spatial understanding The ability to perceive oneself and other natural and human-made things in space.

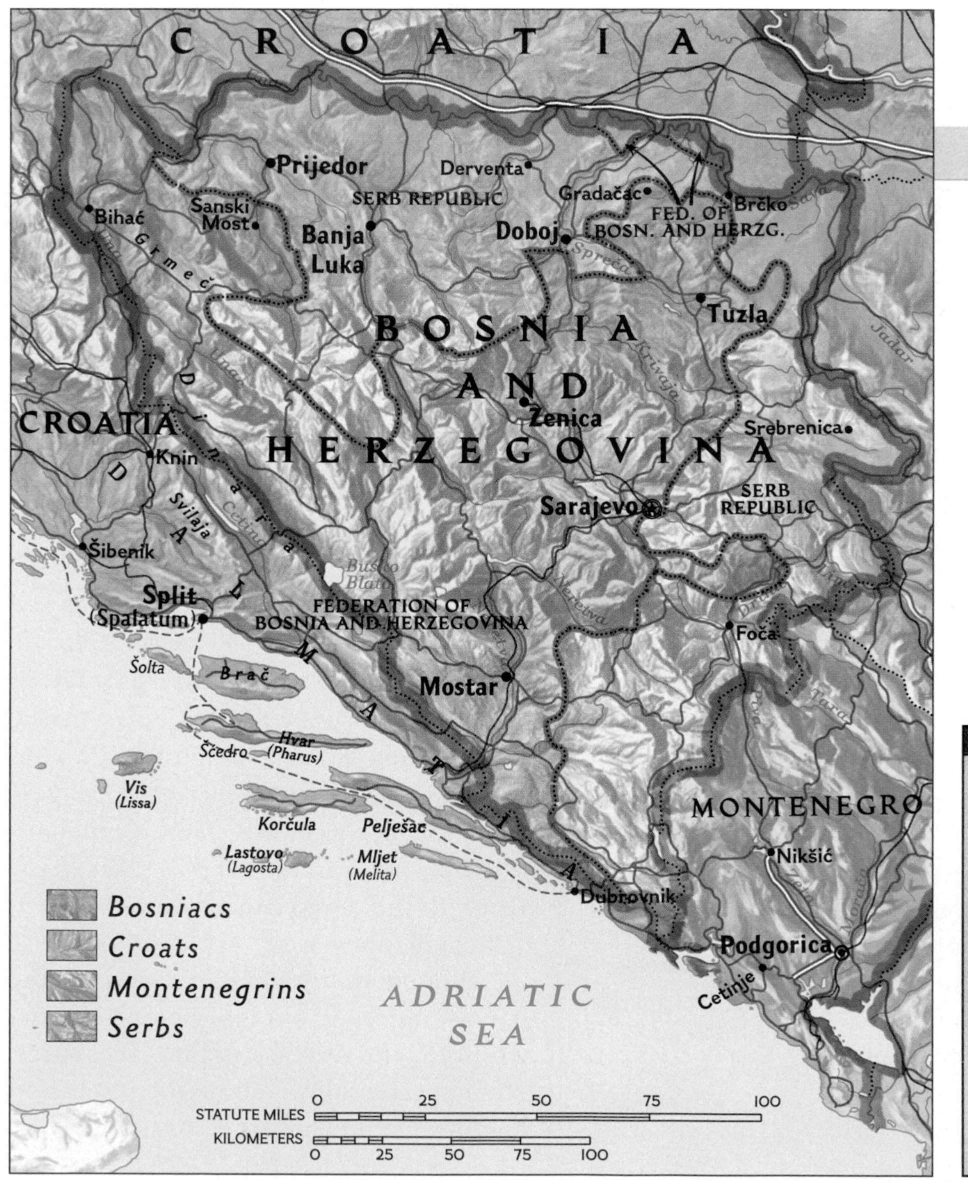

FIGURE 6.2

Describe the spatial and human geographic information that is portrayed on this map of Bosnia-Herzegovina.

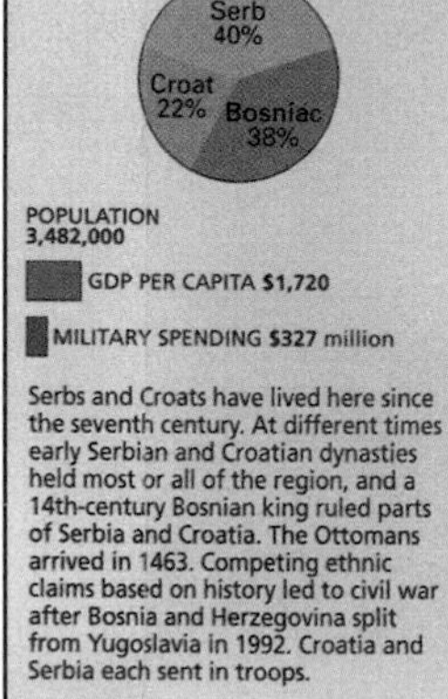

Systems are combinations of related elements that fit together and, in geography, take form as cultural or physical. Geographic **cultural systems** describe how and why people move or settle in places and describe how we conduct economic and social life. **Physical systems** describe nonhuman structures, such as weather and landforms.

All of these approaches to developing geographic knowledge in some way illustrate interaction. Consider the images in **FIGURE 6.3** of places in Bosnia-Herzegovina.

These two images suggest very different forms of interaction, yet the cities are less than 50 miles apart. Ask students to examine these photos to uncover similarities (e. g., both locations have hilly terrain and similar building materials) and differences (e. g., population density and related infrastructure). Point out to students that these impressions make sense only in the context of human interaction with the physical world. Have students consider how life would be different in these two places. How is it possible that landscapes such as these could be so apparently different, yet so close in distance and other characteristics?

Cultural systems How or why people move or settle in places and how they conduct economic and social life.

Physical systems Non-human structures such as weather and landforms.

FIGURE 6.3

A Nisici, Bosnia-Herzegovina

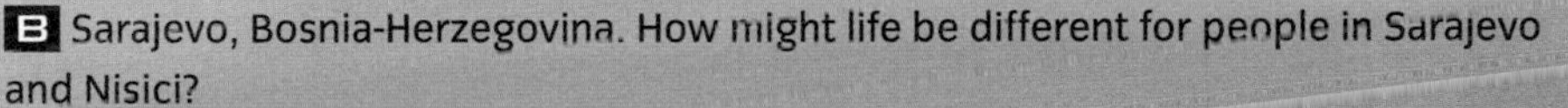

B Sarajevo, Bosnia-Herzegovina. How might life be different for people in Sarajevo and Nisici?

HOW CHILDREN RELATE TO PLACES

It's important for children to consider how they relate to places that they are learning about. Our relationships with places are often very emotional and meaningful. People talk about place using words such as "home" and phrases such as "the place I am from." We form powerful connections to places and use these connections, in part, to define ourselves.

Region A specified district, territory, or other often continuous place on Earth's surface.

We define places such as **regions**, countries, communities, or neighborhoods by the experiences and interactions we have in them. Of course, sometimes we limit our understanding by rigidly valuing one place over another. For example, we might not be willing to learn about a neighborhood in another part of town if we think it is a bad part of town. The same might be true of a region or even a nation. The more closely we associate ourselves, through experience, with a place the more likely we are to be willing and able to study that place. Ultimately, we must expand our horizons and create new appreciations of places that seem strange or different in order to better understand those places and the world in general.

Teachers have to help their students expand on the attachment children and adults have to their home. The most powerful way to do this is to nurture students' feeling about their home places, while facilitating their exploration of places outside the home. In many ways, standard social studies curriculums recognize this need and are structured to facilitate a careful exploration of "other" places while maintaining a focus on the home. In fact, the traditional expanding horizons curriculum in social studies enables children to study their home and community life in the earliest elementary grades and broadens the focus outward in successive years to in-

FIGURE 6.4

A A San Bushman and son hunt with bow and arrow on a savanna. Namibia.

B This image depicts an ancient settlement in South Africa called Umtata, where Bantu-speaking people live to this day. The long history of migration of Bantu-speaking people has shaped the development of Africa, which is marked by intense conflict and significant movement.

clude the study of more distant places and experiences. The expanding horizons curriculum is structured to nurture children's experiences with "other" places by gradually introducing them to places that are further and further away from the child both in distance and in time.

GEOGRAPHY AS THE STARTING POINT FOR SOCIAL STUDIES

Southern Africa is home to a complex human system that has for hundreds of years embodied change and conflict. Evidence of human life dates back millions of years.

Teachers can introduce children to the highly charged topics of colonialism and South African apartheid by looking at these subsystems from a geographic perspective. This might include a study of the place and its climate; the study of the movement of Bantu-speaking Africans and European whites into the area; and the study of settlement patterns in southern Africa over the last 400 years. How do the images in FIGURE 6.4 depict those changes and patterns, or what do they suggest about the changes and patterns?

Social studies at the elementary school level typically does not formally mention geography. Instead, geographic content is often woven deep into the social studies curriculum. This means that students might develop a limited understanding of what geography actually is and what it includes. As noted earlier, teachers often mistakenly communicate to their students that geography is simply the study of maps and development of related skills.

An argument can be made for geography being the best academic context for elementary social studies. Geography can support students' understanding of the past. It can serve as a useful context for learning about cultures. Geography is well suited for the study of problems in society. As we have already seen, geography is even at the core of the common expanding horizons curriculum structure in elementary grades.

C Climate and soil make parts of southern Africa highly desirable. Places such as this tea plantation in the Pungwe Valley of Zimbabwe are the source of conflict between Bantu-speaking people migrating from the north and Europeans arriving by sea. After the arrival of permanent European settlers in the 17th century, a complex, sometimes problematic, human system emerged in southern Africa.

Let's look at an example of how a common topic in the elementary social studies curriculum, North American Native Indians, can be studied using geography as a starting point. In the state of Washington, for example, children in primary grades (K–3) are expected to examine the cultural traditions of local tribes. In the Northwest, Native Americans carve totem poles to honor their ancestors, publicize their clan's standing and accomplishments, and record memorable ceremonies and experiences. A totem is an animal, plant, or natural object that serves as an emblem representing a person, a group, or a clan. As students investigate totem poles such as the one pictured in FIGURE 6.5, they will need to examine cultural traditions that are represented in totem pole carving. This investigation, which in many ways is geographic in nature (FIGURE 6.5B), would draw on work done by historians, anthropologists, and sociologists.

How do other disciplines contribute to the geographic study of this topic?

- Historians tell us that when Europeans first saw totem poles, they thought they were religious symbols and objects of worship. They are not, but these original misconceptions linger today.
- Anthropologists have uncovered some of the story-like meaning conveyed in some totem poles, particularly as these stories relate to cultural happenings such as weddings.
- Sociologists help us understand the complex cultural phenomena that are represented on totem poles. For example, the arrangement of totems as the pole proceeds upward may reflect social hierarchy.

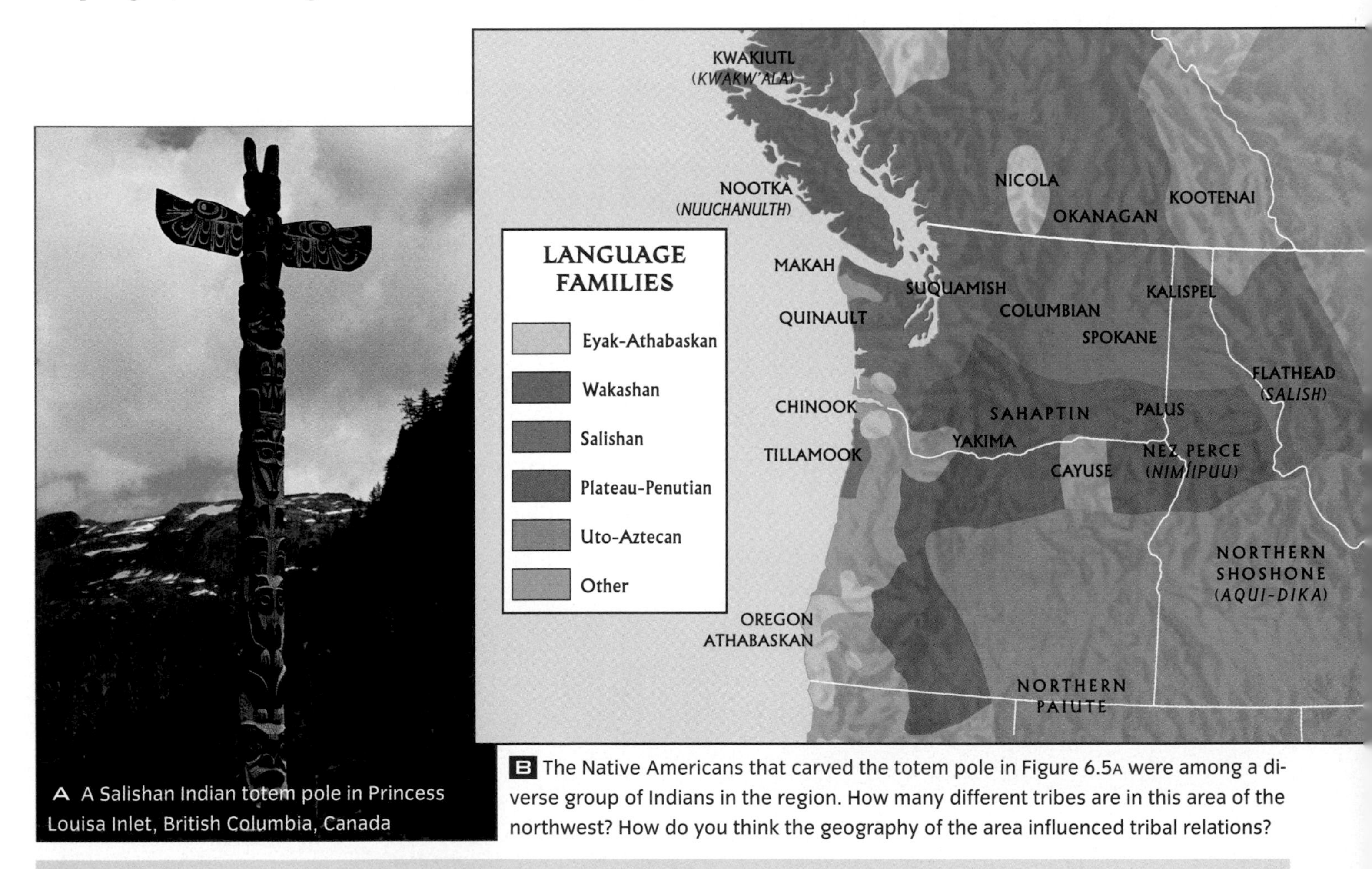

A A Salishan Indian totem pole in Princess Louisa Inlet, British Columbia, Canada

B The Native Americans that carved the totem pole in Figure 6.5A were among a diverse group of Indians in the region. How many different tribes are in this area of the northwest? How do you think the geography of the area influenced tribal relations?

FIGURE 6.5

LEARNING HOW TO USE MAPS

Although geography is about more than just maps, maps and related reasoning skills play an important role in geography instruction. Maps are physical representations of data and information. They have spatial characteristics and can be used to explain concepts that are either too large or too complex for us to understand. Maps can be much more than depictions of places; they can also show ideas, concepts, relationships, and time. The map in **FIGURE 6.6** illustrates information about human development in three ways: as "disturbed land," as "built up areas," and as "irrigated land."

FIGURE 6.7

An early 16th-century Nahuatl glyph map of Aztec migration from Aztlan to Tenochtitlán illustrates imperial Aztec history and was produced by Aztec Indians right about the time of their contact with Europeans.

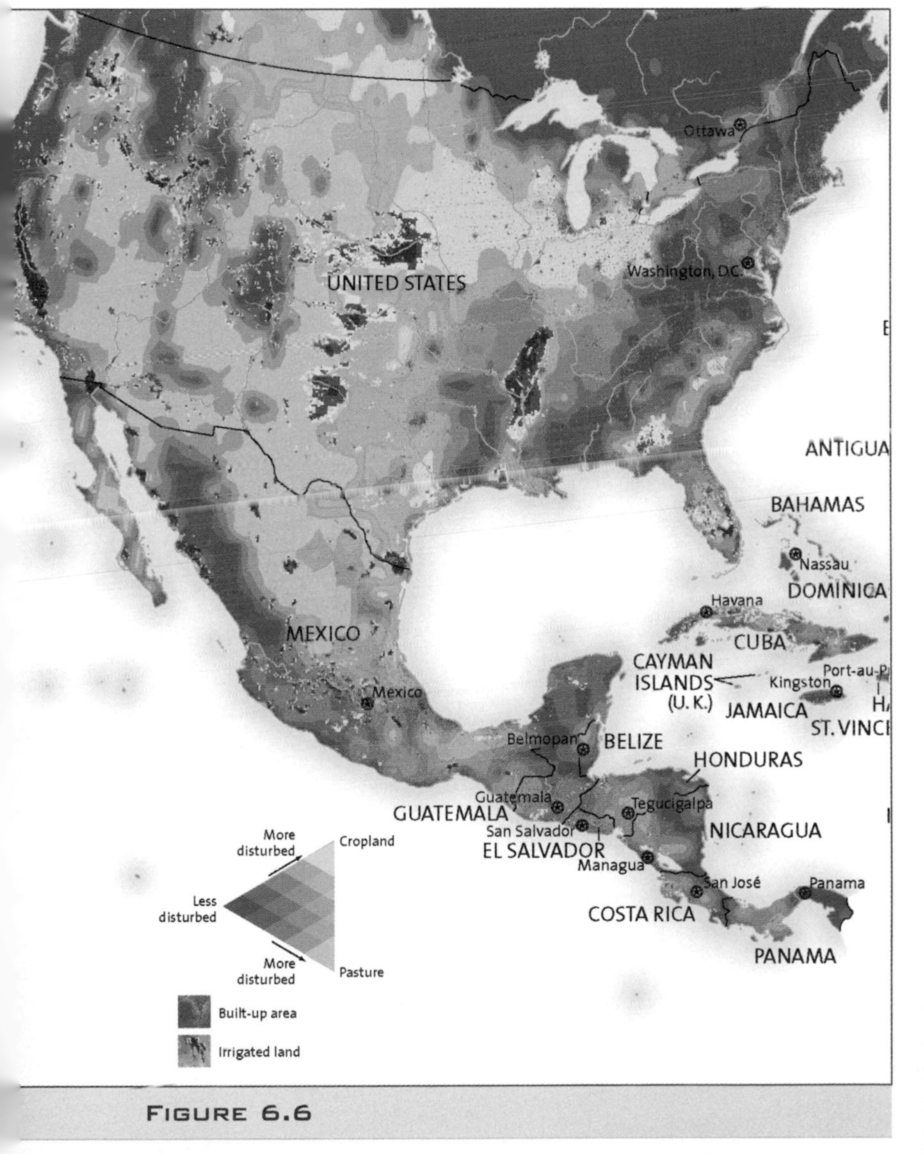

FIGURE 6.6

This map illustrates geographic information in several areas. How are these sources of information related? What does the map help us understand about the United States?

Virtually anything can be mapped. For example, we could construct a map of the totem pole in the previous section. Such a map might display the relative location of the emblems on the totem pole and represent more generalizable characteristics of totem poles. The sixteenth-century Native American map in **FIGURE 6.7** is a good example of how ideas and events can be depicted in a map. The map was created by pre-Columbian natives living along the coast of the Gulf of Mexico around the Yucatan Peninsula. It illustrates a series of conquests and achievements. The map represents these activities by positioning them on the map and showing their relationship to one another.

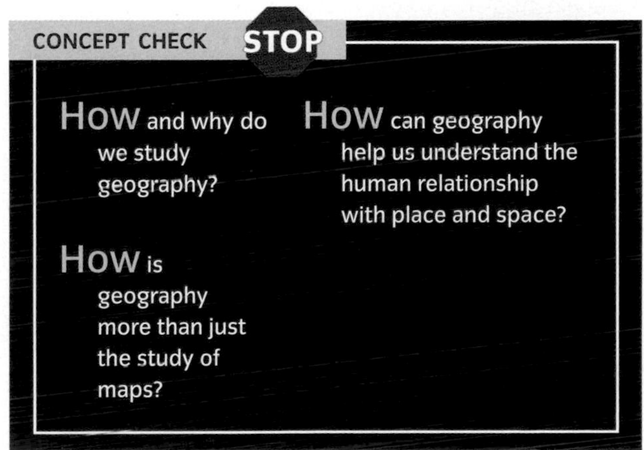

How Children Develop Geographic Awareness

LEARNING OBJECTIVES

Recognize how we become aware of our geography.

Compare human and physical approaches to geography.

Consider the ways in which children make geographic sense of their surroundings.

Children develop geographic awareness through the study of people and places. Geographic study is best when it starts with people and the experiences they have in the world. Learning geography helps explain the world around us.

HUMAN AND CULTURAL GEOGRAPHIC AWARENESS

The study of **human culture** occupies a central place in the social studies curriculum. These cultural studies cross all of the academic disciplines, but are particularly relevant in geography. In fact, much of the geography taught in elementary social studies focuses on culture. The United Nations Educational Scientific and Cultural Organization (UNESCO) (2002) describes culture as "the set of

Human culture Social patterns, arts, beliefs, institutions, and all other products of human work and thought that contribute to a common way of life for a group of people.

These traditional costumes are exciting and fun for children to explore, but as representations of culture they are very limited. What else do students need to know about the people in these pictures and about the places in which they were photographed?

Culture is much more than costumes. According to National Geography Standard number 10, geography includes "social structure, languages, belief systems, institutions, technology, art, foods, and traditions of particular groups of humans." Culture is concerned with ways people live. Students study culture so that they might understand a wide variety of cultures and appreciate and value cultures different from their own.

A Tenth International Children's Folkdance Festival, Sliven, Bulgaria, 2006

distinctive spiritual, material, intellectual, and emotional features of society or a social group, and that it encompasses, in addition to art and literature, lifestyles, ways of living together, value systems, traditions and beliefs." The National Geography Standards address culture directly, suggesting that overlapping cultural experiences across the world create a cultural mosaic. Elementary school social studies teachers need to prepare students for life in this cultural mosaic. The United States has a particularly unique experience in this cultural mosaic. The vast number of cultural experiences in the United States necessitates an understanding and appreciation of the concept of cultural diversity. **FIGURE 6.8** "Visualizing: Cultural Geography" provides images that might spur discussion of Native American cultural geography. "In the Classroom," page 150, focuses on New Zealand as a context for understanding physical and cultural place.

The study of culture can be a powerful way to organize instruction for children. "Social and Cultural Explorations" on pages 152–153, looks at soccer—the world's most popular sport—as a way to encourage student interest in geography. But the study of culture also has its pitfalls if taught using an approach that is too narrow or stereotypical. There is a tendency to simplify the study of culture by focusing on cultural pageants or role-playing, sampling of foods from different places, and dressing in traditional costumes associated with cultures. While these exercises can be meaningful, they must occur within a broader consideration of beliefs, social structures, and institutions.

Visualizing

Cultural Geography FIGURE 6.8

B This child is a participant at Mosaic, part of the annual Rainbow of Cultures celebration in Regina, Canada.

Mount Cook, South Island, New Zealand

A Maori tribesman wears a cloak made of kiwi feathers in Rotorua, New Zealand. Consider the differences in the climate between this jungle scene and the snow-capped mountains in the picture of Mount Cook.

When explaining to children how human life develops and is sustained in a given place, social studies teachers need to prompt their students to consider both physical and cultural elements. For example, New Zealand has a remarkable physical geography and a complex cultural story.

An investigation of Maori culture and the physical geography of New Zealand might result in students addressing questions such as these:

- What are the people like in New Zealand?
- Where did they come from?
- What does the country of New Zealand look like?
- Where is it?
- What is the land like?

Students in elementary grades can engage these questions more effectively when the questions are cast in real-life contexts that reflect a range of geographical knowledge. When considering the Maori culture in the context of the physical geography of New Zealand, students can begin to understand how the physical lay of the land and cultural dynamics interact to shape life. Teachers might explore social contexts with students by having them research the controversies over the preservation of Maori culture. This project involves both physical and cultural geography.

Rotura

Mount Cook

HOW CHILDREN UNDERSTAND THE WORLD AROUND THEM

What does it mean to talk about the "world"? A child in kindergarten may think the world is mostly within her or his physical grasp. Children may be unable to describe to an adult or in an adult-like way what the world is, but they do conceive of places like the world. Psychologists such as Jean Piaget have given us theories to explain how a child understands concepts such as the world. Piaget suggested that children progress through various stages (sensorimotor, preoperational, concrete operational, formal operational) as they build their cognitive sophistication. These theoretical models provide some guidance for understanding how children perceive the world. In addition, teachers need to use their judgment and skills to help children develop an understanding of place.

We often read that children under the age of 11 cannot engage in the spatial reasoning skills that are required to understand global patterns and relationships. While this may be true, students are nonetheless trying to create meaningful understanding and can be nurtured in their understanding. It would be a mistake to disregard geography in elementary school. Instead, the goal should be to engage children given their theories of how the world is structured and enable them to progress using resources that they understand.

Children are particularly adept at representing their ideas and values in unique ways. The interesting map in **FIGURE 6.9** was created by an 8-year-old girl living in America and is another example of how children can represent ideas and relationships using maps.

FIGURE 6.9

A map of the world drawn in 2003 by then 8-year-old Emily Carroll of Burleigh Elementary School in Brookfield, WI. How does this student represent the world, particularly the relationships between places in the world?

Literature can also be a powerful context in which to engage children in geographic subject matter, as can images. Nigel Grey's children's book, *A Country Far Away*, is the story of two boys, one in America and one in Africa. The story unfolds in parallel succession as each boy tells of his school, family, and play experiences. Teachers in kindergarten and first grade can use the book to introduce the differences and likenesses between the United States and Africa and possibly begin to help children develop a more acute understanding of Africa.

CONCEPT CHECK STOP

Why is geography less prevalent in the social studies curriculum, particularly in elementary grades?

How do the geographic features inherent or implied in this image relate to the Social and Cultural Explorations on pages 152–153?

Men and boys play soccer while waiting to unload cotton at a textile facility in Asuncion, Paraguay.

Elements of Geographic Understanding: Spaces, Places, and Systems

Learning Objectives

Identify and describe the four elements of geographic understanding.

Describe the importance of spatial understanding.

Understand that places and regions are distinguished by their unique charateristics.

Distinguish human systems from cultural systems.

There are four elements in our geographic understanding: spatial understanding, places and regions, human systems, and physical systems. These elements are interdependent and interrelated. Each one of these elements encompasses a perspective on human experience given some organization of people or places. An exploration of each of these four elements can help in developing a more complete understanding of how we can construct geographic learning.

SPATIAL UNDERSTANDING

As we saw earlier, spatial understanding involves making the nature of space knowable. In this instance we are talking about space as the area that something occupies, not "outer space." Spatial structures can be as enormous as the Earth or as minuscule as personal space. Geography provides us with tools and skills to understand space and the relationships between things in space. Maps are the most common of the tools, but any physical or mental representation of spatial structures is valid.

There are many reasons to include spatial reasoning in elementary grades. Children will likely engage in some forms of spatial reasoning whether we help them or not. Well before kindergarten, children are encouraged to draw pictures to develop spatial skills.

As children grow, they need opportunities to engage increasingly complex spatial structures. Consider a complex space such as Jerusalem (FIGURE 6.10). The physical space of the city is home to Muslims, Christians, and Jews.

All three religions claim a special relationship with Jerusalem as a spiritual center of the religion. Children as young as those in first grade can depict these structures with simple drawings and then place them in general proximity to one another. These types of exercises

FIGURE 6.10

An aerial view of Jerusalem depicting holy sites for Muslims, Christians, and Jews.

will begin to give children an opportunity to learn how close the religions are to one another in both space and, given their shared monotheistic traditions, structure.

PLACES AND REGIONS

Most humans understand the large spaces around them according to generally agreed-upon place and regional distinctions. These distinctions include unique names and often shared physical and cultural characteristics within them. Streets, neighborhoods, cities and towns; the North and the South, West Coast, and Midwest; Asia and sub-Saharan Africa; the European Union and the developing world; online, the campus, and inside—all these are places and regions. Some are amorphous and some are very distinct. Place and regional distinctions need only human imagination and consistent and distinctive use to be meaningful.

Children need to develop an understanding of the characteristics of places and regions as well as the distinctions of these areas. Many children will develop some very powerful and value-driven associations with places. We need to nurture these feelings while attempting to broaden students' vistas.

Consider the manner in which the students in FIGURE 6.11 are developing an identification with place. Teachers routinely engage elementary school students in activities related to national holidays and regional celebrations. As we continue to help students build self-awareness, we must also extend their awareness of other places and regions. The study of geography can help in this process.

HUMAN SYSTEMS

Human systems are made up of people and their cultural and settlement patterns. The relationships between people are in constant flux, marked by changing levels of cooperation and conflict (FIGURE 6.12). Children understand the most basic elements of human systems, and we can use their experiences to build additional knowledge about how people live in large and small systems.

Human systems typically involve three forms of action: movement, cooperation, and conflict. The Lesson from *National Geographic Map Essentials*, pages 156–163, on Population Density illustrates how teachers can plan for instruction on the topic of movement.

FIGURE 6.11

In Jayuya, Puerto Rico, students at Jayuya Elementary School celebrate Puerto Rican Discovery Day with a parade of the three cultural roots of Puerto Rico: Taino Indians, West African slaves, and the Spanish.

FIGURE 6.12

Women form a human chain to carry bricks used in the reconstruction of Dresden, March 1946, after Allied bombing had destroyed the city in February 1945. The steeple of the wrecked Roman Catholic cathedral can be seen in the background.

Population Density

Population Density

Key Ideas

Population density is the number of people who live in a square mile or square kilometer area.

What's the difference between New York City and the far northwest of Alaska? Look at the land-use map on page 55 to learn one answer. The environment of New York City is urban, with lots of manufacturing activity. Northern Alaska, with a landscape of ice and snow, has little economic activity. Another big difference is people. Areas of difficult physical environments have few people. In northeastern Alaska, you can walk for miles without seeing a single person. In New York City, everywhere you go there are people!

The number of people who live in a set area is called population density. Density means thickness. New York City is one of the most densely populated areas in the United States. Northern Alaska is among the least densely populated.

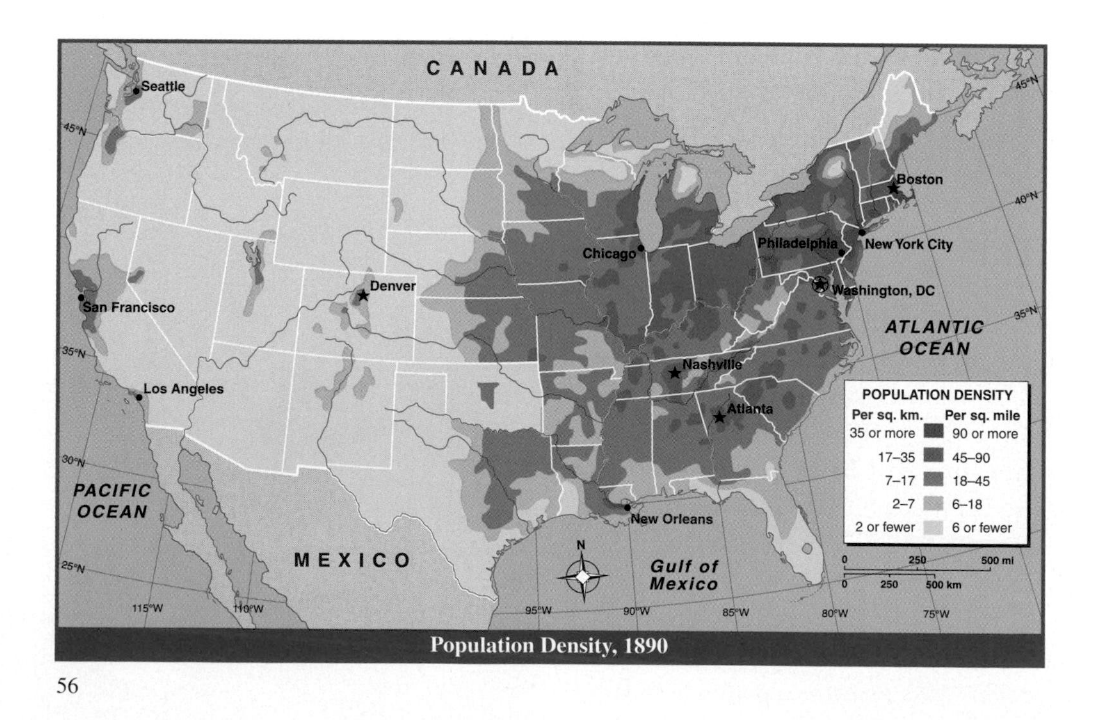

Population Density, 1890

56

- Population density maps show how many people live in an area. Study the map on this page. The map shows, in ranges, the number of people per square mile or square kilometer. Study the key. What is the lowest range of population density?
- Look at the map on page 56. It shows population density in the United States in 1890. You will notice that the range in the key is the same as the map on this page. Look at the shading on this map. What difference do you see between this map and the one of 1990?
- Population-density maps help to show where urban and rural areas are. Would you expect the population to be denser in an urban or a rural area?
- By comparing population-density maps from different years you can see how a population changes over time. The population of the United States was 62 million in 1890 and was almost 249 million in 1990. It is no surprise that the 1990 map shows greater population density overall. Find Los Angeles on both maps. What do you notice?
- Look at the coastal areas on the map on this page. Compare these two areas to the interior of the country. What patterns do you see? What do you think are the reasons for the patterns?
- Find New Jersey and Rhode Island on the map on this page. They are the most densely populated states in the country. Both are small states with few rural areas.
- These maps also show that patterns of population density have changed over time. On the 1890 map the eastern half of the country is much more densely populated than the western half. In 1990, the East was more densely populated than the West, but the difference was not as great. Where in the West has population density increased the most? The least?

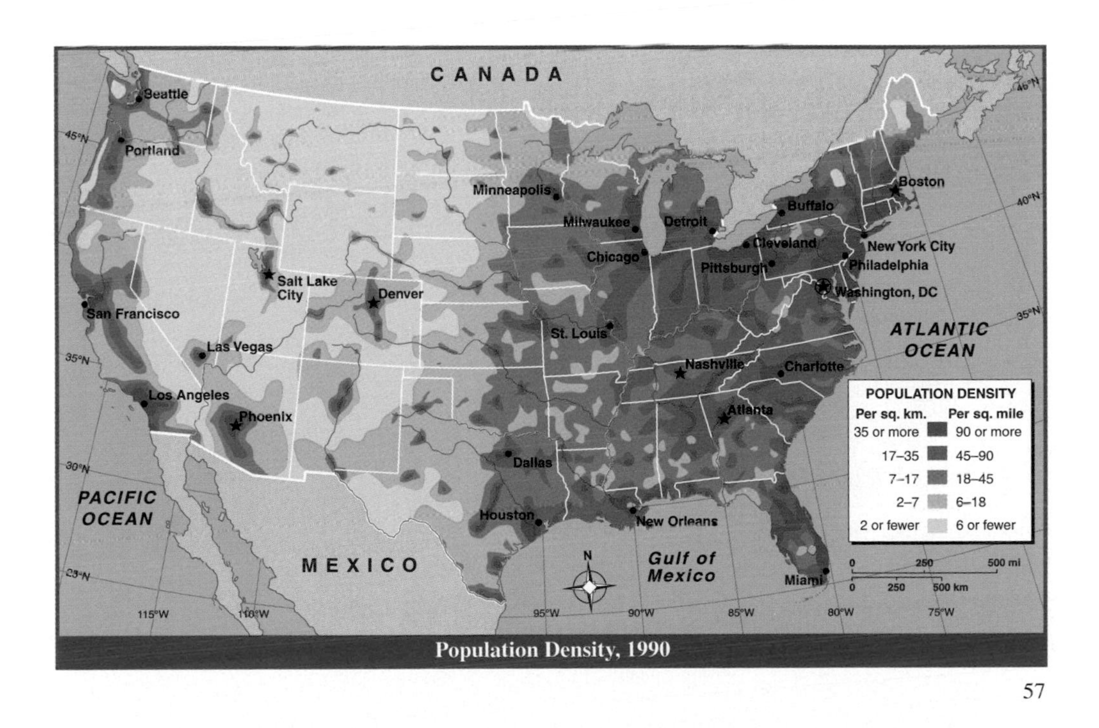

Population Density, 1990

LESSON

Population Density (cont.)

A Changing Population

The population of the United States has changed by more than just numbers in the last one hundred years. People from many different countries and continents have immigrated to the United States. In 1990, nearly 8 percent of the U.S. population was born in another country. The pie graphs on this page show the country or continent of origin of newcomers to the states of California and New York.

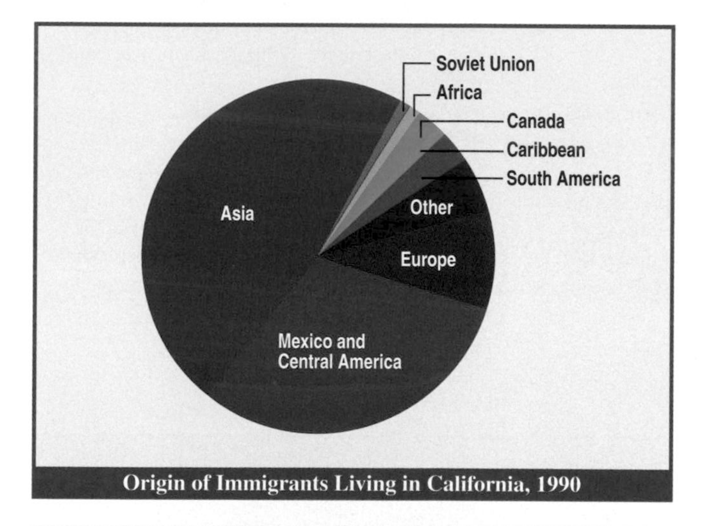

Origin of Immigrants Living in California, 1990

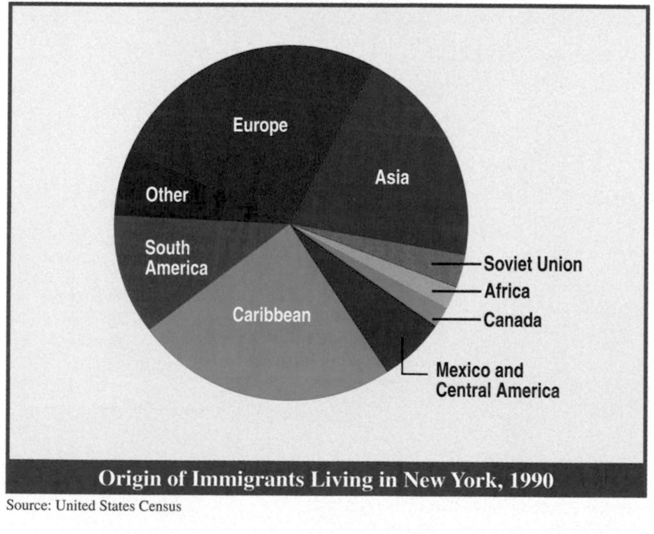

Origin of Immigrants Living in New York, 1990

Source: United States Census

- More than 6 million of the approximately 30 million people in California in 1990 were born in another country or continent. From which area did the largest number of immigrants come?
- New York State had almost 18 million people in 1990. About 3 million of them were immigrants. Look at the pie graph for New York. The largest number of immigrants came from Europe.
- By comparing these graphs, you can see different patterns of immigration to these two states. What patterns do you notice? Explain these patterns. (Hint: The World Map on pages 70–71 will help you explain the patterns.)

58

On Your Own

Use pages 56-58 to help answer the questions.

1. What does a population-density map show? How is it used?
2. What was the population density of most of the state of Montana in 1990?
3. From which country or continent did the second largest number of immigrants come to California in 1990?
4. Were there more immigrants in California or New York in 1990?

Think Like a Geographer

5. Look at the 1990 map areas that are the least densely populated. Then find these areas on the land-use map on page 55. What is land use like in these areas?
6. Why do you think there are more immigrants from Asia, Mexico, and Central America in California and more from Caribbean countries in New York? Explain.
7. Since 1950, more people have moved to the "sunbelt" area of the United States, which includes the states of the South and Southwest. How do you see this movement of people reflected in the population-density map of 1990?
8. Suppose you have a friend who wants to move from a crowded urban environment to a place that has few people and lots of open space. What are five states that you would recommend?

This satellite image of Los Angeles shows the majority of people live in the flat areas and along the water. The mountains appear to have few people.

Field Study

Create a simple population density map by doing a survey of the number of students in each classroom in your school. First, create a floor plan, or simple map, showing the classrooms in all or part of your school. Then do a survey to find out how many people, including students and teachers, are in each classroom. Create a color-coded key for population density for each class. Include other school areas, such as the office and cafeteria, in your map by counting the number of people who work in each of these places. Create another map showing population density 30 minutes after school is out. Compare and contrast the two maps.

Population Density (cont.)

PLANNING GUIDE

WHY IT'S ESSENTIAL

By using this skill, students learn how demographic information can be conveyed in map form. Demographic information is vital to government and business. Government uses it for such things as voting and distribution of funds. Businesses might use it to locate their potential customers. The ability to analyze a population density map will enable students to understand where the United States population lives.

Objectives

- Interpret population density information presented in map form.
- Compare population density maps from different time periods.
- Analyze immigrant population data in the form of pie graphs.

Blackline Master

- Activity Master 20

Optional Resources

- Transparencies 3,3F

Pacing

30–50 minutes

Correlation to Standards

- Geography Standard 9: The characteristics, distribution, and migration of human populations on Earth's surface
- Geography Standard 10: The characteristics, distributions, and complexity of Earth's cultural mosaics
- Social Studies Standard 3d: Estimate distance, calculate scale, and distinguish other geographic relationships such as population density and spatial distribution patterns

For more details, see pages 8–9.

Internet Link

- For teacher resources, visit the National Geographic Society website at: www.nationalgeographic.com/education

1. INTRODUCE

Begin by defining population as the number of people in a specific area.

Ask: *What is the population of our classroom?* (Answer will depend on the number of students in the classroom.)

Then explain the term "density" as meaning "thickness." Population density means "thickness of population" or how closely people live to one another in a specific area.

Remind students about the difference between rural and urban areas, since these are key concepts to understanding population density.

Ask: *Would you expect the population of the United States to have become greater or smaller in the last 50 years? Why?* (greater, because the population has grown, but the area of the country remains the same)

2. TEACH

Suggestions for page 56

Have students look at the map on page 56. Explain that this map shows 48 states and is a historical map as well as a population density map.

Ask: *How can you tell that this is a historical map?* (The date 1890 appears in the title.) *How are different population densities shown on this map?* (Different colors show different ranges of population density.)

Suggestions for page 57

Display Transparencies 3 and 3F for students, or use the map in the Student Book on page 57. Have students look for patterns to describe states and areas of the country that have relatively high and relatively low population densities.

Have students compare the map on page 57 with the map on page 56. Have them locate the area where your hometown is situated and determine the population density in 1890 and 1990.

Ask: *Did the population density increase or decrease from 1890 to 1990?* (probably increased)

Ask: *What generalization can you make about how the population density in the United States changed from 1890 to 1990?* (it increased)

Lead a discussion about why population density maps are useful and who might use them.

Suggestions for page 58

Direct students' attention to the graphs on page 58.

Ask: *How is the information on these graphs similar to and different from the information on the population density maps?* (The graphs also give information about population. The graphs describe where immigrants come from.)

3. CLOSE/ASSESS

Using Activity Master 20 To review and assess the skill, have students complete the Activity Master by creating a line graph showing population changes of California and New York. Students should then compare their graphs with the two maps in this activity.

EXTENSION ACTIVITIES

RETEACH

Using Transparency 3F or the map on page 57, practice the skill by giving students a population density range from the key and asking them to find a place on the map with that population density.

CHALLENGE

Have students locate a place on the map where the population density has increased dramatically from 1890 to 1990 (by more than two color ranges). Then have them research this area of the country in an effort to find some reasons behind the significant increase in population.

ANSWERS TO ACTIVITY 20

Page 57

- The lowest range of population density is 6 or fewer per square mile.
- The population in 1990 was denser than in 1890.
- Urban areas have denser populations.
- The population density of Los Angeles has increased.
- Coastal areas have denser populations. These areas were settled first and cities formed there. Coastal cities grew fast because of access to shipping. They also served as an entry point for those entering by boat.
- The population density has increased most in California and has increased the least in Montana.

Page 58

- Most came to California from Asia.
- Answers may include: a greater percentage of New York immigrants came from Europe; few immigrants came to either state from Canada or Africa compared to other groups.

Page 59

On your Own

1. the number of people who live in a set area, such as a square mile or square kilometer; to understand the distribution of the population across the country
2. six or fewer people per square mile
3. Mexico and Central America
4. California
5. Western mountain states are among the least populated areas of the country. Land use in these states is mostly forest and grazing.
6. Asia, Mexico, and Central America are closer to California, and the Caribbean countries are closer to New York.
7. The population density has increased in these areas.
8. Answers may include: Nevada, Utah, Idaho, Montana, Oregon, New Mexico, South Dakota.

Arctic
GREENLAND
(DENMARK)
RUSSIA
ALASKA
(U.S.)
ICELAND
C A N A D A
North
Pacific
Ocean
UNITED STATES
North
Atlantic
Ocean
TROPIC OF CANCER
HAWAII
(U.S.)
MEXICO
BAHAMAS
WESTERN SAHARA
CAPE VERDE
SENEGAL
GAMBIA
GUINEA-BISSAU
SIERRA LEONE
Area shown below
VENEZUELA
COLOMBIA
GUYANA
SURINAME
FRENCH GUIANA
EQUATOR
ECUADOR
KIRIBATI
0
2400 mi
0
2400 km
Scale at the Equator
Winkel Tripel projection
BRAZIL
PERU
SAMOA
BOLIVIA
FRENCH POLYNESIA
South
Pacific
Ocean
PARAGUAY
TONGA
CHILE
TROPIC OF CAPRICORN
ARGENTINA
URUGUAY
South
Atlantic
Ocean
CUBA
MEXICO
HAITI
DOM. REP.
PUERTO RICO
(U.S.)
ANTIGUA AND BARBUDA
BELIZE
JAMAICA
ST. KITTS AND NEVIS
GUAT.
HOND.
DOMINICA
EL SAL.
NICARAGUA
ST. LUCIA
ST. VINCENT AND THE GRENADINES
BARBADOS
GRENADA
COSTA RICA
TRINIDAD AND TOBAGO
PANAMA
COLOMBIA
VENEZUELA
ANTARCTIC CIRCLE
ANTARCTIC

20°E
40°E
60°E
80°E
100°E
120°E
140°E
160°E
Ocean
80°N
60°N
40°N
20°N
0°
20°S
40°S
60°S
NORWAY
SWEDEN
FINLAND
RUSSIA
Area shown below
KAZAKHSTAN
MONGOLIA
ARMENIA
UZBEKISTAN
KYRGYZSTAN
TURKMENISTAN
TAJIKISTAN
TURKEY
AZERBAIJAN
NORTH KOREA
SOUTH KOREA
JAPAN
North Pacific Ocean
CHINA
TUNISIA
CYPRUS
SYRIA
LEBANON
ISRAEL
JORDAN
IRAQ
IRAN
AFGHANISTAN
PAKISTAN
BHUTAN
NEPAL
BANGLADESH
TROPIC OF CANCER
TAIWAN
LIBYA
EGYPT
KUWAIT
BAHRAIN
QATAR
UNITED ARAB EMIRATES
SAUDI ARABIA
OMAN
INDIA
MYANMAR (BURMA)
LAOS
THAILAND
VIETNAM
CAMBODIA
PHILIPPINES
NIGER
CHAD
BURKINA FASO
TOGO
BENIN
NIGERIA
SUDAN
ERITREA
YEMEN
DJIBOUTI
CAMEROON
CENTRAL AFRICAN REP.
ETHIOPIA
SOMALIA
SRI LANKA
MARSHALL ISLANDS
PALAU
FEDERATED STATES OF MICRONESIA
BRUNEI
MALAYSIA
GUINEA
GABON
CONGO
RWANDA
UGANDA
KENYA
DEMOCRATIC REPUBLIC OF THE CONGO
BURUNDI
TANZANIA
MALDIVES
SINGAPORE
EQUATOR
NAURU
KIRIBATI
INDONESIA
SEYCHELLES
PAPUA NEW GUINEA
SOLOMON ISLANDS
SAO TOME AND PRINCIPE
ANGOLA
COMOROS
Indian Ocean
TUVALU
ZAMBIA
MALAWI
MOZAMBIQUE
ZIMBABWE
BOTSWANA
NAMIBIA
MADAGASCAR
MAURITIUS
VANUATU
FIJI
TROPIC OF CAPRICORN
SOUTH AFRICA
SWAZILAND
LESOTHO
AUSTRALIA
NEW ZEALAND
10°W
0°
10°E
20°E
30°E
NORWAY
SWEDEN
ESTONIA
LATVIA
RUSSIA
UNITED KINGDOM
DENMARK
LITH.
RUS.
BELARUS
IRELAND
NETH.
POLAND
GERMANY
BELGIUM
50°N
CZECH REP.
UKRAINE
LUX.
SLOVAKIA
AUSTRIA
MOL.
SWITZ.
HUNGARY
FRANCE
SLVN.
LIECH.
CROATIA
ROMANIA
YUG.
BOSNIA
BULG.
PORT.
SPAIN
ANDORRA
ITALY
MAC.
ALB.
TURKEY
40°N
GREECE
MALTA
20°E
40°E

PHYSICAL SYSTEMS

The Earth has many physical features such as mountains, rivers, oceans, and valleys. These physical features are not static. The physical characteristics change; they are affected by the atmosphere, plants, and animals. These features and characteristics are what we mean by physical systems. Human and physical systems interact to shape how places look and are used by humans. For example, consider a place like the Redwood Forest in California.

The aerial photo in **FIGURE 6.13** shows a lumber plant, near the Redwood National Park in Crescent City, California. A redwood tree logging area is in the foreground—a place in which human activity is reshaping a physical system. Students can study physical systems in contexts such as this one to learn the physical characteristics of places and how humans interact with those places.

In the National Geography Standards publication *Geography for Life*, the following questions are posed as reasons for studying physical systems:

- What does the surface of Earth look like?
- How have its features been formed?
- What is the nature of these features and how do they interact?
- How and why are they changing?
- What are the spatially distinct combinations of environmental features?

The NGS suggest that physical processes shape physical places. There are four processes at work on the Earth:

- The atmosphere (i.e., climate and meteorology)
- The lithosphere (e.g., plate tectonics, erosion, and soil formation)
- The hydrosphere (e.g., the circulation of the oceans and the hydrologic cycle)
- The biosphere (e.g., plant and animal communities and ecosystems)

These purposes for studying physical geography and processes of physical geography can be used to shape curriculum or adapt existing curriculum. Social studies elementary teachers need to pay special attention to aspects of the curriculum that directly deal with physical places and consider the questions and ideas posed here. For example, in Indiana, third-grade students are expected to meet the following standard:

> Identify the continents and oceans, the equator, the Northern and Southern Hemispheres, and the Eastern and Western Hemispheres.

Students might learn about the continents and oceans by learning that these features are part of the lithosphere or hydrosphere, but they both interact with the atmosphere and support the biosphere.

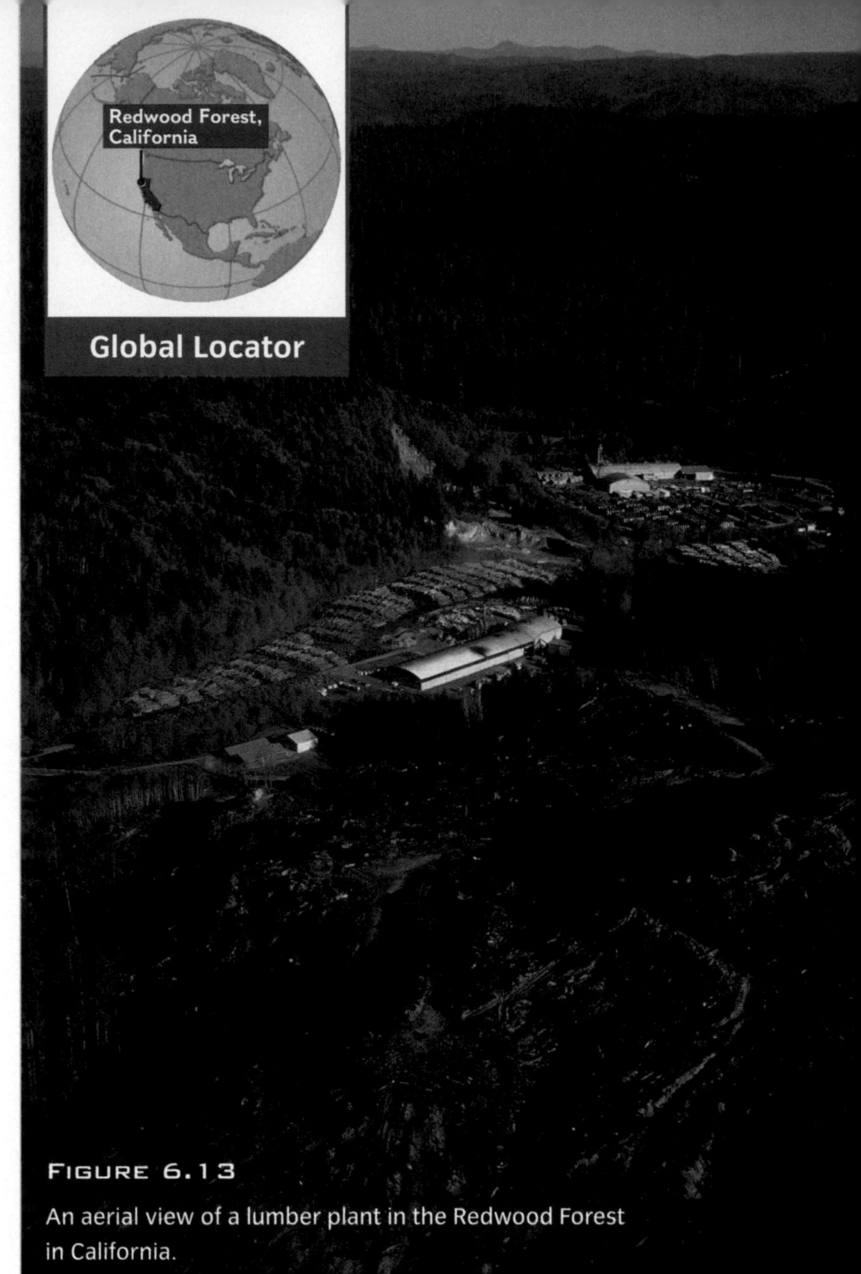

FIGURE 6.13
An aerial view of a lumber plant in the Redwood Forest in California.

FIGURE 6.14

Singapore lies at the tip of the Malay Peninsula.

Now, look at the image of the island city-state of Singapore (**FIGURE 6.14**). In Singapore, international banks stand next to corporate headquarters in a forest of high-rises in the city's business/financial district. In the background is Singapore Harbor, the world's busiest port. Students might try to describe the physical systems that are at work in Singapore, based on looking at the photo.

CONCEPT CHECK **STOP**

What are some of the characteristics in the human and physical system portrayed in this image and the image in Figure 6.14?

How might we use the context of this place—Singapore—to teach about human and physical geographic systems?

A trishaw rider with an empty cart leads traffic down a busy Singapore street that is lined with Chinese signs and shops and ends with the golden domes and minarets of the Sultan Mosque.

Using Maps to Teach Geographic Awareness

LEARNING OBJECTIVES

Recognize specific approaches to teaching for geographic awareness.

Consider how maps might be used to develop students' geographic awareness.

Analyze the relationship of geography to the past.

USING MAPS AND OTHER GEOGRAPHIC REPRESENTATIONS

Maps are the lingua franca of geography. In other words, maps enable people to communicate geographic knowledge and enable understanding when it might otherwise be difficult or impossible. Maps convey meaning and values. They give shape to information and can help children make sense out of the murkiness of raw data.

We make a map when we display information using spatial information and physical representations. For example, we might know that there are a certain number of miles between given places in a community. We can map the community using the reference points and a scaled-down measure.

Maps help us represent places, but they can do so much more. Maps can portray ideas, relationships, and movement, as well as places. (See Process Diagram: Constructing Maps with Children, **FIGURE 6.15**.) Given these varied uses, we cannot simply construct maps without concern for what and how they represent places and ideas.

DEVELOPING SPATIAL REASONING SKILLS

When children actively use maps in school, they are developing spatial reasoning skills. **Spatial reasoning** enables us to mentally organize information about people, places, and environments. We think in spatial terms when we use the components of spatial representations on maps—points, lines, and areas.

Spatial reasoning
The ability to mentally organize information about people, places, and environments.

One of the primary goals for geography educators should be to help children develop spatial reasoning skills. To do this we have to provide children opportunities to apply their skills in creative and meaningful settings.

USING GEOGRAPHY TO UNDERSTAND THE PAST

Geography can play a central role in the study of history. How and why do places change? What events in the past influenced these changes? When students study exploration, they can make extensive use of maps. These maps not only convey meaning about the location of explorers' voyages, but historical maps also tell us something about the past.

The simple map in **FIGURE 6.16** illustrates the path of the first manned balloon flight in North

FIGURE 6.16

The path of the first manned balloon flight in North America by Jean-Pierre Blanchard

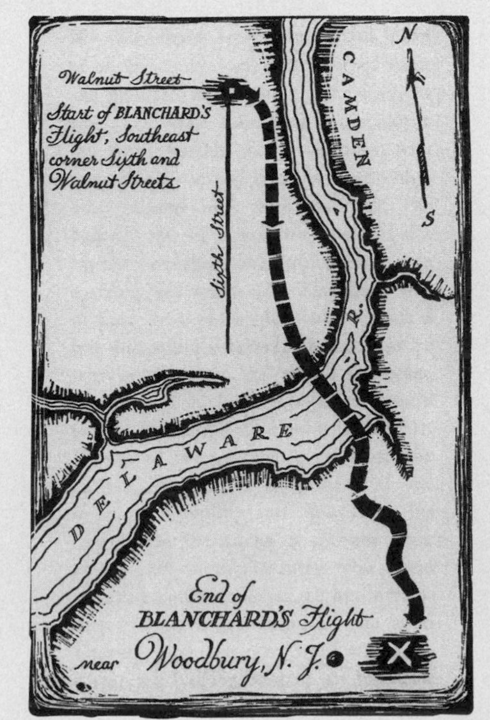

Constructing maps with children FIGURE 6.15

Children reason best with maps when they have some role in constructing them. This may involve labeling a map or some creative coloring with a pre-drawn map. Children should also be encouraged to use maps to explain information. Interaction with maps helps children to learn about places and to form mental images of places.

The following process can guide planning an activity in which students construct a map and develop specific map skills. The process involves three steps:

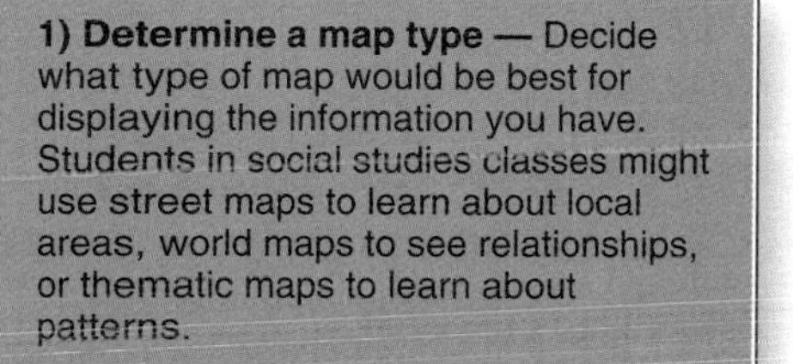

1) Determine a map type — Decide what type of map would be best for displaying the information you have. Students in social studies classes might use street maps to learn about local areas, world maps to see relationships, or thematic maps to learn about patterns.

2) Select information that will be on the map — Maps cannot show everything, so carefully selecting the information to display is very important. If students are creating a street map, they will need to decide what level of detail to include. Information that is conveyed on a map for learning should be selected with a focus on student learning, and additional information should be kept to a minimum. For example, a map depicting cities should not include information about natural resources or average rainfall unless that information helps illustrate something relevant for the study of cities.

3) Determine how information will be highlighted on the map — Maps communicate information, so it is important to highlight important details or features on the map. After carefully selecting the information that is presented on the map and limiting additional information, the most relevant information needs to be highlighted. The important information should clearly stand out on the map.

PARTICIPATING AND TAKING ACTION IN DEMOCRATIC COMMUNITIES

For many children, their most meaningful experiences in school will be project-based activities that allow them to be involved in the community. These might be small-scale activities, such as a trip to a local community center, or more involved activities, perhaps even focused on some dramatic and public effort to change public policy on an issue. Many examples exist of elementary school-aged children who have taken some action in their community after being prompted by a social studies teacher. For example, children in an elementary school in Rome, Georgia, organized a public drive to have the state legislature recognize the tree frog as the official state amphibian. After much effort, including directly lobbying state lawmakers, the students were successful.

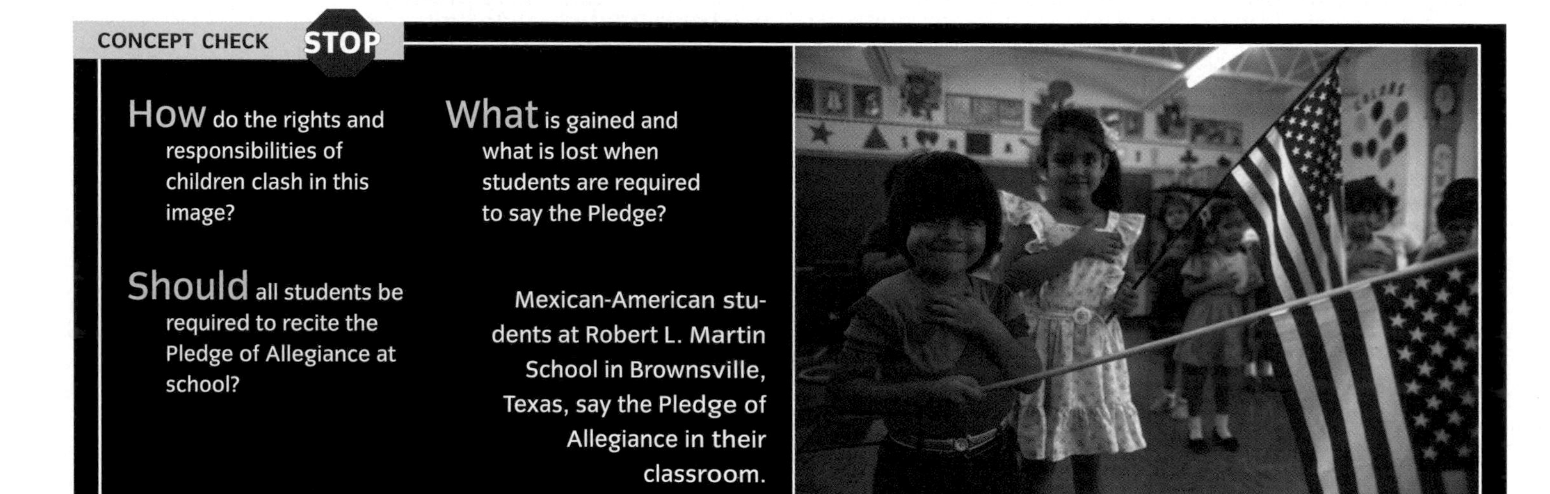

CONCEPT CHECK STOP

How do the rights and responsibilities of children clash in this image?

Should all students be required to recite the Pledge of Allegiance at school?

What is gained and what is lost when students are required to say the Pledge?

Mexican-American students at Robert L. Martin School in Brownsville, Texas, say the Pledge of Allegiance in their classroom.

Promoting Civic Competence

LEARNING OBJECTIVES

Recognize the role of stories in teaching civics and government.

Compare how civic knowledge and civic activity can emerge from teaching activities on specific subject matter.

Identify how ideology can influence civics curriculum and teaching.

USING STORIES TO COMMUNICATE CIVIC VALUES

As we learned in Chapter 5, stories have powerful communicative value. Teachers can use stories to help children develop civic competencies. Stories can convey important responsibilities. Through storytelling, teachers can help children understand the roles and processes of government. Stories can be a resource for exploring civic diversity and for reasoning in multicultural democratic contexts. Some stories can even provide a context for critical exploration of social issues and potentially for encouraging social activity.

Elementary social studies teachers can use a variety of storytelling techniques including tales, parables, and fables to convey ideas, concepts, and values to students. Tales tend to be simple stories that may or may not have a message. Parables typically have no story structure, but convey a special and sometimes hidden message. Fables are perhaps the most useful pedagogical tool of the three in that they combine the story structure of a tale with the message of a parable. Teachers can make effective use of the famous fables assembled under the legendary (and probably fictional) Aesop. These fables are culled from a wide range of African and European sources and date in some cases back thousands of years. Fables such as "The Tortoise and the Eagle," about the tortoise who complains that he cannot fly and is then lifted aloft by an eagle only to be dropped and eaten by the eagle, might convey to children the value of appreciating their own talents and traits.

Such stories help teachers to illustrate important values in cultural contexts that are part of social studies curriculum. Almost all cultures across the globe have their own traditions of fables and storytelling. The African tales of the Ashanti and the tales of African American slaves collected by Joel Chandler Harris in Uncle Remus Tales convey powerful messages through imagery and African animal mythology. Indian fables focused on the mystery and beauties of the Vedic-Hindu tradition convey important cultural characteristics. Similar culturally situated tales have emerged in Korea, Japan, and China and throughout the Pacific region, as well as in the Caribbean and Central and South America.

Books and stories about the processes of government are very important. Elementary school students will only develop a rudimentary knowledge of the details of how government works, but the generalities are very important at this age. David Catrow's book, *We the Kids: The Preamble to the Constitution*, is a clever adaptation of the Preamble of the United States Constitution, which explores government as an idea, as well as the rights and responsibilities of citizens and the processes of government.

The subject of multicultural democratic life is one of the most vibrant subgenres of children's social studies literature. Books ranging across the spectrum of multicultural topics are available, including books on cultural appreciation, individual achievement against cultural odds, cultural pluralism, and respect for cultural differences (see **TABLE 7.2**). In order to develop a sense of respect for a culture, it's important to include books that present culturally valid images of individuals or groups of people that reinforce some indigenous value.

Social studies teachers may use stories or books to explore social issues and to potentially encourage social activity. Lois Lowry's powerful 1993 book, *The Giver*, might be used in upper elementary classes (preferably fifth grade) to explore social issues related to historical memory, such as how people value differences and how we live with our past. In the book, the main character, a 12-year-old named Jonas, lives in a utopian world that knows nothing of its past, except for one person who holds this sacred but potentially destructive knowledge. When Jonas is selected to replace this person and is given knowledge of the past, he is unable to remain and flees the utopian community and its life of sameness for a new life where traditions and the past are known and differences are valued.

Sample of books with different multicultural foci TABLE 7.2

Book title	Author	Multicultural topic
Tenzin's Deer: A Tibetan Tale	Barbara Soros	Cultural appreciation
Sequoyah: The Cherokee Man Who Gave His People Writing	James Rumford	Individual achievement against cultural odds
My Name Was Hussein	Hristo Kyuchukov	Cultural pluralism
Babushka Baba Yaga	Patricia Polacco	Respect for cultural differences

SOCIAL STUDIES CONTENT, TEACHER AND STUDENT OPINIONS, AND IDEOLOGY

What opinions might emerge from a consideration of the image of the Greenpeace protest in FIGURE 7.10? How might one's political ideology or perspective influence how one teaches about the military or defense spending and preparation?

Ideology, or one's view of the world, appears in many places in social studies, but the most obvious place is in civics and government. In elementary school social studies, students might learn about the political parties and might begin to understand that people have different beliefs about democratic ideals such as justice and liberty. These representations become ideological in that they explain the world.

Ideology
A world view or set of beliefs that explains human action and behavior.

Beyond the subject matter for instruction, ideology affects curriculum and instruction. Ideological perspectives influence how specific curriculums are developed. Evidence of the ideological character of curriculum can be found in the recent contentious debate over the national history standards. Ideology also influences teachers' development of instructional ideas. Some teachers might not even know they are acting ideologically when planning for instruction and teaching. Simple decisions such as what resources to use are often made using judgments informed by ideology. For example, consider a teacher who is planning an Earth Day activity. A simple decision over whether to focus on a topic such as global warming, a topic that generates much controversy, might reflect an ideological belief.

Ideology may be present in social studies content, but those involved in education often attempt to mask its influence. Publishers go to great lengths to remove ideological overtones from textbooks. In a market as narrow as the social studies textbook market, very few companies would risk sales by claiming to be driven by a particular ideology. Likewise, social studies teachers are generally very careful to avoid revealing their political opinions, and most often attempt to hide their personal ideology behind their pedagogical practice. Great care needs to be taken to identify your own ideology as a teacher and continually check yourself to see whether that ideology unduly influences what you teach and the way you teach. Knowing your own ideological stance requires reflection and serious consideration of what you believe about seminal contested issues (school choice, abortion, prayer in schools, etc.) and basic systems (e.g., free and market economies).

NUCLEAR
WEAPONS
OUT OF ITALY
GREENPEACE

FIGURE 7.10

Greenpeace activists hold reproductions of B61 atomic bombs outside the Italian Parliament during a protest, in Rome, Friday, November 24, 2006. The activists are protesting against the holding of B61 atomic bombs in NATO headquarters in Italy, in view of the upcoming NATO summit in Riga, Latvia.

FIGURE 7.11

Martin Luther King, Jr., with other civil rights leaders on August 28, 1963, during the March on Washington

One common story in social studies with an ideological focus is the story of Martin Luther King, Jr. Read the following excerpt from King's speech, "I Have a Dream." Think about King's call for social action and the ideology reflected in this famous speech during the 1963 March on Washington (**FIGURE 7.11**).

> We cannot walk alone. And as we walk, we must make the pledge that we shall march ahead. We cannot turn back. There are those who are asking the devotees of civil rights, "When will you be satisfied?" We can never be satisfied as long as the Negro is the victim of unspeakable horrors of police brutality. We can never be satisfied as long as our bodies, heavy with the fatigue of travel, cannot gain lodging in the motels of the highways and the hotels of the cities. We cannot be satisfied as long as the Negro's basic mobility is from a smaller ghetto to a larger one. We can never be satisfied as long as a Negro in Mississippi cannot vote and a Negro in New York believes he has nothing for which to vote. No, no, we are not satisfied, and we will not be satisfied until justice rolls down like waters and righteousness like a mighty stream.

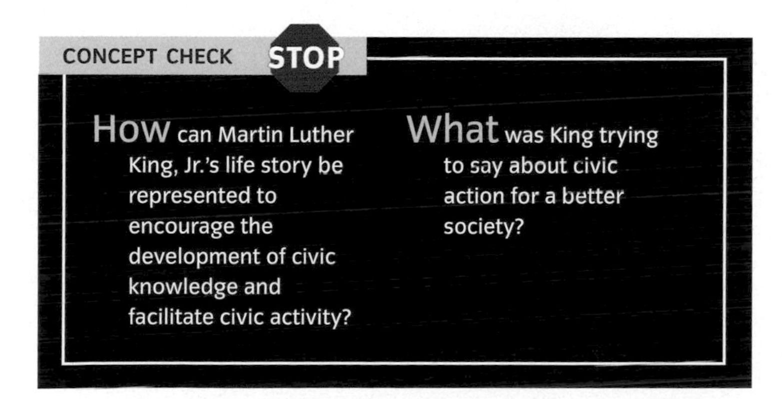

Many teachers feel comfortable using didactic or direct instructional methods. These direct approaches, which include lecture, independent student work, and guided whole class instruction, provide teachers with the utmost control over the learning pace and classroom interaction. The primary goal of this chapter is to consider various effective direct instructional methods and the most appropriate and meaningful contexts for implementing these techniques. We give special attention to specific reasons why direct instruction is important in social studies. Lecture plays an important role in social studies and so we cover it in depth in this chapter.

Direct Instruction and Teacher-Directed Instruction

LEARNING OBJECTIVES

Consider how teachers use direct instruction in their practice.

Describe the broad characteristics of teacher-directed instruction.

Compare formal direct instruction and generalized teacher-directed instruction.

Think about how a teacher might direct students toward a specific subject matter–related learning goal associated with the image in FIGURE 8.1. For example, the teacher might say that the children and animals depicted in this image live in the Egyptian desert. The teacher might then prompt the students to notice what the children are wearing and ask why they think the children are dressed this way.

The teacher might continue by providing students opportunities to think of other deserts in the world, even giving several examples of desert dress (FIGURE 8.2). This work becomes a form of practice with each succeeding example helping to further advance students' knowledge.

This example of teacher-directed or **didactic** instruction is just one of many ways to use that teaching method. All of these approaches to teaching position the teacher at the center of the instructional process, with the teacher delivering instruction through closely managed techniques aimed at encouraging learning of specific

Didactic
Another word for a teacher-centered approach to teaching; also can mean a form of moral instruction.

FIGURE 8.1
Boys and camels at Pushkar camel fair in India

Desert life in Algeria FIGURE 8.2

and focused subject matter. Teacher-directed instruction takes form in precise ways, including specific educational practices such as the direct instruction method.

WHAT IS DIRECT INSTRUCTION?

Direct instruction Closely developed series of exercises that provide learners continual interaction with limited, fundamental subject matter.

Direct instruction is a specific method of teaching that enables teachers to take students through a series of exercises that provide the learners with continual opportunities to interact with limited but fundamental subject matter and skills. The method was developed by Siegfried E. Engelmann (Engelmann & Carnine, 1991) in the late 1960s and has been continually refined and adapted since. Although the direct instruction method is most commonly associated with math, it has an interdisciplinary application. Direct instruction requires teachers to closely develop activities that proceed with care given to learning outcomes.

One of the names most closely associated with direct teaching is Madeline Hunter (1982). A method of direct teaching that she developed demonstrates in simple form some of the hallmarks of direct instruction. See the Process Diagram (FIGURE 8.3) on page 206 for the steps involved in teaching via direct instruction using the Hunter method.

Teacher-directed instruction Teaching approach focused on clearly defined and organized teaching tasks and measurable incremental learning.

WHAT IS TEACHER-DIRECTED INSTRUCTION?

Teacher-directed instruction is a much broader way of thinking about teacher-centered instruction. As opposed to direct instruction, teacher-directed instruction is not a prescribed procedure. Instead, it is a flexible approach to instruction that incorporates four major priorities.

Priorities for Teacher-Directed Instruction

1. The teacher needs to be very clear about the subject matter that will be learned.
2. Students should learn subject matter or skills through repetition and should demonstrate their knowledge in multiple formats.
3. All students should be actively learning the same thing in the activity.
4. The subject matter should be situated in meaningful contexts that will encourage students to learn the subject matter given what they already know.

In social studies, teacher-directed instruction often takes the form of a lecture, but it might also include memorization, reading comprehension, map skills exercises, directed inquiry, role-play, group decision-making, and problem-solving exercises. Each one of these approaches to teaching could be adapted and taught as student-centered activities if any of the four priorities were not taken into consideration.

Lecture is perhaps the most common approach to teaching social studies. Although lecture can sometimes be overused, well-planned lecture as a form of teacher-directed instruction is an essential part of social studies. See "In the Classroom" on page 208 for an example of how a fourth-grade teacher in Montana prepares for a 15-minute lecture on the purpose and various levels of government.

As Ms. Rankin planned her lecture, she used multiple examples to support her explanations. Teaching by example is an effective and manageable way to enliven and enrich lecture and teacher-directed instruction. Providing examples is a way to follow up on previously introduced subject matter. Another way teachers might reinforce subject matter in a teacher-directed activity is through group work on topics that were previously introduced through lecture, or through whole group discussion and whole class reading activities. Following are additional teacher-directed instructional approaches to support active and meaningful student learning.

- The teacher describes the context surrounding an inquiry question that students will be working on.
- The teacher presents background information to prepare students for a simulation.
- The teacher explains concepts and issues that will prepare students for a debate.
- The teacher offers a lecture as a way to initiate a whole class discussion.

found. Quickly, with almost no time to spare, Mrs. Madison ordered the picture frame to be smashed and the painting to be cut from the frame, a task that was completed by White House servants. Mrs. Madison, her staff, the important papers, and the picture of George Washington all made it out unharmed—due in large part to the courage and determination of Dolley Madison.

TAKING IT APART: HIGHER-ORDER THINKING SKILLS

In addition to direct explanation and storytelling, teacher-directed instruction can incorporate activities for students to analyze ideas. Analytical activities help students develop higher-order thinking skills. Conducting an analysis means breaking down or taking apart a whole idea or concept into its component pieces. By focusing on how something can be "taken apart," students conduct a specific analysis of the subject matter at hand, and also learn how to conduct analyses in general.

One common analytical task in elementary social studies is to ask students to analyze opportunity costs in personal economic decisions. Simply put, **opportunity cost** is the value of what we decide *not* to spend our money on. In other words, when we make an economic decision, there is always a next best alternative. The value of this next best alternative is opportunity cost. Students can learn how to analyze opportunity costs by taking apart any decision they might make to spend money.

> **Opportunity cost** The value of things not selected in an economic situation.

A teacher can direct students' learning about opportunity costs by creating a classroom economy and paying students with classroom currency for good behavior or for completing classroom tasks such as cleaning up. At the end of a week, the teacher can open a class market with goods such as pencils and notebooks for sale. After students spend their classroom money, the teacher can direct students to analyze their spending for opportunity costs. Prior to this student work, the teacher can model his or her own thinking and opportunity costs related to some recent economic decision. Students make a list of the items they wanted to buy, in order from the most desired to least desired, and then list a reason why they wanted to buy the item. The reasons listed for all the items that were not purchased are ranked opportunity costs and represent the analysis of students' purchasing rationale.

OTHER TEACHER-DIRECTED ACTIVITIES

Helping Children Understand "Why?"

Children love to ask "Why?" Their natural curiosity can create opportunities in the classroom. Teachers need to respond to students' curiosity and desire to understand the meaning of things. When students raise questions, teachers should be as responsive as possible, looking to standards and curriculum for opportunities to provide students with answers to questions about why.

Decision Making

An important higher-order social studies skill involves making decisions. Children in elementary grades are learning how to make well-informed decisions. In this teacher-directed activity, students and teachers work together to make a decision about a problem that emerges from subject matter in the curriculum. For example, students might consider various historical decisions that resulted in two countries or two groups of people engaging in conflicts. The more students can be involved in the process of recognizing the significance of the problem, the more they will be involved in the problem-solving activity. These problems can emerge from student interests and prior knowledge. Each problem, such as the one the United States faced in 1917 regarding whether to enter World War I, needs to be set in the context of students' own understanding or interests.

Direct Concept Development Teaching

Children develop knowledge of concepts at very early ages. In social studies, examples of these concepts include history, shelter, home, citizenship, common good, earth, place, money, and scarcity. Each one of these concepts can be developed in the mind of a child through teacher-directed instruction. Concept-development requires careful attention to definitions and representations of the concept in various contexts.

Transportation is a very important concept and organizing theme in elementary social studies. What does the image in FIGURE 8.8 tell us about how the Mississippi River is used for transporting people and goods? How might you teach about transportation on the Mississippi River using direct concept development or another teacher-directed approach?

FIGURE 8.8

Aerial view of barges traveling the Mississippi River past St. Louis.

CONCEPT CHECK STOP

Make a list of three topics related to shelter that would be best suited for storytelling.

How might you plan three different teacher-directed activities on the concept of shelter?

An Italian peasant couple in the late 19th century in front of a hut in the Basilicata region. The hut was used as a day shelter only—the workers returned to town at night.

Ethnic Karen women and children in Myanmar (Burma) in front of their bamboo hut in the village of Ei Htu Hta, Myanmar, Tuesday, May 9, 2006, near the Salween river along the Myanmar-Thai border. The refugee village sprang up after more than 13,000 ethnic Karen fled persecution by the Myanmar Army.

ncouraging students to be actively involved in class is not always easy. Too much involvement and students might get off task. Not enough involvement and they are probably not learning much.

How can we encourage students to be involved in class without going too far? Interactive instruction is one solution. When interacting in the classroom, students work with one another in controlled instructional contexts without sacrificing the individual student's responsibility to learn.

Enabling students to work in interactive learning environments is a powerful means to promote active student learning (**FIGURE 9.1**). At the center of interactive approaches to teaching and learning is this notion that children learn best when they interact. Consider how frequently we use knowledge in interaction. In fact, most of us almost never apply our knowledge outside of interactive or social contexts. In this chapter, we consider interactive instruction as an essential means for supporting active and meaningful learning in social studies.

FIGURE 9.1

Elementary school students in Schenectady, New York, use blocks and paper to create imaginary community.

What Is Interactive Instruction?

LEARNING OBJECTIVES

Define interactive instruction.

Describe the structure of interactive instruction.

Explain the role of assessment in interactive learning.

Interaction is fundamental to education. Imagine learning in isolation, without the help of others. Self-guided learning, while important, is always constrained by individual limitations. When we interact we have the potential to extend our limitations and expand our learning opportunities. Although students must be accountable for their own learning, interaction enables social engagement and heightens our appreciation for others. Ideally, we will always seek a balance between individual and interactive learning.

DEFINING INTERACTIVE INSTRUCTION

Interactive instruction is an approach to teaching that enables children to benefit from each other in dynamic environments. Classroom interaction can heighten students' interest and involvement in the learning process. Interaction can also help students learn to value similarities and differences. Most interactive instruction takes place in small to medium-size groups, but interactive instruction is not just about group work. Instead, it draws on the strengths of individuals in group settings.

Interactive instruction
A teaching approach that uses a combination of group and individual work; it enables students to benefit from each other in dynamic environments.

Interactive instruction is framed by the work of educational psychologist Lev Vygotsky (1978). In the early part of the 20th century, Vygotsky developed a theory of learning that suggested that learning occurs in social settings. His theory of social cognition holds that society influences both what students learn and how they learn. The children depicted in **FIGURE 9.2** in Firozabad, India, work ten hours a day, seven days a week making bracelets. The parents send their children to work and receive cash from the workshop owner. How might the context of these children's social condition affect the way they learn?

Children learn within the context of culture, and that culture determines what knowledge is important. One of the ways these cultural contexts influence what children learn is through the development of curriculum. Children also learn in society by interacting with others. Vygotsky claimed that children initially interact with parents and other adults as they learn and adapt to their culture. Later, this learning becomes more independent, a process psychologists call adaptation.

When children interact in the classroom they are adapting to cultural expectations about knowledge in a controlled environment. Through interactive instruction, teachers give students an opportunity to develop knowledge in social settings while also promoting the independence that is necessary for children to internalize what they are learning. During interactive instruction, students must maintain a dual focus on themselves and on the larger group. In fact, the most important aspect of interactive instruction is that each learner is ultimately responsible for his or her own learning. Individual responsibility for learning means that students will also have to account for their actions in the classroom, and this allows teachers to assess more fairly and consistently.

Children working in Firozabad, India FIGURE 9.2

THE STRUCTURE OF INTERACTIVE INSTRUCTION

Interactive instruction should be dynamic, active, and meaningful. These three distinguishing characteristics inform the development of interactive instructional activities as well as the management of time and materials. The dynamic characteristics of interactive instruction require a flexible approach to organizing materials for instruction. Active involvement on the part of learners in interactive learning environments results from engaging other students. Children feel the learning is meaningful because they have worked together in an environment that parallels their everyday lives.

What does interactive instruction look like? Consider this example. Chris Steele teaches fourth grade at an innovative elementary school where teachers are expected to teach in an interactive manner. One of Chris's interactive lessons focuses on the effects of change in the students' town and how they might predict and plan for future changes.

- In order to get students' interest, Chris asked the class to describe their favorite place in town. She followed up by working with students to make a list of things they liked and disliked about their town.
- Next, students individually wrote a brief description of their town and drew a picture of one important place in their community.
- After this individual work, Chris's class and another class in the school constructed four learning stations:
  - two stations, which represented two different historical times in their community;
  - a third station, which presented information on the current community;
  - and a fourth station, which focused on the future in their town.
- The students constructed the learning stations while working in cooperative groups. The learning stations included images, drawings, and text that described the particular time or explained the future.

Characteristics of Interactive Instruction

LEARNING OBJECTIVES

Identify the conditions for active and meaningful learning during interactive instruction.

Examine how and why interactive approaches to instruction should be dynamic.

Describe ways to make instruction with challenging subject matter more effective with interactive instruction.

s we learned earlier, interactive instruction should involve active, meaningful, and dynamic experiences with challenging subject matter. These characteristics are consistent with the National Council for the Social Studies (1992) description of the central features of ideal social studies as meaningful, integrative, value-based, challenging, and active. In this section we look at each of the characteristics of interactive learning as they relate to one another.

ACTIVE AND MEANINGFUL LEARNING DURING INTERACTIVE INSTRUCTION

When students learn about the political leaders in their community, they can engage meaningful material in an active manner by visiting city hall or by writing letters to civic leaders. This type of active and meaningful learning engages students in subject matter and requires them to adapt information for personal use. When developing interactive lessons that encourage active involvement, teachers should plan for students to work together to achieve personal learning goals.

Active learning requires that students construct their own knowledge by manipulating information as opposed to learning passively by simply receiving information. Active learning exercises are typically at higher thinking levels than passive activities. This is not because active learning has to be at higher levels. But in most cases, passive learning does not allow for higher-order thinking.

Consider the difference between an activity that requires students to listen to a story about Thomas Edison and one that requires them to actively consider how Edison and George Eastman worked together to develop and popularize photography. FIGURE 9.4 depicts the father of popular photography, George Eastman (left), in 1928 as he confers with the wizard of light, Thomas Edison, about an early motion picture camera. What do you know about these men, and how might their expertise have contributed to developing motion picture technology?

In a lecture on Thomas Edison, students would receive information and perhaps engage in some dialogue. In an interactive activity, the teacher might ask students to describe how motion picture cameras work. Students might first work individually to brainstorm ideas and then move into groups to study Edison and Eastman. The group work could focus on Edison's work with light and Eastman's work with film. The teacher could then place students in new groups with a mixture of people who learned about Edison and Eastman so they could share what they learned about these men. They might then reconsider the original question about motion picture cameras. The goal would be for students to realize that Eastman and Edison collaborated on how to properly use light and film to record moving images. Students here work in a variety of settings (indi-

FIGURE 9.4

In 1928, the father of popular photography, Eastman Kodak Company founder George Eastman (on the left), confers with Thomas Edison about an early motion picture camera.

In the Classroom LEARNING ABOUT CIVIC LEADERS

Jere Gravitt enjoys teaching his fourth-grade students about local government. His involvement in the local community makes this particular lesson very meaningful for Mr. Gravitt. In an effort to transfer that sense of meaningfulness to his students, Mr. Gravitt developed an interactive lesson in which students work together to collect information about a local issue and then personally lobby a city council member.

The issue this year was zoning. The city wanted to change the rules for zoning some local property to include more high-density dwellings. This change would result in a greater number of apartments and town homes in the community. At the time of the proposal, most of the residential developments in town were single-family homes. Mr. Gravitt described the role of the city council in determining what gets built where and gave his students their task. They were to research the zoning issue and write a group report on how the zoning process works. They also had to research arguments for and against the proposal. Each group had five members and there were five tasks in the group.

Mr. Gravitt developed the tasks to take into account differing levels of prior knowledge among students. He wanted a student in the group with a high level of prior knowledge to write the section of the report describing the zoning procedure. A second student, also preferably with a high level of prior knowledge, would describe the specific zoning issue. Another student would describe the composition of the city council and the voting procedure. The other two students would list pros and cons for the zoning proposal. Once the report was complete, students would each develop their own position on the issue and write a brief letter to their councilperson outlining their position.

This lesson enabled students to work together to develop knowledge about a meaningful topic. Mr. Gravitt situated the activity in the context of students' personal lives. He started the lesson by describing what people had suggested would be the positive and negative consequences of changes in zoning and required students to individually describe these consequences. Many of the consequences would affect students in their schools by increasing enrollment. While this might result in overcrowding, it would also result in increased tax revenues and potentially mean more government services. The larger schools would also receive more money to buy additional equipment.

Mr. Gravitt encouraged students to take a stand on a public issue and to write a letter to a real person. Students were able to follow the issue after they completed the activity, thereby connecting their school life with life outside the school. Students were also individually responsible for their learning. Mr. Gravitt's primary objectives were to enable students to learn about their local city council and to observe it in action. These goals were achieved when students wrote their letters.

Two young girls helping out in their community painting a fence

vidual and group). Their work with an uncertain or emerging topic is representative of interactive learning.

In this series of individual and small group activities, students can actively construct their own knowledge of motion picture technology given their developing knowledge of Edison and Eastman. This context enables a more powerful and potentially more meaningful learning experience. Research suggests that such experiences result in more residual knowledge. In other words, students are more likely to remember what they learned in the active experience than in the passive one.

DYNAMIC INSTRUCTION AND ACTIVE LEARNING

Unlike more scripted forms of teacher-directed instruction, interactive instruction requires a dynamic approach. When teaching in interactive contexts, teachers must constantly adapt their lessons. As groups work together, you will find that some students need more assistance than others. Some groups will not work together in the way you expected. Groups will complete parts of activities at different times, and additional work or shortened work will be necessary. Of course, these problems may also be present in individual work, but grouping makes addressing problems more urgent. When groups are unable to complete a task, or if they finish work early, they may become disruptive. Being able to adapt a lesson is critical to keeping students focused and on task.

A teacher's ability to keep up with students working in groups is tied to the teacher's knowledge of the subject matter. Often students have subject matter–oriented questions, which when addressed will enable them to get back on task. A teacher's ability to find or adapt materials is often tied to subject matter knowledge.

Consider an activity in which groups of students are working to develop profiles of the Hindu gods such as Shiva, Parvati, and Brahma (FIGURES 9.5 and 9.6). Students in each group are required to prepare a profile of one of these religious figures.

Prior to this group work, students individually learned about the monotheistic nature of Hinduism. During the work, a student stops because she cannot understand how the Hindu religion can have so many gods while at the same time maintain a belief in a single Supreme God. The teacher who doesn't have enough knowledge of Hinduism might not be able to provide a meaningful answer.

An appropriate response might be to tell the students that Hindus believe that each god is a representa-

FIGURE 9.5

The Hindu gods Shiva and Parvati

FIGURE 9.6

The Hindu god Brahma

FIGURE 9.7

President Ronald Reagan riding with his wife, Nancy, on his California ranch

tion of a Supreme God. In other words, God takes form in a number of ways for Hindus. If the teacher does not know how to respond because her subject matter knowledge is weak, she can be honest with students and work as quickly as possible to find the information students need.

Sometimes students are off task because they are not interested in the subject matter or the task. This problem is more difficult to address during instruction. A well-planned lesson should take into account students' interest, but if during the lesson students exhibit a lack of interest, the teacher might re-cast the task around something the students find interesting.

INTERACTIVE INSTRUCTION AND CHALLENGING SUBJECT MATTER

Not all subject matter is easy to present in a meaningful context. How can teachers engage students in an active and meaningful interactive lesson when the subject matter is seemingly uninteresting, complicated, or challenging? The first step is for the teacher to know and appreciate the subject matter. With an in-depth understanding of subject matter, teachers can bring a level of enthusiasm that is simply not possible otherwise, but enthusiasm is not enough. Without intriguing instructional methods, even the most enthusiastic teachers will likely find themselves struggling to maintain student interest in a lesson focused on subject matter that is obscure or irrelevant for students.

For most students, an inability to engage with subject matter in a meaningful way is often due to an inability to see how the material relates to them. Teachers can find ways to relate the subject matter to their students' lives using interactive instructional settings.

Subject matter that has been problematized is by nature more interesting. For example, students may be uninterested in memorizing the names of the presidents of the United States. However, when presented as an interactive problem-based activity, this subject matter is far more interesting.

FIGURE 9.7 depicts popular former President Ronald Reagan riding a horse on his California ranch. How does this image influence our perception of President Reagan?

To enliven the subject matter, teachers might ask students to rank-order presidents or list the top ten and bottom ten. They might want to analyze presidential backgrounds for birthplace, prior occupation, or experience in politics. Other options include looking at historians' judgments of presidents, or public opinion of presidents when in office, or learning how popular representations of U.S. presidents shape our current opinion.

CONCEPT CHECK STOP

How can a lesson on the shapes of U.S. states be active, meaningful, and dynamic?

Why are some U.S. states small and others large?

Why do some states have regular borders and others have irregular borders?

How might you create an activity about the shapes of U.S. states?

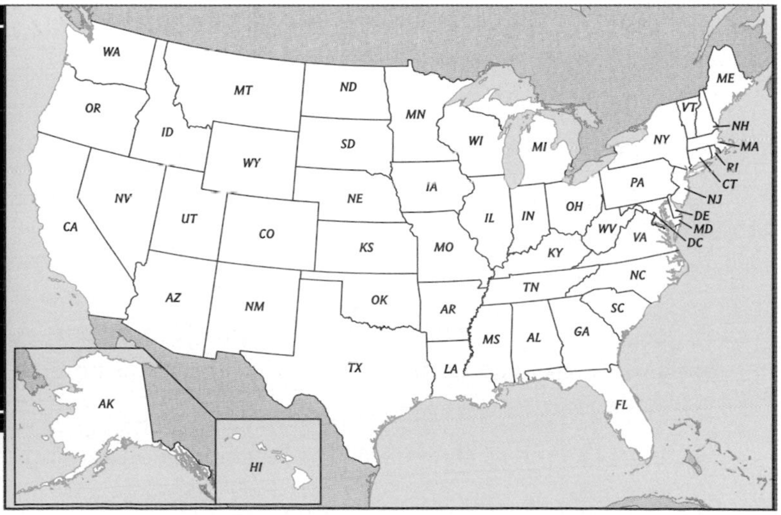

Types of Interactive Instruction

LEARNING OBJECTIVES

Recognize types of interactive instruction.

Describe some of the pedagogical approaches to interactive instruction.

Consider appropriate subject matter for specific interactive instructional approaches.

Interactive instruction may take several forms. As you learned earlier, interactive instruction should be active, meaningful, and dynamic. What are some specific interactive activities that social studies teachers can use in their class? In this section we will review several specific types of interactive instruction.

SOLVING PROBLEMS TOGETHER

Solving problems helps us to succeed in life. In social studies, we can give students authentic opportunities to solve problems in interactive settings. With interactive problem solving, the individual students are ultimately responsible for the solution they pose for their problem, but each student is part of a group of fellow students who can help support their understanding.

There are four components to an interactive problem-solving activity:

1. Identify a problem that is situated in a meaningful and authentic context.
2. Work with others in a group to develop an understanding of the dimensions of the problem.
3. Work within a group to develop possible solutions to the problem.
4. Individually select a solution to the problem and estimate the consequences of implementing the solution.

Interactive problem solving is unique because students work with each other to build an understanding of the problem and develop possible solutions, but when it comes time to solve the problem each student is accountable for his or her own work.

There are countless problems that can serve as contexts for problem-solving activities. Of course, if we are to use a specific problem in class it must fit within the boundaries of curriculum. One common curriculum area is natural resource usage. Developing and sustaining usable water supplies is one of the most vexing natural resource use problems in the world. Sometimes it seems as if water is everywhere we don't want it and in short supply where we need it. In **FIGURE 9.8A**, flood waters surround a village at the intersection of the Jamuna and Padma Rivers in Bangladesh, a country in which the average annual rainfall is between 100 and 400 inches a year. At the other extreme is the Sahel region in the Sudan as seen in **FIGURE 9.8B**. This area on the southern rim of the Sahara desert is experiencing desertification as a result of drought, overgrazing, and deforestation. The encroaching desert has forced many to relocate in search of food, water, and shelter.

An interesting problem-based interactive lesson might focus on the uneven availability of water in various places in the world. Students could work individually at first to develop an understanding of the problem in places like Bangladesh and the Sudan, and then come together in groups to propose solutions to the general problem. Each student would then select what he or she believes to be the best solution to the problem.

MAKING DECISIONS TOGETHER

Decision making is an important skill. In free-market democracies such as the United States, people are continuously faced with decisions about how to spend their time, energy, and money. Children need to learn how to make good decisions in carefully constructed academic environments. Far too often, we make decisions without adequately considering other options and the consequences of our decisions. In an interactive deci-

The uneven availability of water Figure 9.8

A Flood waters surround a village at the intersection of the Jamuna and Padma Rivers in Bangladesh.

B The Sahel region in the Sudan

sion-making activity, these two considerations—options and their consequences—are front and center. Let's begin with a question and proceed in an iterative fashion through a series of possible decisions given the consequences (Figure 9.9)

During a decision-making activity, a set of possible decisions should be evident from an investigation of the question or situation. Each of the potential decisions has consequences. As we evaluate these consequences, we discard some of the possible decisions and retain others. Ultimately, we select a single, best decision. Although there is not always a "right" decision, a decision should be made and supported based on opinions and consequences.

The situation for which a decision is to be made must be interesting and meaningful for students as well as being curriculum-based. Once the teacher has generated a question or situation, students work together in groups to develop a list of possible decisions. They then evaluate each possible decision for potential consequences. Each individual student takes into account the consequences of the decisions, and each student selects his or her own best decision.

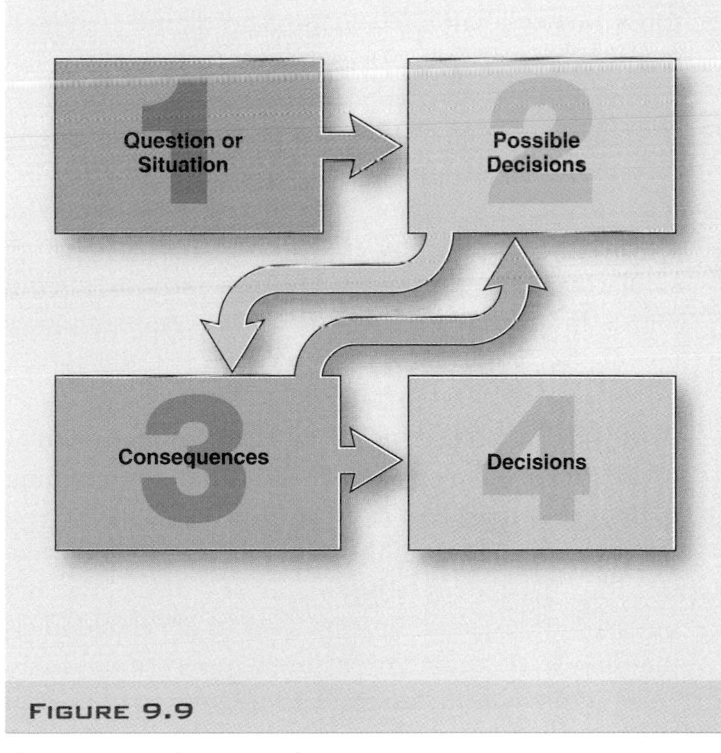

Figure 9.9

The interactive decision-making process.

PUTTING THINGS TOGETHER

One of the most underappreciated high-order thinking activities available in social studies is synthesis. We spend tremendous time and energy encouraging analysis, but rarely consider its antecedent. **Synthesis** is an important skill that enables children to develop a whole understanding when material is presented in fragments. The concept attainment/development models of Jerome Bruner (1956) anf Hilda Taba (1962) are based on synthesis. These approaches to developing concept knowledge are inductive and involve students recognizing examples and non-examples of a concept as a way to develop knowledge of the concept.

Synthesis
The process of combining ideas or objects to form a new whole thing.

Synthesis activities work in a similar way, enabling interaction that is dynamic and active. All of the following interactive synthesis activities involve students working together to meet individual learning goals.

What's in Common? In this activity, students begin with a collection of seemingly disconnected facts about famous people, places, or events. Teachers assign students in groups one of the facts, and the students work to determine the identity of their person, place, or event. After making the identification, students begin to work in the groups to determine similarities. The teacher can provide the group with a chart for listing similarities and differences. The final outcome should be an individual finding—namely, some similarity among the people, places, or events.

The Big Picture One of the things we try to do in social studies is help students understand overarching themes and storylines. Far too often, teachers and students become mired in the details of discrete information. In this activity, students must construct a "big picture" understanding from a series of related ideas that they have studied over time. Opportunities to do "big picture" synthesis occur frequently in the social studies curriculum.

Curriculum often calls for students to learn about specific Native American tribes or, at best, similarities among regional Indians. It is rarer for students to consider Native American Indians as a whole. Since all synthesis-related activities need to have a central focus, an activity on Native Americans might focus on Indian dwellings such as the ones illustrated in FIGURES 9.10 and 9.11.

This activity requires students to use several sources of information, such as these images of Caribou and Anasazi dwellings, to develop a whole understanding of some aspect of Native Indian life. FIGURE 9.10 shows two Caribou Inuit women sitting inside a cozy igloo, and FIGURE 9.11 shows a view inside ancient Anasazi Indian cliff dwellings. Students can use these sources to develop general statements about home life among Native American Indians. This means that students will synthesize—they will identify similarities among dwellings related to topics such as size, construction materials, and purpose. Students bring these findings together to construct substantive statements about Native Indian dwellings in general.

FIGURE 9.10

Two Caribou Inuit women sit inside an igloo.

FIGURE 9.11

A view inside ancient Anasazi Indian cliff dwellings.

OTHER APPROACHES TO INTERACTIVE ACTIVITIES

At its best, interactive instruction is creative. Teachers must create activities that reflect their students' and their own interests and talents. In this section, we present several interactive activities as examples of the variety inherent in interactive instruction. Consider these pedagogical approaches as creative sparks for developing your own approaches to interactive instruction.

The Buzz Children love to talk and, like adults, their talk often follows trends and fashions. We might think of this talk as buzz or what everyone is talking about. This instructional approach takes advantage of our tendency to be attracted to gossipy talk. To start this activity, identify some curriculum-based subject matter. Also, focus the subject matter topic to reflect student interest. First, plant an idea with one student or a small group and facilitate interesting talk about the idea. As the talk proceeds, have students consider how the focus changes, comparing where they started to where they end. The goal is to demonstrate how talk can affect what we know, while learning about some substantive subject matter.

It's a Mystery "It's a mystery" is an activity to use when you have an issue or topic that contains some element of uncertainty. For example, students could study the mystery of the disappearance of Amelia Earhart and the emergence of women in traditional male roles such as an aviator. Have students assemble in groups of three or four, and provide each group a one- or two-sentence description of the mystery. You could give each group a slightly different version. Once all the students have read their passage, create new groups with members from each of the previous groups. In these new groups have students share their version of the story. Each individual should then select the one version they think is most credible.

What Do You Know About It? This activity should relate to an issue or topic in social studies that is complex or difficult to understand—such as the concept of freedom. Ask students to share with each other what they know about freedom. Then, have students share their definition of freedom in small groups and come up with one example of freedom. Students could record each one of the ideas shared in the group, then move to new groups and share what they learned in their first group. This outcome should be an expanded understanding of the meaning of freedom.

Young children will often hold an absolute or ideal belief about freedom. In practice, freedom is limited and conditional.

For and Against In this activity, students pair up and take opposing views on some controversial issue. The idea is that each student will have a script of sorts and will try to convince the other that they are right. The central characteristic of this activity is its structure. Be sure to give students a focused topic for discussion and a set of rules for trying to convince one another that they are right.

The concept of economic choice is a good topical area for developing a "for and against" activity. Offer students two choices for to how to spend a sum of money. Have each student develop all or some part of an argument in favor of one choice. They would deliver their arguments in a controlled setting, perhaps each student having one or two minutes to present. The activity can take place in pairs, small groups, or as a whole class.

What's the Question? Students are very familiar with the routine of answering questions posed by their teachers. In this activity, the tables are turned, and students ask the questions. In this activity, students formulate questions from teacher-delivered prompts. The goal of the activity is to encourage students to work together imagining the question that some information is answering. For example, students might be prompted to develop questions about the history of the founding of their local community. Such questions might focus on why people came to the area, how the community has changed since its founding, and the names and activities of the people who founded the community. As with all interactive activities, this approach should enable students to share possible questions, but ultimately each student should be responsible for selecting what he or she thinks is most correct.

CONCEPT CHECK STOP

Last Chance Gulch in Montana Territory is shown in a period photograph. It is one of hundreds of boomtowns created by the gold rush, which began after a miner found gold near Pikes Peak.

What interactive activities might emerge that are related to the gold rushes in the United States in the 19th century?

What might be the impact of the timing of the gold rushes in 1828 (Georgia), 1848 (California), and 1858 (Colorado) given other events occurring in the United States?

Last Chance Gulch, in Montana Territory in the 1860s.

Grouping Strategies

LEARNING OBJECTIVES

Recognize some reasons for grouping.

Identify methods for grouping students for interactive instruction.

Compare various goals for grouping students.

Grouping is a very important part of interactive instruction. Although not all interactive instruction is conducted with groups, it is the most significant configuration of learners in interactive instructional settings. In "Visualizing: Grouping Based on Subject Matter" on page 244, we look at organizing groups around subjects such as history, politics, or geography.

WHY GROUP STUDENTS?

There are two reasons for grouping students. First, grouping enables students to interact in a social environment. This means the physical characteristics of the grouping should meet the social needs of the group. If students are expected to talk in their group, they should face one another. If they need to share materials, they will need an area in which they can do this easily. If they are expected to read together, they will need the proximity that comes with being read to or reading to someone.

The second reason for grouping is to facilitate instructional objectives. Interactive instruction requires that students work together, in a group, on some portion of an assignment. When planning an interactive activity, teachers need to consider the instructional needs of the group to determine the size, composition, and form of interaction for the group.

HOW TO GROUP STUDENTS

There are as many grouping strategies as the imagination can conjure. To manage the task of setting up groups, we can use three interrelated considerations: (1) the size of the group, (2) the purpose of the activity, and (3) the level of understanding needed by each student.

How many students should be in each group? The size of the group cannot be determined solely from the context of the activity and the individual learning goals for students. For example, a four-person group will not work if the instructional goal is for the group to vote by a majority on some issue. Here are some considerations that might determine the size of a group.

1. Are there specific roles or tasks for group members? If so, the number of these roles will determine the group size.
2. Will the group members be discussing information? Depending on the subject matter, smaller groups may be better. If the teacher expects all students to participate in the discussion or if the subject matter is particularly dense, smaller groups are better.
3. Are the group identities tied to subject matter? If they are, the number of groups and thus the group size will be influenced by the subject matter arrangement. For example, if students are studying the climates in North America, the teacher may want each group to represent a different climate type, which will influence the number of groups.
4. Will groups be rearranged for some extended activity? This regrouping will influence the size and number of groups.
5. Will the groups present information to the whole class? If presentations are a part of the activity, the number of groups will be influenced by the amount of time for presentations and the length of each presentation.

SPECIFIC GROUPING STRATEGIES

There are a number of ways to group students for learning experiences. The following sections address some of these approaches. These grouping strategies are organized as general forms of grouping, specialized

Specialized Groupings

Subject-matter based grouping Occasionally, you may want to form groups based on subject matter. For example, if students are studying ethnic immigrant groups the teacher could form groups based on historic immigration patterns. If students are studying immigration to the United States, teachers could group students by ethnic immigrant groups such as the Chinese immigrant children in FIGURE 9.14 in San Francisco. Another group might represent Vietnamese immigrants, as seen in the photo of four Vietnamese children in FIGURE 9.15 who are holding drawings of their homes. How might a teacher create other subject-matter based groups in an exercise on immigration? Perhaps students could be grouped according to the time immigrants arrived. FIGURE 9.16 shows a group of newly arrived immigrants after their long journey to the United States as they await official approval here in 1917.

Subject-matter grouping enables student groups to focus on specific subject matter and is useful in jigsaw activities. It also enables the actual grouping to serve as an instructional element, with group identities, such as ethnic immigrant groups, informing students about some subject-matter structure.

Ability grouping Grouping students by their ability must be done very carefully. A general rule is to never group by ability unless the ability is based on something that will not result in students feeling inferior. Instead of simply putting the brightest students in one group and struggling learners in another, use ability grouping based on specific abilities. For example, some students might be better at math and others might be better at writing. You can place the students who are good in mathematics together if this group has a task that requires advanced math skills.

Student interest grouping Often the group task will concern something that is interesting to students. If groups have different tasks, it might make sense to group students according to their interests. This approach might be a good first grouping for a jigsaw activity.

Multiple intelligence grouping The theory of multiple intelligences holds that children have tendencies to be stronger in certain cognitive areas such as verbal expression or kinesthetic ability. Grouping based on students' dominant or stronger intelligence may enable them to better use their peers' strengths in the group work.

Learning style grouping Scholars suggest that students have different learning styles. Some students learn best by hearing information (audiotapes), others absorb and retain information better when there is visual presentation (DVD, film). These learning styles might be a good context for grouping given some subject matter task that demands a particular learning style.

FIGURE 9.14

Chinese immigrant children in San Francisco about 1900.

FIGURE 9.15

These children are members of Oklahoma City's immigrant Vietnamese community, known as Little Saigon.

FIGURE 9.16

Immigration officials examining an immigrant family at Ellis Island in 1917 in a photo by Lewis Hine.

Instructional Groupings

Instructional grouping involves placing students in groups based on a particular instructional activity. There are several grouping techniques that relate to specific instructional approaches. Following is a review of some of these instructional approaches to grouping.

Inquiry groups As we learned in Chapter 3, inquiry involves students asking questions and using a prescribed method to answer these questions. Inquiry is typically done individually, but in groups the inquiry experience can be enhanced. When students conduct an inquiry in a group, individuals in the group can contribute specialized findings to a whole understanding. The best approach is to give the group a single inquiry question that can be simply segmented into multiple research tasks. Each task outcome should contribute in some way to the findings.

Problem-based learning groups As we learned earlier, problem-based learning is very important in social studies. Some problems might be best addressed in group settings. Each group might address the same problem, completely different problems, different but complementary problems, or even components of a single problem.

Task grouping This approach to grouping focuses on specific tasks that must be completed by different groups. You might use task grouping when you have multiple activities that need to be completed in order for a whole understanding to be developed. For example, groups might need to have a person who records information and another who reports for the group. These grouping techniques are very useful when you want to utilize individual talents or to ensure that each student in a group has a specific role during group work.

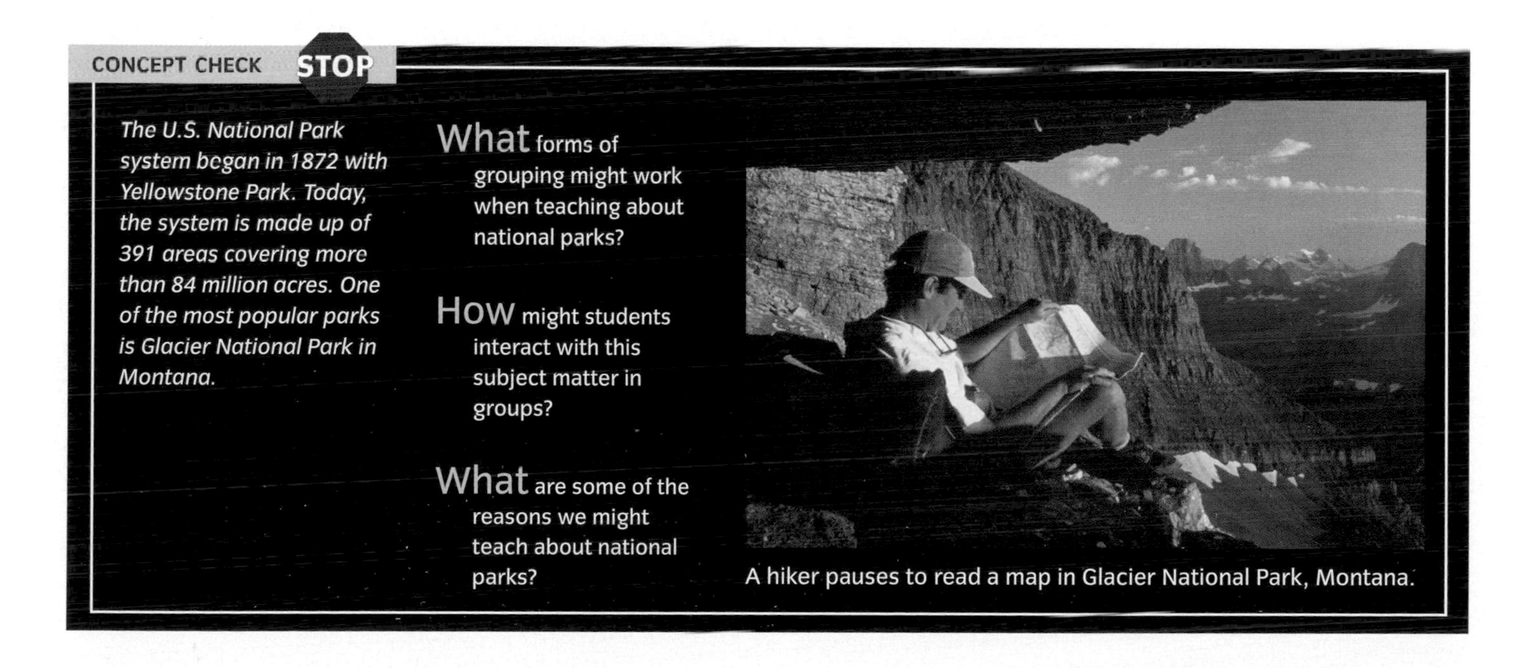

CONCEPT CHECK STOP

The U.S. National Park system began in 1872 with Yellowstone Park. Today, the system is made up of 391 areas covering more than 84 million acres. One of the most popular parks is Glacier National Park in Montana.

What forms of grouping might work when teaching about national parks?

How might students interact with this subject matter in groups?

What are some of the reasons we might teach about national parks?

A hiker pauses to read a map in Glacier National Park, Montana.

Interactive Instruction and Learners

LEARNING OBJECTIVES

Distinguish between collaborative and cooperative learning and interactive instruction.

Identify how the conditions for interactive instruction affect learners differently.

Recognize reasons why interactive instructional activities must be adapted for some learners.

COLLABORATION AND INTERACTIVE INSTRUCTION

As we have seen, most of the learning that takes place in interactive environments is group oriented. Much attention has been given to group learning in educational settings over the last several decades. Often referred to as cooperative or collaborative learning, group-based learning is a mainstay of school today. Interactive instruction is closely tied to collaborative and cooperative forms of learning, but also has some very important differences.

Cooperative learning occurs when students work together to accomplish shared learning goals. In cooperative learning activities, small groups of learners work together as a team to solve a problem, complete a task, or accomplish a common goal. Educational researchers David Johnson and Roger Johnson (1975) promote cooperative learning, but they argue that cooperative learning is a sort of sink-or-swim proposition, with students being dependent on one another for success.

Cooperative learning An approach to learning in which students share learning goals and work as a team toward achieving these goals.

The primary criticism of cooperative learning is that learning will sink to the level of the weakest participant in the group. Proponents of cooperative learning argue that the cooperative learning process is a better approximation of real life. They contrast cooperative learning with competitive and individualistic approaches to learning and believe that for sociological reasons children need to learn to cooperate more than to compete.

Interactive instruction recognizes the power and authenticity of cooperative and collaborative learning, but preserves an element of individual autonomy. How do these individual and collaborative elements compliment each other in an instructional setting? Think about the work the children in FIGURE 9.17 are doing. How might their work differ if it is interactive as opposed to being exclusively cooperative?

ADAPTING INTERACTIVE INSTRUCTION

Some students are more suited for interactive instruction than others. What can we do about students who are reluctant to participate in interactive activities? First, remember that with interactive instruction children are individually responsible for their learning. If students are reluctant to be involved in the activity and are thus limited in their ability to construct knowledge, we must find ways to facilitate their learning.

Because interactive instruction is dynamic, teachers can address unforeseen circumstances that emerge when students interact. This may involve adapting for individual learners' needs.

When adapting instruction, consider how you can address any discomfort a student may have with others. If a student is uncomfortable with specific students in the group, changing groups may resolve the problem. If the student is simply shy, then there needs to be a safe and comfortable environment in which he can express his ideas. The student may need you, the teacher,

FIGURE 9.17

Children working together in a group as part of a larger interactive activity

to be at his side. Or you might allow the student to work by himself or to work with different materials, using images or even written materials. Some students may be uninvolved because they are having difficulty working with the materials, in which case they can be provided with other resources.

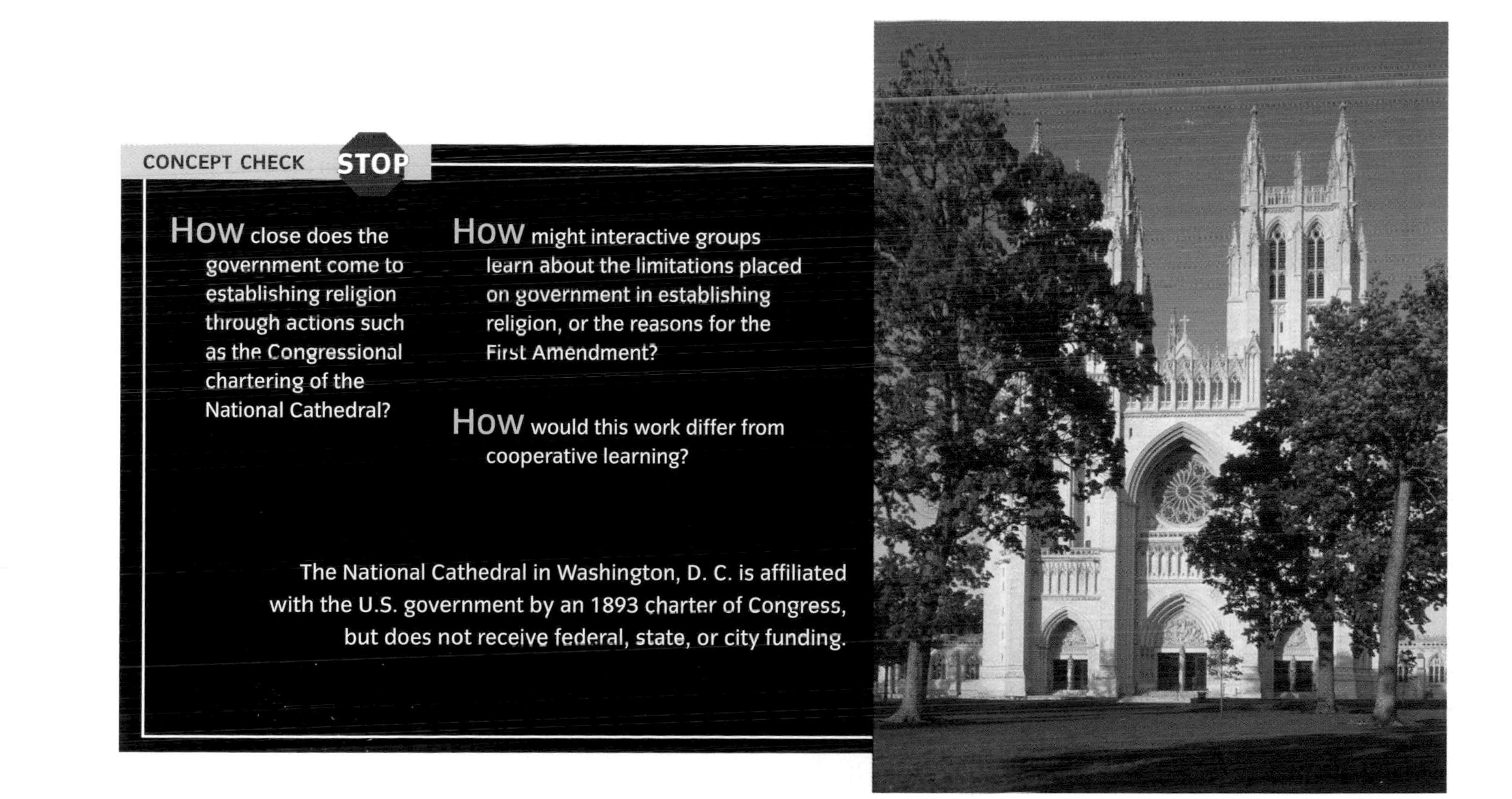

CONCEPT CHECK STOP

HOW close does the government come to establishing religion through actions such as the Congressional chartering of the National Cathedral?

HOW might interactive groups learn about the limitations placed on government in establishing religion, or the reasons for the First Amendment?

HOW would this work differ from cooperative learning?

The National Cathedral in Washington, D. C. is affiliated with the U.S. government by an 1893 charter of Congress, but does not receive federal, state, or city funding.

Using Textbooks in Social Studies

LEARNING OBJECTIVES

Recognize the role of textbooks in elementary social studies.

Describe the limitations of social studies textbooks.

Consider methods for using and supplementing social studies textbooks.

Textbooks are very important in social studies. No other resource is as widely available and commonly used as the textbook. Novice teachers may even use textbooks to learn content themselves. It is important to carefully consider how to use textbooks in the classroom. In this section, we look at some general approaches to using textbooks as well as a procedure for determining the potential uses of textbooks.

THREE APPROACHES TO USING TEXTBOOKS

Although there are many ways to use textbooks in the social studies classroom, we will focus on three distinct approaches. Think about how each of these approaches can be adapted and how the ideas described relate to one another and might even overlap.

Background Reading

Textbooks can provide children with a rich source of background on subject matter featured in a classroom activity. In fact, one of the most common homework assignments in social studies is to read from a textbook in preparation for the next day. While this might be a good strategy (particularly for upper elementary grades), the teacher must take several things into consideration. No textbook-reading homework assignment should be made without introducing the materials and conducting a pre-reading activity. Pre-reading activities may include any number of scaffolding designs to support student readings, such as:

- Guiding questions—A set of questions designed to either heighten students' awareness or target their reading.
- Outline—A simple listing in outline form of the main and subtopics in a reading passage.
- Main idea—A presentation of the main idea(s) presented in the textbook passage.

Consider the book about Abraham Lincoln that the young man in FIGURE 10.8 is reading. What are some guiding questions that might serve as a pre-reading activity about Lincoln's biography? How about an outline or main idea from the same text?

Background textbook reading can also take place in class as preparation for an activity. There are numerous strategies for reading in class. One good thing about reading in class is the assurance that all students have a direct opportunity to engage the text. Also, the closeness in time between the reading and the follow-up activity may be helpful. Of course, classroom reading takes up time, and some teachers may think textbook reading outside the class is more efficient. The decision about when to read should follow a consideration of two factors. First, if reading the textbook material is essential to success on some follow-up activ-

FIGURE 10.8

Fourth grade student reads book about Abraham Lincoln. How can teachers use textbooks such as this one for background reading?

ity, then it makes sense to read in class. Second, if the teacher wants to work directly on reading skills, then it also makes sense to read in class.

Challenge Reading Sometimes the textbook is insufficient as a resource for student learning. In fact, textbook information can be out of date, misleading, or even inaccurate. In his bestselling book, *Lies My History Teacher Told Me,* James Lowen critiques several leading high school textbooks. His findings suggest that textbooks are well behind on leading scholarship, often reflect narrow mindedness, and can be culturally insensitive. The extent to which elementary textbooks suffer from the same problems has been equally well documented (see Bracey, 1993 for one such study).

Given the limitations of textbooks, teachers may want to have students read certain passages in an effort to challenge and possibly revise ideas put forth by the authors. Of course, with young learners such activities require careful attention to the children's desire to know and be confident with their answers. Challenge reading should not focus on questioning the truth. Instead it should be about specific facts or ideas that might be out of date, misleading, or even inaccurate.

For example, consider the very common yet evolving and complicated story of the first appearance of humans in North America. The 1927 discovery in Folsom, New Mexico of fluted projectile points embedded in the rib cage of an extinct ancient bison cemented long standing claims that humans lived in North America before these animals went extinct. Megafauna (large animals) like the ancient bison became extinct during the last ice age at the end of the Pleistocene Era about 11,000 years ago. For decades, elementary textbooks have told the story of humans migrating across an ice bridge between modern Alaska and Russia about 12,000 years ago. Humans quickly migrated to the southern edge of the ice shield where they populated the Americas—or so the story goes.

A mounting collection of evidence today suggests that humans may have been in North and even South America 20,000, 30,000, even 40,000 years ago. Teachers must stay abreast of these new discoveries and can explore these with their students using textbook passages as starting points to inquiries into the expanding story of human life in North America.

FIGURE 10.9

These artifacts were found at the Topper archaeological site near Allendale, South Carolina.

More recent research has been conducted by archaeologists who used carbon-dating of carbon found near human-made artifacts such as the ones shown in FIGURE 10.9. The carbon-dating suggests that humans existed in North American perhaps 50,000 years ago. Although this finding is controversial and not fully accepted in the archaeological community, the data present a strong challenge to the existing belief that the earliest human life in North America goes back only 12,000 years.

Reading for Skills: Vocabulary and Pre-Reading Teachers can use textbooks as a source for developing reading skills. Although textbook material may not be suitable for learning about narrative elements such as plot and character, textbooks can be used to help children develop their vocabulary and learn how to decode. John Hoge (1986) has described two common problems with textbooks, including what he calls the "heavy technical concept load" of textbooks and the "thin" descriptions that may accompany content explanations. Difficult concepts are often identified by textbook writers and listed as vocabulary terms, but teachers must also scan textbook materials for terms and words that might be unfamiliar to their students.

Thin descriptions are a product of the economics of textbook publishing and the desire to address as much curriculum-based content as possible. Pressure to include as much content as possible results in shallow and often underdeveloped content. Teachers must supplement textbook material with pre-reading activities and other scaffolds such as direct explanation.

TEXTBOOK STRUCTURE AND ANALYSIS

No two textbooks are alike. Teachers must be adept at determining the unique value of their textbooks. Having said this, we can address some commonalities among textbooks, particularly revolving around methods for organizing material. Beginning in the earliest grades, students need to learn that a book consists of a spine, a front cover, a title and author page, a table of contents, and an index, as well as sections or chapters. Students need to learn to read material, both text and visual, from left to right and top to bottom. They need to understand how pages are numbered and where to find the page number on the page. Later, students need to learn how to scan a book and locate material within a book using an index, outline, or table of contents. Students can learn to recognize features in books and know how to use these features.

LIMITATIONS OF THE TEXTBOOK

No single social studies resource is as important and as maligned as the textbook. The textbook is the only resource that all children are guaranteed to have at almost all times under almost all circumstances. In many ways, the textbook represents the official wisdom of the field. Its position as a learning resource is unmatched. Having said this, textbooks are often looked down upon as inadequate and unrepresentative of knowledge in the field that they represent. Why this inconsistency? There are several answers, which can help us understand how best to use textbooks in social studies instruction.

Teams of authors often write social studies textbooks. Although there may be a single author on the cover, there are likely multiple contributing authors. Textbook publishers and lead authors want to make use of expertise in specialized areas, but the consequence is often unevenness. The authors' voices have to be muted for the sake of consistency. This generally makes textbooks less interesting and less narrative. At the same time, it enables us to use textbooks in segments. Unlike a novel or a work of history by a single author, textbooks are easily broken into small standalone parts. With most textbooks, teachers can assign short passages to students, without having students read text prior to the selection.

Another limitation of the textbook results from the market and social forces that drive publication. Textbooks are purchased by local school systems through a public system of vetting that includes input from all interested parties. Textbook publishers have to target large markets where they can sell a lot of books and make a profit. Most states require that local school systems buy books from a preapproved list. If a book doesn't make the list in a state, it cannot be purchased. Consequentially, textbook publishers work hard to get on the list in large states such as Texas and California. The approval process involves interested groups (public and private) lobbying textbook makers to include "their story" or to be sensitive to issues that they find important. The process is very democratic, but often results in a distilled book designed more to not offend than to challenge.

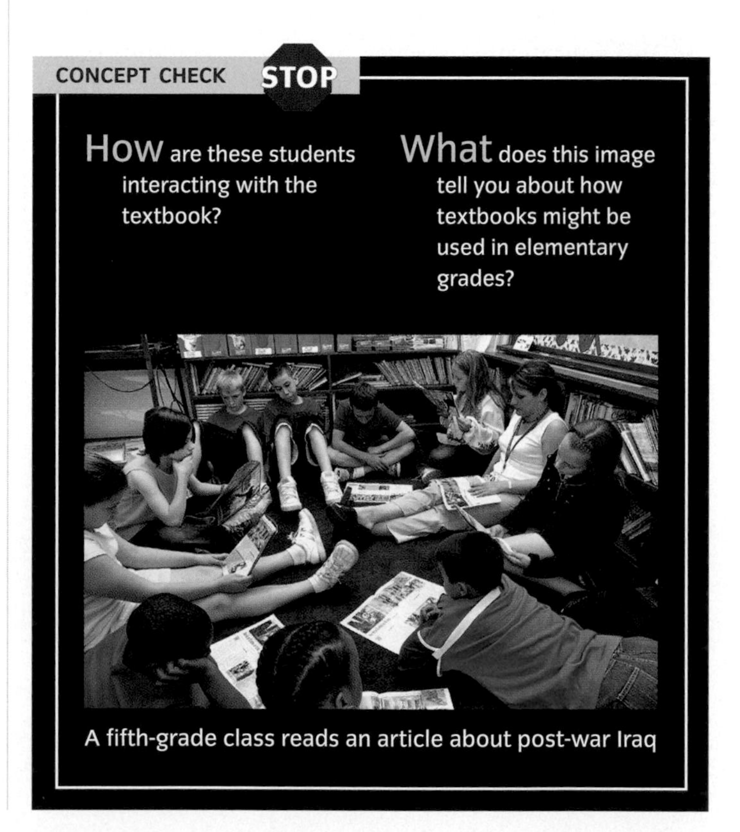

A fifth-grade class reads an article about post-war Iraq

Using Authentic Texts in Social Studies

LEARNING OBJECTIVES

Recognize the importance of authentic texts in social studies.

Recognize the characteristics of authentic intellectual work.

Identify various authentic learning materials.

Teachers must strive to make social studies as authentic as possible. The floating classroom depicted in **FIGURE 10.10** is an example of an authentic classroom context.

In the early part of the 20th century when social studies was in its infancy, John Dewey described authentic learning experiences as the real-life activities that when undertaken provide learners with powerful learning opportunities. Dewey found fault with psychologists' efforts to remove human action from its context. This belief led him to argue for learning to take place in the context of knowledge use such as the learning taking place in the floating classroom in **FIGURE 10.10**. For Dewey, learning in social studies required that learners engage the places where social knowledge is constructed—places like a kitchen, a factory, or an office. Learning in these environments requires some of the following conditions.

- Students are interested in the subject matter.
- Student learning is directly connected to the real world outside the classroom.
- Students are actively inquiring, using higher-level skills, about a question or problem.
- Learning is not tied to one discipline, but is instead interdisciplinary.
- Students share or act on what they have learned.

AUTHENTIC INTELLECTUAL WORK

Fred Newmann has written extensively about authentic teaching and learning in social studies. His work on authentic pedagogy and school restructuring (Newmann and Associates, 1996) led Newmann to develop a concept he calls **authentic intellectual work** (Scheurman & Newmann, 1998). Authentic intellectual work involves three criteria.

Authentic intellectual work Learning activities that enable students to develop knowledge in real-world contexts.

1. Construction of knowledge: learning through analysis, evaluation, and other active high-level tasks.
2. Disciplined inquiry: in-depth learning on focused topics.
3. Value beyond school: the production of usable knowledge that has "personal, aesthetic, or social" significance outside of school.

Authentic intellectual work requires that students make use of a range of literacy skills as they interpret, analyze, evaluate, and otherwise work with materials and information. To illustrate the relationship between literacy and authentic intellectual work, let's look at a third-grade lesson on customs around the world, "In the Classroom: Authentic learning about customs," on page 272.

FIGURE 10.10

This floating classroom was part of Geography in Action/Rivers in 2001 and took place aboard an Earth Conservation Corps boat on the Anacostia River, which runs through Washington, D.C. and Maryland.

Students can look for central ideas, plots, potential uses, and the characters that might have used the artifact. They can consider what the artifact tells us about the person or people who created it. All of these "reading" activities can be completed by looking at or investigating the artifact. Like a reading activity, artifact reading may require support and scaffolds in the form of pre-reading, questions, or reading guides.

The artifact in **FIGURE 10.12** "says" a great deal. For one, its steel construction is evidence of the dramatic advantage the Spanish had over the Incas. Although outnumbered 40,000 to 300, how were the Spanish able to conquer the Incas? How is this sword evidence of a possible answer to this question?

FIGURE 10.12

A sword bearing the initials "FP" is exhibited in the Gold Museum of Lima, Peru. It belonged to the conqueror of the Incas, Francisco Pizarro.

Newspapers and Magazines Social studies teachers can make active use of newspapers and magazines. These reading resources provide valuable subject matter for learning as well as opportunities for students to learn how to engage resources that enable them to better function in society.

Web Sites and Web Logs A wide range of new resources is available on the World Wide Web. Because of the low barriers to publication, the quality of these resources is sometimes questionable. Having students engage Web sites and Web logs (blogs) enables teachers to present and teach critical media skills that will enable students to make effective use of these resources. Of course, very careful attention must be given to the use of the Web in elementary settings. All activities must be very closely monitored and limited. Resources must be carefully vetted, and students must not be allowed to venture outside confined parameters established by the teacher and administrators in the school.

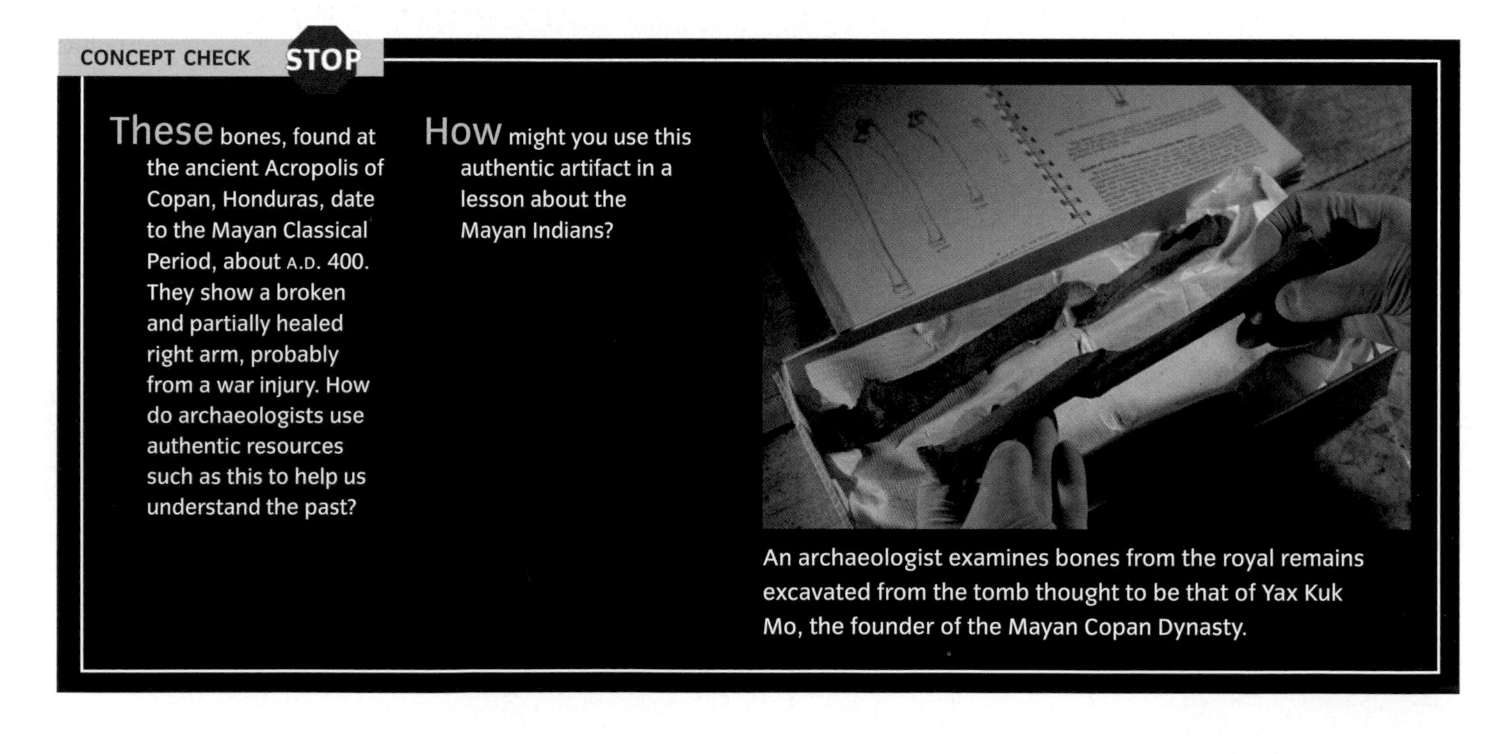

CONCEPT CHECK STOP

These bones, found at the ancient Acropolis of Copan, Honduras, date to the Mayan Classical Period, about A.D. 400. They show a broken and partially healed right arm, probably from a war injury. How do archaeologists use authentic resources such as this to help us understand the past?

How might you use this authentic artifact in a lesson about the Mayan Indians?

An archaeologist examines bones from the royal remains excavated from the tomb thought to be that of Yax Kuk Mo, the founder of the Mayan Copan Dynasty.

Writing in Social Studies

LEARNING OBJECTIVES

Consider the importance of writing in social studies.

Identify ways students can learn social studies through writing exercises.

Compare approaches to writing for learning in social studies.

Writing plays a central role in social studies. It is the most common form of expression for students when they are conveying their knowledge. Virtually all social studies activities should include some element of writing. Student writing might simply consist of taking notes or answering questions. Outside of formal language arts, social studies is probably the most important class for the development of students' writing skills.

WRITING FOR SOCIAL STUDIES

In this section, we examine how to integrate writing into social studies—using the writing process, and with attention to national standards. Writing in social studies should include three basic processes: pre-writing, drafting, and revising as shown in the "Process Diagram: The Writing Process". National standards for reading and

The writing process FIGURE 10.13

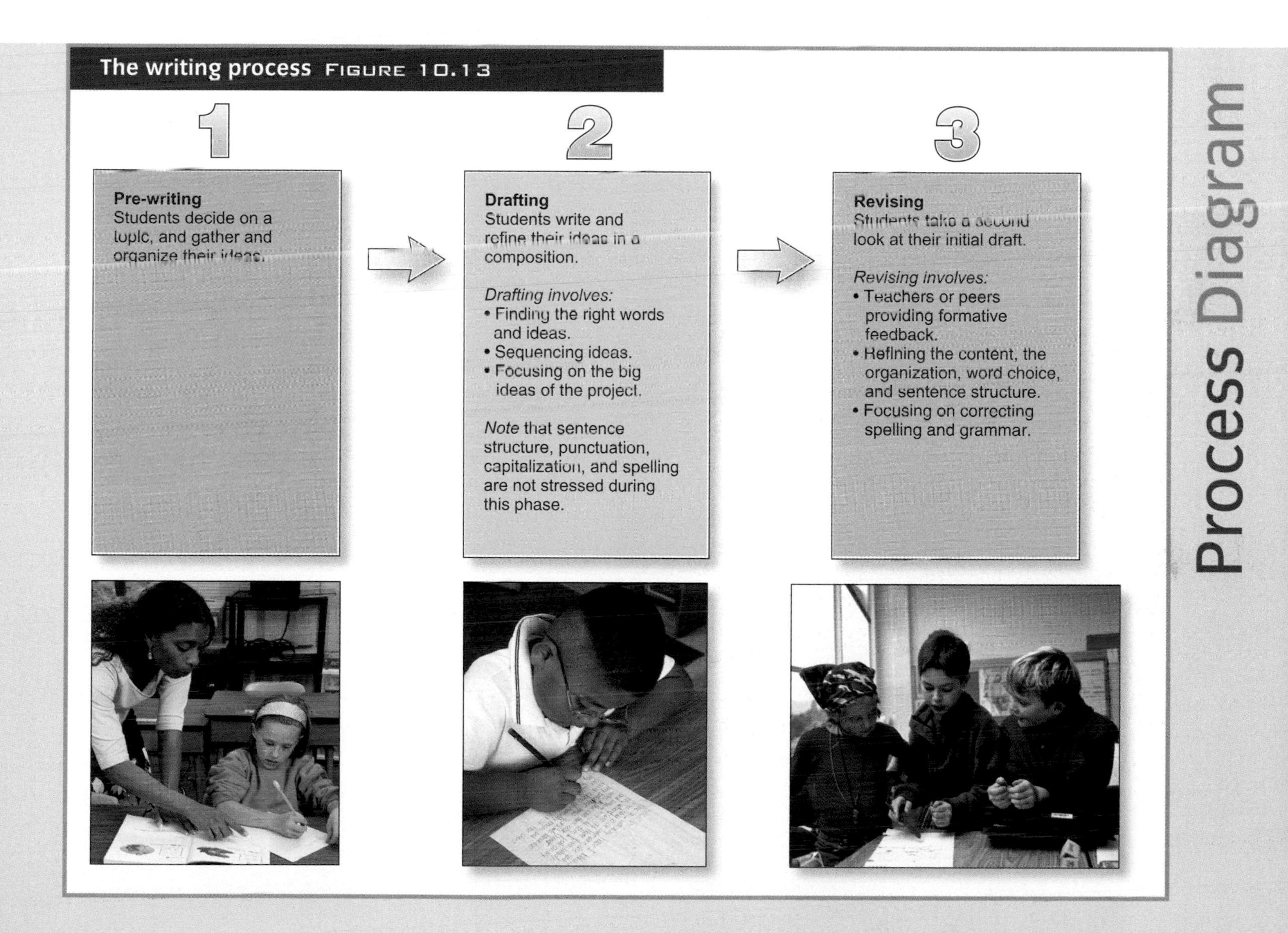

writing can guide your planning for incorporating reading and writing in social studies contexts.

The National Council for Teachers of English (NCTE) and the International Reading Association (IRA) jointly developed Read Write Think (www.ReadWriteThink.org), a powerful compendium of resources and information about literacy. Although primarily aimed at language arts, this resource can provide valuable guidance in planning for writing activities in social studies. A collection of standards for reading and writing form the core of the collaborative work of NCTE and IRA. Two of these standards directly address writing.

> *Standard 5* Students employ a wide range of strategies as they write and use different writing process elements appropriately to communicate with different audiences for a variety of purposes.

> *Standard 6* Students apply knowledge of language structure, language conventions (e.g., spelling and punctuation), media techniques, figurative language, and genres to create, critique, and discuss print and nonprint texts.

The application of these standards in social studies activities should be a priority. Social studies is a subject that can provide students with valuable opportunities to further develop knowledge and skills learned in language arts. The social studies lesson, "Lesson: Using Writing Skills to Argue Alternative Energy Power," on pages 278–279, incorporates these standards. Like many consumers in the United States, fifth-grade teacher Vincente Diaz's daily budget is affected by the price of oil. Mr. Diaz's interest in oil prices motivated him to develop a social studies lesson for his class on alternative fuel sources.

WRITING FOR LEARNING

Writing serves multiple purposes. Some people write as a way to express an emotion or feeling. Others write in order to communicate to an audience. Still others write just to reflect or think through problems. In elementary social studies, teachers should encourage all forms of writing. Writing helps children form opinions and beliefs. Writing can help children think and develop knowledge, but most important, it enables children to develop an understanding of subject matter. Peter Elbow (1981, 2002) calls this process "writing for learning." It differs from writing that is meant to be a demonstration of what a student has learned. When students write for learning they are collecting thoughts and organizing ideas. Writing for learning is a process that students use as they develop their knowledge. Elbow's work focuses in part on how teachers can most effectively use writing to help students learn.

There are a number of approaches teachers can use to encourage writing for learning. Following are some practical classroom approaches for writing to learn.

Writing Aloud When we think aloud, we verbalize ideas in our head that reflect our emerging knowledge or ideas about something. Writing aloud is similar to this process; only students write down thoughts that are emerging as or just after some subject matter is presented. Writing aloud exercises should be short and focused and conducted as subject matter is presented.

Concept Writing When students are learning about a new concept they can track the development of their understanding through writing. In concept writing activities, students begin by writing what they know. Then students write a second version of their understanding of the concept. After the second writing, the teacher asks students to share their ideas about the concept. The teacher guides students toward some common understanding of the concept. After the discussion, students write a third explanation of the concept.

Writing It Out In this activity, the teacher gives the students three to five solutions to a problem. The students then begin to write about the prospects of each solution. The goal is to have students write about each solution and through their writing realize a best solution.

CONCEPT CHECK STOP

What are some specific "writing for learning" topics that might relate to the American Revolution? Think about the entire period, not just the winter at Valley Forge.

How might an elementary teacher engage students in each of the three writing strategies in an activity about the American Revolution?

This image of the American Revolution depicts some of the suffering during the winter of 1777 at Valley Forge, Pennsylvania by soldiers in the American Continental army under the command of George Washington.

Planning for Active Learning

11

Patrick Lowry, a student teacher in Anna Joliet's fourth-grade classroom, was concerned that the students weren't involved enough. "Sometimes they just don't seem to care," Patrick told his cooperating teacher. Anna had heard this before, and knew that involving students in classwork is vital to success.

Patrick was particularly concerned about a planned lesson focused on work. He was not sure how to get students interested in the topic. Ms. Joliet suggested, "Let's put our students to work. We'll create an office and have each student complete a job." Patrick began to plan the lesson and decided to have a factory and an office. Students would experience both work settings. Ms. Joliet cautioned Patrick, "Remember, we only have a certain amount of time each day for social studies." For Patrick, the subject matter was interesting; he researched, prepared materials, and read about factory and office workplace structure.

The next day, Patrick gave Ms. Joliet a plan that involved the teacher talking for most of the time and students completing tasks the teacher created. Ms. Joliet liked the attention to subject matter, but reminded Patrick, "You were concerned that the students were not interested in the class. Do you think this will help?" Patrick admitted that his lesson might not interest students. He revised the lesson to give students more voice in how the factory and the office were set up—even letting the students decide what they would produce. Students had to learn how offices and factories operate and had creative opportunities to learn the material.

Afterward, Patrick and Ms. Joliet agreed that the students enjoyed the lesson. Patrick learned how to think about teaching from the students' point of view, and how to involve students by giving them something to do.

What are the people in this picture doing? How do these jobs illustrate certain kinds of work? How does this work compare to other forms of work in the United States? What might elementary school students need to learn about working in the 21st century?

NATIONAL GEOGRAPHIC

Middelgrunden Wind Park off Copenhagen, Denmark

teacher should apply specific criteria for assessment, which should be provided to students before they begin their writing. The criteria could be as follows:

- Letters to the newspaper should address specific issues, include a summary of your position on the issue, and offer some proposed action on the issue.
- Poems should have words that are clear and use words describing the senses (see, smell, taste, feel, hear), rhythm, and emotion, and should focus on an original topic.
- Magazine-style essays should include an overview of an alternative energy issue and a description of some example of how the issue affects people in the world.
- A policy briefing should include an introductory summary and five points describing a particular position on alternative energy.
- A short story should have a beginning, middle, and end, as well as a minimum of three characters and an important/dramatic event.

Literacy and the Social Studies Curriculum

Learning Objectives

Identify the ways that social studies curriculums address writing.

Distinguish among approaches to writing in social studies as inferred from the curriculum.

How does the social studies curriculum lend itself to the inclusion of literacy instruction? In elementary grades, we might argue that social studies is, more than anything else, about literacy. Social studies teachers have important decisions to make about the manner in which they take content highlighted in the curriculum and turn that into something teachable.

As we have seen in previous chapters, teachers must evolve social studies content in subject matter suitable for instruction. If teachers are required to emphasize literacy skills, then it makes sense for them to include these skills in social studies lessons.

LITERACY IN THE CURRICULUM

Local and state social studies curriculums present opportunities for students to engage in literacy activities. All curriculums either directly or indirectly require students to read textbooks as well as additional stories or books. Teachers must make decisions about how their students will learn about specific curriculum content, and this often includes reading.

Think about how a first-grade teacher might plan instruction about national symbols and monuments. In the Henrico County, Virginia first-grade social studies curriculum, students are expected to "recognize the symbols and traditional practices that honor and foster patriotism in the United States by identifying the bald eagle, Washington Monument, and Statue of Liberty."

How can we put this standard into pedagogical action? One option is to have students read about national monuments. A series of books by Lloyd G. Douglas, written for emerging readers, tells about monuments and symbols in the United States such as the bald eagle depicted in **FIGURE 10.14**. Douglas's books include *The Bald Eagle, The White House, The Statue of Liberty, The Liberty Bell*, and *The American Flag*. All of these can be incorporated into a lesson or lessons about national monuments and symbols.

Curriculums also set forth expectations that students use specific written skills to express their knowledge. This writing might focus on social studies subject matter or might be writing in social studies aimed at developing writing skills. Developing writing skills through writing in or about social studies serves multiple purposes and is now a common expectation in elementary schools.

The Visualizing feature includes guidelines for revising and editing that can be used to improve students' writing skills.

FIGURE 10.14

Why is the bald eagle such an important symbol in the United States? How can we teach children the importance of this and other symbols? What should students read about the symbolism of the bald eagle?

Writing in social studies should focus on the development of writing skills. Such activities might include revising and editing. How might we situate a writing activity in a social studies class on the history of Walt Disney? The global reach of American culture, in this case Disney, is extensive. Look at the display in this Hong Kong taxicab dashboard. What do these figurines say about the reach of Disney? We might ask students to write about how these figurines illustrate Disney's cultural influence.

In the writing process, teachers can use the following guidelines to scaffold students in revising and editing. Students would use the checklists to check their own work.

Sample Revision Checklist

- ❑ Is the beginning interesting?
- ❑ Did I include enough supporting details?
- ❑ Is my conclusion logical?
- ❑ Can new ideas be added?
- ❑ Should some ideas be rearranged?

Sample Editing/Proofreading Checklist

- ❑ I correctly spelled all words.
- ❑ I wrote each sentence as a complete thought.
- ❑ I began each sentence with a capital letter.
- ❑ I used capital letters correctly in other places.
- ❑ I indented each paragraph.

Taxi interior with McDonald promotional cartoon figures on a street in Hong Kong

LITERACY, SOCIAL STUDIES, AND LANGUAGE ARTS

Language arts occupies a very important place in elementary school. Compared to social studies (comparisons are unavoidable) language arts is by many estimations more important. This reality is reflected in testing, time allotted to instruction, teacher training and expertise, as well as resources allocated for classroom materials. Instead of bemoaning the fact that social studies plays a lesser role in the elementary classroom, we must consider how social studies can support the important and central work of literacy education in language arts. Teachers can accomplish this by using social studies materials in language arts lessons and by using language arts and literacy objectives in social studies lessons.

Although the primary goals of the subjects might differ, the opportunities for overlap are great. The National Council for the Social Studies has emphasized the importance of the connections between social studies and language arts in the NCSS Position Statement, "A Vision of Powerful Teaching and Learning in the Social Studies: Building Social Understanding and Civic Efficacy" (1992):

> Social studies is the integrated study of the social sciences and humanities to promote civic competence.

The connections between social studies and language arts are numerous. Some of the more important connections include the following:

- Focusing on the comprehension of various forms of printed material
- Using text, visual, and graphical media for expression of knowledge
- Developing communicative skills

Social studies and language arts share ground in the humanities. Both subjects are sources of knowledge and human creativity.

CONCEPT CHECK STOP

Describe an activity involving both social studies and language arts that focuses on the concept of family.

How might students write about this family at Ellis Island in a language arts / social studies interdisciplinary activity?

A German immigrant family of one daughter and seven sons, at Ellis Island, New York, in about 1905.

What is happening in this picture?

- How might a child in the first or second grade read this image?
- What would children need to know in order to have the most meaningful understanding of this image?

This cartoon drawing, done in commemoration of Alexander Graham Bell's 100th birthday, shows that children of that period might have wanted to use the telephone to reach Santa Claus.

VISUAL SUMMARY

1 The Importance of Literacy

Literacy is at the heart of all instruction. It has been defined narrowly as reading and writing skills. More broadly, literacy skills include a host of things students do when they are locating and using learning materials. In social studies, literacy skills enable students to consider problems and issues and make decisions about how they should solve or address these problems.

VISUAL SUMMARY

2 Reading in Social Studies

Given the importance of text in social studies, reading plays a central role in social studies instruction. When teachers make pedagogical decisions about reading materials they must consider the subject matter, the curriculum, the amount of time available, and if they use a reading source, they must then adapt that source for use in the classroom. There are a number of reading methods that can be used in the classroom including popup reading, reading buddies, a reading festival, and shadow reading. When selecting and adapting reading materials, teachers can use specific tools to determine reading levels, including the Flesch-Kincaid grade-level reading scale.

$$(.39 \times \text{ASL}) + (11.8 \times \text{ASW}) - 15.59$$

ASL = average sentence length (the number of words divided by the number of sentences)

ASW = average number of syllables per word (the number of syllables divided by the number of words)

3 Using Textbooks in Social Studies

Textbooks play a central role in all classroom instruction. There are several ways to incorporate textbooks into elementary social studies instruction, including using the textbook for background reading as well as reading for analytical and skills-based purposes. Textbooks can be useful, but also have significant limitations. Textbooks typically have little narrative value, and they often lack the coherence of historical fiction and other single-author works.

4 Using Authentic Texts in Social Studies

Authentic texts include resources that were produced by people who participated in the subject of the texts; or the texts are about something that will resonate with learners given the learners' life experiences. The use of authentic texts enables authentic learning related to students' lives. Newmann calls such work authentic intellectual work and argues that this includes knowledge construction, disciplined inquiry, and some value beyond school. Authentic texts might include historical documents, newspapers, maps, or Web-based resources.

5 Writing in Social Studies

In addition to reading, writing also plays a central role in social studies. The application of standards for writing instruction such as the Read Write Think program can be integrated into social studies instruction. Writing in social studies serves the purposes of communicating, emoting, expressing, thinking, and understanding. Social studies teachers might use specific writing strategies such as writing out loud and concept writing.

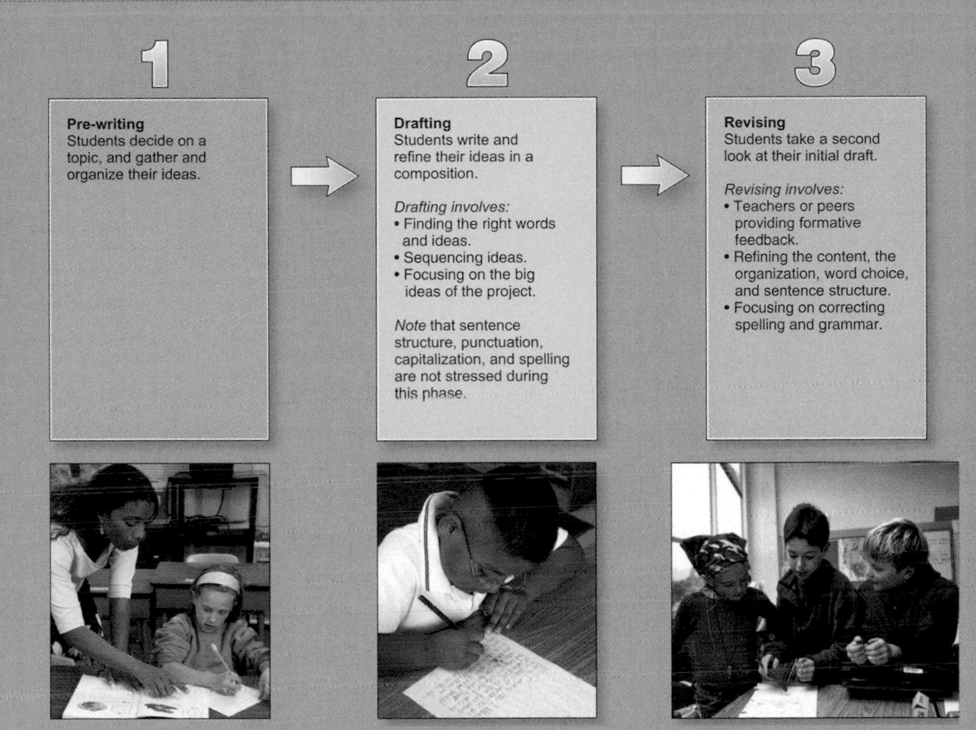

6 Literacy and the Social Studies Curriculum

The elementary social studies curriculum offers plenty of opportunities to engage students in literacy-related activities. Given current national efforts to emphasize reading and writing skills, social studies should include student experiences in both of these areas. The connections between language arts and social studies provide interdisciplinary opportunities to explore a wide range of related activities.

KEY TERMS

- **literacy,** p. 258
- **authentic intellectual work,** p. 271
- **artifact,** p. 273

CRITICAL AND CREATIVE THINKING QUESTIONS

Literacy in social studies involves critical thinking. When students think critically, they ask questions that help them better understand some poorly understood or misunderstood idea or thing.

- Is there anything unusual about the photo below?
- How does this photo further demonstrate the influence of American culture?

A cartoon of Donald Duck in a car with one of his nephews is painted on the side of a building in Amman, Jordan.

SELF-TEST

1. What is literacy?

2. Why is literacy important?

3. What are the literacy skills that the National Council for the Social Studies says are important in social studies?

4. Which of the following is *not* a strategy for enhancing students' understanding of text as they read?
   a. the activation of prior or background knowledge
   b. active engagement in the content
   c. metacognition
   d. defining vocabulary words

5. What are the literacy skills related to the work of the archaeologists who make arguments about human history based on artifacts such as these?

6. How can each of these pre-reading activities better position students for meaningful reading experiences?
   a. guiding questions
   b. outline
   c. main idea

7. What did John Dewey suggest were some of the conditions for authentic learning?

8. Label the three main steps in the writing process on the figure below.

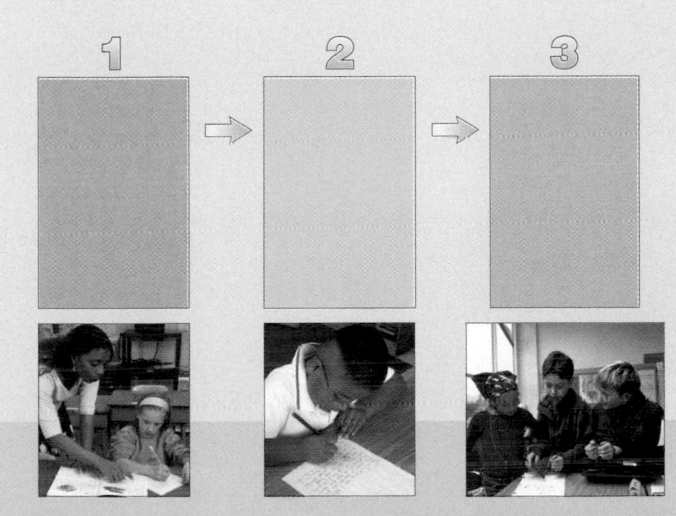

9. How are classrooms such as this one authentic?

10. How can social studies teachers work with language arts teachers to focus on the development of literacy skills? What sort of literacy is needed to "read" a map such as this one?

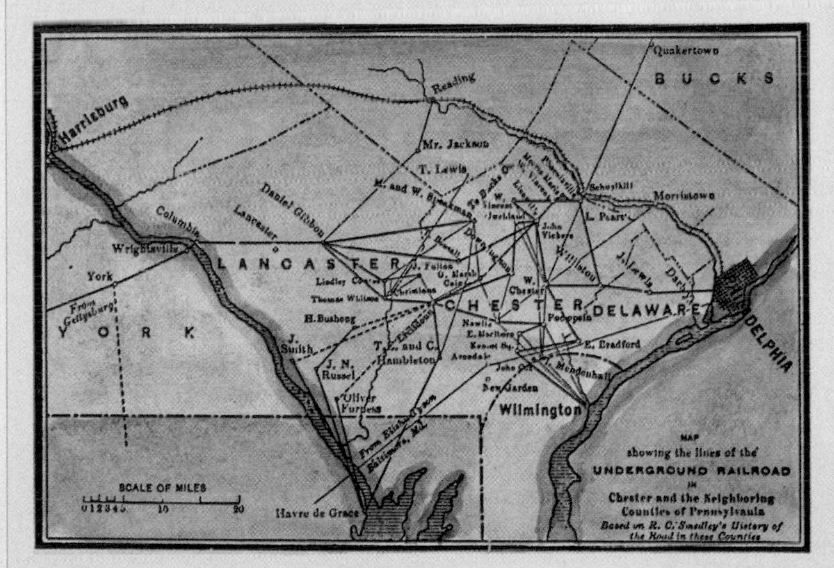

Planning for Active Learning 11

Patrick Lowry, a student teacher in Anna Joliet's fourth-grade classroom, was concerned that the students weren't involved enough. "Sometimes they just don't seem to care," Patrick told his cooperating teacher. Anna had heard this before, and knew that involving students in classwork is vital to success.

Patrick was particularly concerned about a planned lesson focused on work. He was not sure how to get students interested in the topic. Ms. Joliet suggested, "Let's put our students to work. We'll create an office and have each student complete a job." Patrick began to plan the lesson and decided to have a factory and an office. Students would experience both work settings. Ms. Joliet cautioned Patrick, "Remember, we only have a certain amount of time each day for social studies." For Patrick, the subject matter was interesting; he researched, prepared materials, and read about factory and office workplace structure.

The next day, Patrick gave Ms. Joliet a plan that involved the teacher talking for most of the time and students completing tasks the teacher created. Ms. Joliet liked the attention to subject matter, but reminded Patrick, "You were concerned that the students were not interested in the class. Do you think this will help?" Patrick admitted that his lesson might not interest students. He revised the lesson to give students more voice in how the factory and the office were set up—even letting the students decide what they would produce. Students had to learn how offices and factories operate and had creative opportunities to learn the material.

Afterward, Patrick and Ms. Joliet agreed that the students enjoyed the lesson. Patrick learned how to think about teaching from the students' point of view, and how to involve students by giving them something to do.

What are the people in this picture doing? How do these jobs illustrate certain kinds of work? How does this work compare to other forms of work in the United States? What might elementary school students need to learn about working in the 21st century?

CHAPTER OUTLINE

Patrick Lowry learned that planning instruction is a continuous process that must include attention to the needs of students. Planning to teach social studies should involve the use of many forms of knowledge, including:

- A teacher's knowledge of subject matter
- The curriculum
- The community
- The purposes of social studies

However, if teachers do not take into consideration the needs of their students, all the planning in the world will not make the lesson effective.

In this chapter, we present planning for instruction as an effort to encourage active student involvement in the learning process. We will look at learning theories and specific ways to plan for active learning in elementary social studies.

When preparing for active instruction, teachers must plan for student-centered activities that require teachers to pay close attention to how students learn and to the progress of individual learning. The chapter begins with an overview of active learning in social studies. Then, we examine specifically how to plan for active learning: initial considerations for planning active learning, actual planning of the instruction, and teaching and reflection involved in active learning.

Active Learning in Social Studies

LEARNING OBJECTIVES

Define active learning.

Explain how active learning emerges from authentic daily social studies instruction.

Analyze the connections between active learning and social studies subject matter.

Imagine planning to teach a class. What are you thinking about—yourself teaching or the students learning? If you are like most teachers, you think first about the act of teaching. There is nothing wrong with planning for instruction by considering the actions of the teacher, but active learning requires student involvement and thus requires careful planning for student activities (**FIGURE 11.1**).

Considerations about how to actively involve students in the learning process are critical to success in teaching. Later, we will look at strategies, but first let's examine some of the theory about why active involvement in learning is so important.

Active learning
A learning process that involves students doing something in order to learn.

Active learning requires students to engage in the learning process rather than passively receive information. Active learning involves doing something other than listening—such as reading, writing, talking or discussing, making decisions, solving problems, working together, planning, organizing, comparing, analyzing, synthesizing, and evaluating. Let's consider what it means to be active in the classroom and begin with our own actions as teachers.

FIGURE 11.1

What does it mean for students to be active? How might you describe the activity of these students?

GOALS FOR ACTIVE INSTRUCTION

Teaching elementary school grades is a very active enterprise. Think about all the actions teachers must take in the course of a typical day. Consider all the movement and talk teachers engage in when teaching. At the end of the day, teachers are often physically tired from all this activity. Students need to have these same opportunities for activity in the classroom, but it is not uncommon for teachers to try to limit their students' activity. Consider two significant classroom management issues in elementary school—too much noise and too much movement. Of course, teachers need to have control over the classroom. They cannot allow off-task or disruptive student activity. At the same time, we know that active students are better able to learn, so how can teachers achieve a balance?

There are four goals that teachers should strive to meet when planning for active instruction in elementary social studies.

1. ***Create interest and excitement about learning.*** By getting children interested in what they are about to study, they will be more likely to engage the activity. Generating interest requires that teachers be creative and adapt curriculum content given their students' interest.
2. ***Have students produce something.*** Most young children love to create, and using this natural instinct enables them to learn otherwise remote or abstract content.
3. ***Give students a role in setting up the procedures for completing their work.*** When students are empowered to make decisions about how they will complete an activity, they are more willing to actually engage in the activity.
4. ***Connect the learning experience to other life experience.*** The more children can see that their school work is connected to and even part of their whole life, the more meaningful that work becomes. As students make these connections, they actively assimilate new knowledge into existing schemas of knowledge.

Let's consider an example of involving students in active learning about work. **FIGURE 11.2** shows the construction of the pyramids in Egypt. This was a monumental effort that required work unlike any another construction project in history. In this image, stone masons work in the outer enclosure of the pyramid of King Se'n-Wosret I (XII Dynasty, reign of Se'n-Wosret I, 1980–1939 B.C.) at El Licht. Some scholars think the heavy limestone blocks that were used to build the pyramids were moved on wooden rails by teams of workers as is depicted in the image. How might you engage students in active learning about the construction of Egyptian pyramids?

FIGURE 11.2

Stone masons work in the outer enclosure of the pyramid of King Se'n-Wosret I (1980–1939 B.C.) at El Lisht, Egypt.

ACTIVE LEARNING AND AUTHENTIC SOCIAL STUDIES

Elementary school teachers must help students understand how actions students take when learning social studies are connected to the real world. These real-world actions might be thought of as authentic. By **authentic**, we mean that students are engaging in learning opportunities that connect to their world and reflect the goal of preparing students for participation in democratic life. In Chapter 10, we read about Fred Newmann and Geoffrey Scheurman's ideas on authentic intellectual work. The idea of authentic intellectual work emerges from the general concept of authenticity in pedagogy and learning. Scheurman and Newmann (1996) have suggested that authentic learning activities should be developed given five standards or considerations. Authentic learning activities should:

Authentic
Situated in the real world and connected to experiences that are a part of daily life.

1. Encourage higher-order thinking.
2. Be an opportunity for students to develop deep knowledge of the subject matter they are studying.
3. Connect to the world beyond the classroom.
4. Include substantive conversation.
5. Allow teachers to provide social support for student achievement.

Each of these standards for authentic learning requires careful planning. An example of how an elementary social studies lesson plan might incorporate these five standards of authentic learning is presented in "Lesson: Weather and the Earth's Movements," on pages 294–295.

ACTIVE LEARNING AND SUBJECT MATTER

Different subject matter demands different forms of active learning. What makes learning about history an active process is different from what makes learning about geography an active process. The key differences are rooted in the disciplines themselves and the manner in which knowledge is created in the disciplines. For example, a historian might use a map differently than a geographer might use it. This is important because if we use resources for purposes that are uncertain or in conflict, our teaching might be uninspired, tedious, or even boring. The general goal of elementary social studies instruction is not to make little historians or little geographers out of students. Instead, the goal is to help them become aware of how experts use knowledge in their field, given the students' needs to learn in authentic and active contexts.

Consider how historians, geographers, political scientists, sociologists, anthropologists, economists, or any other social studies experts might consider a social issue such as world population distribution. Different experts might use the same resources to address similar problems in different ways (FIGURE 11.3).

- A historian might consider trends in population migration across the Earth and study a map of the Earth for clues about why and how people move from place to place.
- A geographer might consider the limitations and possibilities presented by physical geography for people living in certain places.
- An economist might consider the availability of labor or capital in different places in the world and represent that information on a map.

Ultimately, social studies draws on all of these experts to study specific subject matter in active and real-life contexts.

The authentic Mesopotamian world map shown in "Concept Check" illustrates a different understanding of the world than we have today. The circular image at the bottom represents what the Mesopotamians knew of the Earth. Babylon was placed at the middle of the map. The lines represent rivers. The small circular areas were other cities. Extending out from the larger circle are triangular points representing islands (only one is shown here).

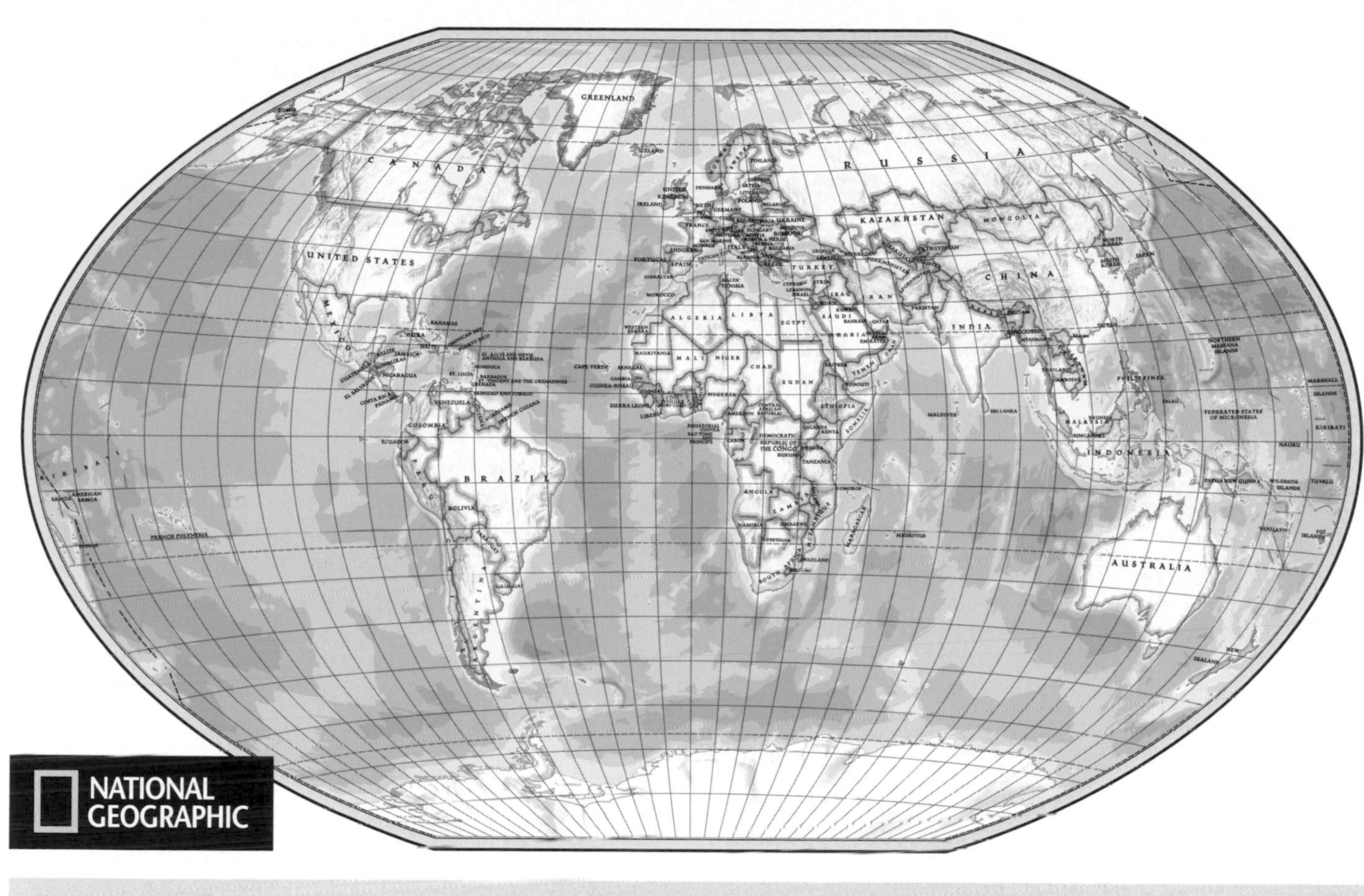

FIGURE 11.3

How would a historian use this map differently than a geographer to study world population? These differences should be evident when students use maps in social studies.

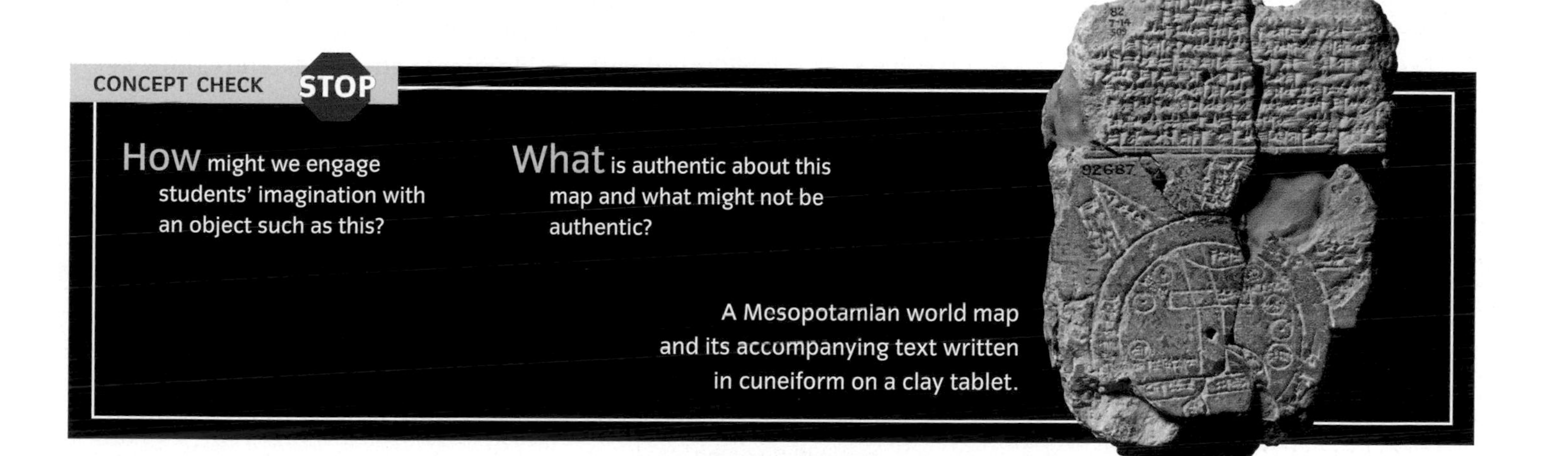

CONCEPT CHECK STOP

How might we engage students' imagination with an object such as this?

What is authentic about this map and what might not be authentic?

A Mesopotamian world map and its accompanying text written in cuneiform on a clay tablet.

Initial Considerations for Instructional Planning

Learning Objectives

Explain how teachers reorganize their content knowledge for planning purposes.

Describe some of the initial considerations teachers must make when transforming subject matter into pedagogical ideas, including curriculum and learner considerations.

Reflect on how teachers weave subject matter into explanative patterns when teaching about different but related topics over time.

nstructional planning involves a number of initial considerations that must be made by teachers before implementing a lesson plan. These considerations include reorganizing existing knowledge for the purpose of teaching, as well as other actions relating to curriculum, the selection of subject for a lesson, the development of instructional goals, making the material relevant for students, selecting materials, and connecting or weaving the ideas together.

REORGANIZING KNOWLEDGE: CONTENT TO SUBJECT MATTER

Planning for instruction should begin with teachers reviewing their content knowledge. The goal is to reorganize knowledge as subject matter. To begin this process, teachers determine important concepts, ideas, themes, events, movements, and people emphasized in their content knowledge.

As we saw in Chapter 10, teachers can distinguish content knowledge from subject matter in a very deliberate manner. Scholars in specific fields develop content knowledge. Subject matter is that content after it has been reorganized for K–12 settings. This reorganization is similar to the work that curriculum committees do when planning what will be taught in schools.

The process of creating subject matter focuses on making decisions about what might be relevant for the student to know. The identification of subject matter should arise from a careful consideration of the relative importance of the subject matter given pedagogical criteria. An example of how teachers might select subject matter from academic knowledge about clothing appears in "Social and Cultural Explorations" on pages 298–299.

TRANSFORMING SUBJECT MATTER INTO PEDAGOGICAL IDEAS

After reviewing academic content and reorganizing it as subject matter, teachers can begin to consider the subject matter in more specific pedagogical contexts. Teachers undertake a number of actions as they transform their knowledge into practical and personal pedagogical knowledge including:

- Considering state and local curriculum
- Narrowing subject matter content
- Justifying the subject matter given the purposes of education
- Personalizing the subject matter for the learners
- Selecting appropriate subject-based resources
- "Weaving" subject matter knowledge

In this section, we examine each of these actions teachers engage in when preparing material for specific pedagogical tasks.

Considering the Curriculum Planning to teach requires that teachers think about local and state curriculum. All teachers must be experts on their curriculum, basically internalizing the scope and sequence of the curriculum and understanding the details. The task at this point in the planning process is not to learn about curriculum, but to apply that knowledge. A firm understanding of the curriculum needs to be in place for teachers to effectively use it in the planning process. Teachers must identify the large bodies of subject matter for which they are expected to plan instruction. Teachers need to develop a sense of comfort with the amount of time they have and the depth to which they can plan for instruction.

Consider content on the North American colonial experience. Most elementary curriculums will include some subject matter focus on American colonies. For example, the fifth-grade curriculum for the public schools in Lexington, Massachusetts, requires that students "describe each colony geographically, economically, culturally, and politically." This simple statement includes large amounts of subject matter that the teacher must carefully narrow prior to planning for instruction.

Narrowing Subject Matter Planning for instruction requires that teachers narrow broad subject matter areas to manageable areas of instructional focus. In the following, "Visualizing: Connecting past to present" (**FIGURE 11.4**), we consider how to narrow the broad topic of Greek history to a manageable lesson.

Visualizing

The Narrowing of Subject Matter: Connecting Past to Present FIGURE 11.4

Let's begin by examining some commonly held beliefs about ancient Greeks. Which of these beliefs do these images conjure up?

How can teachers narrow the focus from this common and broad vision of Greek history to something more focused and instructional? One possibility is to make connections between the past and the present.

What are some obvious characteristics of Greek life that are both ancient and modern and result from the geography of Greece? Given knowledge of the geography of Greece, how might we even more clearly focus the subject for a lesson on ancient Greek history?

A Classic night view of the Parthenon and surrounding Acropolis in Athens, Greece.

B Statues of Socrates and Apollo in front of the Academy of Athens.

C This modern view of one of the three ancient harbors of Piraeus captures some clues about ancient life in Greece.

What to know about what to wear

In elementary school grades, children learn about clothing. In many states, including Texas, Wisconsin, Kentucky, and Nebraska, children in early grades are expected to distinguish various human needs including clothing. In Kentucky, elementary school students are expected to "recognize language, music, art, dress, food, literature, and folktales as elements of culture."

There is plenty of content knowledge related to the idea of dress and clothing. Learning expectations such as these require teachers to plan for instruction that will enable students to understand a wide range of cultural characteristics, including dress. Scholars have studied clothing and dress patterns in history in terms of how clothes function, and the social and cultural phenomena of clothing. But in Kentucky, the explicit connection between clothing and culture should compel teachers to focus on the cultural aspects of clothing.

In a lesson on the cultural characteristics of clothing, students might focus on dress in the United States at specific times as it reflects different cultural trends. Students might investigate forms of dress for adults and young people at specific times such as 1850, 1900, and 1950.

These three images depict typical dress at three different periods of time. An elementary social studies lesson on the topic of dress over time in the United States should focus on subject matter culled from larger bodies of content in areas of interest for students. The following questions might interest elementary school students:

- What materials were clothes made out of at different periods in history, and why?
- How long were clothes expected to last?
- What function did different clothes serve?
- How did clothing styles reflect culture and society?

Teachers would plan activities directed at helping students answer these questions. The result is the subject matter focus of the lesson. The subject matter focus might include the following ideas:

- Cloth was more expensive and hard to come by in the 19th century.
- Clothing materials are made from a range of natural, treated, and artificial materials.
- Clothing styles reflect cultural expectations for group: people, available resources, and status.

Such subject matter focus reflects only a small part of the available content knowledge on this topic. For a teacher, however, it is a meaningful and productive pedagogical context for learning about changes in clothing over time.

A portrait of three members of a family taken around 1849. The tight bodices of the women's dresses are typical of the style worn by women in the mid-1800s. The style reflected cultural expectations for women. What might some of these expectations have been?

Immigrants from Bulgaria at Ellis Island around 1905. The clothes, all dresses, were most likely homemade from the same swath of cloth. What cultural message does the style of dress portrayed in this image send?

A family in the early 1950s. How had cultural standards shifted in the 1950s relative to the 19th century?

Once a general curriculum focus has been determined, teachers should narrow subject matter content for emphasis in a lesson. This process, as simple as it sounds, is actually quite complex. It is an important outgrowth of a teacher's knowledge of scholarly content and the reorganization of that content into subject matter.

Not all subject matter knowledge on a topic is suitable for inclusion in a lesson. For example, a lesson on the 13 original British North American colonies might include subject matter on differences between the colonies with respect to political, economic, or geographic characteristics. Such a lesson might focus on the political, social, or economic development of the colonies over time. Or, the focus might be on the original purpose of the colonies, or the success of the colonies in achieving founding goals. Each of these foci is comparative, but a bit different. Teachers have to make specific decisions about their focus, consequentially narrowing the focus to meet the constraints (e.g., time, resources, etc.) of the lesson.

Setting Learning Goals Given Subject Matter Selections Establishing learning goals for an instructional activity is an important part of the planning process. Teachers may set learning goals given the curriculum or as a result of students' interest. Teachers may also be driven to construct learning goals that match their own interests and knowledge. Transparent learning goals enable students to understand exactly what they are learning and why they are learning about it.

Let's return to the example of the 13 colonies. In this example, the teacher wants students to learn about the differences between two colonies, specifically Maryland and South Carolina. Comparisons are powerful heuristics for learning specific subject matter. At the same time, comparisons sometimes oversimplify or lead students to overemphasize differences or likenesses. For this activity, a learning goal might be for students to compare obvious differences and not-so-obvious similarities between the two colonies.

The activity focuses on two people from the colonial era, Henry Middleton and William Paca. Henry Middleton was a member of the First Continental Congress. He came to own a large plantation in South Carolina through marriage (see **FIGURE 11.5**). The Middletons' son was one of the signers of the Declaration of Independence. The Middleton plantation continues to be known for its elaborate 60-acre formal gardens. It also was a highly productive rice farm. William Paca was a signer of the Declaration of Independence and later governor of the state of Maryland. Using money he inherited, Paca built a large estate that is maintained to this day (see **FIGURE 11.6**). The grounds, known for their elaborate gardens, are situated on two acres in Annapolis, Maryland.

FIGURE 11.5
Middleton Place, a mid-1700s plantation home on the Ashley River near Charleston, South Carolina

FIGURE 11.6
The Paca House and Gardens, built in 1763 by William Paca in Annapolis, Maryland

Consider the similarities between the men Middleton and Paca. Both were wealthy statesmen. Both owners inherited their wealth: Middleton from his wife and Paca from his father. Both were involved directly or indirectly with the Declaration of Independence. An activity on this subject matter might highlight these similarities while pointing out the important differences—namely, that the South Carolina gardens of Middleton were on a plantation, while Paca's gardens were in a city surrounded by other houses. The political, social, and economic differences between South Carolina and Maryland were also significant. These might be summed up as the differences between the more agrarian and slave-holding South and more industrial North. At the same time, students need to recognize the similarities between the colonies as exemplified by South Carolina farmer Henry Middleton and Maryland politician William Paca. Both men were privileged by birth or marriage, and both were able to use their wealth to rise to the political stage as important actors in the early history of the United States.

Personalizing Subject Matter for Students If we expect students to be motivated to learn, they must be able to relate to the subject matter. When we fail to connect subject matter to what students already know or what they like, we often have to resort to external motivators or what are called behavioral reinforcements. Unfortunately, the effects of these reinforcements are often temporary and spotty. Some students will respond to an external motivator such as a grade. Others may complete work for a small gift, candy, time off, and so on, but the work completed for these rewards is often shallow and detached. The most effective way to encourage students to learn is by situating the subject matter they will learn about in such a way that it becomes personal. Personalizing subject matter requires that teachers consider why students need to know about the subject, given who they are, and given where they are (geographically and in the sense of time).

Selecting Appropriate Resources for Students Countless resources are available for teaching. Some of these resources are so well constructed that a teacher might be tempted to use the resources just for the sake of using them, and because the teacher thinks they'll be easy to use. No matter how irresistible resources are, if they do not match instructional needs, then the resource distracts from the goals of the lesson. For this reason, teachers need to carefully identify appropriate and useful resources.

Weaving Subject Matter into the Curriculum How does the subject matter fit into the larger curriculum? This consideration is essential in order to avoid detaching the subject matter from its context. As teachers plan and teach lessons, they should consistently return to a whole body of knowledge to consider how new knowledge fits in. These reconsiderations allow teachers and students to expand existing understanding and begin to build a robust network of subject matter ideas.

CONCEPT CHECK STOP

How might you plan instruction about Native American relations with settlers at the lost colony of Roanoke?

How is the subject matter implied in these goals part of the body of knowledge of U.S. history?

What subject matter might you select given curriculum and student interests?

This 1590 engraving depicts the landing of the English at Roanoke Island in 1585.

Planning Instruction for Active Learning

LEARNING OBJECTIVES

Describe approaches to developing procedures for lesson plans.

Explain how the selection and use of instructional resources relate to student learning.

Identify approaches to assessment that support active learning.

DEVELOPING PROCEDURES FOR FACILITATING STUDENTS' LEARNING

The most obvious and important part of planning for instruction is the development of instructional procedures. The Process Diagram in **FIGURE 11.7** describes an approach to developing procedures for active instruction. Such procedures enable students to engage subject matter through their work with specific resources and their interactions with other students and teachers. The teacher needs to adapt these resources and then tailor them to meet the needs of students. Teachers need to orchestrate or at least outline interactions prior to the class. The planning process for these activities involves adapting subject matter content resources and developing specific procedures for students to engage these resources and interact with each other and the teacher. Teachers must also plan or anticipate how they might tailor the resources for use by students with different needs.

Procedures for a lesson will emerge from the details of the instructional technique selected for the lesson. To some degree, instructional techniques also emerge from subject matter content. In order to be successful in the process of developing lesson plans, teachers need to have a well-rounded understanding of instructional methods and, more important, teachers need practice adapting the generic instructional techniques given the particular subject matter content. Following are some generic instructional techniques that might be included in a lesson plan.

- Lecture
- Discussion
- Simulation
- Role-playing
- Inquiry
- Problem solving
- Debate

These instructional techniques can be incorporated into a lesson using direct instruction, indirect instruction, collaborative, experiential, and independent methods. When planning to teach, several factors influence the instructional approaches selected:

- The amount of time available
- The resources available
- The scope of what is being taught
- The strategies that have proven productive in the past given the students in the class
- The skills of the teacher
- The experiences that the class has had to date

Let's consider how to plan a lesson on renewable and nonrenewable natural resources. A **renewable resource** is a natural resource that is depleted at a rate slower than the rate at which it regenerates (i.e., solar energy). **Nonrenewable resources** are resources for which there are no reasonable ways to replenish the supply (i.e., fossil fuels). The first step is to reorganize relevant content knowledge into relevant subject matter knowledge. Content knowledge about renewable and nonrenewable resources might focus on what scientists have learned about the biological and physical differences between natural resources. Experts also study the political and economic impact of using renewable and nonrenewable resources. As teachers reorganize their understanding of content knowledge, this takes the form of subject matter.

Planning instruction for active learning FIGURE 11.7

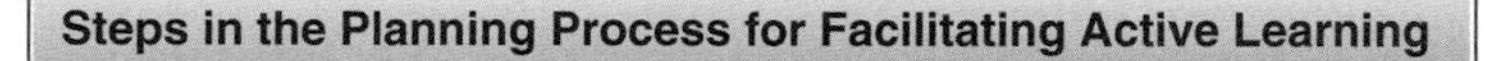

Steps in the Planning Process for Facilitating Active Learning

1. Organize content knowledge into subject matter knowledge while considering...
- Curriculum
- Community
- Social studies

2. Transform subject matter into pedagogical ideas by...
- Considering curriculum
- Narrowing subject matter
- Personalizing the subject matter
- Getting students interested
- Having students produce something
- Helping students connect to life experience

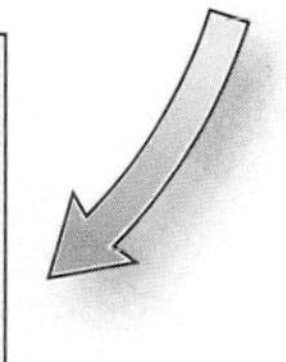

3. Develop relevant procedures such as...
- Role playing
- Problem solving
- Debate

4. Select resource materials that...
- Support learning goals
- Are appropriate for student grade level
- Can be adapted to student needs

5. Assess student learning by having students produce...
- A letter
- A report
- A research paper

With petroleum production estimated to peak in coming decades, some experts say we must develop alternative power sources, including renewable sources of energy like wind, solar power, and biofuels (FIGURE 11.8A). Given what you know about the subject matter, what general instructional approach might you use to teach about solar power?

A common subject matter approach to this topic is to focus on the differences between everyday renewable and nonrenewable resources. Other initial considerations might result in a focus on resources that can be found in the house, such as water. A teacher might want students to determine how we use household resources and whether everyday products are made from renewable or nonrenewable resources (FIGURE 11.8B).

Another approach might be for students to evaluate the consequences of their consumption of different resources. Have students brainstorm about resources that they use on a daily basis. You or a student can make a list of these resources on the board, which will enable the students to benefit from each other's ideas about everyday resources.

Next, consider a teacher-directed introduction of the concepts of renewable and nonrenewable resources. This subject matter will probably be new for students, so the approach used by the teacher is very important. You may want to start by using metaphors or some other figure of speech to introduce the topic. Consider approaching the topic by asking students to think of renewable and nonrenewable resources as common things. Renewable resources might be thought of as being like our hair. When we cut it off, it always grows back. Nonrenewable resources are like the days of the week. Once a day in our life passes, it is gone forever. This part of the activity might only take a few minutes, but it is extremely important.

Next, consider having students work independently to determine whether the resources listed on the board are renewable or nonrenewable (FIGURE 11.8C).

Prior to this activity, students will have to separate human-made from natural products. Students will need

Lesson Planning: Renewable and Nonrenewable Resources FIGURE 11.8

A Sheep graze near solar energy panels—is solar energy a renewable or nonrenewable resource?

to think about the resources that are used to make the products they have listed. The goal is to get them focused on natural products. A final activity could involve students working in pairs to think about the consequences of using each product on their list. These consequences should be determined given guidelines the students create. This might be a separate whole class activity situated between the independent work and the work in pairs.

SELECTING AND USING RESOURCES

Selecting resources for use in a lesson is a very important part of the planning process. Resource selection should be guided by three considerations.

1. Does the resource support the learning goals for the lesson?
2. Is the resource appropriate for students given their prior knowledge, reading ability, and maturity?
3. Can the resources be adapted and tailored to meet the specific needs of students?

Answers to these questions will help determine whether the resource will work with the lesson. Then teachers must still adapt the resource for use in the lesson and actually plan for its use. Adapting the resource means limiting the amount of the resource being used, changing the layout or order of the material in the resource, or even adding some supporting material to the resource. For example, teachers often use film in social studies. Tailoring a resource occurs when the teacher makes adjustments during instruction to meet individual needs given emerging contexts in the classroom.

Films convey powerful emotions and often depictions of content that are easy for children to understand. However, most often films are not intended to be educational. They must be highly adapted and eventually tailored to meet individual students' needs. Unless the circumstances are unusual, only a portion of a film should be shown in class. A film clip of five or ten

B Is water a renewable resource? How would content experts determine whether water is renewable? What content knowledge about water as a resource is important for elementary social studies?

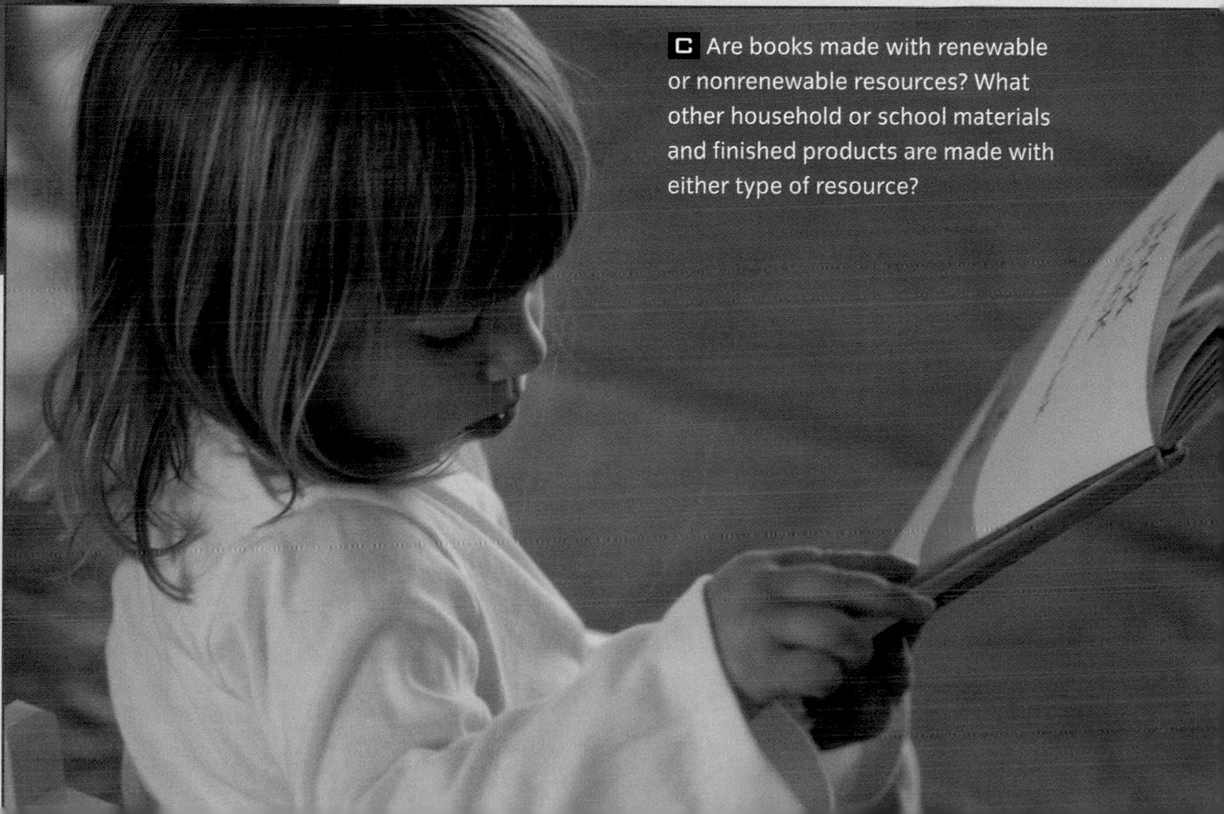

C Are books made with renewable or nonrenewable resources? What other household or school materials and finished products are made with either type of resource?

FIGURE 11.9

Children need to be provided with support and scaffolding when interacting with media resources.

minutes is usually enough. Also, films must be contextualized and scaffolded. Students need to understand why they are watching the film and take some action during or after viewing the film clip.

Robert Kubey (2004) claims that social studies teachers have a special responsibility to prepare students to be critical consumers of media resources such as newspaper and film. When interacting with these resources, students use specific skills that need to be supported and scaffolded. Consider the interaction the boy in FIGURE 11.9 is having with the newspaper. How is this child using media literacy skills as he reads the newspaper? What types of support do you think he might need as he reads?

Most of the media resources that teachers use in elementary social studies are printed or viewed on computer and whiteboard screens. These resources typically also require significant adaptation and tailoring. Most print resources, whether they are primary source documents, original maps, literature, or pictures, will need to be in the form of an excerpt. In fact, the process of excerpting text from primary sources and literature will be necessary for almost every resource.

CHOOSING MEANINGFUL ASSESSMENT TECHNIQUES

The assessment of students' acquisition of subject matter content knowledge is one of the most important tasks in teaching. For each instructional technique or procedure developed, teachers need to develop a corresponding assessment that documents students' learning. Planning for assessment requires clearly described learning goals or objectives. It also means providing instruction that is designed to position students to be successful at achieving the learning objectives. When teachers plan instruction, they try to develop activities that will result in concrete evidence of students' progress. This typically means having students complete some task(s) while engaging subject matter resources and/or interaction with other students. Assessment can also involve informal observation of students' work, but for most activities students should be producing something (a short paper, a letter, a report, etc.). Integration within a lesson plan and creativity are important components of all assessment strategies, and Chapter 13 deals with these ideas in depth. The criteria for determining the quality of students' work and the means by which to provide feedback are equally important and should be described in lesson plans.

CONCEPT CHECK STOP

Consider a lesson with the goal of understanding how money supply is determined.

What procedures might a teacher plan?

What effect does the printing of money have on the value of money?

What procedures might students follow in order to learn specific subject matter?

Money is inspected after being printed at the United States Bureau of Engraving and Printing.

Lesson Plans and Reflection

LEARNING OBJECTIVES

Describe two basic approaches to writing lesson plans.

Explain the reasons why a teacher would develop a formal lesson plan.

Identify what goes into a lesson narrative.

Compare lesson plans to lesson narratives.

Eighteenth-century Scottish poet Robert Burns wrote in his poem "To a Mouse" that "The best laid schemes o' mice an' men/Gang aft a-gley." From this old Scottish line, comes the familiar saying, "even the best laid plans go wrong." Maybe Burns tapped into our concern about being able to control what will happen in the future. As in all ventures, even the best laid teaching plans sometimes go wrong. Of course, that does not mean we should abandon efforts to plan for instruction. No matter the potential problems, instructional plans are essential to quality learning experiences.

Imagine teaching without a plan. What would happen? Most likely, the teacher would fall back on what he knows and maybe tell a story or recite some easy-to-remember subject matter for students. He might use a prepackaged activity or worksheet that seemed to be on the same topic as the curriculum suggests. We know that such teaching techniques do not result in productive learning for students. Productive learning results from active student engagement, and this requires careful planning.

WRITING LESSON PLANS

There are at least two methods for developing lesson plans. Typically, teachers spend most of their time specifying and writing procedures for students to follow. These procedures are often coupled with behavioral objectives, lists of resources, and descriptions of assessment activities. These lesson plan elements take form as an *outline lesson plan.* Outlines are good because they convey the essentials of a plan for instruction in a well-understood format.

Look at FIGURE 11.10. How might we use this element of mystery to plan for a lesson on ancient Native Americans, using an outline lesson plan? The amazing drawings on a 50-foot-tall flat rock comprise one of the largest known collections of petroglyphs. The petroglyphs are believed to have been carved by natives, possibly the Anasazi, between the first and fifth century A.D., but dating the rock carvings is difficult. Mystery surrounds the meaning and the purposes for the carvings.

Sometimes, we need to probe our pedagogical understanding more deeply than an outline will permit. For these occasions, we can use another method, *instructional narratives,* which go into more depth in exploring some theme or idea being conveyed in the teaching and learning experience. Often, instructional narratives focus on subject content knowledge and how the teacher selected and developed certain pedagogical strategies to enable students to learn specific subject matter content. The focus of lesson narratives is describing, rather than simply conveying a list of procedures. A person who reads an instructional narrative may still need an accompanying lesson plan in order to implement the lesson,

FIGURE 11.10

Ancient petroglyphs at Newspaper Rock, Utah

but she will know much more about the thinking that went into the plan after reading the narrative.

One maxim that seems to hold true is that the more intricate the learning experiences, the more detailed the plans must be and, consequently, the more important planning actually becomes. Lessons that involve in-depth planning include:

- Students using resources or completing a sequence of activities
- Differentiated instruction (different learning goals and activities for different students)
- Self-paced learning activities
- Group work
- Research projects
- Simulations
- Other student-centered learning activities

Often, teachers construct mental teaching plans, but novice teachers especially need to spend time writing plans. Written lesson plans enable a form of professional communication that is vital for professional growth. Writing is also a form of learning and thinking, and the writing process may very well result in higher-quality lessons.

Students learning about technology might be interested in learning about how societies react to the introduction of new technologies. How might a teacher plan for a lesson in which students investigate the issue of how new technologies are adapted by people in different cultural settings (FIGURE 11.11)?

Lesson Plans Outline lesson plans typically contain five or six sections.

1. Introduction
2. Objectives
3. Related standards and curriculum goals
4. Materials being used
5. Procedures (sometimes including a separate lesson opening and closing)
6. Assessment strategies

FIGURE 11.11

Residents of the Australian aborigine settlement of Balgo in the Great Sandy Desert, spending the evening watching television. The government provides them with houses, but many still prefer to live in the open air and, except during winter, use their houses for storage.

Behavioral objective A learning goal specifying observable actions students must demonstrate to indicate that learning has occurred.

The sequence of these lesson plan elements is quite logical. After an introduction that summarizes the content of a lesson, teachers must consider what they want students to learn. These take form as **behavioral objectives**. Well-crafted behavioral objectives typically include four parts.

1. The skill/knowledge to be gained
2. The action students undertake when demonstrating their skill or knowledge
3. The conditions under which the students will exhibit their skill or knowledge
4. The criteria used to determine the quality of students' skill or knowledge

Objectives need to encompass relevant subject matter that has been selected for the lesson and should be within the expectations of standards and curriculum. The process of planning activities for successful learning includes selecting pertinent materials and a set of procedures to facilitate student learning. These are typically recorded in a lesson plan as a list of items needed for the lesson and a sequence of teacher and student actions. Most lesson plans include a separate section detailing assessment strategies and the criteria for evaluating students' work.

Lesson Narratives Lesson narratives are much more impressionistic than lesson plans. A good lesson narrative tells the story of a lesson idea. Narratives have a beginning, middle, and end, as does the process for planning and implementing a lesson. Using narrative structure, teachers can describe the processes they undertook as they developed subject matter knowledge and transformed that knowledge into pedagogical subject matter knowledge. The transformations can be written about as an idea for how and what is taught.

Although a narrative lesson plan may lack the sequential detail of an outline lesson plan, a well-written lesson narrative can be very enlightening. Teachers can reveal their thinking, ambitions, and expectations in lesson narratives. A fully formed lesson narrative should include:

- An introduction that addresses the emergence of the teacher knowledge about the subject matter of the lesson
- An exploration of the teacher's ideas about what students in the class should learn and why
- An explanation of how the featured subject matter fits with standards and curriculum

The narrative provides a structure to describe the manner in which the lesson addresses standardized subject matter. Lesson narratives should flow from section to section, with the writer describing procedures as imagined events that are interwoven and purposeful. Within the description of these imagined class events, rich descriptions of assessment and plans for evaluation and reflection should be described. Lesson narratives might also be written after a teaching episode. Such work might be considered reflective and can be an important part of the teaching process.

REFLECTION

Planning to teach does not stop when teachers implement a lesson. Constant reflection is a critical component of planning. Reflection enables teachers to determine whether their plan for instruction is working. More often than not, lesson plans need to be adjusted. Sometimes these adjustments must take place in the middle of instruction. At other times, adjustments can be made between activities, during breaks, or even over a period of days. There are at least three questions teachers should consider when reflecting on a lesson plan.

1. *Are all students receiving the opportunities the teacher envisioned when planning for instruction?* The answer(s) to this question emerge from assessment. Typically, informal assessment can be used to make quick judgments about whether students are benefiting from the instruction that was planned. If students are not "getting it," then the teacher must make adjustments in the lesson.
2. *Is the time allotted for instruction appropriate given the realities of the actual implementation?* Teachers sometimes overplan for a class. There is nothing

inherently wrong with this as long as the teacher realizes the problem and then adjusts the activities to maximize students' work. Sometimes, the opposite occurs and a teacher underplans. In such situations, there are a number of options. The teacher can begin the next planned activity or lesson, even if it was planned for the next day. The teacher might also extend the completed lesson and provide students additional opportunities to learn about the subject matter. This might even involve planning to teach "on the fly." Sometimes teachers use filler activities that address important or valued skills and/or knowledge. Teachers should not assign "busy work" that is unconnected to either curriculum or realistic learning goals.

3. *Are the materials and resources that were adapted and prepared for the lesson being used the way the teacher planned?* One of the most important teacher actions that occurs during class is the explaining and tailoring of materials. Sometimes students do not understand material that is being presented or the resources they are working with. This confusion should not be unexpected. Children are learning about subject matter they may be partially or completely unfamiliar with. A teacher's ability to tailor the instruction and the materials that support their instruction is essential. Much of the tailoring process is a product of the teacher's informal assessment, again highlighting the importance of continual assessment.

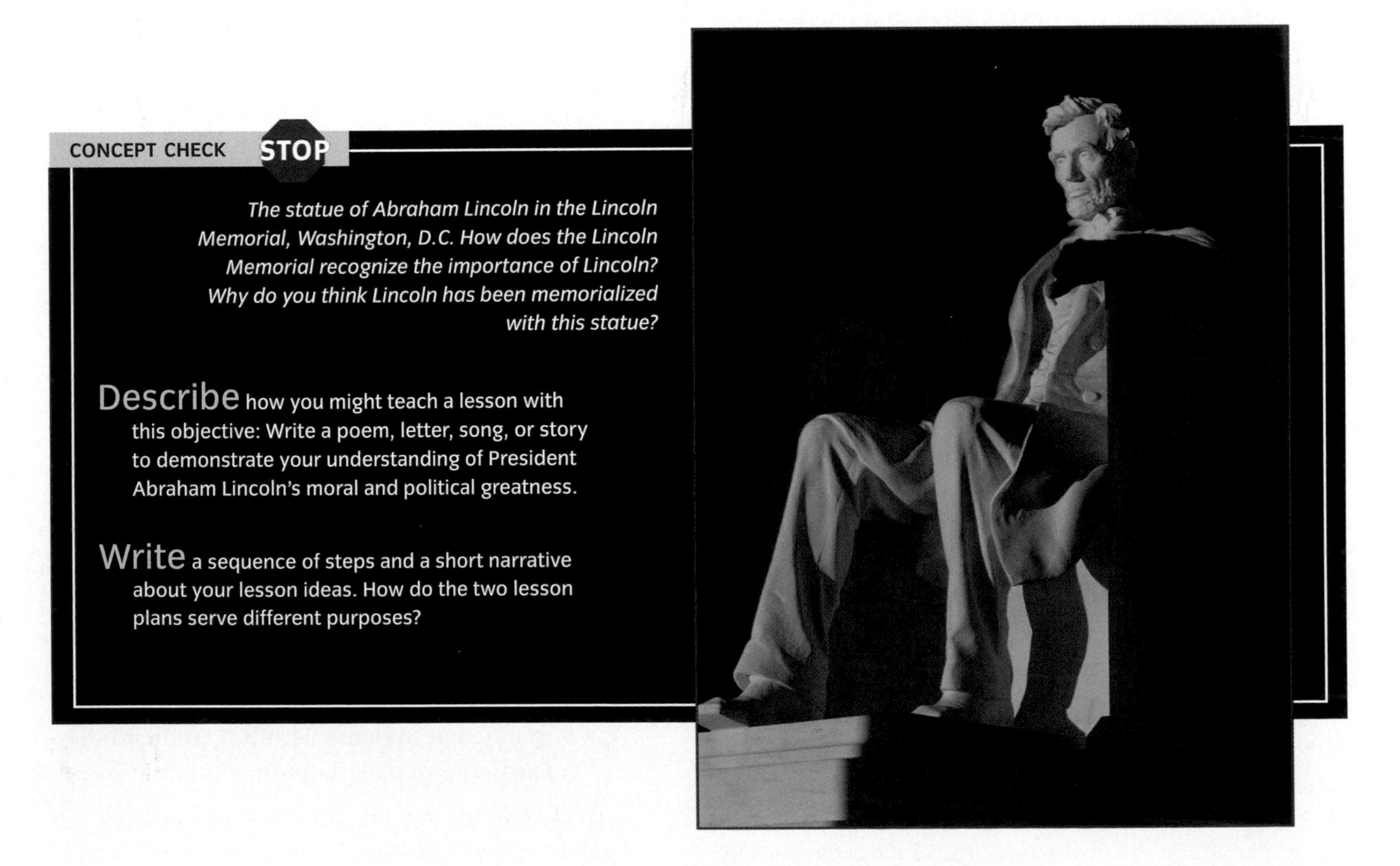

CONCEPT CHECK STOP

The statue of Abraham Lincoln in the Lincoln Memorial, Washington, D.C. How does the Lincoln Memorial recognize the importance of Lincoln? Why do you think Lincoln has been memorialized with this statue?

Describe how you might teach a lesson with this objective: Write a poem, letter, song, or story to demonstrate your understanding of President Abraham Lincoln's moral and political greatness.

Write a sequence of steps and a short narrative about your lesson ideas. How do the two lesson plans serve different purposes?

What is happening in this picture ?

- When new technology meets traditional culture interesting contrasts come to mind. What are some of the contrasts evident in this image?
- How might an investigation of early music technology be fashioned into an active learning experience?

VISUAL SUMMARY

1 Active Learning in Social Studies

Active learning requires that students be active in the pursuit of knowledge. Active learning occurs when teachers create interest and excitement about learning. When students produce something, have a role in setting up the activity, and see the connections to their life, the experiences are even more active. The more authentic the learning experience, the more active the learning experience will be. In social studies, teachers draw on a number of authentic social studies disciplinary areas and resources to enable their students to actively learn.

ll teachers must be prepared to teach in diverse environments. Like Mr. Gonzalez, we have to expect diversity to take many different forms. Social studies is particularly well suited for discovering diversity and for helping children understand and value diversity. In this chapter we present various characterizations of diversity and suggest techniques for how to use social studies content when teaching about and within a diverse social context.

Teaching Children in Diverse Environments

LEARNING OBJECTIVES

Define diversity.

Describe the forms of diversity that exist in elementary schools.

Explain how diversity in society is reflected in the schools.

Expectations shape much of our actions. Think about the children depicted in **FIGURE 12.1**. How do you think these children's school experiences are affected by their culture? If this question is hard to answer, what do you need to know about the children or their culture in order to answer it? If we expect students to perform at a certain high level given their culture, we may subconsciously provide them more opportunities to succeed than other students for whom we do not have such high expectations. Such teacher expectations must be shaped by knowledge of individuals, and our knowledge must develop in the context of life and school in a diverse society.

FORMS OF DIVERSITY

Diversity Natural and social differences that emerge from meaningful and unique human characteristics.

Diversity can take form in a number of ways. Some forms of diversity have a direct bearing on educational aims and methods. Other forms are less influential, but at minimum worthy of recognition. Following are several forms of diversity and recommendations for how to incorporate these diversities into planning and teaching elementary social studies.

FIGURE 12.1

Do you have any expectations based on what you can tell about the culture of these children from this photo?

Natural Diversity

Natural forms of diversity include gender age, size, and any other traits that are a product of some natural or biological development. Social studies teachers like to include subject matter that is specifically focused on these natural forms. For example, having students study about children their own age can be an effective strategy. The same might be true for gender studies, particularly the study of women. Given the relative lack of information about women in elementary social studies curriculums and textbooks, girls and boys might find women's studies interesting.

Socially Constructed Diversity

All societies construct institutions and classifications that result in a wide diversity of human experiences. Institutions such as religion and nationality as well as classifications such as **race** and **ethnicity** are all socially constructed. Much like natural forms of diversity, socially constructed forms of diversity can be found in the social studies curriculum. For example, students learn about social groups of people such as the black African Catholics pictured in FIGURE 12.2. Children are usually interested in learning about people who are in groups like their own. For example, immigrant children from China might be interested in studying Chinese American experiences in history. Elementary social studies teachers can use those interests to encourage learning, but should also try to balance the curriculum so that multiple groups are represented and so that children have opportunities to learn about a wide range of social groups.

Race A group of people united or classified together based on common history, geographic distribution, and similar physical traits.

Ethnicity A group of people who share a common and distinctive racial, national, religious, linguistic, or cultural heritage.

FIGURE 12.2

At an African Catholic mission, this Zairian Mbuti tribal leader and village neighbors parade to church on Palm Sunday. How do the social constructs of religion and race depicted in this image confound expectations about religion and race?

Learning Diversity

Another form of diversity, learning diversity, refers to each child's unique learning traits and habits. Learning traits and habits include specific learning styles and intelligences (one child may be particularly good with language, another has high math skills) as well as learning preferences or abilities. Some differences in learning styles include an aptitude for visual learning, or motor skills. Elementary school teachers should try to meet the needs of children with unique learning traits and habits.

Personality-Related Diversity

The personality of each student is unique, but certain patterns of behavior enable teachers to describe and sometimes predict personality. Learning personalities are unique and individual and reflect natural as well as socially constructed differences related to learning habits and traits. Teachers should take into account only those personal traits that relate to learning, such as a student's willingness to work individually or in groups.

DIVERSITY IN SCHOOL

Diversity is a term used to suggest difference and uniqueness. As we have seen, diversity might be measured using natural and socially constructed characteristics such as age, ethnicity, gender, nationality, race, and religion, as well as educational aptitude. With regard to schooling, diversity might be classified as either cultural or individual.

Cultural diversity is mostly a social construction, and it is what people often think of when they think of diversity. The descriptive characteristics of cultural diversity have historical and political dimensions. Schools have been in the foreground of historical and political action that recognizes cultural diversity and, when needed, schools have addressed inequalities resulting from cultural diversity. For example, the desegregation of public facilities in the United States was in part initiated in the public schools.

Race is the most continuous and problematic of the socially constructed forms of cultural diversity in the United States. The image of Elizabeth Eckford in **FIGURE 12.3** is from an important period in U.S. history when schools were at the forefront of the fight for racial equality. The image illustrates the tension surrounding the forced integration of the Little Rock, Arkansas, school district in 1956. Eckford was one of the nine black children who integrated Little Rock High School.

Individual diversity reflects natural as well as learning or personality-related traits that are sometimes

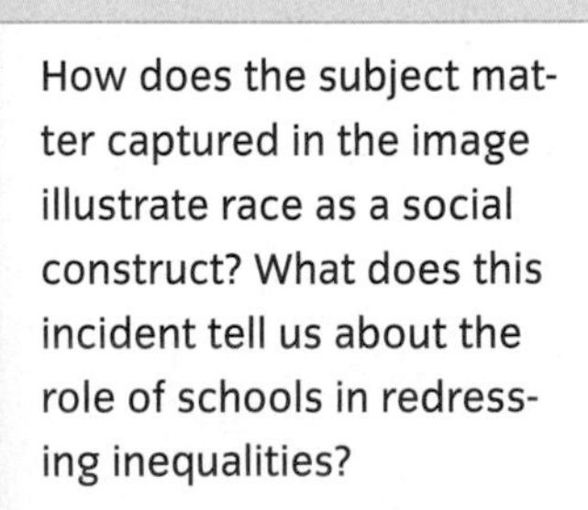

FIGURE 12.3

How does the subject matter captured in the image illustrate race as a social construct? What does this incident tell us about the role of schools in redressing inequalities?

hard to compare and categorize. At its simplest, it says that each person is unique. For teachers, this means that each child deserves individual attention and has unique needs. These needs may be educational, emotional, or behavioral. Teachers must know their students as learners. They must be aware of their students' background knowledge and their abilities as learners, but they must also be aware of their students' other needs. These include the emotional and behavioral needs that teachers can meet with specialized instruction and attention or through support personnel in the school and community.

DIVERSITY IN SOCIETY

Diversity is complicated and often controversial. The United States and other nations such as France, Australia, and India are becoming increasingly diverse. Although countries like the United States are made up of many cultural and personal experiences, the idea of being an "American" at least suggests assimilation and likeness. Political groups disagree about the extent to which diversity should be emphasized in the schools, and much of this disagreement has taken form around the idea of **multiculturalism**. Let us consider diversity as it impacts culture and society.

> **Multiculturalism** Many cultures existing together in a locality, without any one culture dominating, and with mutual acceptance of differences aimed at overcoming racism, sexism, and other forms of discrimination.

As illustrated in FIGURE 12.4, Australia is becoming more culturally diverse. The same thing is happening in the United States. Some on the political right want to deemphasize cultural diversity or multiculturalism in favor of a more assimilated cultural American identity. This view might be best represented by Arthur Schlesinger, Jr., in his book *The Disuniting of America: Reflections on a Multicultural Society* (1998). In the book, Schlesinger argued that a "cult of ethnicity" was strangling the liberal vision of America and fracturing the common bonds of the American liberal democracy. Schlesinger was building on the early 20th-century notion of America as a melting pot and generally lamenting the disappearance of this vision of American culture. As illustrated in FIGURE 12.4, the trend toward cultural diversity is not unique to the United States.

Those on the political left generally believe that diversity in society is a productive outgrowth of a uniquely American form of pluralism. Nathan Glazer presented this view in his book, *We Are All Multiculturalists Now* (1998). Glazer argued that cultural diversity—or what we sometimes term multiculturalism—is a product of the Euro-centric notion of America as a melting pot. His theory suggests that European immigrants who assimilated into an American culture never intended for non-Europeans, particularly black Africans, to be part of the American culture they were creating. The result was the emergence of distinct and separate cultural identities that came to exist alongside a European white cultural tradition.

FIGURE 12.4

Buddhist Vietnamese children stand in front of Phuoc Hue Temple in a suburban area of Sydney, Australia called Wetherill Park. In one generation, Sydney has been transformed from a parochial city to a model of cultural diversity. How do such transformations challenge notions of what it means to be Australian?

DIVERSITY IN LEARNING: INTELLIGENCES AND LEARNING STYLES

How should elementary school teachers respond to issues related to diversity? First, it is critical to view diversity in its broadest sense. As presented earlier in this chapter, diversity is much more than multiculturalism. It includes cultural and personal dimensions as well. Teachers must identify and plan for diversity in their classroom, and this requires careful attention to the needs of individual students as well as groups of students in the class.

There are a number of sources for information about students. Teachers should have access to previous grades as well as to standardized test scores. These should be used to get a general sense of the academic achievement levels of students. We must always keep in mind that each of these assessment records is simply a record of achievement at a given time under certain circumstances. Overreliance on previous grades and test scores can have a stifling effect on students' potential for intellectual growth.

Inventories and surveys are another way to determine the unique abilities and skills of students. A number of instruments have been developed that can be used to determine students' learning styles or types of intelligence, such as Howard Gardner's (1983) theory of multiple intelligences. (See FIGURE 12.5, "Visualizing: Multiple Intelligences".) Gardner proposed that there are seven human intelligences, later adding an eighth. These eight intelligences are:

1. Linguistic intelligence: understanding words, their meanings, and the order of text-based language
2. Logical-mathematical intelligence: skill in mathematics and other complex logical systems
3. Musical intelligence: abilities to understand and create music
4. Spatial intelligence: abilities to visualize the world and create representations of the world on paper
5. Bodily/kinesthetic intelligence: being able to use the body for some expressed and purposeful task
6. Interpersonal intelligence: abilities to perceive and understand other people
7. Intrapersonal intelligence: a heightened ability to understand and use emotions
8. Naturalist intelligence: abilities to recognize and classify plants, minerals, and animals

Other theories about learning can help us understand and account for differences among learners. Following is a list of some of the major learning-style theories and their implications with regard to diversity.

David Kolb's (1976) learning styles model described models of learning based on four learning styles.

1. Diverging learners think deeply about experiences and then diverge from the experience to multiple ways of thinking about it.
2. Converging learners think about problems, then try out their ideas or solutions.
3. Accommodating learners explore new knowledge with actions, rarely pausing to think or theorize prior to acting.
4. Assimilating learners think through the entire process preferring to think instead of to act.

Brain-based learning models represent a collection of learning theories and theories about how the brain works when we are learning. These theories suggest that there are multiple approaches to learning. Herrmann (1980) has suggested a four-part model for explaining brain-based learning that focuses on the idea that the left and right parts of the brain function differently.

1. Left brain, cerebral: logical, analytical, quantitative, and factual learning
2. Left brain, limbic: sequential, organized, planned, and detailed learning
3. Right brain, cerebral: visual, holistic, and creative learning
4. Right brain, limbic: emotional, interpersonal, sensory, and kinesthetic learning

Another source of information comes from the assessment of students' knowledge and skills. These can take form as pre-tests, initial unit activities, or even informal questioning sessions. The knowledge that teachers develop about their students' abilities and their

Given Howard Gardner's idea that people learn differently according to various types of intelligence, consider how student learning might differ with the drawing and text below.

- How might elementary school–aged children with a proclivity for linguistic intelligence learn from this image?
- What about a visual learner or a spatial learner?
- Would learners with other strengths be able to learn something about the winter of 1886 or the artwork of Charles M. Russell?

A watercolor of a starving steer in a blizzard on the OH Ranch in 1886 by Charles M. Russell, famed western artist. The painting is attached to a letter of the period by a friend of Russell's trying to report to a rancher on the condition of the cattle. On the left side of the card it says: "This is the real thing painted the winter of 1886 at the OH ranch. CM Russell." On the right it says: "This picture is Charles Russell's reply to my inquiry as to the condition of my cattle in 1886. LE Kaufmann."

prior knowledge of specific content can help in general planning as well as adapting for individual students.

Larger and more group-based measures of diversity might help in the planning process as well. If groups of students are from particular parts of the country or other nations, teachers can adapt the curriculum to take advantage of their students' cultural experiences. If a number of students have particular learning traits or dispositions, the teacher can take advantage of these characteristics as well when teaching.

CONCEPT CHECK STOP

How would students with different learning styles describe the actions depicted in this scene?

How would students with different intelligences approach this activity?

A view of an ancient Egyptian mourning scene on papyrus.

Cultural Diversity and Social Studies

LEARNING OBJECTIVES

Identify how the social studies curriculum reflects cultural diversity.

Evaluate the extent to which cultural diversity should influence instruction in elementary social studies.

Identify the purposes and approaches of culturally responsive teaching.

Examine the role of teachers in implementing culturally responsive teaching strategies.

Cultural diversity is an idea that values multiple cultural experiences. We can expand that idea to suggest that various cultural experiences coexist in modern American culture. Cultural experiences influence how children learn and must therefore be understood and nurtured.

HOW DOES THE SOCIAL STUDIES CURRICULUM REFLECT CULTURAL DIVERSITY?

Curriculum is many things to many people. To those concerned about issues related to cultural diversity, the curriculum provides an opportunity to broaden children's exposure to and experiences with various cultures and their associated values. The social studies curriculum offers teachers ample opportunities to explore topics that can reflect the diversity within the United States and within specific classrooms.

Of course, no single curriculum can fit everyone's needs. When national curriculums such as the National History Standards were developed, groups with vested interests in particular cultural perspectives worked to have their stories included. This pattern plays out on the state level in places like California, whose legislature has passed or considered several resolutions requiring that the state standards and curriculums include the perspectives of specific groups and interests. On another level, local school systems will often strive to represent the diversity within their communities.

State and local curriculums and standards typically reflect local diversity-related needs. For example, in New Mexico students in kindergarten learn about "the customs, celebrations, and holidays of various cultures in New Mexico." In the second grade, students are expected to "describe the cultural diversity of individuals and groups and their contributions to United States history (e.g., George Washington, Ben Franklin, César Chávez, Rosa Parks, the National Association for Advancement of Colored People [NAACP], tribal leaders, American Indian Movement [AIM])." The inclusion of individuals on this list reflects the diversity of New Mexico, which includes large Hispanic and Native Indian populations.

At the classroom level, teachers must implement the curriculum, which provides teachers another opportunity to reflect the diversity in their school and classroom. For example, an elementary grade teacher in Cibola County, New Mexico may choose to emphasize Native American contributions to U.S. history, given that almost half of the population of the county is Native American. Teachers in Cibola might develop a lesson about the legend of the Seven Cities of Cibola. The legend grew out of the travels of Alvar Nunez Cabeza de Vaca, a 16th-century Spanish explorer who shipwrecked in 1528 off the modern-day Texas coast. Cabeza de Vaca and his crew lived among the native Indians in the area for a number of years. In 1532, he and his companions left the coast in search of the Spanish in Mexico. Four years later after traveling through modern-day Arizona, New Mexico, and northern Mexico they found a small Spanish party on a slave-trading run. Cabeza de Vaca described how they had seen bison and repeated rumors about rich Indian pueblos. The rumors became the legend of the Seven Golden Cities of a land called Cibola. This legend spurred further exploration by the Europeans such as Francisco Coronado (**FIGURE 12.6**).

FIGURE 12.6

This painting depicts Francisco Coronado, Spanish explorer, with his party in 1540 exploring the American Southwest in search of the Seven Cities of Cibola, which were thought to be rich in gold and jewels. How does this subject matter have a special cultural relevance in the American Southwest?

CULTURAL DIVERSITY AND INSTRUCTION IN SOCIAL STUDIES

When teaching social studies, elementary school teachers can provide instruction that addresses various cultural needs. Curriculum sets the stage for such instruction, but teachers must plan individual lessons and then implement them. There are several things we can do when teaching in classrooms that are culturally diverse. Following are a few of these ideas.

1. Try to get involved in or at least attend community-based cultural events. At minimum, develop an understanding of the cultural characteristics of the neighborhoods in which your students live.
2. Get to know the students and their parents, perhaps through parent nights or other extracurricular activities. Invite parents and family to the school, and always keep parents informed about what is happening in your classroom.
3. Carefully encourage students to share their own experiences with the class. Make sure that students are comfortable doing this, and never single children out based on their cultural identity. This sharing should always be positive and should reflect some relevant subject matter. Avoid asking students to explain their culture or their traditions. Focus instead on sharing. Also, be willing to model such cultural sharing.
4. Mix students when they work in groups. Heterogeneous (mixed) grouping is important on a number of levels. With regard to culture, it gives children experience working with children who may have cultural backgrounds different from their own.
5. Review all materials used in class for representativeness and accuracy. The goal is to include a range of materials and to avoid resources that are overly representative of a single cultural tradition.
6. Avoid expectations based on race or ethnic group. Reading and learning about groups often results in generalizations about these groups. Despite what we might expect from a group member, remember that each individual is unique and might be very different from the norm. Get to know your students to avoid stereotyping them.

CULTURALLY RESPONSIVE TEACHING AND LEARNING

One systematic approach to teaching children in culturally diverse contexts is an approach called culturally responsive teaching and learning. Geneva Gay (2000) describes culturally responsive teaching and learning as being reflective of cultural knowledge, students' prior experiences, and the performance styles of diverse students. The general idea is to teach to the strengths of students given the cultural contexts that have shaped their learning experiences and styles.

Culturally responsive teaching addresses the needs of students by motivating them through learning experiences that value the students' identity. Such approaches to teaching require that teachers first explore their own cultural identity and the values they associate with different cultural identities. Culturally responsive teaching values cultural differences, and a teacher who teaches in such a way must develop not just a respect for other cultures but an understanding of those cultures and how they influence learning.

Culturally responsive teaching should never be divisive or separatist. The idea is to consider the cultural uniqueness of children for the express purpose of improving teaching and learning. Cultural differences that are harmful or destructive are not likely to be educative. For example, traditions of distrust or intolerance on the part of various religious groups cannot be used as a context for learning. Instead, teachers have to find positive elements within cultural traditions to support learning in the classroom.

Children learn about the days of the week and months of the year in their earliest learning experiences. Most children come to elementary school with this knowledge firmly developed. But do we ever consider why we have a calendar system, how it was developed, or other ways of organizing the passage of time? Look at, "In the Classroom: Teaching about calendars" for how to teach on this topic. A lesson on these questions provides social studies teachers in early elementary grades an opportunity to explore culture.

In the Classroom TEACHING ABOUT CALENDARS

The calendar we use in North America and most of the world is called the Gregorian calendar. It was named for Pope Gregory XIII, who in 1582 issued an order that all Christian Catholic countries should use a newly configured calendar, correcting the Roman Julian calendar, which was several days out of sync with the seasons. The Gregorian calendar, like other calendars such as the Aztec calendar, is based on the time it takes the Earth to revolve around the Sun. Protestant countries (including England and the American colonies) did not adopt it until 1752. When the American colonies converted to the Gregorian calendar, 11 days were eliminated in order to catch up, resulting in September 2, 1752, being followed by September 14, 1752. In this activity, students would compare three calendars and consider the lost days of 1752.

Calendar Activity 1: Why do different people use different calendars?

In China the official state calendar is different from the Islamic Calendar widely used in the Middle East, which is different from the Jewish calendar used in Israel, which is of course different from the Gregorian calendar used in most Western countries.

Why do these different people use different calendars? The answer to this question lies in history. Students can explore the origins of the four calendars mentioned here and learn about each culture.

- Arrange students in groups of four and have each student in the group be responsible for finding the current year in their calendar as well as the event that marks the first year in the calendar.

Calendar Activity 2: The lost 11 days of 1752

What days would you skip if we had to eliminate 11 days from the calendar?

This is the question that faced British and colonial American leaders in 1752. They selected September 3 through 12, some say because no religious holidays fall on those days.

- Have students pick 11 consecutive days that they would eliminate one time from the year, then provide reasons for their decisions. The reasons might very well reflect the cultural interests and background of the students.

Teachers can use students' reasoning as a way to learn more about them and potentially as a way to extend the activity to focus on cultural views and distinctions.

A closeup of the center of the 20-ton Aztec Sun Stone, which depicts the sun god and the four epochs of the creation and destruction of the universe in Aztec mythology. Other symbols represent the 20 days of the Aztec month, the source of the popular name Calendar Stone. Why do you think different cultures have different calendar systems?

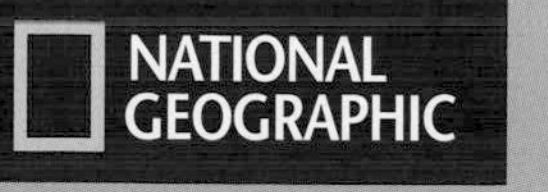

CONCEPT CHECK STOP

HOW does the tradition of Nyepi illustrate the cultural uniqueness of Indonesia?

HOW might knowledge of this tradition alter or expand children's conceptions of the culture of New Year celebrations?

Young girls in Bali, Indonesia prepare for Nyepi, the New Year holiday in Bali. The Balinese people celebrate the New Year with absolute stillness and quiet, just the opposite of the traditions of revelry in the West and in China.

Individual Diversity and Social Studies

LEARNING OBJECTIVES

Describe the diversity inherent in individual learning personalities.

Describe how individual diversity can influence teaching and learning in elementary social studies.

Explain some limitations of individual diversity.

No two children are the same, and no two children learn the same. This simple idea has enormous consequences for teaching and learning. When we plan for elementary social studies instruction and implement those plans, we should take into account the idea of individual diversity. Individual diversity is the idea that students differ as individual learners, and we must respect and account for these differences when teaching.

DIVERSITY AND INDIVIDUAL LEARNING PERSONALITIES

Imagine a class of 20 third-grade students. Each student is completing a map exercise by labeling, coloring, and illustrating land and water forms in the state. One student starts by coloring the entire map red. Another student carefully labels each land form in green and each water form in blue. A third student is slow to start, preferring to study the map and look at resources the teacher has provided to help students. The other 17 students proceed in their own unique way. Individuals, such as the students in this class, differ in countless ways. In the classroom, each child has a learning personality. These individual learning personalities are shaped by environment and experience that may be the same, but each learning personality is ultimately unique.

In order to best meet the individual needs of students, teachers must address individual learning personalities. These personalities are marked by four distinct dimensions. The Process Diagram (FIGURE 12.7), "The elements of individual learning personalities," shows how teachers can address each of these dimensions in their planning.

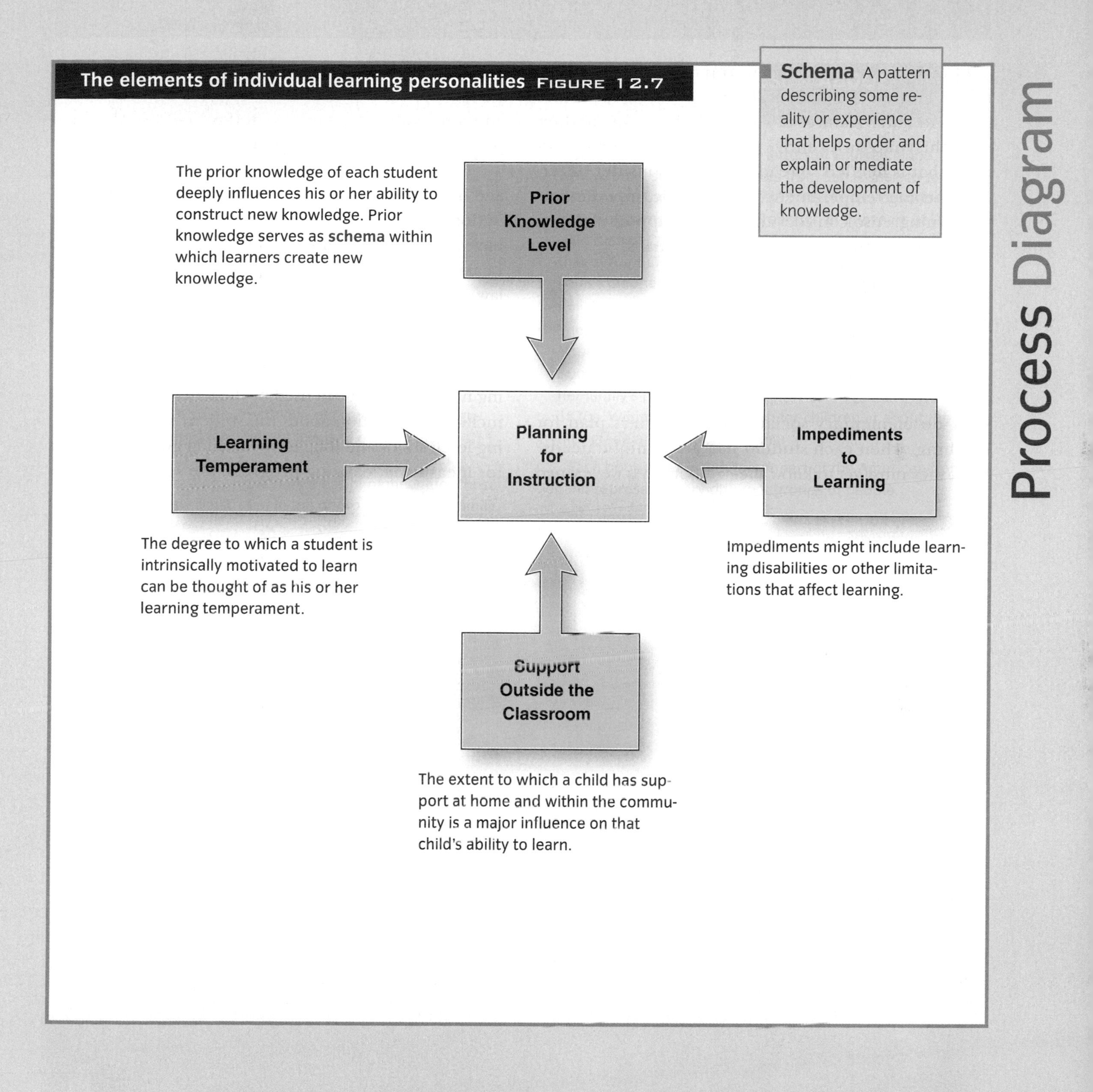
The elements of individual learning personalities FIGURE 12.7
Schema A pattern describing some reality or experience that helps order and explain or mediate the development of knowledge.
Process Diagram
The prior knowledge of each student deeply influences his or her ability to construct new knowledge. Prior knowledge serves as schema within which learners create new knowledge.
Prior Knowledge Level
Learning Temperament
Planning for Instruction
Impediments to Learning
The degree to which a student is intrinsically motivated to learn can be thought of as his or her learning temperament.
Impediments might include learning disabilities or other limitations that affect learning.
Support Outside the Classroom
The extent to which a child has support at home and within the community is a major influence on that child's ability to learn.

that will be provided, the extent the child will work outside of the regular classroom, modifications for formal assessments, the dates of special services, the process for informing parents/guardians of the child's progress, and plans for the reduction of services at age 16.

ILPs tend to be more informal and idiosyncratic. Although they are similar to IEPs, an Individual Learning Plan assumes that all of the student's learning needs can be met in the classroom with existing resources. The general idea is to have a plan for how to specialize instruction for a child given his or her learning personality. The plan can be quickly written using a format that includes the four dimensions of learning personalities reviewed in the previous section.

CONCEPT CHECK STOP

If teaching about the cultural institution of marriage, how can we represent the various traditions of marriage across the globe in a way that meets the individual needs of students in the class?

Are there any limits as to how concepts such as marriage might be considered in different cultural contexts?

This marriage of Selma and Khaled Sadek strengthened the ties between their families as the two are cousins. Most Saudi marriages are alliances between families, although Islamic law gives a woman final approval over her family's choice. A Saudi man is allowed as many as four wives, if he can treat them all equally.

Teaching in Schools with Homogeneous Social and Cultural Characteristics

LEARNING OBJECTIVES

Recognize the learning distinctions present in schools with homogeneous social and cultural characteristics.

Describe best teaching practices given limited social and cultural diversity.

Consider the consequences of certain approaches to teaching in schools with limited social and cultural diversity.

Despite the diversity present in many schools, some are strikingly homogeneous in terms of social and cultural characteristics. While numbers are hard to come by, every state has large pockets of homogeneous populations. Given that school populations are typically drawn from surrounding neighborhoods, schools in neighborhoods that are culturally similar are likely to also be culturally similar. There are exceptions that result from school system efforts to diversify student populations, but these efforts are typically limited to areas that have a history of racial discrimination.

GENERAL CONSIDERATIONS FOR TEACHING IN HOMOGENEOUS SETTINGS

How do teachers meet the needs of children when the social and cultural characteristics of the student body are relatively homogeneous? There are several things to keep in mind before you plan for any teaching experience in such schools.

1. Remember that all children are unique and have unique needs.
2. Never assign to an individual the characteristics of a group.
3. If you are not familiar with the cultural traditions of the community in which you work, take time to get to know what happens in the community.
4. Incorporate opportunities for children to use their cultural traditions as a context for learning new subject matter.
5. Carefully consider the cultural traditions that have shaped your students' learning personalities. Think how those learning personalities can be expanded and enriched.
6. Try to include information about other cultural traditions as subject matter in the lessons.

What might different groups of students in different schools know about life in a big city like New York (FIGURE 12.9)?

Consider students in a school in rural parts of Alabama or North Dakota. How might you approach teaching children who have limited experiences with urban areas about life in a city?

FIGURE 12.9

This aerial view shows New York with Brooklyn in the foreground and the skyscrapers of Manhattan in the background. Can you expect that children growing up here might have unique learning personalities that are reflective of their life in a large urban area?

Teaching about Timbuktu

The very name "Timbuktu" conjures up an image of distance and mystery. Most people know the name and understand it to be someplace far away. Children might have heard adults say something like, "Where is your friend's house?" "Oh, it's way out of town. It's in Timbuktu." How did these ideas about Timbuktu arise? This lesson is about the origin of the legend and the reality of the place called Timbuktu.

Timbuktu is a city in Mali, Africa, on the southern rim of the Sahara desert. Over one thousand years ago, the city was a flourishing settlement on the trade route between the sub-Sahara and North Africa. It was a city of wealth and a seat of Islamic learning. Its aura came from the inability of Europeans to visit this place. An overland route was impassable because of the desert, and until the late 15th century sea travel was impossible. Despite their lack of physical contact, the word and legend of Timbuktu grew. Eventually, in the 15th century and later, Europeans encountered Timbuktu, but by then it was quickly receding in power and glory. After Europeans made contact with Timbuktu, a young Alfred Lord Tennyson wrote a poem in 1829 called "Timbuktoo" essentially mythologizing the place.

As children learn about the real Timbuktu or any other place that is distant or remote, they may also be influenced by stereotypes and distanced by the lack of familiarity with people from the place being studied. Teachers must work to overcome these perceptions and help children appreciate and recognize the values of people from places that are, at first, strange and distant.

A view of the modern Timbuktu in the Saharan region of Mali. Timbuktu was once the hub of Africa where camel caravans met Niger River canoes. What do you know about Timbuktu? How does your prior knowledge influence your interest in learning about this place?

CURRICULUM AND HOMOGENEOUS CULTURAL SETTINGS

As we learned earlier, most social studies curriculum planners want to include a wide range of cultural subject matter in their curriculum. The actual development of curriculum can sometimes be continuous, but at minimum even a limited curriculum can be supplemented to include a rich set of cultural experiences for elementary school students. This should happen in all school settings, no matter how homogeneous the school population might be. However, special attention should be placed on implementing curriculum when in homogeneous cultural educational settings.

Teachers should try to balance a need to reflect the community's values and ideals through the curriculum with a goal of diversifying children's experiences through educational experiences. Many communities will already value cultural diversity no matter how little diversity there is in the community. But even when the community does not seem to value such diversity, teachers need to try to incorporate multiple cultural experiences into the curriculum. The goal is to honor the wishes of the community by attending to its cultural traditions while expanding the scope of what students experience by deliberately including information on other cultures in lessons.

CONCEPT CHECK **STOP**

What should social studies teachers take into consideration when teaching in homogeneous schools?

How should a teacher who is teaching about Islam in a mostly Jewish neighborhood school situate the study?

What special considerations must a teacher make for the lack of diversity in such settings?

More than two million Muslims prostrate themselves at the Grand Mosque in Mecca each year during the hajj. Tens of thousands pray on their knees in this photo.

CRITICAL AND CREATIVE THINKING QUESTIONS

- What might elementary students think about the sensibleness of living so close to an active volcano?
- How might American children relate to such a danger?
- How might their cultural geographic experience influence their understanding?

Outrigger canoes on Luzon Island in the Philippines rest on shore with the volcanic Mount Mayon rumbling in the background. Since 1616, Mayon has erupted 47 times, killing thousands of people. The most recent eruption in 1993 killed 93 people and led to the evacuation of more than 60,000.

SELF-TEST

1. What are the four forms of diversity? Which form of diversity is displayed in this image?

2. How have schools played a role in the expansion of opportunities to diverse groups of people in the United States?

3. Which is not a unique need for diverse learners?
   a. educational
   b. emotional
   c. behavioral
   d. biological

4. What is multiculturalism?

5. Label the elements of individual learning personalities on the figure below.

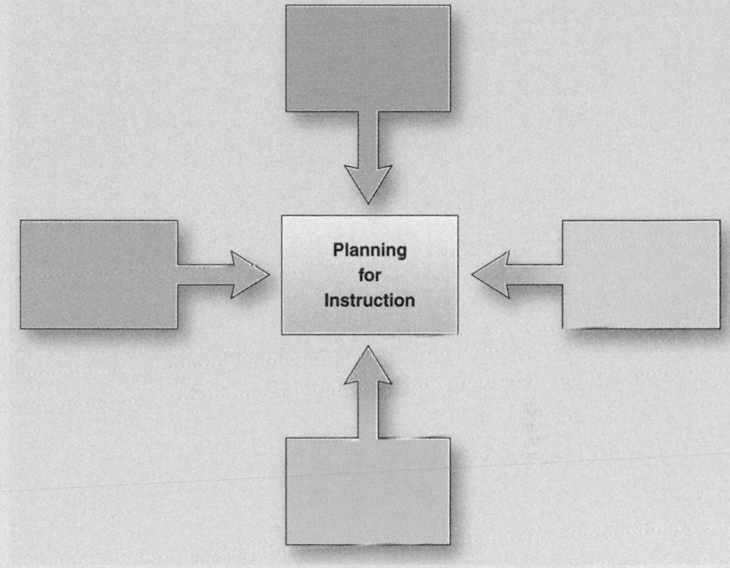

6. List Howard Gardner's eight multiple intelligences.

7. Which of the following describes the degree to which a student is intrinsically motivated to learn?
   a. learning temperament
   b. prior knowledge level
   c. support outside the classroom for learning
   d. impediments to learning

8. Describe three ways teachers can meet the needs of children when the social and cultural characteristics of the student body are relatively homogeneous.

9. What is the difference between an Individual Education Plan (IEP) and an Individual Learning Plan (ILP)?

10. How should teachers approach the challenge of teaching in a diverse manner in homogeneous cultural settings?

Assessing Learning

The United Nations–sponsored International Day of Peace provides an opportunity for elementary school students to explore the ways that nations around the world cooperate to solve problems and prevent conflicts. This day of recognition is celebrated in September on the first meeting day of the United Nations' General Assembly. It was started by the UN General Assembly in 1983 to "devote a specific time to concentrate the efforts of the United Nations and its Member States, as well as all people, to promoting the ideals of peace and to giving positive evidence of their commitment to peace in all viable ways." Schools all over the world participate in International Peace Day.

In Bridgeville, Delaware, students at Cedars Academy celebrated a recent International Day of Peace by making pinwheels for peace. The Malezi School in Langata, Kenya, just outside Nairobi was one of hundreds of schools in fifty countries that planted trees as a symbol for environmental protection and international cooperation.

Like other holidays and celebrations, International Peace Day in an elementary school classroom can include fun and memorable activities that children look forward to. How can teachers structure activities on such days so that the planned learning activities are meaningful and students' learning can be assessed? Whenever teachers plan to teach, they must consider how they will determine whether their students have learned what was expected.

The activity in which students make peace pinwheels might have students display specific things on their pinwheels. A teacher could ask students to include a definition of peace that they learned from another class activity, or an example of how people worked out a peaceful solution in a world event or in their personal lives. The teacher can set criteria for these requirements, and then check students' work to ensure that their definitions match that learned in class and that their examples are reasonable and clearly presented.

Children celebrating the International Day of Peace outside the United Nations headquarters in New York. How might you assess a definition of peace?

CHAPTER OUTLINE

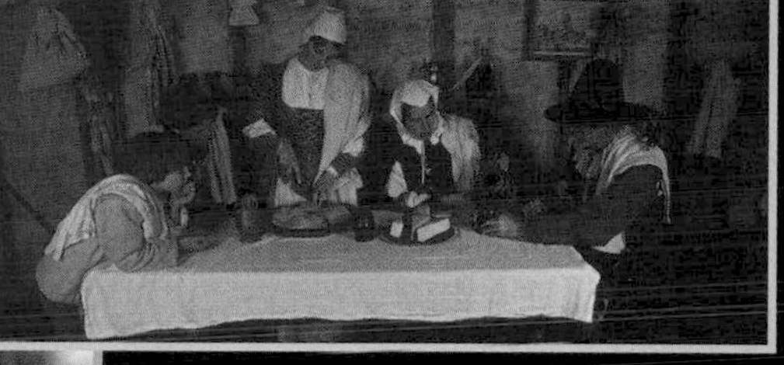

he assessment of learners' knowledge of subject matter is one of the most important things a teacher considers when planning and implementing instruction. In this chapter, we present student learning as a process that includes the teacher's effective and consistent use of assessment data. The chapter focuses on methods for collecting concrete evidence of learners' progress toward short- and long-term educational goals. Various forms of assessment and specific techniques are also presented.

As we consider assessment, note that assessment means different things to different people. Often, teachers view assessment data as a static body of information that simply serves to inform students of their progress. Viewing assessment this way only helps students know about their relative success on a task. In this chapter, assessment data are presented as a two-way process, which informs both teachers and students about what is happening in the classroom. This approach requires reflection on instruction and student learning given their progress as determined through assessment. In this chapter, case studies of specific assessment experiences highlight some of the ways that teachers can use assessment data to improve teaching and learning. Specific assessment techniques are also presented with special attention to subject matter and cognitive level.

Types of Assessment

LEARNING OBJECTIVES

Define assessment.

Describe the various types of assessment that might be used in elementary social studies.

Explain how assessment is a part of the teaching cycle.

hat did you learn today at school?" How many times do children hear this question from parents and others interested in their learning? The question gets at the heart of the school experience. Children attend school to learn, and everyone with a stake in the process is interested in that outcome. Consider the children in **FIGURE 13.1**. They are in school to learn and their teacher is informally assessing their learning by asking questions. By understanding the purpose and structure of assessment, teachers can begin the process of ensuring that their students have the best opportunity possible for learning and can answer questions about what they learned with confidence.

FIGURE 13.1

A fourth-grade teacher works with students on an English/language arts lesson about essay writing

WHAT IS ASSESSMENT?

Assessment is an ongoing process that involves the collection and analysis of information about student learning. Assessment is part of instruction and can occur at any time during a lesson. The information collected in the assessment process is rich and purposeful. Teachers use this information as data to make instructional decisions about the relative success of instruction, as well to make decisions about the direction the instruction will take going forward. When teachers assess learning they are taking the pulse of the class, so to speak. They are determining the progress of students in attaining some knowledge given the circumstances at the time and adjusting existing plans or making new plans about future instruction. Educational assessment in some ways is like what a sailor does when he checks the weather. If the sailor determines there are high winds, he will probably choose a smaller sail than if the winds are light. The sailor is acting on his assessment of conditions and, in much the same way, teachers must act on their assessment of students' learning.

Assessment
A continual instructional process for collecting and analyzing information about student learning.

Do not confuse assessment with evaluation. When educators evaluate students, they are typically trying to measure a specific student achievement so that it can be reported. Evaluation is often conducted to help policymakers and educational stakeholders make determinations about the relative success of instructional programs. Evaluation is much less a part of everyday teaching and learning than assessment. Unlike evaluation, assessment is continuous and routine. The general purpose of assessment is to improve student learning. Assessment is part of a holistic instructional process. It fits within the teaching and learning cycle, which views teaching and learning as an ongoing process. Assessment helps teachers and learners understand where to go next. Often, assessment prompts further interest on the part of a learner. When done effectively, assessment can encourage learners to seek out knowledge and to fill holes in their existing knowledge schema. Assessment helps teachers understand what their students know and do not know given specific learning objectives and should compel them to create new pedagogical opportunities given their students' assessed knowledge.

The reflective teaching cycle, which was introduced in Chapter 2, includes opportunities for assessment and conditions that require assessment data to be considered and acted upon. Teachers plan for assessment and implement those plans during instruction. Any activity has assessment potential, and the depth of any assessment is dependent on factors such as the amount of time available and the importance of the subject matter being learned in the activity. After conducting the assessment, teachers can use what they have learned about their students to rethink and reflect on the lesson. These considerations should lead teachers to develop new knowledge of the subject matter and new ideas about what to teach. The instruction that follows an assessment should be influenced by what the teacher learns in the process of assessing previous learning. This may result in reteaching or remediation for some or all students. Later in this chapter, we will look more closely at reteaching and remediation, and assessment as a part of instruction.

FORMAL AND INFORMAL ASSESSMENT

There are two main types of assessment: formal and informal. **Formal assessment** includes assessment activities that a teacher has designed for all the students in the class. These assessments are a kind of one-size-fits-all activity that often involves having students create something that can be turned in and graded. The procedures for grading students' work in formal assessments are guided by criteria that are provided to students in advance of their work and are held constant for all students completing the assignment.

Formal assessment
Consistent assessment approaches used for all students in a class to evaluate specific learning stages.

In early grades, children learn the value, purpose, and obligations of friendship. In social studies, the study of friendship can help children understand how

FIGURE 13.2
Alaskan Yupik Eskimos meeting with Russian Eskimos in the early 1980s

people organize social life. The picture in FIGURE 13.2 shows Alaskan Yupik Eskimos meeting with Russian Eskimos in the early 1980s before the fall of the Soviet Union. The two Eskimo groups shared deep cultural bonds, but were separated by the political differences between the United States and the Soviet Union. The meeting was billed as a meeting of friends designed to promote peace between the United States and the U.S.S.R. What can we learn from this story about friendship, and how might a teacher formally assess her students' learning on such a topic?

Informal assessment
Low-key and unintrusive teacher actions focused on determining whether students are learning during an activity.

Informal assessment is typically an in-progress effort by teachers to determine how well students are learning during a given activity. Teachers often conduct informal assessments through a simple question-and-answer procedure. Informal assessment is sometimes so continuous as to occur on a minute-by-minute basis. Teachers need to make informal assessments a seamless part of their instruction.

There are a number of formal and informal approaches to assessment. Below are examples of formal and informal assessment techniques with descriptions of how each might be implemented in an instructional setting.

Formal Assessment Techniques

Written assessments Teachers can use a wide variety of writing exercises to assess students' understanding of subject matter. Writing is an important form of expression in social studies. Teachers can use writing

FIGURE 13.3

Keys to the Bastille prison in Paris, France.

exercises as opportunities for their students to convey their understanding in a short period of time. There is virtually no limit to the kinds of writing assessments teachers might create. Students can write letters, journal entries, essays, structured paragraphs, articles, reports, reflections, stories, poetry, and any number of other forms. Teachers can also use a variety of contexts for writing assignments. The more authentic or real-life the context, the more likely students will be to engage the activity and succeed in their work.

Quizzes A short or focused quiz is a staple of most teachers' assessment systems. Quizzes consist of questions in some regular format that students can complete in a short period of time. Quizzes can provide teachers with quick and easy-to-grade opportunities to get feedback on their students' progress toward understanding low-level information. Quizzes normally focus on recall and identification, as well as classification and comparison. Unlike writing assignments, quizzes cannot easily be made authentic, but a quiz can help teachers motivate students to learn essential information that might be needed in more authentic assignments. Quizzes should not be confused with tests, which are typically more lengthy and standardized.

Expressive assessments Students need opportunities to express their knowledge in nontraditional formats. Both writing and quizzes are limited with regard to the extent to which they can get at what students might know about a topic. An expressive assessment is a technique that provides students an opportunity to demonstrate their knowledge in a variety of forms. Using various expressive formats, students can demonstrate their knowledge through oral presentations, graphical displays, illustrated portrayals, poetic renderings, stories, songs, or even staged events.

Consider **FIGURE 13.3**, which shows a view of the keys to the Bastille prison that fell to Parisians and militiamen on July 14, 1789. This day, much like July 4, 1776 in the United States, is celebrated in France as the symbolic beginning to the French Revolution.

- How might students express their knowledge of the famous storming of the Bastille, when French revolutionaries freed fellow patriots in the last years of the reign of King Louis IV?

Think of specific expressions that students might create such as drawings, poems, or plays. What kinds of knowledge can teachers assess from such expressive student work?

As is the case with written assessments and quizzes, teachers must have fixed expectations for student performance when using expressive formats. These expectations can take form as assessment rubrics. We discuss the topic of rubrics later in this chapter.

Informal Assessment Techniques

Questioning Engaging students with questions is an important method for informally determining their progress toward some learning goal. Questioning can be conducted in a verbal or written format. When asking questions, teachers should try to follow a few simple guidelines. First, they should try to construct questions in such a way as to elicit meaningful responses. Assessment-oriented questions should be open-ended and inviting. Second, teachers need to wait an appropriate amount of time before responding with an answer or a follow-up. Teacher responses to unanswered questions should always be in the form of a clarification or re-statement. Even when answering their own question, teachers should try to elicit students' cooperation in formulating the answer. Third, teachers should call on a mix of volunteers and nonvolunteers.

Polling When teachers want a quick check of how many students understand a topic or of any disagreement that might exist regarding uncertain content, they can use polling techniques. A student poll is simply a public showing of agreement or understanding of a teacher-directed question or idea. Polling can be a useful way to determine how many students agree with certain opinions or a quick way to see whether they understand simple concepts and ideas.

Seat check Sometimes teachers need to use less intrusive ways to check students' progress toward a learning goal. Questioning and polling require all students to pay attention to the teacher. If the work is student centered, then teachers can use assessment techniques that will not disrupt the flow of students' work. A seat check is such a method. The seat check involves the teacher moving around the room and checking students' work in progress as they continue to work. The seat check assessment requires that teachers have a particular set of criteria or items that they are looking for when they visit a student's desk or work area. If students are not making progress, teachers should take the opportunity to redirect, correct, or otherwise help them.

FORMATIVE AND SUMMATIVE ASSESSMENT

Assessment can serve two general purposes. It can provide learners with formative feedback on their progress toward some learning goal or it can be a summative end product designed to inform students and other educational stakeholders of students' achievement level at a given time. The Visualizing feature describes an activity with both formative and summative assessment procedures. Consider how these methods can complement one another in daily instruction.

In the Visualizing example about climates (**Figure 13.4**), Ms. Jones needed to decide how she wanted to assess her students. In the minute-to-minute instruction in the classroom, Ms. Jones used questioning as a way to find out what her students were learning. She adapted her instruction for the whole class and tailored it for individual students based on how they were progressing. Most classroom assessments are formative. Formative assessment includes any type of assessment that is directed at helping children advance their knowledge. Both formal and informal assessments can be formative. The key is for teachers to use the assessment process to help children understand both what they do not know and how they can come to know what they do not know.

Summative assessment serves a very different purpose. Instead of focusing on process, summative assessments are product oriented. Tests—both high-stakes and low-stakes—are summative, but other more creative assessments such as the one Ms. Jones gave her students can also be summative. Since summative assessment occurs toward or at the end of a learning period, teachers might not return to the subject matter for some time. Of course, if an evaluation of students' work on the summative assessment turns up significant problems, the teacher may want to include additional opportunities for students to learn the material. Teachers often share the results of summative assessments with parents and the larger community of educational stakeholders. High-stakes tests that might determine a child's ability to move on to the next grade are summative in nature. These assessments attempt to capture a student's grasp of a large body of knowledge in a fair and even-handed fashion.

Consider how teachers might plan for formative and summative assessment in a lesson on money. What happens to your money when it is deposited in a bank? Children commonly ask that question in elementary school. Some children might imagine their money going in a large safe such the one in the Concept Check image, but in reality most banks have a small fraction of the money their clients have deposited in actual cash. United States law requires that banks keep some of the money deposited on reserve. The rules for these

Visualizing

Teaching and Assessing about Climate Types FIGURE 13.4

In Celeste Jones's third-grade class, students learn about climate types using maps and pictures. Ms. Jones starts the lesson by introducing the five major climate types:

1. Tropical
2. Dry
3. Temperate
4. Continental
5. Polar

She shows students pictures and asks them to identify the climate type depicted in each photo. Ms. Jones then follows this with two more activities, one focused on similarities and differences in the five climates and the other on what it is like to live in each climate. The climates present striking differences in temperature and plant and animal life, but interesting similarities such as topography.

Ms. Jones conducts numerous assessments while teaching this topic. Some of these assessments are quick and help students apply their knowledge of climate types. For example, when a student was struggling to understand why humans would live in a polar environment, Ms. Jones used this as an opportunity to reinforce why most people live in temperate climates. Ms. Jones knew her student was unsure because she asked questions designed to assess her students' developing knowledge. As students answered the questions, Ms. Jones adapted (changed for the whole class) and tailored (changed for a student) her instruction.

At the end of the activity, students completed a summative assessment activity. Students wrote a short description of a day in the life of a person living in one of the five climates. Students described at least three characteristics of the climate. Through formative assessment such as questions and summative assessment at the end of class activity, Ms. Jones's students learned about the five climate types.

A A polar bear rests on an icy patch in arctic Canada.

B A man hoes a tropical field near Parc des Volcans in Rwanda.

reserves are set forth in the Federal Reserve Act and are governed by the Federal Reserve Board, sometimes known as "the Fed." The amount of money banks are required to keep "on reserve" or in cash ranges from 0 to 10% depending on the amount of the deposit. The larger the deposit is, the larger the reserve requirement.

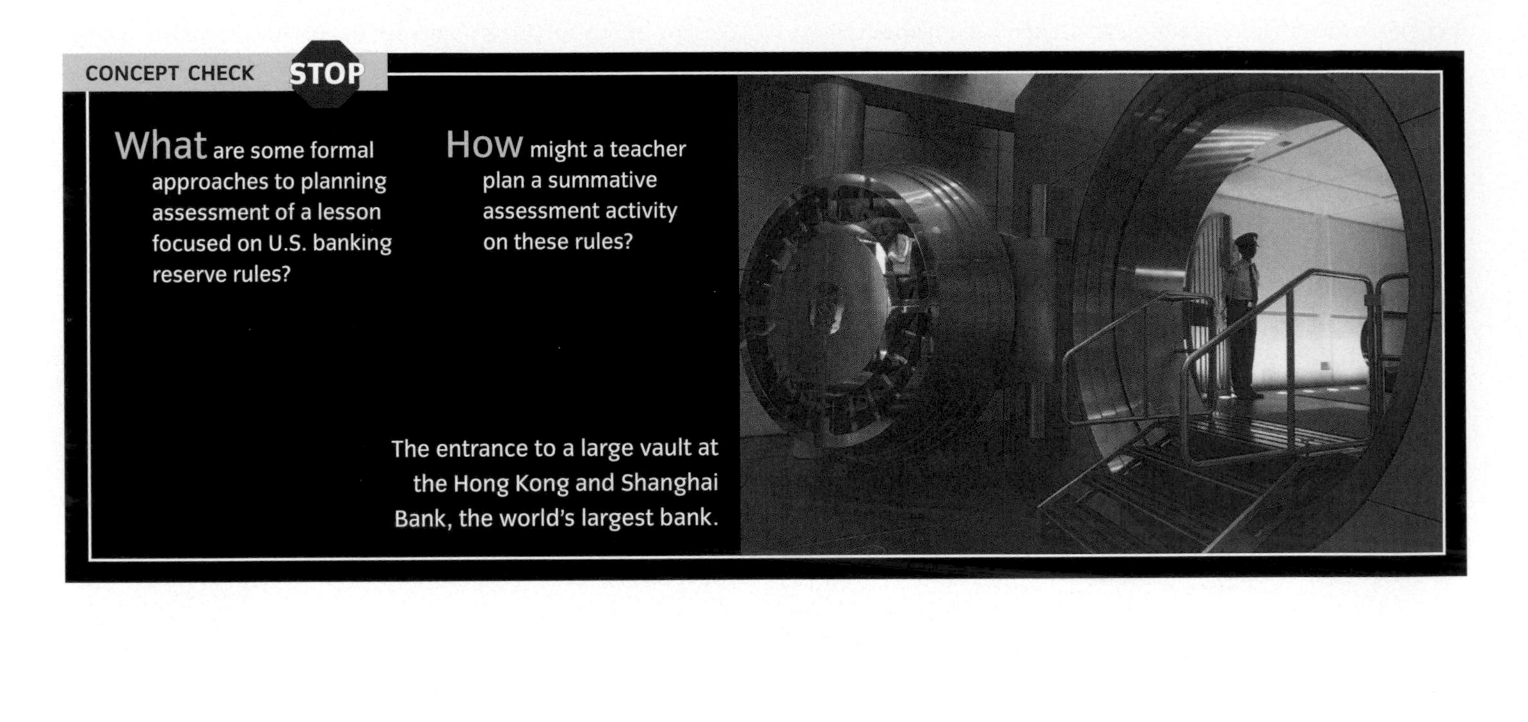

What are some formal approaches to planning assessment of a lesson focused on U.S. banking reserve rules?

How might a teacher plan a summative assessment activity on these rules?

The entrance to a large vault at the Hong Kong and Shanghai Bank, the world's largest bank.

Assessment as a Part of Instruction

Learning Objectives

Identify how assessment fits into the teaching cycle.

Evaluate various approaches to planning for assessment.

Identify effective means for implementing assessments.

Good instruction includes continuous and meaningful assessment. As an ongoing part of instruction, assessment provides teachers with opportunities to enhance student learning. When conducted with deliberate attention to the needs of individual students, assessment is a meaningful part of instruction. When planning for instruction and implementing these plans, teachers sometimes think of assessment as detached from instruction or as something that occurs after it. In this section, we consider assessment as a part of instruction by looking at how assessment fits in a teaching cycle and by considering planning and actual teaching examples of assessment as instruction.

ASSESSMENT IN THE TEACHING CYCLE

The reflective teaching cycle reviewed in Chapter 2 includes a four-part sequence of events. After developing subject matter knowledge, the teaching cycle includes three events that are directly related to assessment: instructional planning, instructional practice, and rethinking the lesson. When planning to teach, teachers must consider how they will determine whether their students are meeting the instructional objectives and goals for the lesson. (See **FIGURE 13.5**, Process Diagram: Assessment in the reflective teaching cycle.)

In Chapter 5, we looked at the myth and reality of the First Thanksgiving by considering how students might use a historical document to understand more

Process Diagram

Assessment in the reflective teaching cycle FIGURE 13.5

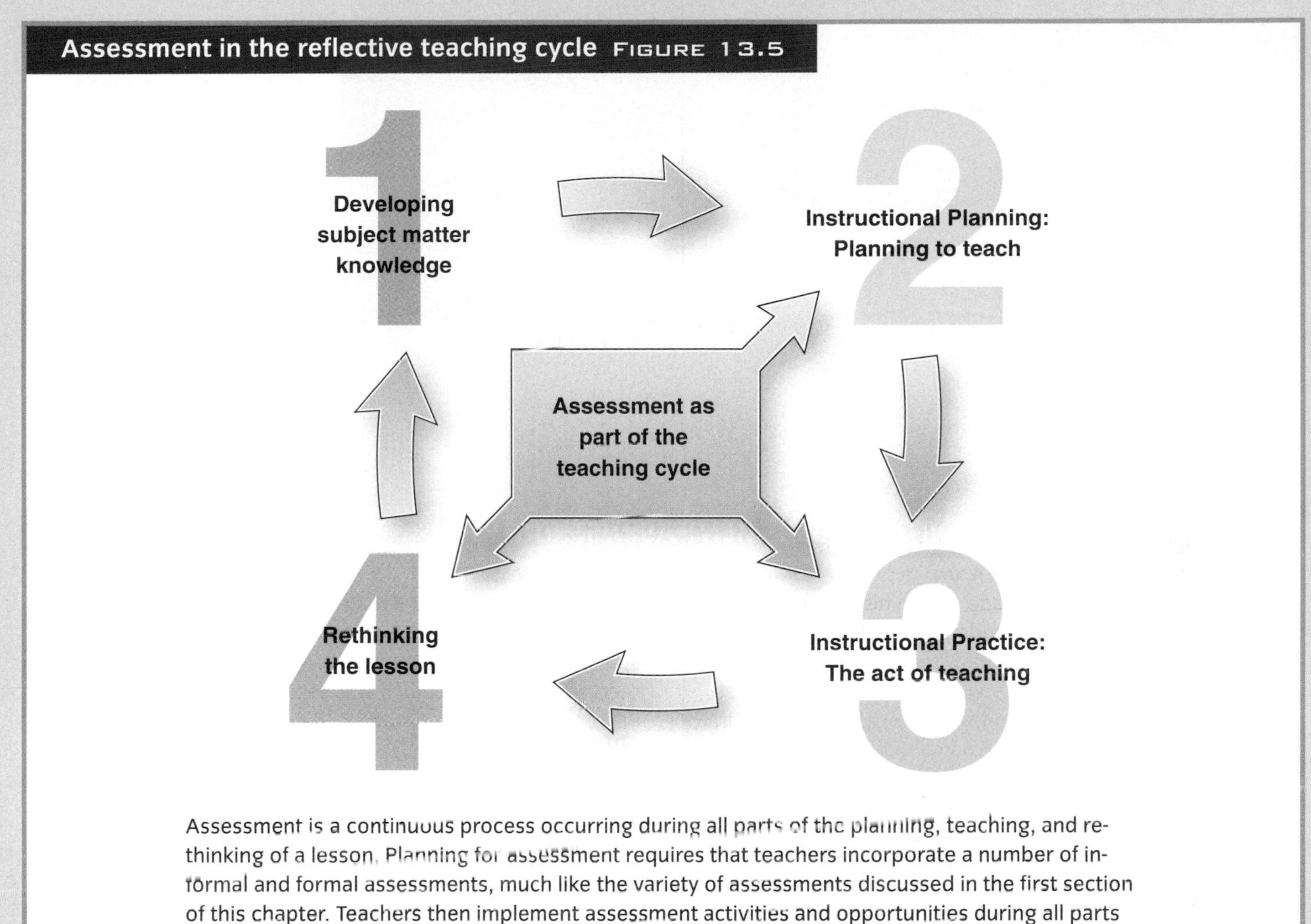

Assessment is a continuous process occurring during all parts of the planning, teaching, and rethinking of a lesson. Planning for assessment requires that teachers incorporate a number of informal and formal assessments, much like the variety of assessments discussed in the first section of this chapter. Teachers then implement assessment activities and opportunities during all parts of the lesson and use the results of their assessment to reflect on and rethink the lesson.

about the event. The story of the First Thanksgiving might be one of the most important and common social studies topics in early childhood grades. From 1630 to 1640, more than 20,000 Puritans settled in the emerging American colonies of New England. This wave of immigration came just 10 years after the establishment of the first Puritan colony in North America at Plymouth (actually settled by a small group of Puritans known as the "Pilgrims"). Plymouth was the first successful New England colony and ushered in the first sustained period of European immigration in North American history. Today, children learn about the Pilgrims and other Puritans in early grades through the Thanksgiving story, but in later elementary grades they might explore in more depth the reasons why Puritans came to North America.

How might we teach about the Pilgrims and Puritans, and how might assessment be a part of such a lesson? Let's look at how one teacher incorporated assessment in a lesson on the Pilgrims and Puritans ("In the Classroom: Assessment as instruction," on page 348).

When teachers plan for informal assessment, they typically plan time for questions and checking students' work. The implementation of these plans is highly dependent on local conditions related to how students are progressing. Informal assessment should also have an immediate effect on the progress of a lesson. If students are progressing successfully toward a learning goal, then the teacher will not need to intervene as much. If students are not having much success, then the teacher may need to adjust the instruction and even dramatically alter the plan for the lesson.

More formal assessment techniques are typically implemented according to fixed plans that normally do not have to deviate far from the existing plan. Such assessments are in fact a part of instruction. Viewing assessment as instruction enables a more transparent and meaningful type of assessment. Instead of directing assessment at simply providing students and their parents or guardians with information on students' progress, assessment as instruction enables teachers to use assessment activities as learning activities.

CONCEPT CHECK STOP

For assessment to be successful and meaningful, teachers must plan for it as an integral part of instruction. Consider a lesson on state flags.

HOW might a teacher assess students at the beginning, during, and at the conclusion of a lesson on symbolism in their state flag?

HOW might consideration of informal assessment affect how the lesson proceeds?

The state flag of Kentucky, like most of the 50 state flags, has symbolic importance. What are the symbols in the Kentucky flag? Who are the two people on the flag or who might they represent? Why is Kentucky called a Commonwealth? What is the meaning of "United we stand, Divided we fall"?

Using Assessments to Improve Teaching and Learning

LEARNING OBJECTIVES

Describe how teachers use assessments to help them understand how to teach more effectively.

Describe the value of assessment case studies.

Explain how reteaching and remediation evolve out of the assessment process.

eachers frequently use assessments to improve teaching and learning. As mentioned earlier in this chapter, adapting a lesson or some form of interaction with students is the pedagogical purpose of assessment. Assessment serves a very different purpose from the public reporting nature of evaluations. Although teachers need to share the results of their assessments with parents just as schools do when they publicize evaluation data from high-stakes tests, the primary use of assessment information is to immediately improve teaching and learning. This section includes a review of strategies for using assessment information to improve teaching and learning.

ASSESSMENT RESULTS AND EFFECTIVE TEACHING

Effective teaching requires that teachers know their students and how they are responding to specific instructional strategies. Some assessment strategies enable immediate feedback for teachers. For example, when questioning students, teachers can know immediately whether students are progressing in their understanding. Other forms of assessment require more time for the teacher to process. When possible, teachers should try to quickly assess students' work so they can make any adjustments that are necessary. Sometimes, the adjustments require just a simple restatement of an idea or concept, while other times more complex pedagogical actions must be taken.

Students in early childhood are often asked to study the past. Unless these studies encourage active learning and/or are collaborative, students might find their work dull. One approach to studying history might involve students thinking about the past as a series of unsolved mysteries. Such an approach can be particularly useful when the subject matter might otherwise be uninteresting.

As teachers collect assessment data, they can begin to develop an understanding of the topics in history that students consistently find hard to engage. Planning mystery-based explorations on subject matter that has proven difficult for students to engage is a good use of such assessment data. For example, an elementary school teacher may find that students have a hard time engaging subject matter related to ancient civilizations. Although students might find certain stories from ancient Egypt or Mesopotamia interesting, the details can often prove to be hard for them to relate to. When studying about ancient civilizations, active and collaborative mystery-oriented activities may encourage students to engage the subject matter in more depth. The Lesson on pages 352–353, "The Death of Tutankhamen," uses the theme of a mystery to explore ancient Egypt.

Pedagogical responses to assessment might be thought of as existing on a continuum from low-level adjustments to high-level adjustments. Low-level adjustments are quick and almost instinctual. They might involve teachers using an example to help students understand a concept, or comparing some misunderstood information to something the teacher believes students already understand. Higher-level adjustments involve reorganizing materials, instructional approaches, or instructional sequence to provide students a better opportunity to learn something. "In the Classroom: A new metaphor," on page 354, gives examples of various pedagogical adjustments teachers might make during instruction as a result of assessment.

6. Teachers introduce new books that provide for specific learning opportunities.
7. Students read the new book, selected by the teacher, using the strategies as listed above.

ASSESSMENT CASE STUDIES

Assessment case studies are in-depth examinations of the progress of a group of students toward learning goals. The assessment case study focuses deliberately on what large groups of students know and what the teacher can do to help them progress toward learning goals. The structure of an assessment case study is straightforward. When conducting an assessment case study, teachers should develop a good understanding of what they want students to learn, how they planned for students to learn, how the plan was implemented, what students actually learned, and how future instruction should be planned or modified given students' existing knowledge. In the feature, "In the Classroom: An assessment case study," a teacher explains what she learned through assessment about a lesson she taught on the inventions of the pencil with eraser, typewriter, and computer.

CONCEPT CHECK STOP

Students in the second or third grade in Georgia learn about Asia, including Japan. When studying Japan, students might learn about origami. This paper-folding art form dates to the beginning of papermaking in China over 2,000 years ago and was transported to Japan in the sixth century A.D.

How might assessment help teachers determine how to best make connections between Japan and origami?

What assessments might you conduct to determine whether students would benefit from learning about Japan through the study of origami?

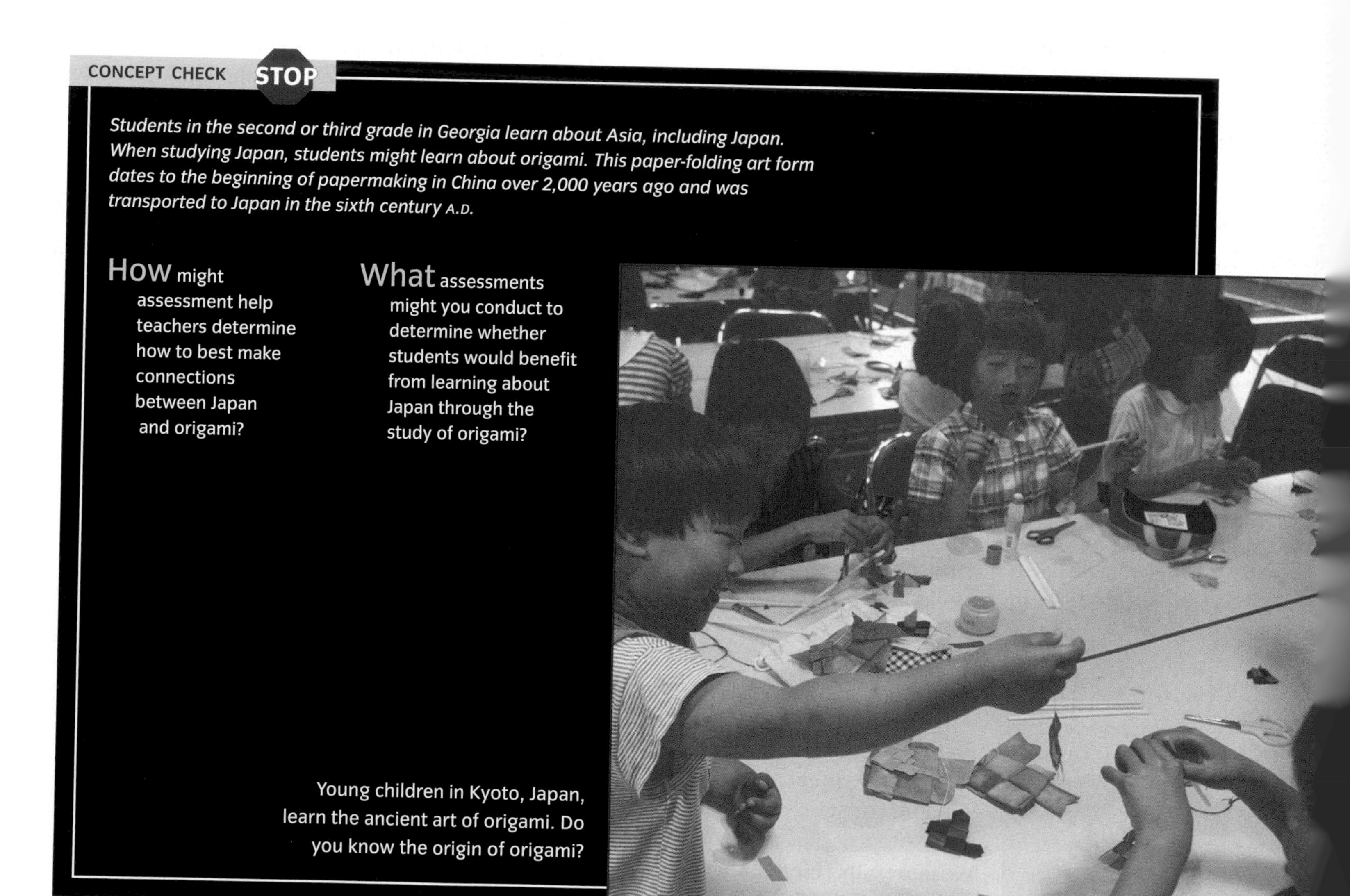

Young children in Kyoto, Japan, learn the ancient art of origami. Do you know the origin of origami?

In the Classroom AN ASSESSMENT CASE STUDY

From Helen, a fourth-grade teacher:

I developed this lesson to help my students learn about inventions related to writing. I began the class with some discussion about the inventing process and then broke students into groups of three and give them pictures of three inventions: the pencil with an eraser (1850s), the typewriter (1870s), and the computer (1940s). Each student was supposed to describe the purpose of the item in their picture and how they think it might have changed the writing process. Individuals then shared their work with the others in their group. The group was then supposed to decide which invention had the biggest impact or was most important and write a short explanation for why. In the explanation they were supposed to include the date of each invention, the way people wrote at the time, and how they thought the invention changed people's writing habits. I then evaluated the organization, accuracy, and content of the papers.

As I looked at the papers, I was checking for identification of the conditions that existed at the time of the invention. I was also looking for the recognition of how specific writing activities were changed by the invention. I explained both of these requirements prior to students' working the assignment and reviewed the information in the opening discussion.

Unfortunately, the students thought the task could be completed without considering the conditions at the time of the invention. The students' grades on the assignment were OK, but not great. Their content was mostly accurate, and their formatting was also pretty good. Although students did well on these parts of the assignment, their arguments were not so good. There was not really a "right" answer, but I did expect that students would understand how each invention impacted writing given what we talked about in class. I explained to students that the pencil with an eraser might have been the most important invention. When the pencil with an eraser was invented, people could now remove what they had written. The need to get it right the first time was suddenly reduced. If you made a mistake, you could just erase it. The typewriter influenced the development of the clerical industry, but not so much the everyday actions of individuals. The same might be said of the computer. Both devices were very expensive when they were invented. Despite the explanation, students focused on how each device is used today, which was good, but went beyond how the devices are used for writing. Almost to a group, they argued that the computer was the most influential writing-related invention.

Through this assessment, I realized that I could have been clearer in my discussion about how big a deal it was that people could erase their pencil marks and that this was a radical change from the entire history of writing. I also realized that I could have used examples of writing and learning to write from what is around us in the classroom and in students' lives. I should have pointed out that there are no typewriters in the room and only three computers, but everyone has a pencil. In fact, everyone is required to have a pencil. All children are taught how to write with a pencil before they are taught to type or use a computer. These realities are evidence of the importance of the pencil with eraser. I resolved to spend a few minutes in class the next day explaining this to students and hopefully helping them better understand the relative impacts of the pencil, typewriter, and computer on writing.

How important an invention was the pencil with an eraser? Was it more important than the invention of the typewriter or computer?

Designing and Using Rubrics

LEARNING OBJECTIVES

Recognize the purpose of assessment rubrics.

Describe the components of an assessment rubric.

Consider various uses of assessment rubrics.

Assessment **rubrics** are devices that enable teachers to determine the quality of their students' work. A rubric can be very simple or can be quite complex. Rubrics are important because they bring together two important elements of assessment—criteria and achievement. This section contains information about the purpose, design, and uses of assessment rubrics in elementary social studies.

Rubric Two-dimensional matrix of criteria that a teacher can use to make judgments about achievement levels for student work.

PURPOSE OF ASSESSMENT RUBRICS

When Joyce sat down to grade her students' work, she realized something was terribly wrong. She did not really know what to look for in students' work. Joyce, a student teacher in a third-grade class, had spent significant time planning her lesson on the Great Lakes and places such as Lake Michigan as shown in FIGURE 13.7.

Joyce's students were interested in the stories about lakes being carved from huge sheets of ice. They answered the questions she posed, and ultimately did a good job working on the 3D diorama projects she assigned.

Joyce had the students' completed projects, but she wasn't sure what to do with them. She wanted to give her students feedback and a grade. She also wanted to be

FIGURE 13.7

An evening view of a small lighthouse on Lake Michigan, one of the Great Lakes. Given this picture, how would you describe the Great Lakes?

fair, but she was unsure how to weight the directions she had given students. Joyce had told her students to create a representation of all five lakes. What if they were missing one lake? She had also told them to not worry as much about the shape being correct as the lakes being in the correct place relative to one another. Some unexpected issues arose as she looked at the projects. She saw that some of the lakes were misplaced. Also, some students had misspelled the names of lakes.

If Joyce had developed an assessment rubric prior to students' work, she might not have had as many problems, if any. Assessment rubrics allow teachers to determine students' grades and serve as a context for teachers to provide students with feedback on their work.

COMPONENTS OF ASSESSMENT RUBRICS

Assessment rubrics detail the criteria for an assignment and the performance level for each criterion. TABLE 13.1 is a graphic of the structure of an assessment rubric. Note that the performance levels are listed as Level A, Level B, and Level C.

These performance levels could be a number, letter, or other indication of performance. The performance levels could even include descriptions such as "excels" or "exceeds." Along the left of the table in the rows are individual criteria. These are the expectations for student work.

Rubrics: Performance Levels TABLE 13.1

	Level A	*Level B*	*Level C*
Criterion #1			
Criterion #2			
Criterion #3			
Criterion #4			

Assessment rubrics help teachers organize their assessment data and report them back to students, but in order for rubrics to function properly teachers need to develop quality criteria. Here's an example of how a teacher might develop criteria for an assessment on student learning about political traditions and holidays in the United States. In Illinois, children in early grades are expected to understand the development of political ideas and traditions in the United States. One specific descriptor requires that students "describe how a holiday such as Veterans Day represents the idea of sacrifice to preserve freedom." The photo in FIGURE 13.8 from the first Veterans Day parade in New York City makes clear the sacrifice that some made during World War I. What are some criteria for a discussion about the origins of Veterans Day and the idea of "sacrifice to preserve freedom"? Think about specific questions you might ask students and how you might expect students to respond to the questions (e.g., in writing, orally, volunteers, nonvolunteers).

FIGURE 13.8

A limping soldier and friends parade in New York City on November 11, 1918, the first Armistice Day (now celebrated as Veterans Day). How does this image illustrate sacrifice?

DEVELOPMENTALLY APPROPRIATE TECHNOLOGY

Each of the guidelines presented in Table 14.1 focuses on a different aspect of technology integration including teacher knowledge, planning and teaching, assessing, and ethics. When planning for using technology, the NCSS Technology Guidelines suggest that elementary teachers should "design developmentally appropriate learning opportunities that apply technology-enhanced instructional strategies to support the diverse needs of learners." Perhaps more than any other area, developmental issues must be considered when integrating technology into social studies.

Most importantly, teachers must ensure that their students are protected when using Web- and Internet-based resources. The **Internet** connects computers around the world via the TCP/IP protocol. Most schools will provide reasonable if not overly cautious safeguards in the classroom. However, opportunities still exist for children to be taken advantage of or to interact with resources that are inappropriate. Teachers must work to ensure that their students understand the risks of the Internet, as well as the advantages. One simple approach is to help students develop their own set of rules that reminds them to be careful when they are on the Internet. As you develop rules for using Internet resources, the following criteria might be helpful.

Internet An interconnected system of networks that connects computers around the world via the TCP/IP protocol.

1. When considering whether a Web resource is appropriate for students, determine who owns or is responsible for the content on the Web site. Web sites or other Internet resources for children should have transparent purposes and operations.

2. Ensure that your students' rights and privacy are protected. If the Web site or other resource requires personal information as a prerequisite for participation, carefully consider how that information will be used. Do not give any personal information about a student.

3. Make sure all information and resources are open and easily accessible. Educational resources for elementary school students should be clearly focused, given specific developmental issues.

4. Often, Web sites and other Internet resources have advertising and links to other sites and services. The teacher should limit these links and check them out ahead of time.

Refugees cross a flooded field during monsoon season

Technological Applications

LEARNING OBJECTIVES

Identify how to best use Web-based resources in social studies.

Describe methods for locating information on the Web.

Recognize the connections between technology, democracy, and human experiences.

FINDING AND USING WEB-BASED RESOURCES AND INFORMATION

he vastness of the **Web** can be overwhelming. Both teachers and students must exercise care when trying to find meaningful resources. Locating resources for use in social studies can be effectively managed by using a three-part strategy. Depending on the age of the student, teachers may need to conduct searches and locate resources for students in advance. Students in upper elementary grades may be able to find some resources themselves using appropriate Web sites, but the following recommendations can be used to scaffold those experiences.

Web World Wide Web (WWW) Electronic resources—text, visual, audio—residing on all Internet servers that use the HTTP protocol, accessible to users via a simple point-and-click computer system.

1. Develop a curriculum or subject matter context for the identification of resources. These contexts are built from curricular and secondary source–derived subject matter knowledge. Contexts can be questions that when answered might help students know whether the information they are looking at is worthwhile.
2. Narrow the search for information or resources given the characteristics of the resource. This should involve developing some guidelines related to subject of the information, the media (text, pictures, video, etc.), and the length.
3. Summarize the information, or represent it in some manner different from how it exists on the Web.

Think about how teachers or students might use this process to locate information on a curriculum-related topic such as celebrations in Mayan civilization as depicted in **FIGURE 14.6**.

FIGURE 14.6

Maya dancers dressed as hunters and a jaguar perform the Deer Dance.

The Process Diagram (FIGURE 14.7) provides more detail on the three strategies for finding Web-based information. Another more detailed exploration of this process of a Web search in social studies is described in the "Visualizing" feature (FIGURE 14.8).

TECHNOLOGY, DEMOCRACY, AND THE HUMAN EXPERIENCE

Technology can play an important role in addressing the commonly agreed upon goal of citizenship preparation for social studies. Technology, particularly Internet-based, can enhance existing civic dialogue and encourage talk that would not have otherwise been possible. Teachers can connect their students with elected representatives using the Internet. They can use **multimedia** to demonstrate places and cultural contexts that make up the multicultural experience in the United States. Using technological resources and communication networks appropriately can minimize boundaries between people and help us see how we are dependent on one another.

Multimedia
The combined use of media, such as movies, music, lighting, CD-ROMs, and the Internet, for education or entertainment.

Process Diagram

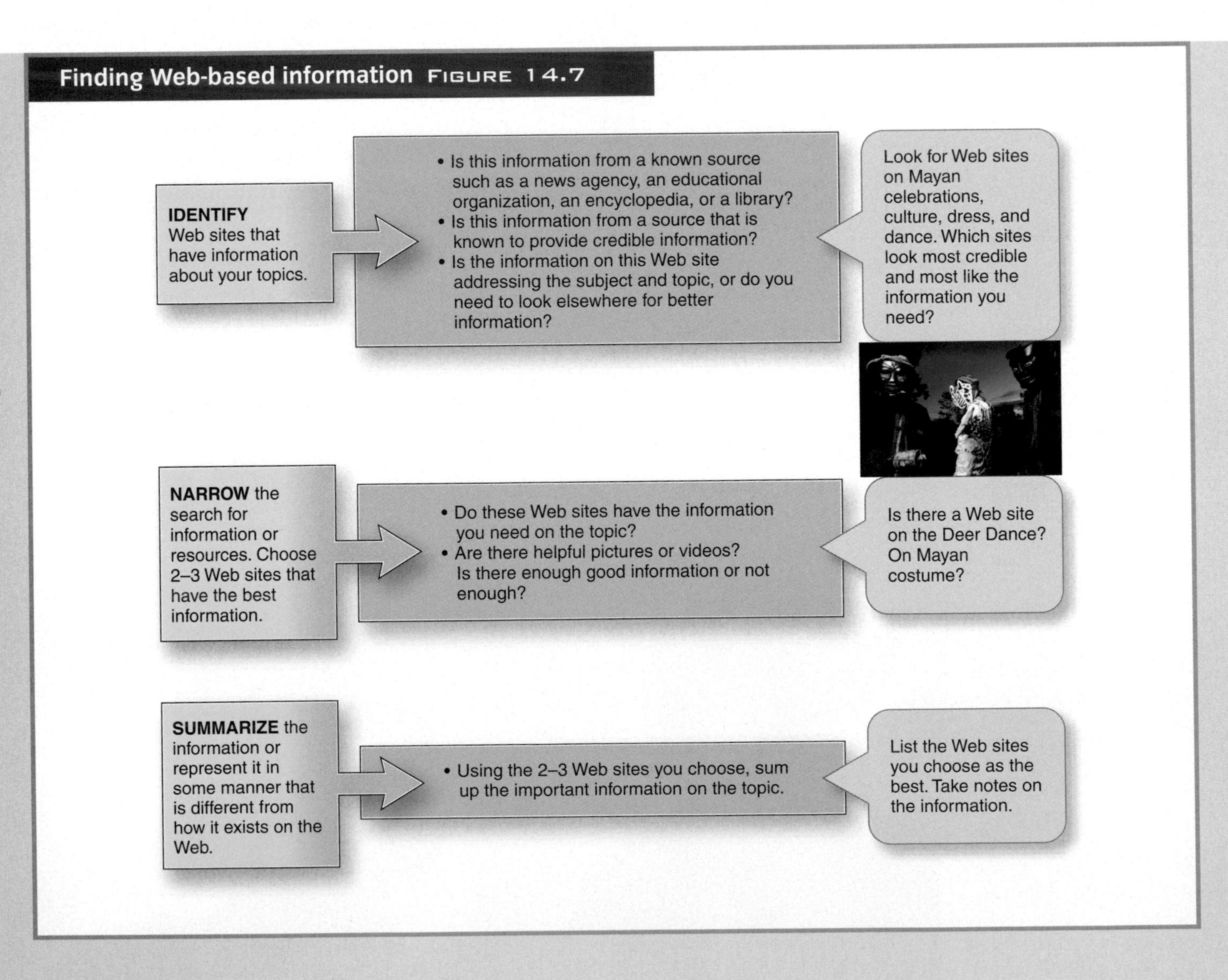

Visualizing

A Web Search in Social Studies FIGURE 14.8

Finding resources on the Web can be like looking for the proverbial needle in a haystack. A good Web search requires a clear purpose and a critical eye. Teachers can help their students find resources online by providing them with supportive scaffolds and models of productive searches. Consider a search for information about humans' uses of horses.

- What types of curriculum context might help students when searching for information about humans' uses of horses? Contexts might include uses that are recreational, work-related, or cultural.
- As students search for information about horses given specific curriculum contexts, what sorts of information or resources might be appropriate for students to use? Students might use general search resources such as Google or reference materials such as Wikipedia or might access specific resources such as www.theultimatehorsesite.com.
- How might students summarize information they find on the Web? Students must be helped to make use of information that is available on the Web in ways that might not have been intended by the author. For example, if students are learning about horses from a Web site focused on caring for horses, the teacher should help students understand what information might be useful and what is not as useful.

Close-action shot of horses racing in the Kentucky Derby

The horse was first acquired by the Nez Perce sometime in the early 18th century, probably through trade with, or theft from, their southern neighbors. A symbol of wealth and pride, horses were an integral part of Nez Perce society and were used for a number of purposes such as hunting, raiding, or traveling from camp to camp.

Terra cotta horses excavated from the third-century B.C.E. Chinese Emperor Qin Shi Huangdi's tomb

Imagine using technology to visit the Hagia Sophia in Istanbul, as seen in FIGURE 14.9A, or the canals of Venice as depicted in FIGURE 14.9B. Using **digital** images, video, and audio, students can have experiences with places that they might not otherwise have.

Digital Expressed in numerical form, especially for use by a computer, and displayed as an electronic representation of some other physical form.

Of course, these experiences are not nearly as powerful as being there, and virtual visits should never take the place of an actual visit, but an experience with a place using technology can begin the process of opening young people's minds to the richness and variety of the human experience.

Other technologies provide students with opportunities to interact with children from places around the world and to learn about diverse human experiences in different countries. The Model United Nations Headquarters at the United Nations Cyberschoolbus Web site (http://www.un.org/cyberschoolbus/) epitomizes this type of student interaction on a wide range of issues. Through this resource, children of all ages can investigate other cultures, study about how people are working together to solve global problems, and express themselves while learning from other young people.

Numerous media and technological resources can facilitate the exploration of democratic themes. For example, the C-SPAN television network provides virtually every minute of every congressional debate, thousands

Virtual explorations FIGURE 14.9

A Side domes and added minarets gather about the great vault of Hagia Sophia in Istanbul, Turkey. This church has been the focus of Christianity for nine centuries and of Islam for five more. The original structure was designed by Isodorus of Miletus and Anthemius of Tralles under the direction and funding of Emperor Justinian I. The historic areas of Istanbul are a World Heritage site.

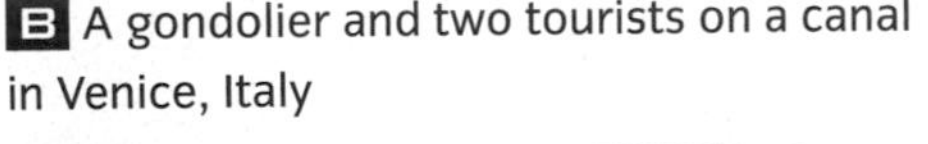

B A gondolier and two tourists on a canal in Venice, Italy

of congressional committee hearings, and countless programs related to political and civic issues and public policy. Social studies teachers can use other resources such as those made available by National Geographic (FIGURE 14.10) to help students learn about a wide range of topics and issues in social studies.

Teachers can have their students engage these programs as active participants in the debate. This may mean simulating the debate in the classroom, participating in role-playing activities, or attempting to solve the problems being addressed. Advocates of issues-based education such as NCSS encourage the use of resources similar to those listed here to conduct issues-based inquiries. This type of inquiry allows students to solve real-life problems using procedures based on the scientific model of observation, hypothesis, experiment, conclusion, and theory.

FIGURE 14.10

Screen shot of National Geographic Web site

CONCEPT CHECK STOP

How can elementary school teachers use technology to teach about the technological changes that influence the development of place?

How does the Masjid-I-Shah Mosque function as a place?

How does technology affect this place?

Exterior view of the Masjid-I-Shah Mosque in Isfahan, Iran

Instruction and Technology

LEARNING OBJECTIVES

Describe four issues to consider when planning to use technology in elementary school social studies.

Explain how to use computer-based games in elementary school social studies.

PLANNING FOR TEACHING WITH TECHNOLOGY

Social studies educators can use technology to promote specific instructional objectives by creating authentic experiences that encourage critical and active student learning in elementary social studies. The Lesson titled "Technology Timeline" describes an activity in which students learn about technology while using technology in authentic ways. Technology offers special opportunities, but also creates unique challenges. There are four issues to keep in mind when planning to teach with technology.

1. If using a computer or some other digital device, determine the number of devices that will be needed. Also consider the consequence of working with a limited number of devices.
2. Think about how long it will take to complete the activity using the technology selected for the activity. Often, technology requires setup and extended directions for students. If the setup work and/or directions take extended time, reconsider whether the activity could be completed without using technology.
3. Consider the extent to which students will be engaged with social studies subject matter as opposed to focusing on a technology or technology device. For example, Microsoft PowerPoint® presentational software can sometimes lead students to focus more on the technology than the subject matter. The general rule should be that the technology improves students' opportunities to learn subject matter without distracting from the subject matter.
4. Think about students' technology skills. If students are at different levels with regard to their skills, consider how you will bring students up to the skill level they will need in order to complete the activity. Sometimes this can be achieved by pairing technologically savvy students with students who have less developed skills.

LESSON

Technology Timeline

INTRODUCTION

For this lesson, students construct an annotated timeline that traces selected technological innovations from the last 2,000 years of human history.

INSTRUCTIONAL GOALS AND OBJECTIVES

Students identify some of the most significant technological advancements in human history and represent these technological advancements in chronological order using a multimedia presentation tool.

PROCEDURE

In 1998, author John Brockman proposed an interesting question to an organization of more than 100 scholars. His question was simply, "What is the most important invention in the past two thousand years?" Responses to this question varied from the somewhat obscure public key inscription system (a security system for computers) to more expected candidates such as the steam engine or the computer. Eleven of the inventions nominated by the scholars are listed here.

1. The printing press
2. The scientific method
3. The computer
4. Numbers
5. Reading glasses
6. The atomic bomb
7. Democracy
8. The steam engine
9. Clocks
10. Plumbing
11. Hay

This activity involves students using the Web to find out the dates of these inventions. Students then construct an illustrated timeline of the inventions. They can base their illustrations on information they find on the Web. The timeline could be a graphic illustration of the occurrence of these events, with notations that accompany the timeline. Depending on the time for this activity and the students' age, notations can be simple or detailed enough to stand alone as narrative descriptions.

These mini-narratives could focus on the impact the innovation had on human history and culture and can include both the positive and negative consequences of the particular innovation.

Suggested resources for this research include standard world history textbooks and the Web resources listed here.

Resources related to inventions:

- *World History: Attitudes and Events, from Early Humanity to Yesterday*, by Frank Smitha, at http://www.fsmitha.com
- Historical inventions at About.com at http://inventors.about.com

ASSESSMENT

As an assessment, students can rank the technological innovations listed. They should base their rankings on criteria developed by the students. They should explain the criteria in a short paragraph.

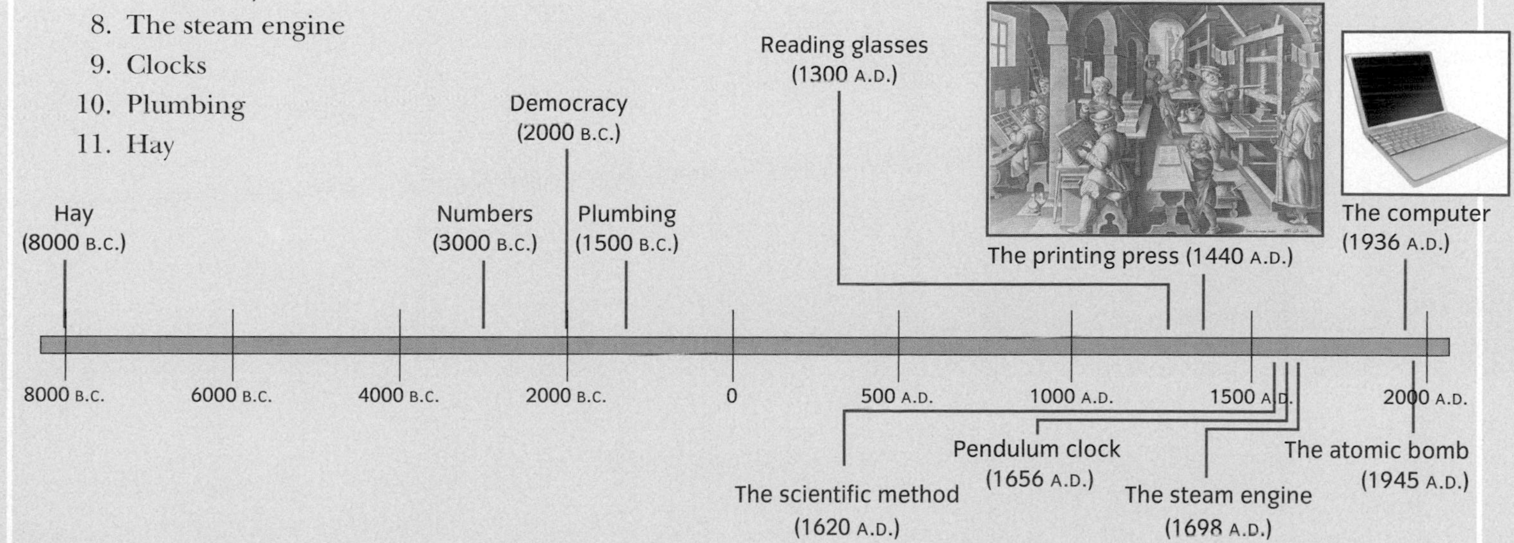

USING COMPUTER-BASED GAMES

When we think of games, we might not think of education, but games do have an important role in elementary social studies. Some of the most powerful and mainstream social studies methods, such as simulations, role-plays, and even discussions, have game-like structures. Games are often characterized as a form of entertainment or amusement, but games also involve rules, strategies, and competition, all of which can be useful in educational activities. Each of these characteristics can be emphasized in social studies activities to enhance learning.

Social studies teachers can use many forms of games, including those that are computer-based. Early computer-based strategy games such as Oregon Trail and Where in the World Is Carmen Santiago? introduced thousands of children to computer technology in the 1980s and 1990s. Today, thousands of games in and out of school compete for children's attention. Games such as Sim City, which requires students to plan and build a city, include fundamental social studies–related concepts. Consider how a game like Sim City might be used to help students understand construction in a city such as Beijing as depicted in FIGURE 14.11. The "In the Classroom" feature describes how one teacher learns about new games from his students and then plans to use these games in his classroom.

How can we use these games in elementary social studies, and what are the characteristics of good elementary-level social studies games? Let's look first at some of the characteristics of educative games.

1. Good social studies computer-based games should have a curricular-based subject matter focus.

FIGURE 14.11

A Beijing, China, street scene showing a shopping mall construction project called Pinyan Road in the background

In the Classroom GAMES AS INSTRUCTION

What is your favorite computer game? Mr. Alexander asks his third-grade students this question when he starts his unit on games. The question is designed to help students make connections between their lives and the subject being studied in class, but it also gives Mr. Alexander an opportunity to find out about new computer-based games.

The students tell Mr. Alexander about games that span a range of interests, and while listening he is constantly thinking about how he might use each game in his class. As he imagines how he can use the games, Mr. Alexander tries to keep three things in mind.

1. Will the game focus students' attention on subject matter that is in the curriculum?
2. How much time will it take to play the game?
3. Can students learn by playing the game?

As the activity continues, Mr. Alexander stores away what he has learned about his students' gaming interests and revisits some of the games in the context of other activities. One particular game that Mr. Alexander decides to use is called Civilization, a computer-based simulation involving building, exploration, discovery, and conquest in both historical and imaginary contexts. The game includes competitive elements and can be very complicated. Mr. Alexander uses the demonstrations from the game to engage his students in themes from ancient civilizations such as Rome that are explored in the game.

A view of Ancient Rome. How might a computer-based simulation game help students learn about exploration and discovery of Ancient Rome?

Constitution of the United States

WE THE PEOPLE of the United States, in order to form a more perfect union, establish justice, insure domestic tranquility, provide for the common defense, promote the general welfare, and secure the blessings of liberty to ourselves and our posterity, do ordain and establish this Constitution for the United States of America.

Article I

Section 1. All legislative powers herein granted shall be vested in a Congress of the United States, which shall consist of a Senate and House of Representatives.

Section 2. The House of Representatives shall be composed of members chosen every second year by the people of the several states, and the electors in each state shall have the qualifications requisite for electors of the most numerous branch of the state legislature.

No person shall be a Representative who shall not have attained to the age of twenty five years, and been seven years a citizen of the United States, and who shall not, when elected, be an inhabitant of that state in which he shall be chosen.

Representatives and direct taxes shall be apportioned among the several states which may be included within this union, according to their respective numbers, which shall be determined by adding to the whole number of free persons, including those bound to service for a term of years, and excluding Indians not taxed, three fifths of all other Persons. The actual Enumeration shall be made within three years after the first meeting of the Congress of the United States, and within every subsequent term of ten years, in such manner as they shall by law direct. The number of Representatives shall not exceed one for every thirty thousand, but each state shall have at least one Representative; and until such enumeration shall be made, the state of New Hampshire shall be entitled to chuse three, Massachusetts eight, Rhode Island and Providence Plantations one, Connecticut five, New York six, New Jersey four, Pennsylvania eight, Delaware one, Maryland six, Virginia ten, North Carolina five, South Carolina five, and Georgia three.

When vacancies happen in the Representation from any state, the executive authority thereof shall issue writs of election to fill such vacancies.

The House of Representatives shall choose their speaker and other officers; and shall have the sole power of impeachment.

Section 3. The Senate of the United States shall be composed of two Senators from each state, chosen by the legislature thereof, for six years; and each Senator shall have one vote.

Immediately after they shall be assembled in consequence of the first election, they shall be divided as equally as may be into three classes. The seats of the Senators of the first class shall be vacated at the expiration of the second year, of the second class at the expiration of the fourth year, and the third class at the expiration of the sixth year, so that one third may be chosen every second year; and if vacancies happen by resignation, or otherwise, during the recess of the legislature of any state, the executive thereof may make temporary appointments until the next meeting of the legislature, which shall then fill such vacancies.

No person shall be a Senator who shall not have attained to the age of thirty years, and been nine years a citizen of the United States and who shall not, when elected, be an inhabitant of that state for which he shall be chosen.

The Vice President of the United States shall be President of the Senate, but shall have no vote, unless they be equally divided.

The Senate shall choose their other officers, and also a President pro tempore, in the absence of the Vice President, or when he shall exercise the office of President of the United States.

The Senate shall have the sole power to try all impeachments. When sitting for that purpose, they shall be on oath or affirmation. When the President of the United States is tried, the Chief Justice shall preside: And no person shall be convicted without the concurrence of two thirds of the members present.

Judgment in cases of impeachment shall not extend further than to removal from office, and disqualification to hold and enjoy any office of honor, trust or profit under the United States: but the party convicted shall nevertheless be liable and subject to indictment, trial, judgment and punishment, according to law.

Section 4. The times, places and manner of holding elections for Senators and Representatives, shall be prescribed in each state by the legislature thereof; but the Congress may at any time by law make or alter such regulations, except as to the places of choosing Senators.

The Congress shall assemble at least once in every year, and such meeting shall be on the first Monday in December, unless they shall by law appoint a different day.

Section 5. Each House shall be the judge of the elections, returns and qualifications of its own members, and a majority of each shall constitute a quorum to do business; but a smaller number may adjourn from day to day, and may be authorized to compel the attendance of absent members, in such manner, and under such penalties as each House may provide.

Each House may determine the rules of its proceedings, punish its members for disorderly behavior, and, with the concurrence of two thirds, expel a member.

Each House shall keep a journal of its proceedings, and from time to time publish the same, excepting such parts as may in their judgment require secrecy; and the yeas and nays of the members of either House on any question shall, at the desire of one fifth of those present, be entered on the journal.

Neither House, during the session of Congress, shall, without the consent of the other, adjourn for more than three days, nor to any other place than that in which the two Houses shall be sitting.

Section 6. The Senators and Representatives shall receive a compensation for their services, to be ascertained by law, and paid out of the treasury of the United States. They shall in all cases, except treason, felony and breach of the peace, be privileged from arrest during their attendance at the session of their respective Houses, and in going to and returning from the same; and for any speech or debate in either House, they shall not be questioned in any other place.

No Senator or Representative shall, during the time for which he was elected, be appointed to any civil office under the authority of the United States, which shall have been created, or the emoluments whereof shall have been increased during such time: and no person holding any office under the United States, shall be a member of either House during his continuance in office.

Section 7. All bills for raising revenue shall originate in the House of Representatives; but the Senate may propose or concur with amendments as on other Bills.

Every bill which shall have passed the House of Representatives and the Senate, shall, before it become a law, be presented to the President of the United States; if he approve he shall sign it, but if not he shall return it, with his objections to that House in which it shall have originated, who shall enter the objections at large on their journal, and proceed to reconsider it. If after such reconsideration two thirds of that House shall agree to pass the bill, it shall be sent, together with the objections, to the other House, by which it shall likewise be reconsidered, and if approved by two thirds of that House, it shall become a law. But in all such cases the votes of both Houses shall be determined by yeas and nays, and the names of the persons voting for and against the bill shall be entered on the journal of each House respectively. If any bill shall not be returned by the President within ten days (Sundays excepted) after it shall have been presented to him, the same shall be a law, in like manner as if he had signed it, unless the Congress by their adjournment prevent its return, in which case it shall not be a law.

Every order, resolution, or vote to which the concurrence of the Senate and House of Representatives may be necessary (except on a question of adjournment) shall be presented to the President of the United States; and before the same shall take effect, shall be approved by him, or being disapproved by him, shall be repassed by two thirds of the Senate and House of Representatives, according to the rules and limitations prescribed in the case of a bill.

Section 8. The Congress shall have power to lay and collect taxes, duties, imposts and excises, to pay the debts and provide for the common defense and general welfare of the United States; but all duties, imposts and excises shall be uniform throughout the United States;

To borrow money on the credit of the United States;

To regulate commerce with foreign nations, and among the several states, and with the Indian tribes;

To establish a uniform rule of naturalization, and uniform laws on the subject of bankruptcies throughout the United States;

To coin money, regulate the value thereof, and of foreign coin, and fix the standard of weights and measures;

To provide for the punishment of counterfeiting the securities and current coin of the United States;

To establish post offices and post roads;

To promote the progress of science and useful arts, by securing for limited times to authors and inventors the exclusive right to their respective writings and discoveries;

To constitute tribunals inferior to the Supreme Court;

To define and punish piracies and felonies committed on the high seas, and offenses against the law of nations;

To declare war, grant letters of marque and reprisal, and make rules concerning captures on land and water;

To raise and support armies, but no appropriation of money to that use shall be for a longer term than two years;

To provide and maintain a navy;

To make rules for the government and regulation of the land and naval forces;

To provide for calling forth the militia to execute the laws of the union, suppress insurrections and repel invasions;

To provide for organizing, arming, and disciplining, the militia, and for governing such part of them as may be employed in the service of the United States, reserving to the states respectively, the appointment of the officers, and the authority of training the militia according to the discipline prescribed by Congress;

To exercise exclusive legislation in all cases whatsoever, over such District (not exceeding ten miles square) as may, by cession of particular states, and the acceptance of Congress, become the seat of the government of the United States, and to exercise like authority over all places purchased by the consent of the legislature of the state in which the same shall be, for the erection of forts, magazines, arsenals, dockyards, and other needful buildings;—And

To make all laws which shall be necessary and proper for carrying into execution the foregoing powers, and all other powers vested by this Constitution in the government of the United States, or in any department or officer thereof.

Section 9. The migration or importation of such persons as any of the states now existing shall think proper to admit, shall not be prohibited by the Congress prior to the year one thousand eight hundred and eight, but a tax or duty may be imposed on such importation, not exceeding ten dollars for each person.

The privilege of the writ of habeas corpus shall not be suspended, unless when in cases of rebellion or invasion the public safety may require it.

No bill of attainder or ex post facto Law shall be passed.

No capitation, or other direct, tax shall be laid, unless in proportion to the census or enumeration herein before directed to be taken.

No tax or duty shall be laid on articles exported from any state.

No preference shall be given by any regulation of commerce or revenue to the ports of one state over those of another: nor shall vessels bound to, or from, one state, be obliged to enter, clear or pay duties in another.

No money shall be drawn from the treasury, but in consequence of appropriations made by law; and a regular statement and account of receipts and expenditures of all public money shall be published from time to time.

No title of nobility shall be granted by the United States: and no person holding any office of profit or trust under them, shall, without the consent of the Congress, accept of any present, emolument, office, or title, of any kind whatever, from any king, prince, or foreign state.

Section 10. No state shall enter into any treaty, alliance, or confederation; grant letters of marque and reprisal; coin money; emit bills of credit; make anything but gold and silver coin a tender in payment of debts; pass any bill of attainder, ex post facto law, or law impairing the obligation of contracts, or grant any title of nobility.

No state shall, without the consent of the Congress, lay any imposts or duties on imports or exports, except what may be absolutely necessary for executing its inspection laws: and the net produce of all duties and imposts, laid by any state on imports or exports, shall be for the use of the treasury of the United States; and all such laws shall be subject to the revision and control of the Congress.

No state shall, without the consent of Congress, lay any duty of tonnage, keep troops, or ships of war in time of peace, enter into any agreement or compact with another state, or with a foreign power, or engage in war, unless actually invaded, or in such imminent danger as will not Top

Article II

Section 1. The executive power shall be vested in a President of the United States of America. He shall hold his office during the term of four years, and, together with the Vice President, chosen for the same term, be elected, as follows:

Each state shall appoint, in such manner as the Legislature thereof may direct, a number of electors, equal to the whole number of Senators and Representatives to which the State may be entitled in the Congress: but no Senator or Representative, or person holding an office of trust or profit under the United States, shall be appointed an elector.

The electors shall meet in their respective states, and vote by ballot for two persons, of whom one at least shall not be an inhabitant of the same state with themselves. And they shall make a list of all the persons voted for, and of the number of votes for each; which list they shall sign and certify, and transmit sealed to the seat of the government of the United States, directed to the President of the Senate. The President of the Senate shall, in the presence of the Senate and House of Representatives, open all the certificates, and the votes shall then be counted. The person having the greatest number of votes shall be the President, if such number be a majority of the whole number of electors appointed; and if there be more than one who have such majority, and have an equal number of votes, then the House of Representatives shall immediately choose by ballot one of them for President; and if no person have a majority, then from the five highest on the list the said House shall in like manner choose the President. But in choosing the President, the votes shall be taken by States, the representation from each state having one vote; A quorum for this purpose shall consist of a member or members from two thirds of the states, and a majority of all the states shall be necessary to a choice. In every case, after the choice of the President, the person having the greatest number of votes of the electors shall be the Vice President. But if there should remain two or more who have equal votes, the Senate shall choose from them by ballot the Vice President.

The Congress may determine the time of choosing the electors, and the day on which they shall give their votes; which day shall be the same throughout the United States.

No person except a natural born citizen, or a citizen of the United States, at the time of the adoption of this Constitution, shall be eligible to the office of President; neither shall any person be eligible to that office who shall not have attained to the age of thirty five years, and been fourteen Years a resident within the United States.

In case of the removal of the President from office, or of his death, resignation, or inability to discharge the powers and duties of the said office, the same shall devolve on the Vice President, and the Congress may by law provide for the case of removal, death, resignation or inability, both of the President and Vice President, declaring what officer shall then act as President, and such officer shall act accordingly, until the disability be removed, or a President shall be elected.

The President shall, at stated times, receive for his services, a compensation, which shall neither be increased nor diminished during the period for which he shall have been elected, and he shall not receive within that period any other emolument from the United States, or any of them.

Before he enter on the execution of his office, he shall take the following oath or affirmation:—"I do solemnly swear (or affirm) that I will faithfully execute the office of President of the United States, and will to the best of my ability, preserve, protect and defend the Constitution of the United States."

Section 2. The President shall be commander in chief of the Army and Navy of the United States, and of the militia of the several states, when called into the actual service of the United States; he may require the opinion, in writing, of the principal officer in each of the executive departments, upon any subject relating to the duties of their respective offices, and he shall have power to grant reprieves and pardons for offenses against the United States, except in cases of impeachment.

He shall have power, by and with the advice and consent of the Senate, to make treaties, provided two thirds of the Senators present concur; and he shall nominate, and by and with the advice and consent of the Senate, shall appoint ambassadors, other public ministers and consuls, judges of the Supreme Court, and all other officers of the United States, whose appointments are not herein otherwise provided for, and which shall be established by law: but the Congress may by law vest the appointment of such inferior officers, as they think proper, in the President alone, in the courts of law, or in the heads of departments.

The President shall have power to fill up all vacancies that may happen during the recess of the Senate, by granting commissions which shall expire at the end of their next session.

Section 3. He shall from time to time give to the Congress information of the state of the union, and recommend to their consideration such measures as he shall judge necessary and expedient; he may, on extraordinary occasions, convene both Houses, or either of them, and in case of disagreement between them, with respect to the time of adjournment, he may adjourn them to such time as he shall think proper; he shall receive ambassadors and other public ministers; he shall take care that the laws be faithfully executed, and shall commission all the officers of the United States.

Section 4. The President, Vice President and all civil officers of the United States, shall be removed from office on impeachment for, and conviction of, treason, bribery, or other high crimes and misdemeanors.

Article III

Section 1. The judicial power of the United States, shall be vested in one Supreme Court, and in such inferior courts as the Congress may from time to time ordain and establish. The judges, both of the supreme and inferior courts, shall hold their offices during good behaviour, and shall, at stated times, receive for their services, a compensation, which shall not be diminished during their continuance in office.

Section 2. The judicial power shall extend to all cases, in law and equity, arising under this Constitution, the laws of the United States, and treaties made, or which shall be made, under their authority;—to all cases affecting ambassadors, other public ministers and consuls;—to all cases of admiralty and maritime jurisdiction;—to controversies to which the United States shall be a party;—to controversies between two or more states;—between a state and citizens of another state;— between citizens of different states;—between citizens of the same state claiming lands under grants of different states, and between a state, or the citizens thereof, and foreign states, citizens or subjects.

In all cases affecting ambassadors, other public ministers and consuls, and those in which a state shall be party, the Supreme Court shall have original jurisdiction. In all the other cases before mentioned, the Supreme Court shall have appellate jurisdiction, both as to law and fact, with such exceptions, and under such regulations as the Congress shall make.

The trial of all crimes, except in cases of impeachment, shall

be by jury; and such trial shall be held in the state where the said crimes shall have been committed; but when not committed within any state, the trial shall be at such place or places as the Congress may by law have directed.

Section 3. Treason against the United States, shall consist only in levying war against them, or in adhering to their enemies, giving them aid and comfort. No person shall be convicted of treason unless on the testimony of two witnesses to the same overt act, or on confession in open court.

The Congress shall have power to declare the punishment of treason, but no attainder of treason shall work corruption of blood, or forfeiture except during the life of the person attainted.

Article IV

Section 1. Full faith and credit shall be given in each state to the public acts, records, and judicial proceedings of every other state. And the Congress may by general laws prescribe the manner in which such acts, records, and proceedings shall be proved, and the effect thereof.

Section 2. The citizens of each state shall be entitled to all privileges and immunities of citizens in the several states.

A person charged in any state with treason, felony, or other crime, who shall flee from justice, and be found in another state, shall on demand of the executive authority of the state from which he fled, be delivered up, to be removed to the state having jurisdiction of the crime.

No person held to service or labor in one state, under the laws thereof, escaping into another, shall, in consequence of any law or regulation therein, be discharged from such service or labor, but shall be delivered up on claim of the party to whom such service or labor may be due.

Section 3. New states may be admitted by the Congress into this union; but no new states shall be formed or erected within the jurisdiction of any other state; nor any state be formed by the junction of two or more states, or parts of states, without the consent of the legislatures of the states concerned as well as of the Congress.

The Congress shall have power to dispose of and make all needful rules and regulations respecting the territory or other property belonging to the United States; and nothing in this Constitution shall be so construed as to prejudice any claims of the United States, or of any particular state.

Section 4. The United States shall guarantee to every state in this union a republican form of government, and shall protect each of them against invasion; and on application of the legislature, or of the executive (when the legislature cannot be convened) against domestic violence.

Article V

The Congress, whenever two thirds of both houses shall deem it necessary, shall propose amendments to this Constitution, or, on the application of the legislatures of two thirds of the several states, shall call a convention for proposing amendments, which, in either case, shall be valid to all intents and purposes, as part of this Constitution, when ratified by the legislatures of three fourths of the several states, or by conventions in three fourths thereof, as the one or the other mode of ratification may be proposed by the Congress; provided that no amendment which may be made prior to the year one thousand eight hundred and eight shall in any manner affect the first and fourth clauses in the ninth section of the first article; and that no state, without its consent, shall be deprived of its equal suffrage in the Senate.

Article VI

All debts contracted and engagements entered into, before the adoption of this Constitution, shall be as valid against the United States under this Constitution, as under the Confederation.

This Constitution, and the laws of the United States which shall be made in pursuance thereof; and all treaties made, or which shall be made, under the authority of the United States, shall be the supreme law of the land; and the judges in every state shall be bound thereby, anything in the Constitution or laws of any State to the contrary notwithstanding.

The Senators and Representatives before mentioned, and the members of the several state legislatures, and all executive and judicial officers, both of the United States and of the several states, shall be bound by oath or affirmation, to support this Constitution; but no religious test shall ever be required as a qualification to any office or public trust under the United States.

Article VII

The ratification of the conventions of nine states, shall be sufficient for the establishment of this Constitution between the states so ratifying the same.

Done in convention by the unanimous consent of the states present the seventeenth day of September in the year of our Lord one thousand seven hundred and eighty seven and of the independence of the United States of America the twelfth. In witness whereof We have hereunto subscribed our Names,

G. Washington-Presidt. and deputy from Virginia

New Hampshire: John Langdon, Nicholas Gilman

Massachusetts: Nathaniel Gorham, Rufus King

Connecticut: Wm: Saml. Johnson, Roger Sherman

New York: Alexander Hamilton

New Jersey: Wil: Livingston, David Brearly, Wm. Paterson, Jona: Dayton

Pennsylvania: B. Franklin, Thomas Mifflin, Robt. Morris, Geo. Clymer, Thos. FitzSimons, Jared Ingersoll, James Wilson, Gouv Morris

Delaware: Geo: Read, Gunning Bedford jun, John Dickinson, Richard Bassett, Jaco: Broom

Maryland: James McHenry, Dan of St Thos. Jenifer, Danl Carroll

Virginia: John Blair—, James Madison Jr.

North Carolina: Wm. Blount, Richd. Dobbs Spaight, Hu Williamson

South Carolina: J. Rutledge, Charles Cotesworth Pinckney, Charles Pinckney, Pierce Butler

Georgia: William Few, Abr Baldwin

The Bill of Rights

The Conventions of a number of the States having, at the time of adopting the Constitution, expressed a desire, in order to prevent misconstruction or abuse of its powers, that further declaratory and restrictive clauses should be added, and as extending the ground of public confidence in the Government will best insure the beneficent ends of its institution;

Resolved, by the Senate and House of Representatives of the United States of America, in Congress assembled, two-thirds of both Houses concurring, that the following articles be proposed to the Legislatures of the several States, as amendments to the Constitution of the United States; all or any of which articles, when ratified by three-fourths of the said Legislatures, to be valid to all intents and purposes as part of the said Constitution, namely:

Amendment I

Congress shall make no law respecting an establishment of religion, or prohibiting the free exercise thereof; or abridging the freedom of speech, or of the press; or the right of the people peaceably to assemble, and to petition the government for a redress of grievances.

Amendment II

A well regulated militia, being necessary to the security of a free state, the right of the people to keep and bear arms, shall not be infringed.

Amendment III

No soldier shall, in time of peace be quartered in any house, without the consent of the owner, nor in time of war, but in a manner to be prescribed by law.

Amendment IV

The right of the people to be secure in their persons, houses, papers, and effects, against unreasonable searches and seizures, shall not be violated, and no warrants shall issue, but upon probable cause, supported by oath or affirmation, and particularly describing the place to be searched, and the persons or things to be seized.

Amendment V

No person shall be held to answer for a capital, or otherwise infamous crime, unless on a presentment or indictment of a grand jury, except in cases arising in the land or naval forces, or in the militia, when in actual service in time of war or public danger; nor shall any person be subject for the same offense to be twice put in jeopardy of life or limb; nor shall be compelled in any criminal case to be a witness against himself, nor be deprived of life, liberty, or property, without due process of law; nor shall private property be taken for public use, without just compensation.

Amendment VI

In all criminal prosecutions, the accused shall enjoy the right to a speedy and public trial, by an impartial jury of the state and district wherein the crime shall have been committed, which district shall have been previously ascertained by law, and to be informed of the nature and cause of the accusation; to be confronted with the witnesses against him; to have compulsory process for obtaining witnesses in his favor, and to have the assistance of counsel for his defense.

Amendment VII

In suits at common law, where the value in controversy shall exceed twenty dollars, the right of trial by jury shall be preserved, and no fact tried by a jury, shall be otherwise reexamined in any court of the United States, than according to the rules of the common law.

Amendment VIII

Excessive bail shall not be required, nor excessive fines imposed, nor cruel and unusual punishments inflicted.

Amendment IX

The enumeration in the Constitution, of certain rights, shall not be construed to deny or disparage others retained by the people.

Amendment X

The powers not delegated to the United States by the Constitution, nor prohibited by it to the states, are reserved to the states respectively, or to the people.

Other Amendments of the Constitution

Amendment XI (1798)

The judicial power of the United States shall not be construed to extend to any suit in law or equity, commenced or prosecuted against one of the United States by citizens of another state, or by citizens or subjects of any foreign state.

Amendment XII (1804)

The electors shall meet in their respective states and vote by ballot for President and Vice-President, one of whom, at least, shall not be an inhabitant of the same state with themselves; they shall name in their ballots the person voted for as President, and in distinct ballots the person voted for as Vice-President, and they shall make distinct lists of all persons voted for as President, and of all persons voted for as Vice President, and of the number of votes for each, which lists they shall sign and certify, and transmit sealed to the seat of the government of the United States, directed to the President of the Senate;—The President of the Senate shall, in the presence of the Senate and House of Representatives, open all the certificates and the votes shall then be counted;—the person having the greatest number of votes for President, shall be the President, if such number be a majority of the whole number of electors appointed; and if no person have such majority, then from the persons having the highest numbers not exceeding three on the list of those voted for as President, the House of Representatives shall choose immediately, by ballot, the President. But in choosing the President, the votes shall be taken by states, the representation from each state having one vote; a quorum for this purpose shall consist of a member or members from two-thirds of the states, and a majority of all the states shall be necessary to a choice. And if the House of Representatives shall not choose a President whenever the right of choice shall devolve upon them, before the fourth day of March next following, then the Vice-President shall act as President, as in the case of the death or other constitutional disability of the President. The person having the greatest number of votes as Vice-President, shall be the Vice-President, if such number be a majority of the whole number of electors appointed, and if no person have a majority, then from the two highest numbers on the list, the Senate shall choose the Vice-President; a quorum for the purpose shall consist of two-thirds of the whole number of Senators, and a majority of the whole number shall be necessary to a choice. But no person constitutionally ineligible to the office of President shall be eligible to that of Vice-President of the United States.

Amendment XIII (1865)

Section 1. Neither slavery nor involuntary servitude, except as a punishment for crime whereof the party shall have been duly convicted, shall exist within the United States, or any place subject to their jurisdiction.

Section 2. Congress shall have power to enforce this article by appropriate legislation.

Amendment XIII (1864)

Section 1. Neither slavery nor involuntary servitude, except as a punishment for crime whereof the party shall have been duly convicted, shall exist within the United States, or any place subject to their jurisdiction.

Section 2. Congress shall have power to enforce this article by appropriate legislation."

Amendment XIV (1868)

Section 1. All persons born or naturalized in the United States, and subject to the jurisdiction thereof, are citizens of the United States and of the state wherein they reside. No state shall make or enforce any law which shall abridge the privileges or immunities of citizens of the United States; nor shall any state deprive any person of life, liberty, or property, without due process of law; nor deny to any person within its jurisdiction the equal protection of the laws.

Section 2. Representatives shall be apportioned among the several states according to their respective numbers, counting the whole number of persons in each state, excluding Indians not taxed. But when the right to vote at any election for the choice of electors for President and Vice President of the United States, Representatives in Congress, the executive and judicial officers of a state, or the members of the legislature thereof, is denied to any of the male inhabitants of such state, being twenty-one years of age, and citizens of the United States, or in any way abridged, except for participation in rebellion, or other crime, the basis of representation therein shall be reduced in the proportion which the number of such male citizens shall bear to the whole number of male citizens twenty-one years of age in such state.

Section 3. No person shall be a Senator or Representative in Congress, or elector of President and Vice President, or hold any office, civil or military, under the United States, or under any state, who, having previously taken an oath, as a member of Congress, or as an officer of the United States, or as a member of any state legislature, or as an executive or judicial officer of any state, to support the Constitution of the United States, shall have engaged in insurrection or rebellion against the same, or given aid or comfort to the enemies thereof. But Congress may by a vote of two-thirds of each House, remove such disability.

Section 4. The validity of the public debt of the United States, authorized by law, including debts incurred for payment of pensions and bounties for services in suppressing insurrection or rebellion, shall not be questioned. But neither the United States nor any state shall assume or pay any debt or obligation incurred in aid of insurrection or rebellion against the United States, or any claim for the loss or emancipation of any slave; but all such debts, obligations and claims shall be held illegal and void.

Section 5. The Congress shall have power to enforce, by appropriate legislation, the provisions of this article.

Amendment XV (1870)

Section 1. The right of citizens of the United States to vote shall not be denied or abridged by the United States or by any state on account of race, color, or previous condition of servitude.

Section 2. The Congress shall have power to enforce this article by appropriate legislation.

Amendment XVI (1913)

The Congress shall have power to lay and collect taxes on incomes, from whatever source derived, without apportionment among the several states, and without regard to any census of enumeration.

Amendment XVII (1913)

The Senate of the United States shall be composed of two Senators from each state, elected by the people thereof, for six years; and each Senator shall have one vote. The electors in each state shall have the qualifications requisite for electors of the most numerous branch of the state legislatures.

When vacancies happen in the representation of any state in the Senate, the executive authority of such state shall issue writs of election to fill such vacancies: Provided, that the legislature of any state may empower the executive thereof to make temporary appointments until the people fill the vacancies by election as the legislature may direct.

This amendment shall not be so construed as to affect the election or term of any Senator chosen before it becomes valid as part of the Constitution.

Amendment XVIII (1919)

Section 1. After one year from the ratification of this article the manufacture, sale, or transportation of intoxicating liquors within, the importation thereof into, or the exportation thereof from the United States and all territory subject to the jurisdiction thereof for beverage purposes is hereby prohibited.

Section 2. The Congress and the several states shall have concurrent power to enforce this article by appropriate legislation.

Section 3. This article shall be inoperative unless it shall have been ratified as an amendment to the Constitution by the legislatures of the several states, as provided in the Constitution, within seven years from the date of the submission hereof to the states by the Congress.

Amendment XIX (1920)

The right of citizens of the United States to vote shall not be denied or abridged by the United States or by any state on account of sex.

Congress shall have power to enforce this article by appropriate legislation.

Amendment XX (1933)

Section 1. The terms of the President and Vice President shall end at noon on the 20th day of January, and the terms of Senators and Representatives at noon on the 3d day of January, of the years in which such terms would have ended if this article had not been ratified; and the terms of their successors shall then begin.

Section 2. The Congress shall assemble at least once in every year, and such meeting shall begin at noon on the 3d day of January, unless they shall by law appoint a different day.

Section 3. If, at the time fixed for the beginning of the term of the President, the President elect shall have died, the Vice President elect shall become President. If a President shall not have been chosen before the time fixed for the beginning of his term, or if the President elect shall have failed to qualify, then the Vice President elect shall act as President until a President shall have qualified; and the Congress may by law provide for the case wherein neither a President elect nor a Vice President elect shall have qualified, declaring who shall then act as President, or the manner in which one who is to act shall be selected, and such person shall act accordingly until a President or Vice President shall have qualified.

Section 4. The Congress may by law provide for the case of the death of any of the persons from whom the House of Representatives may choose a President whenever the right of choice shall have devolved upon them, and for the case of the death of any of the persons from whom the Senate may choose a Vice President whenever the right of choice shall have devolved upon them.

Section 5. Sections 1 and 2 shall take effect on the 15th day of October following the ratification of this article.

Section 6. This article shall be inoperative unless it shall have been ratified as an amendment to the Constitution by the legislatures of three-fourths of the several states within seven years from the date of its submission.

Amendment XXI (1933)

Section 1. The eighteenth article of amendment to the Constitution of the United States is hereby repealed.

Section 2. The transportation or importation into any state, territory, or possession of the United States for delivery or use therein of intoxicating liquors, in violation of the laws thereof, is hereby prohibited.

Section 3. This article shall be inoperative unless it shall have been ratified as an amendment to the Constitution by conventions in the several states, as provided in the Constitution, within seven years from the date of the submission hereof to the states by the Congress.

Amendment XXII (1951)

Section 1. No person shall be elected to the office of the President more than twice, and no person who has held the office of President, or acted as President, for more than two years of a term to which some other person was elected President shall be elected to the office of the President more than once. But this article shall not apply to any person holding the office of President when this article was proposed by the Congress, and shall not prevent any person who may be holding the office of President, or acting as President, during the term within which this article becomes operative from holding the office of President or acting as President during the remainder of such term.

Section 2. This article shall be inoperative unless it shall have been ratified as an amendment to the Constitution by the legislatures of three-fourths of the several states within seven years from the date of its submission to the states by the Congress.

Amendment XXIII (1961)

Section 1. The District constituting the seat of government of the United States shall appoint in such manner as the Congress may direct:

A number of electors of President and Vice President equal to the whole number of Senators and Representatives in Congress to which the District would be entitled if it were a state, but in no event more than the least populous state; they shall be in addition to those appointed by the states, but they shall be considered, for the purposes of the election of President and Vice President, to be electors appointed by a state; and they shall meet in the District and perform such duties as provided by the twelfth article of amendment.

Section 2. The Congress shall have power to enforce this article by appropriate legislation.

Amendment XXIV (1964)

Section 1. The right of citizens of the United States to vote in any primary or other election for President or Vice President, for electors for President or Vice President, or for Senator or Representative in Congress, shall not be denied or abridged by the United States or any state by reason of failure to pay any poll tax or other tax.

Section 2. The Congress shall have power to enforce this article by appropriate legislation.

Amendment XXV (1967)

Section 1. In case of the removal of the President from office or of his death or resignation, the Vice President shall become President.

Section 2. Whenever there is a vacancy in the office of the Vice President, the President shall nominate a Vice President who shall take office upon confirmation by a majority vote of both Houses of Congress.

Section 3. Whenever the President transmits to the President pro tempore of the Senate and the Speaker of the House of Representatives his written declaration that he is unable to discharge the powers and duties of his office, and until he transmits to them a written declaration to the contrary, such powers and duties shall be discharged by the Vice President as Acting President.

Section 4. Whenever the Vice President and a majority of either the principal officers of the executive departments or of such other body as Congress may by law provide, transmit to the President pro tempore of the Senate and the Speaker of the House of Representatives their written declaration that the President is unable to discharge the powers and duties of his office, the Vice President shall immediately assume the powers and duties of the office as Acting President.

Thereafter, when the President transmits to the President pro tempore of the Senate and the Speaker of the House of Representatives his written declaration that no inability exists, he shall resume the powers and duties of his office unless the Vice President and a majority of either the principal officers of the executive department or of such other body as Congress may by law provide, transmit within four days to the President pro tempore of the Senate and the Speaker of the House of Representatives their written declaration that the President is unable to discharge the powers and duties of his office. Thereupon Congress shall decide the issue, assembling within forty-eight hours for that purpose if not in session. If the Congress, within twenty-one days after receipt of the latter written declaration, or, if Congress is not in session, within twenty-one days after Congress is required to assemble, determines by two thirds vote of both Houses that the President is unable to discharge the powers and duties of his office, the Vice President shall continue to discharge the same as Acting President; otherwise, the President shall resume the powers and duties of his office.

Amendment XXVI (1971)

Section 1. The right of citizens of the United States, who are 18 years of age or older, to vote, shall not be denied or abridged by the United States or any state on account of age.

Section 2. The Congress shall have the power to enforce this article by appropriate legislation.

Amendment XXVII (1992)

No law varying the compensation for the services of the Senators and Representatives shall take effect until an election of Representatives shall have intervened.

The Declaration of Independence

IN CONGRESS, July 4, 1776.
The unanimous Declaration of the thirteen united States of America,

When in the Course of human events, it becomes necessary for one people to dissolve the political bands which have connected them with another, and to assume among the powers of the earth, the separate and equal station to which the Laws of Nature and of Nature's God entitle them, a decent respect to the opinions of mankind requires that they should declare the causes which impel them to the separation.

We hold these truths to be self-evident, that all men are created equal, that they are endowed by their Creator with certain unalienable Rights, that among these are Life, Liberty and the pursuit of Happiness.—That to secure these rights, Governments are instituted among Men, deriving their just powers from the consent of the governed, —That whenever any Form of Government becomes destructive of these ends, it is the Right of the People to alter or to abolish it, and to institute new Government, laying its foundation on such principles and organizing its powers in such form, as to them shall seem most likely to effect their Safety and Happiness. Prudence, indeed, will dictate that Governments long established should not be changed for light and transient causes; and accordingly all experience hath shewn, that mankind are more disposed to suffer, while evils are sufferable, than to right themselves by abolishing the forms to which they are accustomed. But when a long train of abuses and usurpations, pursuing invariably the same Object evinces a design to reduce them under absolute Despotism, it is their right, it is their duty, to throw off such Government, and to provide new Guards for their future security.—Such has been the patient sufferance of these Colonies; and such is now the necessity which constrains them to alter their former Systems of Government. The history of the present King of Great Britain is a history of repeated injuries and usurpations, all having in direct object the establishment of an absolute Tyranny over these States. To prove this, let Facts be submitted to a candid world.

He has refused his Assent to Laws, the most wholesome and necessary for the public good.

He has forbidden his Governors to pass Laws of immediate and pressing importance, unless suspended in their operation till his Assent should be obtained; and when so suspended, he has utterly neglected to attend to them.

He has refused to pass other Laws for the accommodation of large districts of people, unless those people would relinquish the right of Representation in the Legislature, a right inestimable to them and formidable to tyrants only.

He has called together legislative bodies at places unusual, uncomfortable, and distant from the depository of their public Records, for the sole purpose of fatiguing them into compliance with his measures.

He has dissolved Representative Houses repeatedly, for opposing with manly firmness his invasions on the rights of the people.

He has refused for a long time, after such dissolutions, to cause others to be elected; whereby the Legislative powers, incapable of Annihilation, have returned to the People at large for their exercise; the State remaining in the mean time exposed to all the dangers of invasion from without, and convulsions within.

He has endeavoured to prevent the population of these States; for that purpose obstructing the Laws for Naturalization of Foreigners; refusing to pass others to encourage their migrations hither, and raising the conditions of new Appropriations of Lands.

He has obstructed the Administration of Justice, by refusing his Assent to Laws for establishing Judiciary powers.

He has made Judges dependent on his Will alone, for the tenure of their offices, and the amount and payment of their salaries.

He has erected a multitude of New Offices, and sent hither swarms of Officers to harrass our people, and eat out their substance.

He has kept among us, in times of peace, Standing Armies without the Consent of our legislatures.

He has affected to render the Military independent of and superior to the Civil power.

He has combined with others to subject us to a jurisdiction foreign to our constitution, and unacknowledged by our laws; giving his Assent to their Acts of pretended Legislation:

For Quartering large bodies of armed troops among us:

For protecting them, by a mock Trial, from punishment for any Murders which they should commit on the Inhabitants of these States:

For cutting off our Trade with all parts of the world:

For imposing Taxes on us without our Consent:

For depriving us in many cases, of the benefits of Trial by Jury:

For transporting us beyond Seas to be tried for pretended offences

For abolishing the free System of English Laws in a neighbouring Province, establishing therein an Arbitrary government, and enlarging its Boundaries so as to render it at once an example and fit instrument for introducing the same absolute rule into these Colonies:

For taking away our Charters, abolishing our most valuable Laws, and altering fundamentally the Forms of our Governments:

For suspending our own Legislatures, and declaring themselves invested with power to legislate for us in all cases whatsoever.

He has abdicated Government here, by declaring us out of his Protection and waging War against us.

He has plundered our seas, ravaged our Coasts, burnt our towns, and destroyed the lives of our people.

He is at this time transporting large Armies of foreign Mercenaries to compleat the works of death, desolation and tyranny, already begun with circumstances of Cruelty & perfidy scarcely paralleled in the most barbarous ages, and totally unworthy the Head of a civilized nation.

He has constrained our fellow Citizens taken Captive on the high Seas to bear Arms against their Country, to become the executioners of their friends and Brethren, or to fall themselves by their Hands.

He has excited domestic insurrections amongst us, and has endeavoured to bring on the inhabitants of our frontiers, the merciless Indian Savages, whose known rule of warfare, is an undistinguished destruction of all ages, sexes and conditions.

In every stage of these Oppressions We have Petitioned for Redress in the most humble terms: Our repeated Petitions have been answered only by repeated injury. A Prince whose character is thus marked by every act which may define a Tyrant, is unfit to be the ruler of a free people.

Nor have We been wanting in attentions to our Brittish brethren. We have warned them from time to time of attempts by their legislature to extend an unwarrantable jurisdiction over us. We have reminded them of the circumstances of our emigration and settlement here. We have appealed to their native justice and magnanimity, and we have conjured them by the ties of our common kindred to disavow these usurpations, which, would inevitably interrupt our connections and correspondence. They too have been deaf to the voice of justice and of consanguinity. We must, therefore, acquiesce in the necessity, which denounces our Separation, and hold them, as we hold the rest of mankind, Enemies in War, in Peace Friends.

We, therefore, the Representatives of the united States of America, in General Congress, Assembled, appealing to the Supreme Judge of the world for the rectitude of our intentions, do, in the Name, and by Authority of the good People of these

Colonies, solemnly publish and declare, That these United Colonies are, and of Right ought to be Free and Independent States; that they are Absolved from all Allegiance to the British Crown, and that all political connection between them and the State of Great Britain, is and ought to be totally dissolved; and that as Free and Independent States, they have full Power to levy War, conclude Peace, contract Alliances, establish Commerce, and to do all other Acts and Things which Independent States may of right do. And for the support of this Declaration, with a firm reliance on the protection of divine Providence, we mutually pledge to each other our Lives, our Fortunes and our sacred Honor.

The 56 signatures on the Declaration appear in the positions indicated:

Column 1
Georgia:
Button Gwinnett, Lyman Hall, George Walton

Column 2
North Carolina:
William Hooper, Joseph Hewes, John Penn

South Carolina:
Edward Rutledge, Thomas Heyward, Jr., Thomas Lynch, Jr., Arthur Middleton

Column 3
Massachusetts:
John Hancock

Maryland:
Samuel Chase, William Paca, Thomas Stone, Charles Carroll of Carrollton

Virginia:
George Wythe, Richard Henry Lee, Thomas Jefferson, Benjamin Harrison, Thomas Nelson, Jr., Francis Lightfoot Lee, Carter Braxton

Column 4
Pennsylvania:
Robert Morris, Benjamin Rush, Benjamin Franklin, John Morton, George Clymer, James Smith, George Taylor, James Wilson, George Ross

Delaware:
Caesar Rodney, George Read, Thomas McKean

Column 5
New York:
William Floyd, Philip Livingston, Francis Lewis, Lewis Morris

New Jersey:
Richard Stockton, John Witherspoon, Francis Hopkinson, John Hart, Abraham Clark

Column 6
New Hampshire:
Josiah Bartlett, William Whipple

Massachusetts:
Samuel Adams, John Adams, Robert Treat Paine, Elbridge Gerry

Rhode Island:
Stephen Hopkins, William Ellery

Connecticut
Roger Sherman, Samuel Huntington, William Williams, Oliver Wolcott

New Hampshire:
Matthew Thornton

APPENDIX B ANSWERS TO SELF-TESTS

Chapter 1: **1.** A patriotic notion of social studies might be inferred from the image, one focused more on the transmission of cultural ideas and knowledge than on critical thinking. One person's view of *social* might influence whether he/she views social studies as focused on the individual or on groups of people.; **2.** b; **3.** a; **4.** b and d; **5.** Most broadly, pedagogy is the act or art of teaching. Pedagogy is also the substance of the knowledge of how to teach.; **6.** Storytelling is a direct method of teaching, investigating is student-centered and focused on unresolved problems, and deliberating is focused on students clarifying and supporting their beliefs and opinions.; **7.** Interdisciplinary teaching makes use of materials and strategies from various disciplines, while disciplinary approaches utilize one disciplinary approach. An interdisciplinary investigation of the Jamestown settlement might include resources and methods from history, archeology, political science, physical sciences, and even cultural sciences.; **8.** interdisciplinary or multifaceted knowledge; **9.** Each of these disciplines has its own approach to the development and confirmation of new knowledge, but thy all deal with similar content that is situated in the actions of humans in social settings.; **10.** Criteria or goals by which one can judge the quality of educational achievement.

Chapter 2: **1.** Reflection is important because it provides teachers with a means to refine their knowledge, adapt to changing educative conditions, and account for new ideas and unforeseen circumstances.; **2.** d; **3.** #1 is developing subject matter knowledge, #2 is planning to teach, #3 is the act of teaching, and #4 is rethinking the lesson; **4.** a; **5.** d; **6.** Reflection during instruction is most often focused on the minute-to-minute teaching actions that might require a lesson to be adapted to or tailored to a given learner needs and reflection on teaching tends to be more holistic in focus.; **7.** c; **8.** b; **9.** Reflective inquiry in a democracy enables students to learn given ever-changing conditions related to that knowledge.; **10.** Case studies entail elements of successful teaching in local situations, and also enable us to explore how the teaching episode can be extended or even improved.

Chapter 3: **1.** Inquiry is a method of teaching and learning that makes use of authentic resources in the investigation of meaningful topics and problems. An inquiry about the petroglygh might begin with the emergence of an interest in the subject, a clarification about what we know about the topic, an examination of resources, and a proposed solution; **2.** authentic or real-world; **3.** b; **4.** b; **5.** (1) emergence, (2) clarification, (3) examination, (4) proposed solution; **6.** Scaffolds are specific forms of support for new learning that allow students to grow as independent learners. These supports are gradually removed as students develop autonomous knowledge.; **7.** c; **8.** Questions serve as a starting point for an inquiry and when properly formed capitalize on the interests young children have in distinguishing between what is real and make-believe. An inquiry question about the Great Depression should invite student interest and enable a number of possible answers.; **9.** c; **10.** b

Chapter 4: **1.** b; **2.** c; **3.** Standards are generalized and public representations of expectations for teaching and learning, while curriculums detail the scope and sequence of subject matter that is to be taught. Standards are typically more general than curriculum, which tends to be specific in comparison; **4.** a; **5.** Academic and skills-based standards developed at the national level are often used to guide the development of state standards, which are used in turn to develop local curriculums.; **6.** Scope is the depth of content covered in a curriculum, and sequence is the order that content is expected to be taught and learned.; **7.** b; **8.** Standards should be developed before tests and should inform the construction of tests.; **9.** High-stakes are usually standardized tests and are used to help determine a final grade or whether students can progress to the next grade level, while low-stakes tests are usually teacher designed to assess students' knowledge in specific content areas on a regular basis.; **10.** Teachers can develop a deep and personal understanding of standards, curriculum, and testing programs and invest in the successful implementation of standards, curriculum, and testing programs.

Chapter 5: **1.** By studying history children can be inspired to act more responsibly, study harder, and even care more about their fellow humans.; **2.** b; **3.** b; **4.** timeline; **5.** Students can understand how immigration has influenced the development of culture in the United States. This type of understanding is called active learning.; **6.** 1) summarize, 2) contextualize, 3) infer, 4) corroborate, and 5) monitor; **7.** introduce characters, beginning events, middle events, and ending events; **8.** b; **9.** Transmission activities provide the background knowledge needed for active learning activities, which should make use of authentic resources.; **10.** Authentic resources are from the time being studied and have a meaningful and real-world quality that is easy for children to understand and relate to. The image of the Emancipation Proclamation is authentic because it has a real meaning today and, as an image of the original, has a real look to it.

Chapter 6: **1.** Geography includes studying human systems, past and present, their governments, economies, and systems of thought; **2.** b; **3.** This map illustrates human-built environments in North America.; **4.** Native Americans carve totem poles to honor their ancestors, publicize their clan's standing and accomplishments, and record memorable ceremonies and experiences.; **5.** b; **6.** Regions; **7.** 1) select a map type, 2) determine information to go on the map, and 3) determine how the information will be highlighted on the map; **8.** b; **9.** d; **10.** The study of history includes the study of places where people lived. The photo suggests that human activity has occurred in this place for thousands of years.

Chapter 7: **1.** Civic competence is understanding of important social issues, participating in dialogues and conversations about public social life, volunteering and serving in public roles, and taking action when problems demand involvement.; **2.** c; **3.** Conscience; **4.** d; **5.** b; **6.** b; **7.** Central to the idea of democratic reasoning is a vision of the United States as a pluralistic society with a vast number of ethnic, religious, and racial groups all vying for attention and acceptance. Children who are thinking about problems in a democracy need to appreciate and understand the importance of equality.; **8.** c; **9.** Ideology frames the way people consider and learn new information and how teachers plan and implement those plans for instruction.; **10.** Democratic reasoning is the thinking and analytical skills that are engaged when addressing social problems in democratic contexts. Students might consider how they or their community could address the problem of water pollution either through direct action or through their representatives in local government.

Chapter 8: **1.** Direct instruction is a closely developed series of exercises that provide learners continual interaction with limited, fundamental subject matter. A teacher could ask students to interpret the actions in the photo through direct questioning; **2.** 1) learning objectives, 2) anticipatory set, 3) teaching sequence, 4) guided practice, 5) lesson closure, 6) independent practice; **3.** b; **4.** scripted; **5.** c; **6.** Answers will vary.; **7.** c; **8.** b; **9.** During the lesson the teacher can facilitate short activities which students individually complete followed by group review or assessment of the work.; **10.** Activities have meaning for students, require them to take action, and reflect their interests.

Chapter 9: **1.** a; **2.** Step 1: subject matter interest, Step 2: initial focus on the individual, Step 3: group activity, Step 4: individual assessment; **3.** b; **4.** a; **5.** d; **6.** 1) question or situation, 2) possible decision, 3) consequences, 4) decisions; **7.** d; **8.** Homogeneous grouping results in students with like characteristics being grouped together, while heterogeneous grouping results in different characteristics among the students in a group.; **9.** Group titles or identities might be subject-matter based. Groups might have subject matter related tasks. Students might be group by periods of immigration to student the history of immigration in the United States.; **10.** Interactive learning requires students to be responsible for the development of their own knowledge, while cooperative learning values a groups' knowledge development.

Chapter 10: **1.** Literacy is knowledge in a particular field or subject and the ability to read and write.; **2.** Literate citizens form the basis of social order and stability. Citizens need literacy skills in order to participate in economic, political, and social life.; **3.** 1) Reading, 2) Studying, 3) Thinking, 4) Decision making, 5) Metacognition, 6) Reference and information search skills, 7) Technical skills in using electronic devices, 8) The ability to organize and use information; **4.** d; **5.** *Answers will vary but should include:* decision making, technical skills; **6.** a. Guiding questions frame reading around specific information that readers are seeking, b. Outlines help create a sense of order and expectation for readers, and c. Main ideas help focus readers on the big picture of a reading passage; **7.** Students are interested in the subject matter. Student learning is directly connected to the real world outside the classroom. Students are actively inquiring, using higher-level skills, about a question or problem. Learning is not tied to one discipline, but is instead interdisciplinary. Students share or act on what they have learned.; **8.** 1) pre-writing, 2) drafting, 3) revisions; **9.** *Answers will vary.*; **10.** *Answers will vary.*

Chapter 11: **1.** *Answers will vary but should include*; 1) create interest and excitement about learning, 2) have students produce something, 3) give students a role in setting up the procedures for completing their work, 4) connect the learning experience to other life experiences; **2.** *Answers will vary.*; **3.** *Answers will vary.*; **4.** Teachers can determine important concepts, ideas, themes, events, movements, and people emphasized in their content knowledge as they reorganize this content as subject matter.; **5.** a; **6.** (1) organize content knowledge into subject matter knowledge, (2) transform subject matter knowledge into pedagogical knowledge, (3) develop relevant procedures, (4) select resource materials, (5) assess student learning; **7.** 1) Does the resource support the learning goals for the lesson? 2) Is the resource appropriate for students given their prior knowledge, reading ability, and maturity? 3) Can the resources be adapted and tailored to meet the specific needs of students?; **8.** Lesson planning serves as a guide for action.; **9.** *Answers will vary.*; **10.** 1) Are all students receiving the opportunities the teacher envisioned when planning for instruction? 2) Is the time allotted for instruction appropriate given the realities of the actual implementation? 3) Are the materials and resources that were adapted and prepared for the lesson being used the way the teacher planned?

Chapter 12: **1.** natural, socially-constructed, learning, and personality-related. The form of diversity on display in the image is socially-constructed; **2.** Schools have often taken the lead as the place where inequalities and issues of diversity are addressed.; **3.** b; **4.** Multiculturalism is many cultures existing together in a locality, without any one culture dominating and with mutual acceptance of differences aimed at overcoming racism, sexism, and other forms of discrimination.; **5.** learning temperament, prior knowledge level, impediments to learning, and support outside the classroom; **6.** linguistic intelligence, logical-mathematical intelligence, musical intelligence, spatial intelligence, bodily-kinesthetic intelligence, interpersonal intelligence, intrapersonal intelligence, and naturalist intelligence; **7.** a; **8.** *Any of the following are correct:* 1) Remember that all children are unique and have unique needs. 2) Never assign to an individual the characteristics of a group. 3) If you are not familiar with the cultural traditions of the community in which you work, take time to get to know what happens in the community. 4) Incorporate opportunities for children to use their cultural traditions as a context for learning new subject matter. 5) Carefully consider the cultural traditions that have shaped your students' learning personalities. Think how those learning personalities can be expanded and enriched. 6) Try to include information about other cultural traditions as subject matter in the lessons.; **9.** ILPs tend to be more informal and idiosyncratic. Although they are similar to IEPs, an ILP assumes that all of the student's learning needs can be met in the classroom with existing resources.; **10.** Teachers should try to balance a need to reflect the community's values and ideals through the curriculum with a goal of diversifying children's experiences through educational experiences.

Chapter 13: **1.** The purpose of assessment is to collect and analyze information in an ongoing manner about student learning.; 2, *Answers should address informal and formal, as well as formative and summative approaches.*; **3.** Formal assessment is a consistent approach used for all students in a class to evaluate specific learning stages, and informal assessments are low-key and unintrusive teacher actions focused on determining whether students are learning during an activity.; **4.** b and d; **5.** questioning, seat check, and polling; **6.** teachers can act on what they learn about their students as a result of the assessment, assessments are fair and consistent, and some assessments should be planned for connecting lessons over a sequence of days; **7.** Assessment occurs during and after the implementation of a plan to teaching.; **8.** 1) Subject matter knowledge development, 2) Instructional planning, 3) Teaching and learning the lesson, 4) Rethinking the lesson; **9.** Remediation results from some assessment and serves to help students when they are having trouble learning.; **10.** Criteria describe what students are to learn and achievement levels differentiate levels of learning.

Chapter 14: **1.** Technology is the application of science to the improvement of the human condition.; **2.** Educational technology is designed with some learning goal in mind.; **3.** The printing press made text and books available to greater numbers of people.; **4.** age; **5.** c; **6.** Through technological innovation humans can improve their condition.; **7.** b; **8.** Identify web sites that have information about your topics, Narrow the search for information or resources, Summarize the information or represent it in some manner that is different from how it exists on the Web.; **9.** develop a curriculum or subject matter context, narrow the search, and summarize the information; **10.** They have a curricular-based subject matter focus and they motivate students to learn.

GLOSSARY

Active Learning Learning that involves students creating their own knowledge in dynamic and focused ways.

Artifact Authentic resource created through human work.

Assessment A continual instructional process for collecting and analyzing information about student learning.

Assessment rubric A method of evaluating learning that includes multiple criteria and performance levels for each criterion.

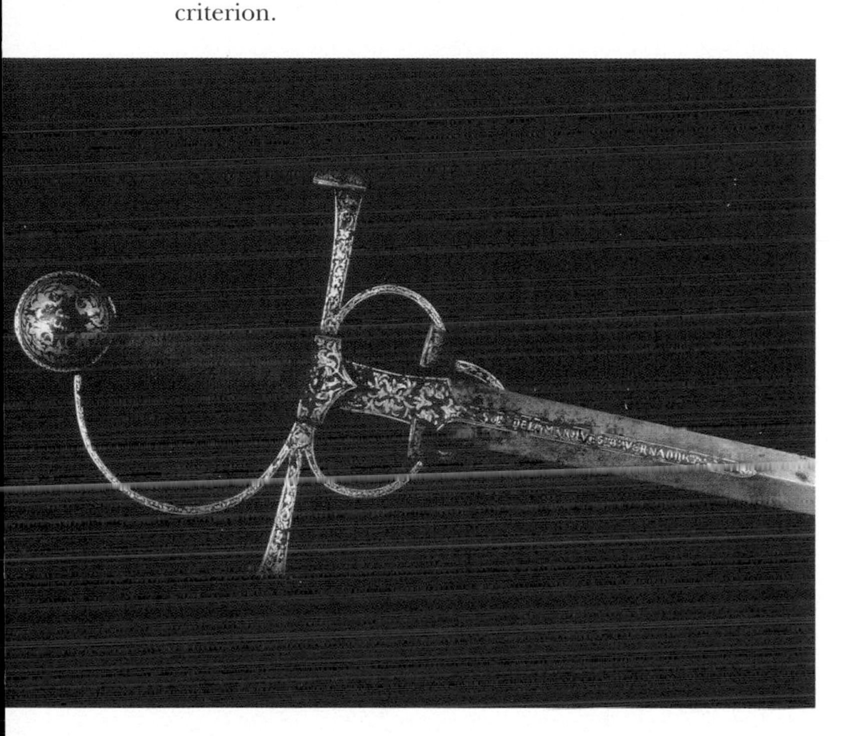

Authentic A reasonable or actual representation of some real-world phenomenon. Situated in the real world and connected to experiences that are a part of daily life.

Authentic materials Materials drawn from real-world contexts that can be used to support learning and instruction.

Authentic intellectual work Learning activities that enable students to develop knowledge in real-world contexts.

Authentic teaching Teaching to accurately represent the real world; how standards become real in the classroom.

Behavioral objective A learning goal specifying observable actions that students must demonstrate to indicate that learning has occurred.

Case studies Descriptions of professional action, such as teaching, that have some explanatory qualities.

Curriculum An organized body of subject matter developed from standards and arranged with consideration for appropriate scope and sequence.

Citizen A member of a sovereign state who incurs certain rights and responsibilities associated with her or his status.

Civic Related to being a citizen.

Civic competence The knowledge and skills needed to actively and productively participate in democratic life.

Civic competence Understanding important social issues, participating in dialogues and conversations about public social life, volunteering and serving in public roles, and taking action when problems demand involvement.

Civic virtue The necessary moral nature of participation in a democracy.

Climate Meteorological conditions, including temperature, precipitation, and wind, that characteristically prevail in a particular region.

Common good The general welfare of all individuals and groups within a community. An agreed-upon vision of what best suits the multiple interests of people in pluralistic societies.

Conscience The willingness and ability to recognize and respect the beliefs or practices of others.

Cooperative learning An approach to learning in which students share learning goals and work as a team toward achieving these goals.

Cultural systems A group consciousness that explains how or why people move or settle in places and how they conduct economic and social life.

Curriculum Courses of study in an academic discipline or the scope and sequence of specific subject matter within a single academic course.

Democracy Most typically thought of as government by the people, either in direct or representative form, but also meant to refer more broadly to principles of social cooperation and individual rights.

Democratic reasoning Thinking and analytical skills that are engaged when addressing social problems in a democratic context.

Didactic Another word for a teacher-centered approach to teaching; also can mean a form of moral instruction.

Digital Expressed in numerical form, especially for use by a computer, and displayed as an electronic representation of some other physical form.

Direct instruction Closely developed series of exercises that provide learners continual interaction with limited, fundamental subject matter.

Disciplinary Relating to the specific field of academic study in which unique rules for acquiring knowledge have been established and are practical.

Discrete knowledge Ideas and concepts that share no obvious characteristics and are understood separately.

Diversity Natural and social differences that emerge from meaningful and unique human characteristics.

Dyad A two-person instructional grouping.

Epistemological A philosophical issue that deals with the nature, origin, and scope of knowledge.

Ethnicity A group of people who share a common and distinctive racial, national, religious, linguistic, or cultural heritage.

Experimentation A form of learning that results from the implementation of a designed set of actions aimed at verifying relationships between phenomena.

Formal assessment Consistent assessment approaches used for all students in a class to evaluate specific learning stages.

Geography The discipline that teaches knowledge about places and environment.

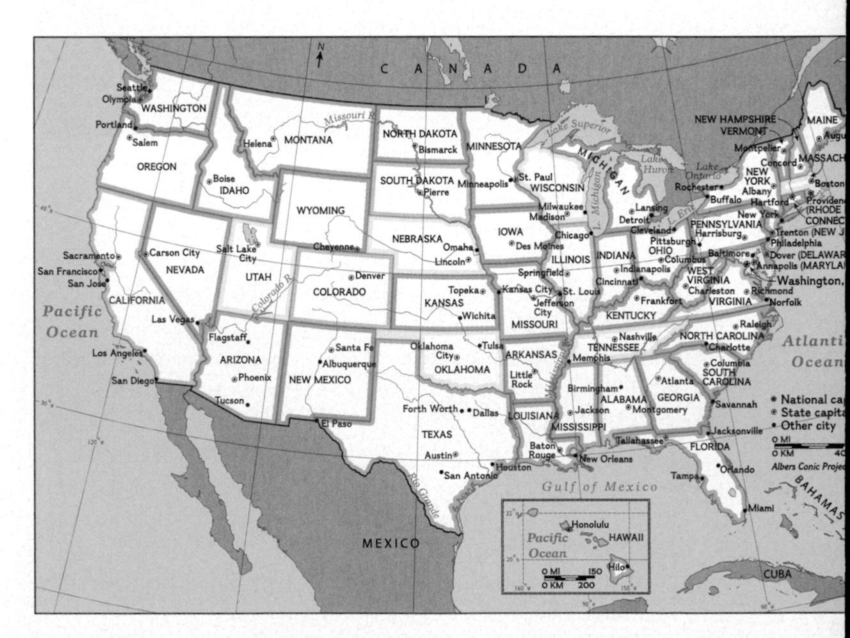

Heterogeneous grouping A grouping strategy that involves students being organized for group work according to different characteristics.

High-stakes tests Standardized assessments of student learning that are used to make decisions about, among other things, students' progress to the next grade level or another course, a school's standing at a local or state level, and/or the need for special services or instructional opportunities for students in a school.

Historical inquiry A specific form of asking and answering questions that makes use of historical resources and particular methodologies in order to construct an interpretation of the past.

Historical thinking Cognitive activities that help students develop historical understanding.

Historical understanding Knowledge of the past that develops out of intrinsic interest and active interpretation.

Homogeneous grouping A grouping strategy that involves students being organized for group work according to like characteristics.

Human culture Social patterns, arts, beliefs, institutions, and all other products of human work and thought that contribute to a common way of life for a group of people.

Human geography A branch of geography that deals with people, their environment, and their interactions.

Ideology A world view or set of beliefs that explains human action and behavior.

Incidental geography The geographic knowledge we have developed from everyday life and experiences.

Informal assessment Low-key and unintrusive teacher actions focused on determining whether students are learning during an activity.

Inquiry A method of teaching and learning that makes use of authentic resources in the investigation of meaningful topics and problems.

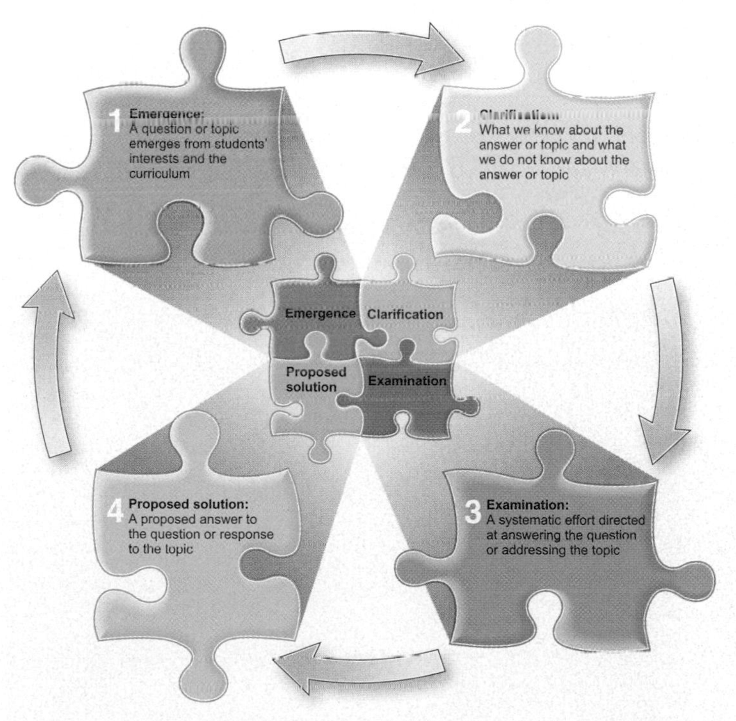

Instructional scope The breadth of instructional activities.

Intentional geography The geographic knowledge that we purposely learn.

Interactive instruction A teaching approach that uses a combination of group and individual work; it enables students to benefit from each other in dynamic environments.

Interdisciplinary Relating to two or more academic disciplines and the relations and connections between these disciplines.

Internet An interconnected system of networks that connects computers around the world via the TCP/IP protocol.

Jigsaw grouping A grouping approach that involves students working in multiple groups on parts of a whole activity.

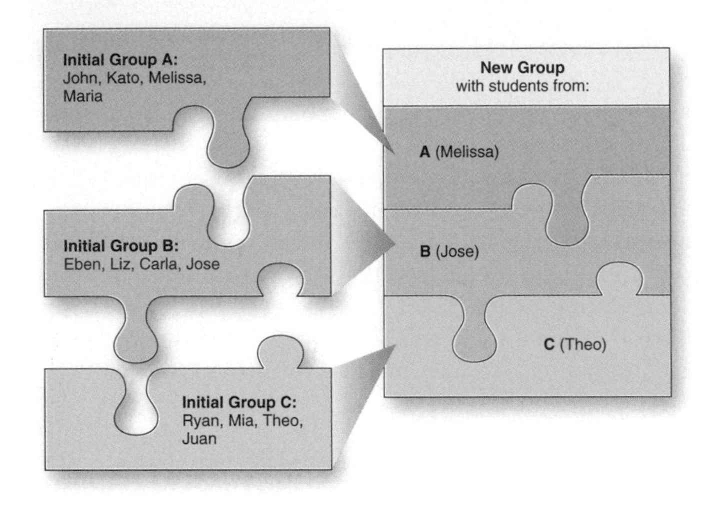

Learning cycle A self-perpetuating learning system in which new learning opportunities result from existing learning experiences.

Literacy Knowledge in a particular field or subject; ability to read and write.

Low-stakes tests Tests that assess students' knowledge in specific content areas on a regular basis so that students learn the state standards throughout the school year, not just in preparation for a one-time annual high-stakes test.

Multiculturalism Many cultures existing together in a locality, without any one culture dominating, and with mutual acceptance of differences aimed at overcoming racism, sexism, and other forms of discrimination.

Multimedia The combined use of media, such as movies, music, lighting, CD ROMS, and the Internet, for education or entertainment.

Opportunity cost The value of things not selected in an economic situation.

Patriotism Generally thought of as love of and devotion to one's country; it may be displayed in countless ways.

Pedagogical content knowledge (PCK) Unique forms of knowledge about how to take into account a teacher's knowledge of subject matter, curriculum, learners, and communities, as well as contexts and ends for education.

Pedagogy Most broadly, the act or act of teaching; also the substance of the knowledge of how to teach.

Physical systems Nonhuman structures such as weather and landforms.

Race A group of people united or classified together based on common history, geographic distribution, and similar physical traits.

Reflection To reflect or think about something carefully; formal reflection may include the use of particular repeatable procedures for careful thinking.

Reflective inquiry A process of developing new knowledge, which is contingent upon a procedure that assumes knowledge is ever changing and evolving.

Region A specified district, territory, or other often-continuous place on Earth's surface.

Remediation The instructional act or process of correcting a fault or deficiency.

Rubric Two-dimensional matrix of criteria that a teacher can use to make judgments about achievement levels for student work.

Scaffolds Specific forms of support for new learning that allow students to grow as independent learners. These supports are gradually removed as students develop autonomous knowledge.

Schema An understanding or pattern that represents a complex set of ideas or experiences.

Social change An action or actions directed at changing society in some positive way.

Social inquiry Inquiry that focuses on the investigation of common problems whose solution will improve the human condition.

Social reconstructionists Activists who aimed to redirect social studies practice toward collective action and social change.

Social science inquiry Inquiry that involves disciplinary investigations focused on observations, hypothesis generation, data collection, and the proposal of a solution.

Social studies The integrated study of the social sciences and humanities to promote civic competence.

Spatial reasoning The ability to mentally organize information about people, places, and environments.

Spatial understanding The ability to perceive oneself and other natural and human-made things in space.

Standards Criteria or goals by which one can judge the quality of educational achievement. The most generalized and public representations of expectations for teaching and learning.

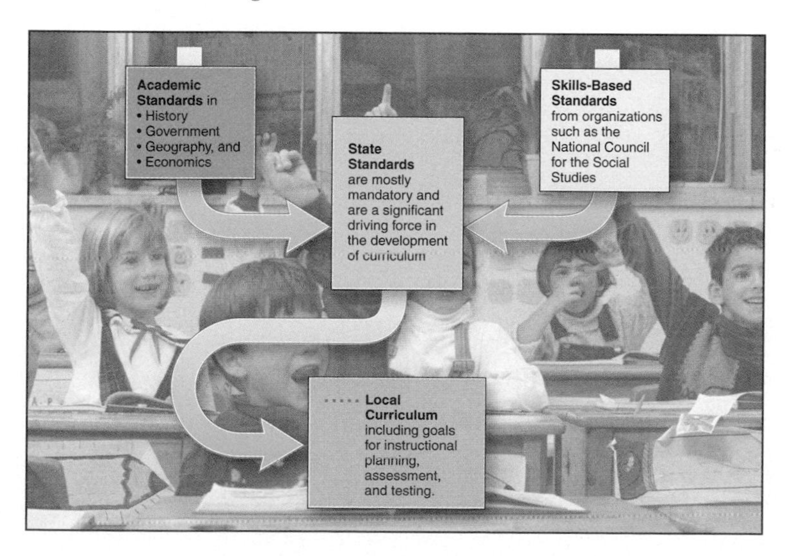

Subject matter knowledge Understanding about content in a specific academic area, such as history.

Synthesis The process of combining ideas or objects to form a new whole thing.

Teacher-directed instruction Teaching approach focused on clearly defined and organized teaching tasks and measurable incremental learning.

Teacher knowledge A formal body of information that comprises our understanding of how to teach.

Teaching cycle A specific four-part sequence of events that encompasses various acts involved in teaching.

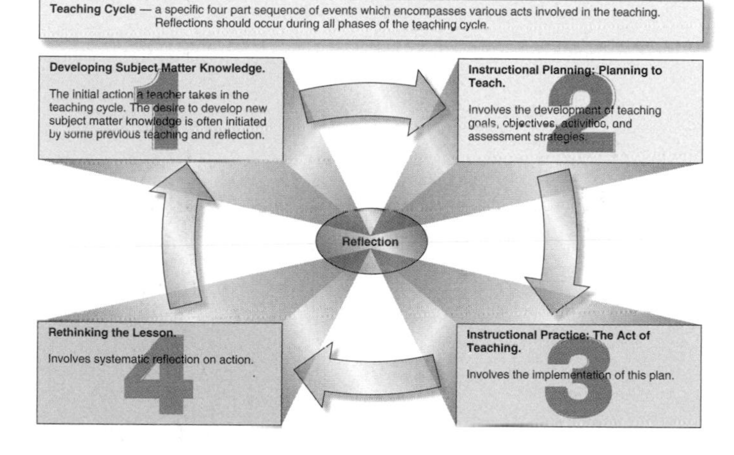

Technology The application of science to the improvement of the human condition.

Tolerance The capacity to recognize and respect the beliefs or practices of others.

Transmission The delivery by a teacher to students of predetermined knowledge intent to be learned as a whole by the student.

Web World Wide Web (WWW) Electronic resources—text, visual, audio—residing on all Internet servers that use the HTTP protocol, accessible to users via a simple point-and-click computer system.

REFERENCES

Chapter 1

Bruner, J. (1999). Folk pedagogies. In J. Leach and B. Moon (Eds.), *Learners and Pedagogy.* London: The Open University.

Levstik, L., and K. Barton. (2001). *Doing History: Investigating with Children in Elementary and Middle Schools,* 2nd ed. Mahwah, NJ: Lawrence Erlbaum Associates.

Saxe, D. W. (1991). *Social Studies in Schools: A History of the Early Years.* Albany, NY: State University of New York Press.

Chapter 2

Dewey, J. (1910). *How We Think.* Lexington, MA: D. C. Heath.

Davis, O. L., and E. Yeager (Eds.). (2005). *Wise Practice in the Social Studies Classroom.* Greenwich, CT: Information Age Press.

Schön, D. A. (1983). *The Reflective Practitioner: How Professionals Think in Action.* London: Temple Smith.

Thornton, S. (2004). *Teaching Social Studies That Matters: Curriculum for Active Learning.* New York: Teachers College Press.

Chapter 3

Bruce, B. C., and J. Davidson. (1996). An inquiry model for literacy across the curriculum. *Journal of Curriculum Studies* 28, 281–300.

Dewey, J. (1991). *How We Think.* Amherst, NY: Prometheus Books. (Originally published in 1910).

Kolb, D. A., and R. Fry. (1975). Toward an applied theory of experiential learning. In C. L. Cooper (Ed.), *Theories of Group Processes.* New York: John Wiley and Sons.

Chapter 4

Center for Civic Education. (2007). *National Standards for Civics and Government.* http://www.civiced.org/stds.html

Center for Media Literacy. http://www.medialit.org/

Joint Committee on Geographic Education of the National Council for Geographic Education (NCGE) and the Association of American Geographers (AAG). (1984). *Guidelines for Geographic Education, Elementary and Secondary Schools.*

Klingel, C. F., and R. B. Noyed. (2002). *Dolley Madison: First Lady* (Spirit of American Our People series). Mankato: MN: The Child's World.

National Center for History in the Schools. (1996). *National History Standards.* http://nchs.ucla.edu/standards/

National Council on Economic Education. (1997). *Voluntary National Standards in Economics.* http://www.ncee.net/ea/standards/

National Council for Geographic Education. (1994). *Geography for Life: National Geographic Standards.* http://www.nationalgeographic.com/xpeditions/standards/

National Council for the Social Studies (NCSS). (1991). *Curriculum Standards for Social Studies.* http://www.ncss.org/standards/

Von Glasersfeld, E. (1995). *Radical Constructivism: A Way of Knowing and Learning.* London and Washington, DC: The Falmer Press.

Chapter 5

Barton, K. C., and L. S. Levstik. (2004). *Teaching History for the Common Good.* Mahwah, NJ: Lawrence Erlbaum Associates.

Stearns, P. N. (1998). *Why Study History?* Available online from the American Historical Association at http://www.historians.org/pubs/Free/WhyStudyHistory.htm

Chapter 6

Golledge, R. (March 20, 2001). Geography and everyday life (again!). *Directions Magazine.*

Piaget, J. (2001). *The Psychology of the Children.* New York: Basic Books.

UNESCO. (2002). Universal Declaration on Cultural Diversity.

Chapter 7

Parker, W. C. (2003). *Teaching Democracy: Unity and Diversity in Public Life.* New York: Teachers College Press.

Yankelovich, D. (2001). *The Magic of Dialogue: Transforming Conflict into Cooperation* (paperback). New York: Touchstone Press.

Chapter 8

Engelmann, S., and D. Carnine. (1991). *Theory of Instruction: Principles and Applications.* Eugene, OR: ADI Press.

Hunter, M. (1982). *Mastery Teaching.* El Segundo, CA: TIP Publications.

Chapter 9

Bruner, J., Goodnow, J., Austin, G. (1956). *A study of thinking.* New York: John Wiley & Sons, Inc..

National Council for the Social Studies. (1992). *A Vision of Powerful Teaching and Learning in the Social Studies: Building Social Understanding and Civic Efficacy.* http://www.socialstudies.org/positions/powerful

Johnson, D., and R. Johnson. (1975). *Learning Together and Alone.* Englewood Cliffs, NJ: Prentice Hall.

Taba, H. (1942) Teacher's Handbook for Elementary Social Studies. Boston: Addison-Wesley.

Vygotsky, L. S. (2006/1930). *Mind in Society: The Development of Higher Psychological Processes.*Cambridge, MA: Harvard University Press.

Chapter 10

Bracey, G. W. (1993). Elementary curriculum materials—still a long way to go. *Phi Delta Kappan* 74(8), 654–656.

Deane, P. (2004). Literacy, redefined. *Library Journal* 129(14), 49–50.

Elbow, P. (1999). *Everyone Can Write: Essays Toward a Hopeful Theory of Writing and Teaching Writing*New York: Oxford University Press, USA.

Elbow, P. (1981). *Writing with Power: Techniques for Mastering the Writing Process.* New York: Oxford University Press, USA.

Fry, E. (1977). *Elementary Reading Instruction.* New York: McGraw Hill.

Hoge, J. D. (1986). *Improving the Use of Elementary Social Studies Textbooks.* Bloomington, IN: ERIC Clearinghouse for Social

Studies/Social Science Education. (ERIC Document Reproduction Service No. ED274582).

Jones, R. C., and S. S. Lapham. (2004). Teaching reading skills in the elementary social studies classroom. *Social Studies and the Young Learner* 17(2), 1–8.

Lowen, J. (1996). *Lies My History Teacher Told Me.* New York: Touchstone.

National Council for the Social Studies. *Notable Trade Books for Young People* (published annually). http://www.socialstudies.org/resources/notable

National Council for the Social Studies. (1992). *A Vision of Powerful Teaching and Learning in the Social Studies: Building Social Understanding and Civic Efficacy* (position statement). Prepared by the Task Force on Standards for Teaching and Learning in the Social Studies. NCSS Board of Directors. Retrieved March 9, 2006. http://www.socialstudies.org/positions/powerful

Newmann, F. M., and associates. (1996). *Authentic Achievement: Restructuring Schools for Intellectual Quality.* San Francisco: Jossey-Bass.

Scheurman, G., and F. M. Newmann. (1998). Authentic intellectual work in social studies: putting performance before pedagogy. *Social Education* 62(1), 23–25.

Thornton, S. J. (2001). Educating the educators: rethinking subject matter and methods. *Theory into Practice* 40(1), 72–78.

Chapter 11

Kubey, R. (2004). Media literacy and the teaching of civics and social studies at the dawn of the 21st century. *American Behavioral Scientist* 46(10), 1–9.

Scheurman, G., and F. M. Newmann. (1998). Authentic intellectual work in social studies: putting performance before pedagogy. *Social Education* 62(1), 23–25.

Chapter 12

Gardner, H. (1983). *Frames of Mind: The Theory of Multiple Intelligences.* New York: Basic Books.

Gay, G. (2000). *Culturally Responsive Teaching: Theory, Research, and Practice.* New York: Teachers College Press.

Glaser, N. (1998). *We Are All Multiculturalists Now.* Boston: Harvard University Press.

Schlesinger, Jr., A. (1998). *The Disuniting of America: Reflections on a Multicultural Society.* New York: Norton and Co.

Chapter 13

Clay, M. M. (1979). *The Early Detection of Reading Difficulties.* Auckland, NZ: Heinemann.

PHOTO CREDITS

Chapter 1

Pages 2–3: Robyn Beck/AFP/Getty Images/NewsCom; page 4: Elyse Lewin/Getty Images; page 5: James P. Blair/NG Image Collection; page 7: (top) Mary Kate Denny/PhotoEdit; page 7: (bottom) ©AP/Wide World Photos; page 8: Library of Congress/NG Image Collection; page 9: ©AP/Wide World Photos; page 10: (left) James P. Blair/NG Image Collection; page 10: (center) Priit Vesilind/NG Image Collection; page 10: (right) Steve McCurry/NG Image Collection; page 11: Augustus F. Sherman/NG Image Collection; page 12: Arthur Shilstone/NG Image Collection; page 13: Library of Congress Prints and Photographs Division; page 14: Chris Johns/NG Image Collection; page 15: (top) Victor R. Boswell, Jr. /NG Image Collection; page 15: (bottom) Winfield Parks/NG Image Collection; page 16: Antonio Mari/NewsCom; page 18: Steve Winter/NG Image Collection; page 20: Ira Block/NG Image Collection; page 21: ©M.SAT LTD/Photo Researchers, Inc.; page 23: (top) Steve Winter/NG Image Collection; page 23: (bottom) William Albert Allard/NG Image Collection; page 24: VICTOR R. BOSWELL, JR/NG Image Collection; page 25: Alexandra Boulat/NG Image Collection; page 26: (top) Peter Newark American Pictures/The Bridgeman Art Library International; page 28: (bottom) Ira Block/NG Image Collection

Chapter 2

Pages 30–31: Imagno/Austrian Archives/Getty Images News and Sport Services; page 33: Robert Warren/Getty Images; page 35: Stephen St. John/NG Image Collection; page 37: NG Maps; page 39: NG Image Collection; page 40: (left) Raymond Gehman/NG Image Collection; page 41: (left) Raymond Gehman/NG Image Collection; page 41: (right) Michael S. Yamashita/NG Image Collection; page 42: (left) NG Image Collection; page 42: (right) Peter Magubane/NG Image Collection; page 43: Kenneth Garrett/NG Image Collection; page 44: (center) NG Image Collection; page 44: (top right) George F. Mobley/NG Image Collection; page 44: (bottom) Michael Lewis/NG Image Collection; page 45: (top) Roy Gumpel/NG Image Collection; page 45: (bottom) Bell Family/NG Image Collection; page 47: Adm. Robert E. Peary/NG Image Collection; page 48: Jim Richardson/NG Image Collection; page 49: REUTERS/Atef Hassan/Landov LLC; page 50: (left) Stephen St. John/NG Image Collection; page 50: (right) Gerd Ludwig/NG Image Collection; page 51: (top) Marc Riboud/Magnum Photos, Inc.; page 51: (bottom) Steve McCurry/NG Image Collection; page 53: Edward Curtis/NG Image Collection

Chapter 3

Pages 54–55: Digital Vision/Getty Images, Inc.; page 54: (inset) ©AP/Wide World Photos; page 56: Debi Treloar/Getty Images; page 58: James P. Blair/NG Image Collection; page 59: (top) AVEENDRAN/AFP/Getty Images/NewsCom; page 59: (bottom) NG Image Collection; page 61: (top) Adam Crowley/Getty Images; page 61: (bottom) Charles Thatcher/Getty Images; page 62: Steve McCraken/NG Image Collection; page 63: (left) Stephen St. John/NG Image Collection; page 63: (right) PhotoDisc/Getty Images/Getty Images; page 64: REUTERS/Mian Khursheed/Landov LLC; page 65: (left) Steve McCurry/NG Image Collection; page 65: (right) James. L. Stanfield/NG Image Collection; page 67: (left) Joel Sartore/NG Image Collection; page 67: (right) Courtesy Tennessee Valley Authority; page 68: MARIANA BAZO/Reuters /Landov LLC; page 69: Purestock; page 71: Hulton Archive/Getty Images, Inc; page 72: Carl E. Akeley/NG Image Collection; page 73: (center left) Otis Imboden/NG Image Collection; page 73: (center right) Michael Lewis/NG Image Collection; page 73: (bottom) Raymond Gehman/NG Image Collection; page 74: Joy Tessman/NG Image Collection; page 75: James P. Blair/NG Image Collection; page 77: David Alan Harvey/NG Image Collection; page 78: (top) David Alan Harvey/NG Image Collection; page 80: Ricahrd Nowitz/NG Image Collection

Chapter 4

Pages 82–83: John Kelly/PhotoDisc/Getty Images; page 85: James P. Blair/NG Image Collection; page 86: PhotoDisc, Inc./Getty Images; page 87: (left) Library of Congress/NG Image Collection; page 87: (right) Thomas Nebbia/NG Image Collection; page 88: Norbert Rossing/NG Image Collection; page 89: Hulton Archive/Getty Images News and Sport Services; page 92: (center left) Paul Damien/NG Image Collection; page 92: (center right) Stephen St. John/NG Image Collection; page 92: (bottom) Richard Nowitz/NG Image Collection; page 93: Stephanie Maze/Getty Images; page 94: Ira Block/NG Image Collection; page 95: Mary Kate Denny/PhotoEdit; pages 96–97: NG Image Collection; page 98: (left) George F. Mobley/NG Image Collection; page 98: (right) Cary Wolinsky/NG Image Collection; page 100: Catherine Karnow/NG Image Collection; page 101: William Albert Allard/NG Image Collection; page 102: (top left) Peter Essick/NG Image Collection; page 102: (top right) Justin Guariglia/NG Image Collection; page 102: (bottom) James P. Blair/NG Image Collection; page 103: NG Image Collection; page 105: (top) ©AP/Wide World Photos; page 105: (center) Justin Guariglia/NG Image Collection; page 105: (bottom) Sarah Leen/NG Image Collection; page 106: (top) Nicole Duplaix/NG Image Collection; page 108: Dick Durrance II/NG Image Collection

Chapter 5

Pages 110–111: Photofest; page 113: James L. Amos/NG Image Collection; page 114: MPI/Hulton Archive/Getty Images News and Sport Services; page 115: (far left and right) Bill Curtsinger/NG Image Collection; page 115: (left) The Granger Collection; page 118: Stock Montage/Hulton Archive/Getty Images News and Sport Services; page 119: (top) James P. Blair/NG Image Collection; page 119: (bottom) Melissa Farlow/NG Image Collection; page 120: James L. Stanfield/NG Image Collection; page 121: (left) Kenneth Garrett/NG Image Collection; page 121: (center) O. Loius Mazzatenta/NG Image Collection; page 121: (right) Medford Taylor/NG Image Collection; page 124: (left) Anne Keiser/NG Image Collection; page 124: (right) Jodi Cobb/NG Image Collection; page 125: (top left) Todd Gipstein/NG Image Collection; page 125: (top right) Library of Congress/NG Image Collection; page 125: (bottom) Mezzotint by Henry S. Sadd, c1845./The Granger Collection; page 127: (top) Sally Greenhill/Alamy Images; page 127: (bottom) Museum of the City of New York/Byron Collection/Getty Images News and Sport Services; page 128: The Granger Collection; page 130: Karen Kasmauski/NG Image Collection; page 131: Picture History/NewsCom; page 132: Maria Stenzel/NG Image Collection; page 133: Joseph F. Rock/NG Image Collection; page 134: (top) ©Collection of the New-York Historical Society, USA/The Bridgeman Art Library International; page 136: Willard Culver/NG Image Collection; page 137: Todd Gipstein/NG Image Collection

Chapter 6

Pages 138–139: David Sutherland/Getty Images, Inc; page 138: (bottom) NG Maps; page 139: (top inset) Gabe Palmer/zefa/Corbis; page 141: Gabe Palmer/zefa/Corbis; page 142: NG Maps; page 143:

(top) James P. Blair/NG Image Collection; page 143: (bottom) Franz Pritz/Alamy Images; page 144: (left) Joy Tessman/NG Image Collection; page 144: (right) James P. Blair/NG Image Collection; page 145: James L. Stanfield/NG Image Collection; page 146: (left) Raymond Gehman/NG Image Collection; page 146: (right) NG Maps; page 147: (left) NG Maps; page 147: (right) The Bridgeman Art Library International; page 148: Alamy Images; page 149: George F. Mobley/NG Image Collection; page 150: (top left) Gordon Gahan/NG Image Collection; page 150: (top right) Frans Lanting/NG Image Collection; page 150: (bottom) NG Maps; page 151: (top) Making the world a better place by Emily Carroll, Age 8, United States, Burleigh Elementary School, Brookfield, WI, 2003. From: The Barbara Petchenik Children s World Map Competition, sponsored by the International Cartographic Association, http://www.icaci.org/.Entries for this competition can be viewed at http://children.library.carleton.ca; page 151: (bottom) O. Louis Mazzatenta/NG Image Collection; page 152: (top) O. Louis Mazzatenta/NG Image Collection; page 152: (bottom) James P. Blair/NG Image Collection; page 153: (top left) Kenneth Garrett/NG Image Collection; page 153: (top right) O. Louis Mazzatenta/NG Image Collection; page 154: Annie Griffiths Belt/NG Image Collection; page 154: (inset) NG Maps; page 155: (top) Amy Toensing/NG Image Collection; page 155: (bottom) Fred Ramage/Keystone Features/Hulton Archive/Getty Images News and Sport Services; page 156: NG Image Collection; page 157: NG Image Collection; page 158: (top) NG Image Collection; page 158: (bottom) NG Image Collection; page 159: Terranova/Photo Researchers, Inc.; pages 162–163: NG Image Collection; page 164: James P. Blair/NG Image Collection; page 164: (inset) NG Maps; page 165: (top) Steve Raymer/NG Image Collection; page 165: (bottom) Dean Conger/NG Image Collection; page 166: Courtesy Penn Mutual Life Insurance Co; page 170: (top) NOAA/Science Photo Library/Photo Researchers, Inc.; page 170: (bottom) Gabe Palmer/zefa/Corbis

Chapter 7

Pages 174–175: The Granger Collection; page 177: Michael Newman/PhotoEdit; page 178: Medford Taylor/NG Image Collection; page 179: (top) David C. Turnley/NG Image Collection; page 179: (center) Jodi Cobb/NG Image Collection; page 179: (bottom) Cary Wolinsky/NG Image Collection; page 182: Karen Kasmauski/NG Image Collection; page 184: Walter Astrada/Getty Images News and Sport Services; page 183: Michael Newman/PhotoEdit; page 185: (bottom) Justin Guariglia/NG Image Collection; page 185: (top) James P. Blair/NG Image Collection; page 186: (top) Tim Platt/Getty Images; page 186: (bottom) Keystone/Getty Images News and Sport Services; page 187: Zephyr Picture/ Index Stock Imagery; page 189: (left) David Alan Harvey/NG Image Collection; page 189: (bottom) Getty Images News and Sport Services; page 192: Danny Lehman/NG Image Collection; page 194: Robyn Beck/AFP/Getty Images News and Sport Services; page 195: Chris Steele-Perkins/Magnum Photos, Inc.; page 196: AP/Wide World Photos; page 197: James P. Blair/NG Image Collection; page 198: (top) Joel Sartore/NG Image Collection; page 200: (top) Corbis Digital Stock; page 200: (center left) PhotoDisc, Inc.; page 200: (center right) PhotoDisc, Inc.

Chapter 8

Pages 202–203: Private Collection/Archives Charmet//Bridgeman Art Library/NY; page 204: (left) Stephen Saks/Lonely Planet Images/Getty Images; page 204: (right) Louise Coleman/NG Image Collection; page 206: SUPERSTOCK; page 208: (left) William Albert Allard/NG Image Collection; page 208: (right) Joel Sartore/NG Image Collection; page 209: Sisse Brimberg/NG Image Collection; page 211: (top) The Granger Collection; page 211: (bottom left) Clifton Adams/NG Image Collection; page 211: (bottom right) Winfield Parks/NG Image Collection; page 212: AP/Wide World Photos; page 213: (left) The Granger Collection; page 213: (right) Breton Littlehales/NG Image Collection; page 214: (left) MPI/Hulton Archive/Getty Images; page 214: (right) AP/Wide World Photos; page 215: The Granger Collection; page 217: (top) Ira Block/NG Image Collection; page 217: (bottom left) Arthur H. Warner/NG Image Collection; page 217: (bottom right) AP/Wide World Photos; page 218: Karen Kasmauski/NG Image Collection; page 219: Peter Macdiarmid/Reportage/Getty Images; page 221: Courtesy USDA, Natural Resources Conservation Service; page 222: (top) Joseph Baylor Roberts/NG Image Collection; page 222: (bottom) Louise Coleman/NG Image Collection; page 224: The Granger Collection

Chapter 9

Pages 226–227: Tim Platt/Iconica/Getty Images; page 228: Ellen B. Senisi/The Image Works; page 229: Jodi Cobb/NG Image Collection; page 233: NG Maps; page 231: (top) Luis Marden/NG Image Collection; page 231: (bottom) Albert Moldvay/NG Image Collection; page 234: ©AP/Wide World Photos; page 235: Jeff Greenberg/PhotoEdit; page 236: (left) James P. Blair/NG Image Collection; page 236: (right) Paul Chesley/NG Image Collection; page 237: (top) Time Life Pictures/White House/Time Life Pictures//Getty Images News and Sport Services; page 237: (bottom) NG Maps; page 239: (left) James P. Blair/NG Image Collection; page 239: (right) Steve McCurry/Magnum Photos, Inc.; page 240: Norbert Rosing/NG Image Collection; page 241: Richard Nowitz/NG Image Collection; page 242: The Granger Collection; page 244: (top) O. Louis Mazzatenta/NG Image Collection; page 244: (bottom) O. Louis Mazzatenta/NG Image Collection; page 246: (left) The Granger Collection; page 246: (right) Penny de los Santos/NG Image Collection; page 247: (top) The Granger Collection; page 247: (bottom) Gordon Wiltsie/NG Image Collection; page 249: (top) Spencer Grant/PhotoEdit; page 250: Louvre, Paris, France/ Lauros / Giraudon/The Bridgeman Art Library International; page 251: Kenneth Garrett/NG Image Collection; page 249: (bottom) James P. Blair/NG Image Collection; page 252: Melinda Berge/NG Image Collection; page 254: (top right) MANDEL NGAN/Getty Images News and Sport Services; page 254: (bottom) Chip Somodevilla/Getty Images News and Sport Services

Chapter 10

Pages 256–257: MANDEL NGAN/AFP/Getty Images News and Sport Services; page 258: David Boyer/NG Image Collection; page 259: Otis Imboden/NG Image Collection; page 260: The Granger Collection; page 261: (top) ©AP/Wide World Photos; page 261: (bottom) Raymond Gehman/NG Image Collection; page 263: Gail Mooney/NG Image Collection; page 264: (right) Phil Schermeister/NG Image Collection; page 264: (left) Steve McCurry/NG Image Collection; page 265: VITALY ARMAND/AFP/Getty Images News and Sport Services; page 266: James P. Blair/NG Image Collection; page 267: NG Maps; page 268: Ellen B. Sinisi/The Image Works; page 269: Kenneth Garrett/NG Image Collection; page 270: Elen Sinisi/The Image Works; page 271: O. Louis Mazzatenta/NG Image Collection; page 272: Alexandra Avakian/NG Image Collection; page 273: Black Stars of Civil War Times by Jim Haskins, general editor. ©John Wiley & Sons; page 274: (top) NG Image Collection; page 274: (bottom) NG Image Collection; page 275: (left) Myrleen Ferguson Cate/PhotoEdit; page 275: (center) Michael Newman/PhotoEdit; page 275: (right) Elizabeth Crews/

The Image Works; page 277: The Granger Collection; page 279: Sara Leen/NG Image Collection; page 280: Paul Nicklen/NG Image Collection; page 281: Jodi Cobb/NG Image Collection; page 282: Frank A. Munsey/NG Image Collection; page 283: (top) NG Image Collection; page 286: Jodi Cobb/NG Image Collection

Chapter 11

Pages 288–289: Jon Feingersh/Getty Images, Inc; page 290: Ellen B. Sinisi/The Image Works; page 291: The Bridgeman Art Library International; page 293: (top) NG Maps; page 293: (bottom) British Museum, London, UK/The Bridgeman Art Library International; page 295: Courtesy NASA; page 297: (top left) Richard Nowitz/NG Image Collection; page 297: (right) Richard Nowitz/NG Image Collection; page 297: (bottom left) Maynard Owen Williams/NG Image Collection; page 298: Dr. Gilbert H. Grosvenor/NG Image Collection; page 299: (top) NG Image Collection; page 299: (bottom) PhotoDisc/Getty Images, Inc; page 300: (left) Raymond Gehman/NG Image Collection; page 300: (right) Howard Castleberry/NG Image Collection; page 301: The Granger Collection; page 304: Sarah Leen/NG Image Collection; page 305: (left) Todd Gipstein/NG Image Collection; page 305: (right) Stacy Gold/NG Image Collection; page 306: (top) Justin Guariglia/NG Image Collection; page 306: (bottom) ©AP/Wide World Photos; page 307: ©AP/Wide World Photos; page 308: Sam Abell/NG Image Collection; page 310: Richard Nowitz/NG Image Collection; page 311: (top) ©AP/Wide World Photos; page 311: (bottom) Ellen B. Sinisi/The Image Works; page 312: (top left) Dr. Gilbert H. Grosvenor/NG Image Collection; page 313: (top) Joel Sartore/NG Image Collection

Chapter 12

Pages 314–315: Dave Nagel/The Image Bank/Getty Images; page 316: MUSTAFA OZER/AFP/Getty Images News and Sport Services; page 317: Jose Azel/Aurora Photos; page 318: Francis Miller/Time Life Pictures/Getty Images News and Sport Services; page 319: Ann Griffiths Belt/NG Image Collection; page 321: Jodi Cobb/NG Image Collection; page 322: O. Louis Mazzatenta/NG Image Collection; page 323: The Granger Collection; page 325: B. Anthony Stewart/NG Image Collection; page 326: Michael Nichold/NG Image Collection; page 328: NG Maps; page 329: MPI/Getty Images News and Sport Services; page 330: Jodi Cobb/NG Image Collection; page 331: Lynn Saville/Photonica/Getty Images; page 332: James L. Stanfield/NG Image Collection; page 333: Reza/NG Image Collection; page 334: (top) Steve Raymer/NG Image Collection; page 336: Paul Zahl/NG Image Collection

Chapter 13

Pages 338–339: Getty Images News and Sport Services; page 340: Bob Daemmrich/The Image Works; page 342: Steve Raymer/NG Image Collection; page 343: James L. Stanfield/NG Image Collection; page 345: (left) Nobert Rosing/NG Image Collection; page 345: (right) Michael Nichols/NG Image Collection; page 346: Jodi Cobb/NG Image Collection; page 349: Klaus Nigge/NG Image Collection; page 350: Stockbyte /Getty Images; page 352: Kenneth Garrett/NG Image Collection; page 353: Kenneth Garrett/NG Image Collection; page 354: Jim Young/Reuters/NewsCom; page 357: Michael S. Quinton/NG Image Collection; page 356: Sisse Brimberg/NG Image Collection; page 358: Will van Overbeek/NG Image Collection; page 359: Hulton Archive/Getty Images News and Sport Services; page 360: Scott Lewis/NG Image Collection; page 361: (top) Medford Taylor/NG Image Collection; page 364: (bottom inset) Bob Sacha/NG Image Collection

Chapter 14

Pages 364–365: Ariel Skelly/Getty Images; page 366: George Steinmetz/NG Image Collection; page 367: The Granger Collection; page 368: (left) MPI/Getty Images News and Sport Services; page 368: (right) Library of Congress/NG Image Collection; page 369: Joel Sartore/NG Image Collection; page 370: James P. Blair/NG Image Collection; page 371: Steve Winter/NG Image Collection; page 373: (center left) Melissa Farlow/NG Image Collection; page 373: (bottom left) Richard Nowitz/NG Image Collection; page 373: (right) Edward Curtis/NG Image Collection; page 374: (left) James L. Stanfield/NG Image Collection; page 374: (right) Taylor S. Kennedy/NG Image Collection; page 375: NG Image Collection; page 376: James P. Blair/NG Image Collection; page 377: (left) Jan van der Straet/Bridgeman Art Library/Getty Images; page 377: (right) Stockybyte/Getty Images; page 378: Justin Guariglia/NG Image Collection; page 379: Taylor S. Kennedy/NG Image Collection; page 380: William Albert Allard/NG Image Collection; page 381: (top) Justin Guariglia/NG Image Collection; page 382: (bottom) Sarah Leen/NG Image Collection

TEXT CREDITS

Lessons on pgs. 96–97 and pgs. 156–163 are from *National Geographic Map Essentials: A Comprehensive Map Skills Program*, courtesy of National Geographic School Publishing.

Table 14.1: Effective Use of Instructional Technology: Guidelines for K-16 Social Studies Educators, from National Council for the Social Studies.

INDEX

N

O

P